A CENTURY
OF STORIES
NEW HANOVER COUNTY PUBLIC LIBRARY
1906-2006

Also by Brian Hicks

Ghost Ship
Raising the Hunley (with Schuyler Kropf)
Into the Wind (with Tony Bartelme)

WHEN THE DANCING STOPPED

The Real Story of the
Morro Castle Disaster
and Its Deadly Wake

Brian Hicks

FREE PRESS
NEW YORK LONDON TORONTO SYDNEY

*f*P

FREE PRESS
A Division of Simon & Schuster, Inc.
1230 Avenue of the Americas
New York, NY 10020

Copyright © 2006 by Brian Hicks

For information about special discounts for bulk purchases,
please contact Simon & Schuster Special Sales at
1-800-456-6798 or business@simonandschuster.com

Designed by Davina Mock

Manufactured in the United States of America

1   3   5   7   9   10   8   6   4   2

Library of Congress Cataloging-in-Publication Data
Hicks, Brian.
When the dancing stopped : the real story of the Morro Castle disaster and its deadly wake/
Brian Hicks. 1966–
p. cm.
Includes bibliographical references and index.
1. Morro Castle (Steamship) I. Title.

VK1257.M6 H53 2006
910.9163'46—dc22   2006047370

ISBN-13: 978-0-7432-8008-2
ISBN-10:   0-7432-8008-3

For Tom, who wanted it told right

CONTENTS

You arrive at New York in the early morning.
It's more than the end of a week . . .
it's the end of an epoch in your life.
You'll date things from "the time I went to Havana!"

—A 1930s Ward Line brochure

Author's Note

This is a work of nonfiction. The quotes used in the narrative come from testimony, interviews, memos, letters or newspaper accounts. Anything inside quotation marks comes from one of those sources. I did not make up dialogue. Nor did I put thoughts in anyone's head, unless that person told me what they were thinking, revealed it in testimony or interview, or there was another clear basis for it. I have not added to the mountains of misinformation on the *Morro Castle*.

I have been back to Asbury Park several times since this voyage began, and have stood on the beach looking at that empty spot where the grand old cruise ship once sat. It seems there is a hole in the ocean there, and I have walked out on a jetty that almost touches the spot. It was as close to the ship as I could get in person, and this book is as close as I could get on paper.

Brian Hicks
Charleston, South Carolina

PROLOGUE

Verdict Imminent

September 24, 1954

After all these years, he could still pack a house.

They loitered on the courthouse lawn, a sea of dark suits, narrow ties and gray fedoras that ebbed and flowed as he was led up to the building. The ones who had given up on a seat inside stood on the sidewalk, leaning against pastel-colored cars and smoking Chesterfields as the golden sky faded to a deep autumnal blue. From there, they could at least get the verdict before moving on to their Friday nights.

The crowd grew thicker as he approached the imposing stone building. So many people fought for a position on the steps, straining for a closer look, it was nearly impossible for his huge frame to squeeze through. Jersey City was buzzing and he felt, once again, like a celebrity.

Inside, the Hudson County Courthouse was chaotic, standing room only. They filled the narrow courtroom benches and spilled out into the second-floor lobby, a mass of gawkers silhouetted against the giant murals of angels decorating the rotunda. The roar of their conversations bounced off the marble floors and dark, wood-paneled walls, filling his head like so much radio static. The noise stopped only when the gold elevator doors closed behind him.

George White Rogers knew almost every person he passed in this voyeuristic crowd. Most of them had come up from Bayonne just to hear the verdict. They were bank tellers, businessmen, a large contingent of police officers—many of them witnesses who had testified against him in the past week. They had no reason to be there but couldn't stay away, lured by the sensational tales in the *Bayonne Times*. It seemed the newspaper could barely fill its pages without him. The *Times* reporter had been there every day, gavel-to-gavel, desperately scribbling down every detail and publishing it on the paper's front page—titillating headlines alluding to stolen money, messages from the grave and, worst of all, the "Death Hammer."

How they had turned on him. These were his neighbors, people he had known for years, who had come into his shop seeking help, given him medals, held parades in his honor. Not a trace of that former courtesy remained. Now they wouldn't greet him when he walked into court, handcuffed to a police officer, a cigarette dangling from his lip. Most of them, in fact, made a point of looking away when he caught their gaze. Only one, the man with the mangled hand, returned his stare.

The significance of the date amused him, although it seemed no one else had noticed. Twenty years earlier—to the day—Rogers had played the Rialto theater on Times Square. On September 24, 1934, the marquee had screamed his name, followed by the most coveted words on Broadway: Sold Out. The audience loved him, lavished him with standing ovations, angled for autographs. Reporters supplied generous reviews. He had enjoyed the attention, and ticket sales did little to dampen his ego. At $1,000 a week during the Depression, a certain cockiness was unavoidable. For a very brief time, it was safe to say, he had been one of the most famous people in the world.

Twenty years. So much had changed in that time. To anyone who had not seen him since his run on Broadway, Rogers would have been barely recognizable. What was left of his hair had turned gray. Time, or perhaps circumstances, had diminished his paunch ever so slightly. Normally joking at all times, even when it was inappropriate, he was now wooden, stolid. As witnesses made horrible accusations, describing terrible things they believed he had done, Rogers had no reaction. It was as if he didn't care what people said or thought anymore, which wasn't entirely true; appearances mattered to him intermittently. He dressed nicely, at least in the courtroom, and still lied about his age.

Rogers had drifted back to better days often during the trial. It was hard not to conjure images of the past as many of the witnesses themselves brought it up. He thought back to the Rialto, how the show had ended after just a couple of weeks. Leave them wanting more—isn't that what they said? So what if he was playing before an Andy Devine movie; he still got more than his share of attention. His name appeared in the papers almost weekly—there was always something else to be said, a reporter with another question. In those days, people would cross the street to speak, come into his radio shop just to gossip. Preachers heralded him in their sermons. It was all so flattering. Once, his hometown newspaper even declared him a historical figure.

They called him a hero.

In 1934, twenty years before he stood trial for double murder, George Rogers won international fame for saving hundreds of lives in one of the deadliest maritime disasters in American history. Off the coast of New Jersey, a luxury liner returning from a Labor Day cruise to Havana caught fire during a tropical storm, just hours after its captain was found dead in his cabin. The ship was incinerated, the passengers tossed into an angry sea. In the chaos of that night, 134 people died.

The tragedy shocked a nation suffering through one of the worst years of the Great Depression, and the entire world quickly took notice. Headlines and hearings followed. J. Edgar Hoover involved his Bureau of Investigation. The drama of the public inquiry, broadcast around the nation, was as popular as a serial—listeners picked their favorite heroes and villains and then inundated them with fan letters, hate mail and an unending stream of advice. As more details emerged, the accident grew even more controversial. Many things had gone wrong before and after the fire, and it appeared there was plenty of blame to go around.

Only Rogers had emerged from the smoldering wreckage unscathed. While nearly every other officer on the ship was tainted by scandal, Rogers was hailed for his bravery in the face of crisis, for keeping his calm when his superiors did not. The country was so desperate for a hero in 1934 that people paid to hear George Rogers recount his last voyage on the most opulent, famous—and tragic—American cruise ship of its time, the turbo electric liner *Morro Castle.*

Whatever notoriety or celebrity George Rogers could still claim as he stood trial in 1954 dated back to his days aboard the *Morro Castle*; in fact, most news reports continued to call him the hero of that disaster.

The ship had been the most luxurious ocean liner in the coastal trade, a well-known icon on the New York waterfront. Designed by a renowned naval architect and powered by state-of-the-art engines from General Electric, the *Morro Castle* shuttled wealthy businessmen and middle-class tourists between Manhattan and Havana on a military-precise schedule. The ship was every bit as prestigious as the steamers on the transatlantic route, as handsome as the finest hotels in Manhattan—even the new Waldorf-Astoria. The Ward Line intended its flagship to be both beautiful and functional, and it quickly lived up to its considerable prelaunch hype. On its maiden voyage, the *Morro Castle* broke the speed record between New York and Cuba. In its time, the ship—elegantly appointed, lightning-fast—held the promise of nothing less than America's own *Titanic*.

The ship's Art Deco–inspired profile, seen daily in the classified advertisements of the New York newspapers, attracted its passengers from a variety of social tiers. While the *Morro Castle*'s largest and best rooms were quietly reserved—and priced—for the wealthy, most of its accommodations were designed for those Americans who had managed to hang on to their jobs at a time when a quarter of the U.S. workforce was unemployed. The Ward Line knew its clientele and catered to them shamelessly. Every week, the haves and have-nots mingled on the *Morro Castle*'s enclosed Promenade Deck, dancing and drinking their way through masquerade balls and parties decorated as if every Friday night was New Year's Eve. In the days before Prohibition ended, the *Morro Castle* had been little more than a floating speakeasy. One advertising man, without a hint of irony, dubbed her weekly cruises "Escape the Depression" vacations.

It was easy to forget about poverty as they flitted about the ship's ostentatious formal rooms decorated in the Louis XVI, Empire and Italian Renaissance styles. The ship reeked of affected taste, an ancestor of the mammoth cruisers that would rule the water by the end of the twentieth century. But beneath its shiny veneer, the *Morro Castle* was a troubled ship. Rogers had smelled that trouble from the moment he first walked aboard. It was a scent he knew well.

The *Morro Castle* struggled with labor problems and allegations that her crew smuggled guns, rum and illegal immigrants. Sailors complained of low wages, poor food and abysmal working conditions, and their efforts to organize a union fueled rumors that Communist sympathizers were on board. By the time Rogers joined the crew in the summer of 1934, the *Morro Castle*'s captain was constantly on guard for mutineers and saboteurs. The Labor Day cruise seemed to validate all of those fears. In a few short hours, Rogers watched as death, fire and nature conspired to doom what the marine journals ominously had once hailed as "the safest ship of her size" ever built. Fire spread through the *Morro Castle* in minutes, destroyed lifeboats and cut off escape routes. That anyone aboard survived September 8, 1934, was nothing short of a miracle.

The incident caught the attention of President Franklin Delano Roosevelt, who insisted on sweeping changes in maritime law. The Bureau of Investigation, urged on by its zealous director J. Edgar Hoover, tried to prove a Communist plot, and then turned its agents on the crew. The fallout ruined the careers of most of the *Morro Castle*'s officers. After an onslaught of hearings, trials and an inquisition by federal agents, some of the men tried to run from their past; others simply gave up sailing. The courts doomed the careers of a few; another attempted suicide. Only Rogers had been acquitted. The judges declared that on the night the *Morro Castle* was lost, he alone did his duty. Although more than 100 people died within a few hours, hundreds more would have perished if not for the actions of George White Rogers. The *Bayonne Times* at the time said Rogers's name would be recorded for history in "the thrilling saga of the sea which bears the names of those who put their own welfare last when danger threatened."

So long ago. Those words had been forgotten by everyone but him. For the two weeks that his trial had unfolded, George Rogers had not seen that quote among any of the thousands of words the *Times* devoted to his case every day. The paper rarely failed to reprint a later quote, however—the one in which Rogers was accused of having "the mind of a fiend."

The evidence they had was proof of nothing, really.

Prosecutors had hauled out a bloody hammer, a ragged pair of pants, a scattering of receipts and some $100 bills. Their case relied on the word of bank tellers and a television repairman. With this scant bit of evidence, the State of New Jersey had charged Rogers with two counts of murder. The victims—an old man and his spinster daughter—had been his neighbors, his "dear friends." But when they turned up dead, he was arrested the very next day. It was so preposterous, Rogers said, that he would not even put up a defense. Through his attorney, Rogers said all the things the accused are supposed to say: that he put his faith in God and that justice would prevail. He would never hurt anyone, least of all his friends.

The man with the mangled hand had been his friend once. They had worked alongside each other, socialized on the weekends, even rode to the office together all those years ago. But over the course of nearly two decades, the man had grown obsessed with Rogers. He was determined to prove that the radioman held a terrible secret, one that went back even farther than the *Morro Castle.* The chase was mostly in the man's mind; Rogers seemed to not run from anything. In fact, the two saw each other often—it was unavoidable in a town as small as Bayonne. Still, the man didn't consider their encounters to be chance. It appeared that Rogers was taunting him, driving by in his old red pickup, his arm hanging out the window. Sometimes the man even thought Rogers waved.

The man kept notebooks on Rogers, interviewed people who had known him before, searched for evidence of a criminal record in other towns. In nearly twenty years, he had compiled notebooks full, like a detective would. He had tried to get the department interested in his case several times, but no one would listen. They accepted his information politely and did nothing. They assumed the man held a grudge for things that could not be undone. They were right, but the man knew that did not make him wrong. He knew George White Rogers was no hero.

The man sat through the entire trial, anxious, waiting to hear something—he wasn't sure what. Perhaps a fact that would relate to all that he had collected. If anyone had taken notice of him, the man might have seemed even nervous. But in truth, his only fear was that, once again, Rogers might get away with it.

At 6:45 P.M., word came that a verdict had been reached. The crowd from the hallway flooded the courtroom and stood along the back wall. They leaned forward, struggling to hear with almost cartoonish exaggeration. The scene reminded Rogers of a photograph he'd seen from the Leopold and Loeb murder trial, when the famous attorney Clarence Darrow defended two young men who had confessed to killing another teenager. Rogers was fascinated by the case and collected every story he could find about the two boys. The radioman also thought of the McCarthy hearings under way in Washington. The country had turned on Senator Joseph McCarthy and his Red-baiting tactics, just as Rogers felt his own community had turned on him.

It was not a good sign that the jury had finished so quickly. Rogers held some small hope that the jurors had been swayed by his unwillingness to put up a defense, a move designed to cast doubt—or show complete disdain—for the prosecution's case. The judge had helped his cause somewhat, noting that Rogers had pleaded not guilty and was not required to take the stand. Maybe the jury would see it his way. Rogers had any number of reasons to not submit to cross-examination, and it was a decision he did not regret. He felt he had testified enough in his life. In the aftermath of the *Morro Castle* disaster, he spent countless hours before committees in license revocation hearings and congressional inquiries. He had even faced the brother of J. Edgar Hoover before a national audience. This trial reminded him of those days—sitting at a heavy wooden table in front of a large crowd, reporters recording his every word. Thinking about it only reminded him again how dramatically his fortunes had changed. In those days, he never sat at the defense table.

Two minutes before sunset, at 6:50 P.M., County Judge Paul J. Duffy welcomed the jury back into the courtroom. As the jurors filed in—weary, somber looks on their faces—Rogers showed the only twinge of emotion he had displayed in two weeks. He wiped a dab of sweat from his pasty brow. If it revealed anything, it was too late to matter.

After a moment of silence, save for the shuffling of people in their seats, Duffy spoke. He had no flair for drama; or if he had, two weeks of listening to this case had extinguished it. He did not even address the jurors formally. He simply asked, "Have you reached a verdict?"

A matronly but well-dressed woman named Mrs. Iff stood up in response. She had been selected the jury's foreman, and it was her job to inform the court of the decision. The room grew quiet, but still the audience strained to hear her soft voice.

"Yes, we have," she said, looking first toward the defense table where Rogers sat and then toward the crowd.

As if for effect, Mrs. Iff paused.

PART ONE

CHAPTER ONE

The Promise of Warmth

He fell in love with her on the East River docks, a ticket to Havana in his hand.

It was an icy day in Manhattan, January 1934, more than a month into the harshest winter Thomas Torresson Jr. had ever experienced. But he was so captivated by her that for a moment he grew oblivious to how the wind off the harbor stung his cheeks, brought a tear to his eye and forced him to bury his hands deep inside his pockets. Nor did he notice the hundreds of people marching by in heavy coats—lugging suitcases, headed for paradise—who were forced to step around him. He couldn't see them, for he was looking high above their heads, mesmerized by her graceful, elegant curves.

Torresson would later remember being most impressed by the sheer size of the *Morro Castle*. The ship towered more than four stories above him and stretched back from the dock more than 500 feet—11,000 tons of sleek black hull and flawless white topsides. She was beautiful, even regal, the winter sun sparkling on her portholes like crown jewels. Her two smokestacks were glossy black with two thin white bands, the trademark of Ward Line ships. In the dark winter of the Great Depression, Torresson rarely saw anything so clean or so wonderful. His instant infatuation with the ship was hardly unusual or even uncommon. The *Morro Castle*, like the other luxury liners moored at the foot of Wall Street, was designed to take passengers not only on holiday, but to transport them to a better time and place. Profits depended on maintaining that illusion.

The golden age of the cruise ship was still steaming along in the winter of 1934, although it had begun to show signs of tarnish. Two dozen of the great liners sailed through New York Harbor every week, each one trolling for a share of business that, despite the moribund economy, was actually growing. Although a quarter of the U.S. workforce was unemployed, more than 72,000 Americans would take pleasure cruises in 1934. Nearly all those people sailed from New York. These ships carried happy people out to sea, then brought them back a week later melancholy, more than a little sad that it was all over. Back to a city of breadlines and beggars, dirty streets and empty storefronts—a world that did not exist on the Atlantic Ocean.

The largest ships competing for space and business in New York Harbor were the transatlantic liners. Their clientele was wealthy travelers immune to economic hardship, and immigrants who found a depressed America still better than their native country. These ships were the descendants of the *Olympic* and the *Titanic,* although the once-great White Star Line—never fully recovered from tragedy—was failing. Within a year, White Star's remaining ships would be sold and added to the fleet of the mighty Cunard Line.

Most of the passenger ships that crowded the harbor—steamers from the Munson, Grace or Clyde lines—never crossed the Atlantic. They sailed down the coast to the Caribbean or South America on shorter and less expensive cruises that catered to middle-class Americans and their modest budgets. Unlike the transatlantic cruisers, there was little or no caste system aboard these ships. Steerage was a word seldom heard on the coastal run. All passengers were treated like first-class passengers—though some more than others, of course.

These ships were quickly changing the perception of an ocean cruise. In the past, these ships had been merely transportation, no matter how grand and opulent they might be. Now, the voyage—the experience of the cruise—was becoming part of the vacation. And the ships with the most to offer attracted the business. Even the smallest steamships were forced to add enticing amenities, overly ambitious menus and an endless schedule of shipboard activities. This competition created an entirely new industry, although its full potential would not be recognized for decades. In the 1930s, the majority of these ships carried passengers only to supplement their cargo business. Among this new generation of hybrid ships, the most

4

luxurious was without a doubt the flagship of the Ward Line, the *Morro Castle.*

Although Tom Torresson attended high school only a few blocks from the dock and his father worked for the company that owned the *Morro Castle,* he had never before seen the ship. Illness afforded him his chance. Pneumonia had kept him out of school and bedridden for weeks, and the weather only made it worse. Tom was luckier than most, however. At a time when many people didn't survive such a harsh infection, the Torresson family was comfortable enough to afford regular visits by the doctor.

When the worst of his sickness passed a few weeks after the holidays, the family physician suggested a cruise. Dr. Sweeney said the sea breeze and Cuba's tropical climate might do the boy good, even speed along his recovery. It was a fairly common notion in those days, but even at seventeen, Torresson knew enough to suspect the doctor was thinking of his mother as well. Winifred Torresson had fretted over her son for more than a month—all through Christmas—and she needed a break. His father booked them a suite on the *Morro Castle* the next day. It was, quite literally, just what the doctor ordered.

Judging from the other passengers, the ship seemed to be the cure for a variety of ailments. As Tom and his mother made their way up the gangplank that Saturday, they passed singles, professionals, secretaries and retired couples—a typical sampling of the *Morro Castle*'s manifest. Businessmen sailed with the Ward Line often, as it was the most dependable form of transportation between two countries with increasingly common interests. These men filled the exclusive cabins on A Deck, suites with expansive views and private baths. Few of the other passengers dreamed so big. Most of them were middle-class—the rich still preferred vacationing in Europe—and a healthy number of them were female. A teenage boy could scarcely have failed to note this. In the ornate "List of Passengers" printed at the beginning of each voyage, the most common courtesy title by far was "Miss." Teachers were the great cliché of the passenger list. When school was out, women outnumbered the men on board by as much as ten to one. On this cruise, Tom mostly saw young ladies taking a break from the steno pool and the cold northeast winter. Their numbers were still sufficient to overwhelm the men in more ways than one.

The ship's foyer was crowded enough that Torresson could not see the checkerboard tile floor, but the cruise was far from sold out. The *Morro*

Castle could carry as many as 532 passengers in its 194 staterooms and cabins, but it was nearly impossible to lure that many people in a single week. Competition among the cruise lines was fierce, sparking ongoing price wars. The Ward Line cut its fares as much as most companies, or more, but still its ships rarely departed more than half full, especially in the winter. Tom's father had not had to pull any strings to get a nice cabin on little notice.

The people who did sail on the *Morro Castle* made up for their modest numbers with a sense of excitement. It was hard not to feel special as they were carried to paradise aboard this floating palace. The ship treated everyone as if they were Vanderbilts. Their rooms were made up every morning and the menus specialized to their cruise. Everybody had their name printed in guest booklets and in the evening found ornate invitations in their cabins, printed color cards that announced "This Evening's Entertainment." These formal cards, decorated with balloons and the Ward Line flag, typically read:

At 9:30 P.M.

Tonight

A BALLOON DANCE

will be held in the DECK BALLROOM

Gentlemen and their partners are

kindly requested to assemble promptly

in Deck Ballroom at 9:30 P.M.

Prizes will be awarded the winning couple.

All are invited.

Most of these travelers had never been treated so specially, and they tried to hoard enough pleasure into one week to last them for years. The ship made them feel they were among the ranks of the lucky few sailing through these hard times untouched. They were in another world, fleeing America's long winter. The *Morro Castle* offered them fun, escape and the promise of warmth.

Tom Torresson found himself most attracted to the ship itself. He could not believe how well the *Morro Castle* was maintained—freshly painted and polished, so proper, so orderly, so *neat*. Even the crew, in pressed dress whites, was picture-perfect, like something out of a magazine. The purser handed out cabin assignments from behind a window that, with its ornate metal scrollwork, looked like a post office counter. Everyone in the ship's office was polite, offered to lock up passengers' valuables and asked if they had any special requirements. It was like being in a first-class hotel, this grand attention to detail, comfort and a guest's needs. Company officials insisted on no less from the pride of the Ward Line.

A purser gave Torresson and his mother adjoining rooms not far from the foyer, a honeymoon suite on C Deck. It was just beyond the elevators and staircases, near the mezzanine overlooking the First-Class Dining Saloon—not the finest address on the ship, but far from the worst. Tom was given a small servant's quarter off the main suite, just a bed and a shower. Despite its size, the cabin afforded him more luxury than many others enjoyed, as a fair number of the rooms on board did not include private baths. He appreciated the nice cabin, but did not plan to spend too much time in it. Although he was still weak, Tom could not rest. Not with so much to see.

The *Morro Castle* sailed promptly at 4 P.M. on Saturdays. The tradition among passengers was to watch the departure from on deck, no matter what the weather. On the ship's maiden voyage, in fact, hundreds had defied thunderstorms that flooded the city and left the decks awash just to see the Statue of Liberty as they sailed by. Tom's cruise was no different, as most passengers braved frigid harbor winds to watch the Manhattan skyline shrink away. As they reached the Verrazano Narrows, they turned their attention to the ship's seductive interior.

At first, some passengers were intimidated by the *Morro Castle*'s public areas, perhaps fearing they had been outclassed. The ship's formal rooms were designed to be imposing, breathtakingly beautiful. The First-Class Lounge featured Louis XVI furnishings; the Smoking Room was decorated in early Italian Renaissance to go along with its ceiling murals; and the Writing Room's décor was an Empire style. The furniture was plush, the walls deeply varnished, the drapery velour—rooms that could have passed for a movie set. Tom wandered around in the same awe as everyone else, craning his neck like a tourist in New York City. From the C Deck mezzanine, he could look down into the First-Class Dining Saloon and be amazed by its walnut paneling, gold light fixtures, white linen tablecloths and upholstered chairs. Everything on the ship had a glistening sheen, the wood and brass from constant polishing, the ship itself from new coats of paint applied every few weeks.

The travel agent brochures claimed that "an unusual atmosphere of refinement" permeated the *Morro Castle,* and Captain Robert Renison Willmott did his best to ensure the ship lived up to that reputation. A native of England, he had been with the Ward Line since becoming a U.S. citizen in 1904. He had spent thirteen of those thirty years at the helm of the first *Morro Castle.* When it was decommissioned in 1924, Willmott jumped at the chance to command the planned flagship that would replace it. He had not been disappointed, telling friends he loved his new ship "like one of my own." In many ways, he *was* the *Morro Castle.*

Passengers fought for an audience with Willmott, checked to make sure he wasn't on vacation before they booked their cruises—he was part of the attraction. Willmott sometimes greeted guests in his private quarters, where he would settle into a plush swivel chair next to his desk and talk about past voyages, the sensitive instrumentation of his ship, the electrical steering wheel.

"There isn't a ship like her," he told many of them.

Willmott—who appeared more seasoned than his fifty-two years—enjoyed playing the role of a gregarious old sea dog, and the grand cruise ship offered him the perfect opportunity to perform. He certainly looked the part: Robert Willmott was a large man who strained the gold buttons of his dress uniform and exuded an air of confidence—Hemingway bravado. He was popular with the ladies, and had even met his second wife, Mathilda, on a cruise two years earlier. Willmott was without a doubt the star of the ship. A seat at his table was the most coveted real estate in the dining room. Every night, he regaled his guests with tales of rounding Cape Horn, leaving his home in London as a deckhand and settling on Long Island. He showed off a watch given to him by passengers the previous September, after he fought for two days to keep the *Morro Castle* afloat in a hurricane off Cape Hatteras. Although they were out of radio contact for nearly two days and had been presumed lost, Willmott bragged that the only damage to the ship was a couple of wet towels. The captain told the story, in part at least, to support the company's hyperbole that the *Morro Castle* was the safest ship afloat.

Willmott had every right to boast of his sailing prowess, for he was no poseur on the bridge. He was a respected mariner in the industry, pursued by other shipping lines and courted by companies marketing new products. In the past year, he had lent his name and endorsement to the Submarine Signal Company's new fathometer visual echo sounding system: "We have used the Fathometer constantly, especially when approaching Matanilla Shoal, on the Bahamas, the Florida Reefs, the Campeche Bank and the Atlantic Coast of the United States south. . . . I consider the Fathometer one of the most valuable contributions to safe navigation."

He also played pitchman for his passengers. At least once on every cruise, Willmott recited the ship's vital statistics to dinner guests who no doubt found the numbers infinitely less interesting than high-seas dramas. But Tom Torresson would never forget the ship's statistics that Willmott recited from memory: gross tonnage, 11,520; displacement, 15,870 gallons; beam, 70 feet, 9 inches; cargo space, 335,000 square feet. This hulking ship was propelled by engines capable of producing 16,000 horsepower.

A mechanically minded young man could hardly help but be awed, so it was of little surprise that Tom was most intrigued by the inner workings of the ship. His father's position as marine superintendent for the Ward Line helped satisfy that curiosity. Shortly after he came aboard, the chief purser promised Tom a tour of the bridge and the engine room. He was not disappointed, for the mechanics of this floating city were more impressive than all the chandeliers and wingback chairs money could buy.

During his brief visit to the bridge, he was amazed by the size of the ship's wheel and all the panels of the newest electronic gear recessed in wood-paneled walls. The bridge's oversized portholes afforded him a view of the bow, which was littered with venting, rope, a foremast and a 25-ton steel derrick. Sometimes cargo was lashed to the deck, although only when the holds were full—which was often. The *Morro Castle* carried all the mail between New York and Cuba, a government contract worth $750,000 a year. The contract was the Ward Line's main source of income; the ship would have made its cruise even if no passengers sailed, cargo being infinitely more profitable than people. In fact, when the *Morro Castle* wandered off its regular route—adding, say, Nassau or Freeport to the itinerary—it was done to make a delivery, not to sell tickets. Still, the Ward Line never failed to capitalize on these detours, advertising such "special cruises" in advance. Sometimes they even printed special flyers for such voyages.

Some of the male passengers, perhaps to impress the women, whispered that the ship smuggled guns for one side or the other in the seemingly endless parade of revolutions and political upheaval in Cuba. The ship did in fact carry guns for various private customers, but it was licensed to do so. Few people knew exactly where these firearms were going, and sometimes they were listed as sporting goods to avoid attracting attention. The liquor was another story. The ship carried some alcohol back to the States, but it was no longer illegal since Prohibition had ended. There were also stories of powerful Cuban stowaways who fled the country in the ship's hold. Some, but not all, of these rumors were unfounded.

Most people, Tom Torresson included, detected nothing insidious on the *Morro Castle*. On the bridge, he was mostly struck by how professional, how impressive, everything seemed. Far from merely functional, the paneled bridge was every bit as handsome as the public rooms. It seemed there was polished wood in every room on the ship. The company wanted to convey an air of elegance, and the bridge was an important symbol of that. Tom's tour was far from exclusive; it was similar to the ones the captain gave nearly every voyage.

The fine wood décor did not extend to the engine room, however. The bowels of the ship were strictly functional—steel bulkhead and gray walls. The *Morro Castle*'s propulsion system was beyond Tom's imagination. The engine room was lined with metal panels featuring more buttons and lights than he had ever seen before. One panel had thirty gauges alone. Chief Engineer Eben Abbott did not hesitate to brag about the *Morro Castle*'s power. Two 8,000-horsepower General Electric Company motors—turbine generators and condenser casings higher than his head—turned the ship's twin propellers at 144 revolutions per minute. These engines made the *Morro Castle* the fastest ship on the coastal run, routinely exceeding 21 knots. Tom had heard about these engine rooms from two of his uncles, who were engineers on other Ward Line ships. Still, they had not told him how complex the engines were. It seemed beyond comprehension that these great ships ran on electricity generated just a few floors below the formal rooms. In advertisements of the day, General Electric declared their investment in the *Morro Castle*'s engines part of "A $10,000,000 Wager" to uphold the prestige of the American merchant marine. The company had, if nothing else, impressed a teenage boy from New Jersey.

By his second day aboard, Tom could feel the air turning ever so slightly warmer. The ship skirted the coast moving south at an average of

20 nautical miles an hour, a pace that had them off the Carolinas by Sunday evening. As the temperatures improved, pale white passengers left the safety and warmth of the enclosed Promenade Deck to venture outside and soak up the first rays of sun that would bake them bright pink. Soon Tom joined them, lying in a deck chair as the warm subtropical winter and the moderate sea breeze sapped the last bit of pneumonia out of him. Dr. Sweeney had been right; he was feeling better. He was enjoying the time away from school, the adventure of his first ocean trip, and the anticipation of Havana. Mostly, though, Thomas Torresson Jr. was amazed by this floating city carrying him there. It seemed unfathomable that man could build such a machine.

At the time, he didn't realize that the most amazing thing about the *Morro Castle* was that it had been built at all.

The Pullman cars arrived in Newport News early on the morning of March 5, 1930. A crew from Universal Newsreels was there to record the occasion as men in custom-tailored suits and serious expressions stepped off the train. The cameras captured their staged greetings, which made the men look—quite accurately—as people who had made a lot of money together over the years. The women were having what fun there was to be had, playfully vamping like characters from an F. Scott Fitzgerald story. They sported cloche hats and skirts that dipped below the knee, which were fashionable once again. The Jazz Age had become a time best forgotten, and short skirts were a style that reflected its bygone gaiety. The cloche hats represented the last vestiges of the era. Within the year, they would be relegated to closets. Hemlines would continue to drop.

These beautiful people, as Fitzgerald would have called them, had traveled to Virginia overnight from Pennsylvania Station in New York—picking up additional train cars of dignitaries in Philadelphia and Washington—to participate in ceremonies for the launch of a grand new cruise ship. This gathering of shipping magnates, congressmen, bureaucrats and diplomats was such a momentous event that newsreels of the occasion would be shown in theaters across Cuba and in selected U.S. cities. The captions, in Spanish and English, would herald "The launching of the Turbo Electric Ward Liner *Morro Castle.*"

If it seemed an odd time to launch such a vessel, a mere five months after the stock market crash plunged America's economy into depression, these people did not show it. They could not afford to: they were depending on the success of this ship, and its twin, to keep their business afloat.

It might have seemed a frivolous bit of government largesse to finance these floating palaces, especially given the times. To be certain, some members of Congress were not so sure of the benefits, and already considered the U.S. Shipping Board the deepest pork barrel in the federal budget. Every shipping company waddled up to the trough, thinking it was owed something special for keeping the merchant marine alive. Congress might have been inclined to cut off the flow of cash had the U.S. Navy not stepped in. Industry regulators apparently gave little thought to political appearance. Members of the U.S. Shipping Board Commission, and even Dickerson N. Hoover of the Commerce Department's Steamboat Inspection Service, were on hand this day for a very public endorsement of the project. If nothing else, it meant jobs for hundreds of people.

It was implied that the ship's construction was at least partially intended to aid the economy—and not only the United States'. During the christening ceremonies, Cuban consul Jesús Álvarez declared that the *Morro Castle* would "play a prominent part of the development of Cuba as an all year-round tourist resort." The statement drew polite smiles from two men: Henry E. Cabaud, first vice president of the Ward Line, and Franklin D. Mooney, president of the Atlantic, Gulf & West Indies Steamship Lines—the Ward Line's parent company. Cabaud and Mooney knew that the ship represented much more than the emerging tourism trade. It would become their flagship, the public image of the company. This luxury liner represented the future of the AGWI Lines. The *Morro Castle* was the company's last chance.

James Otis Ward, the son of a Massachusetts farmer, had started the company with sailing ships in 1846. Mostly, Ward's freighters hauled sugar and rum up the coast, although he did carry some passengers. He added steamships to his fleet in 1870, when it became apparent there was money to be made with service to the West Indies. Ward's son built the fleet into one of the largest in New York, effortlessly navigating the age of steam. The Ward Line became so profitable that other shipping agents invested in it, and when company officials could no longer run it privately, they incorporated as the New York & Cuba Mail Steamship Company. Despite the new name, the company continued to be called the Ward Line. It had become a name brand.

During the Spanish-American War, most of the company's ships were requisitioned by the U.S. Navy. But as more Americans discovered Cuba, the Ward Line expanded its service with fourteen steamships, including the *Orizaba,* the *Santiago,* the *Esperanza* and even one called the *Morro Castle.* The ship was named after the imposing fortress at the entrance to Havana Harbor, which had become the island's iconic image.

The early 1900s economy forced some steamship companies out of business, but the Ward Line survived by merging with the Clyde, Mallory and New York & Porto Rico lines to form the Atlantic, Gulf & West Indies Steamship Lines. This pooling of resources kept all their ships afloat. And when the economy rebounded, cruises to the Caribbean were suddenly in vogue, and the ignoble experiment of Prohibition only accelerated their popularity. American's thirst for alcohol could not be abated—it was the taste that launched a thousand ships. Demand sparked supply. The AGWI Lines expanded their fleets, and their ships became little more than oceangoing bars. A cruise became the most comfortable place to get a drink without looking over your shoulder.

In the late 1920s, Cunard threatened to steal Cuban tourists from the Ward Line, even though it had agreed to charge higher fares and not carry cargo to subsidize the route. It was not enough of a concession for the Ward Line, and company officials asked the United States Shipping Board to intervene. The board approved the Ward Line's plans to add still more ships to its Cuban run.

Then, a bit of luck. In 1928, Congress passed the Jones-White Act. The new law, dressed up as economic development, offered shipping companies low-interest loans to build new liners. Washington officials had their reasons for such generosity: the ships had to be built to specifications that would allow quick conversion to warships or troop transports. The merchant marine had been depleted through war and a roller-coaster economy, leaving the country's defenses in a vulnerable position. To be blunt: the United States government needed ships it could commandeer. Officials with the U.S. Navy said that its battleships could not operate without sufficient support vessels.

Congress acted with uncharacteristic swiftness. By late 1930, the government had doled out $107 million in construction loans. The *Morro Castle* and its sister ship, the *Oriente,* were the first two vessels approved for loans by the United States Shipping Board. The Ward Line got $6.8 million toward their construction, about 75 percent of their total price tag. They would be the most expensive ships built under the government program. But Congress was not finished. To protect its investments, the government increased subsidies for ships that carried U.S. mail between foreign countries, eventually to levels well above market prices. It was a blatant act of corporate welfare.

The Newport News Shipbuilding & Dry Dock Company built the cruise ships for $4.35 million each, and Ward Line officials could not have been more pleased. The 500-acre shipyard at the mouth of the James River had built hundreds of commercial vessels and a healthy number of U.S. warships dating back to the 1880s. The company was, in fact, the largest nonmilitary shipbuilder in the world. Its proprietors knew quite a bit about cruise ships as well, including their frailties: fifteen years earlier, the Newport News shipyard president, Albert L. Hopkins, was among the passengers who died on the *Lusitania.*

If the *Morro Castle* evoked memories of the *Lusitania* or even the *Titanic* on the day of its christening, no one said so. But it could hardly have escaped the mind of Robert Willmott. The man who would be captain of the *Morro Castle* was living at the shipyard, memorizing every dimension, every feature of his future ship. He knew the dangers of the sea firsthand, for he had been standing on the deck of a Ward Line ship in New York Harbor the day the *Carpathia* sailed into port carrying *Titanic*'s survivors. Their relief at the sight of land had been recognizable even from a distance, and Willmott had never forgotten it.

Such sea disasters—and there were more than Willmott cared to recall—only inspired men to build better ships. His new ship was proof of that. The *Morro Castle* incorporated lessons from several major maritime disasters in its design. In a respectful nod to the *Titanic,* the ship had nine watertight bulkheads and carried enough lifeboats and rafts to evacuate 2,000 people—nearly three times the number of passengers and crew the ship was designed to carry. After a blaze gutted the *General Slocum* in 1904 in New York's East River, new fire-detecting systems were added to all ships, and the latest in that technology would be aboard the *Morro Castle.* The ship had a network of tubes to detect smoke in its cargo hold, engine room and most staterooms. Notably, however, these features did not extend to the ship's numerous public rooms.

It seemed the shipwrights had learned everything they could from the mistakes of their predecessors, except perhaps for errors of hubris. Forgetting the promise of the *Titanic*'s builders—which declared her practically unsinkable—writers at *Marine Engineering* magazine had dubbed the *Morro Castle* and *Oriente* "the safest ships afloat." The Ward Line did nothing to discourage the label.

No doubt the ship was well built, given its famous architect. At the launch, the newsreels captured his image—strong brow line, prominent features and bald head—as he stood apart from the festive crowd. Theodore E. Ferris had the best résumé in the business, a reputation for innovation and delivering the impossible. He had designed more than 1,800 ships and was just what the Ward Line needed. To keep its lucrative mail contracts, the Ward Line's new ships had to make the trip from New York to Havana in 60 hours—12 hours better than any ship had done before. The instructions to Ferris, if daunting, were at least fairly simple: build a ship that could carry at least 489 passengers, 240 crewmen and make 20 knots. The speed was almost unheard-of for a ship of its size. The only possible challenger afloat was the Grace Line's new *Santa Clara*.

Ferris's design for the new ship included features most shipbuilders had not yet tried. He molded the *Morro Castle*'s bowline to include a large bulb on its lower end. The bow would push the ship's wake farther back on the hull and thus cut down on water resistance. He shaped streamlined, balanced rudders that Ferris was convinced—along with the massive turbo electric engines—would make a pace of 20 knots or more possible, even probable.

The rest of the ship was a classic design, sleek and sturdy with a tough steel hide and a rigid prow that only enhanced its formal air. The ship's beauty attracted passengers, but Ferris's pride came from his technical innovations. Although the ship had huge refrigerated compartments in its hold, there was no air-conditioning on the ship. To keep the staterooms cool in the tropics, Ferris designed ducts that ran behind false, wood-paneled cabin walls, allowing air to circulate throughout the ship. The Ward Line shamelessly promoted this crude version of air-conditioning, proclaiming the *Morro Castle* was "Sea Cooled." It may have been a cheap promotion, but it wasn't entirely false advertising, either. In many ways, the ship was ahead of its time.

Ferris's bulbous bow was in plain sight on the newsreels as workers released the track pins that held the ship in dry dock that morning. The men had greased the ways earlier, but frigid temperatures froze the grease. For a while they feared there would not be a launch, but sheer force of will finally triumphed. At noon, dock workers gave the signal and Ruth Eleanor Mooney, the daughter of AGWI president Franklin Mooney, swung a champagne bottle at the hull. Despite Prohibition, many reporters speculated Ms. Mooney had used real champagne. Whatever was in the bottle had its effect. On cue, the ship began to slide down the ways.

Six months later, many of the same people who had been there for the launch returned for the *Morro Castle*'s speed trials. The ship had been completed two months ahead of schedule, and interest in its first test run was high enough to attract the attention of the *New York Times*. It was a less ceremonious event, as Ferris, Cabaud and officials with the shipbuilding company boarded at 4 A.M. for the trip offshore. In a long day, they dropped the anchors, took depth soundings and tested the gyroscope. The ship handled fairly well, covering 70 miles in a few hours. No one was more pleased than Ferris. Off the Virginia Cape, the *Morro Castle* clocked nearly 22 knots.

The publicity from this successful test complemented the advertisements the Ward Line ran in the New York papers, and the good press continued all week. A few days later, more than two hundred dignitaries and local leaders turned out for a three-hour luncheon aboard the *Morro Castle* in Manhattan. The *New York Herald Tribune* reported that maritime experts who toured the ship called it "the finest example of the American shipbuilders' art." It was a great relief for Franklin Mooney, who had been at the helm of the AGWI company for ten shaky years. Finally, it seemed he had a hit. Mooney told the audience he was so certain anyone who saw the ship would want to sail on her that he would open it for public tours the next day. One thousand free passes would be available at the Ward Line offices. This show of pride was also a calculated bit of market research: the tours would help gauge interest in the ship, which was recording only a fair number of bookings.

The passes were gone in minutes. Even though the prices advertised were out of the reach of most people—$140 and up for most cruises—it seemed the Great Depression had not cost people their dreams. When 1,000 free passes proved inadequate, 500 more were printed. When those were exhausted, the ticketing system was abandoned and anyone who walked up was allowed aboard. Company officials later guessed that about 2,000 people toured the *Morro Castle* that day.

On August 23, 1930, a rainstorm flooded the Northeast and threatened to overshadow the *Morro Castle*'s maiden voyage. The eighteen-hour downpour flooded homes along the Jersey shore, lightning knocked out power in Queens and Brooklyn, and a New York girl was killed when her car hit a bridge near Trenton. High winds battered the waterfront. The Ward Line could not have realistically expected a sellout, not ten months after the stock market crash, but were pleased by the strong bookings. More than 340 passengers—including a handful of local officials—joined hundreds of spectators to watch the rain and confetti stick to the pennants strung between the ship's masts.

Henry Cabaud, who along with his wife was among the first passengers, was delighted by the turnout. The docks were not only crowded, but most of the passengers stood on the rain-soaked decks as the ship pulled away and slowly floated past Ellis Island and the Statue of Liberty. In their cabins, these soggy passengers found a special souvenir issue of the *AGWI Steamship News.* The magazine gushed about the new ship and offered a rosy history of the Ward Line. Among the magazine's boasts was one comforting statistic: "During its seventy-five years of continuous service, the Ward Line has lost but two ships, and it has never lost a passenger."

Just before the ship left port, Captain Joseph Jones—who had seniority over Willmott and would command the *Morro Castle* until the *Oriente* was ready—bragged that he would make Havana in sixty hours, nine hours better than any ship had before. That afternoon, hours after the ship had passed through the Verrazano Narrows and out to sea, the *New York Times* carried the headline, "*Morro Castle* Sails in Quest of Record."

The ship reached Havana Harbor just over two days later, clocking in with an elapsed time of 58 hours, 40 minutes. A new era in the cruise industry had begun.

By the time Thomas Torresson Jr. sailed on her more than three years later, the *Morro Castle* had lost very little of her luster. Willmott, who had taken over on the ship's eleventh voyage, maintained an unflagging pride. Every day, he walked the decks, inspecting every last detail right down to the polish on the rails. He had a reputation for being as hard on his crew as he was easy on his guests. But these days, Willmott was making the effort for fewer and fewer passengers. Since the ship had to sail even if it didn't carry a single passenger, the company had drastically reduced its fares to lure more tourists. On its maiden voyage, the cheapest cabins were advertised "from $140." Now the finest suites aboard the *Morro Castle* could be had for $140 to $200, and its most economical rooms on the lower decks rented for $65 or $70 a person—about the equivalent of $900 in early twenty-first-century dollars. It was the only way the Ward Line could keep its customers from taking their business to one of the cheaper steamship companies.

There was always a new gimmick, a new promotion to lure people aboard. Lately the *Morro Castle* had gotten a lot of mileage out of its "Sea Spray" attraction. Because the ship had no pool, vacationers had little opportunity to use the bathing suits most of them carried. If they went to the beach in Havana, company officials knew, they wouldn't spend money on the tours that the line arranged—and got kickbacks for booking. The solution was simple, cheap and, as luck would have it, wildly popular. The crew pumped hundreds of gallons of seawater onto the game deck, giving passengers a good excuse to splash around and get wet. Photographs of attractive young people cavorting in the spray soon adorned most Ward Line's advertising brochures, which hailed these high-pressure showers as "the newest and most popular trick in tropic sailing!"

The ship was becoming very much like a floating Catskills summer resort. Much of its success depended on the crew's coming up with ways to keep passengers entertained. In the spring, the ship promoted its "Gala Easter Cruise," a nine-day trip to Havana, Miami and Nassau. The price of passage started at $95, and for that price everybody on board rented their own paradise. One of the countless single females aboard that voyage wrote that she loved the islands and wearing sleeveless dresses before spring. But it was the ship's crew that most impressed her.

"This boat has a cruise staff of five fellows," Minnie wrote to a friend in New York on Ward Line stationery. "Their duty is to take care of the shore trips and entertain the passengers. They get up the deck tournaments, run the horse races and dance with those who want them to. They had a big masquerade Sunday nite. Very clever costumes."

On his winter cruise, Tom Torresson did not get the entire *Morro Castle* experience. It was too cold for the Sea Spray, and he didn't really find a clever costume for the masquerade ball. And luck of the draw in dining room table assignments gave him no opportunity to meet any of the unattached young ladies on board. Tom and his mother were seated with three other people: a Catholic priest named Father Murphy, his recently widowed sister and a woman who was traveling with them. The ladies were friendly enough, but Tom found the priest stiff—he wore his collar every second of the day. In Havana, Tom and his mother invited the two women to go on one of the standard Valdez Tours that the cruise line arranged. Father Murphy would not go with them into the hedonistic back streets of Havana, which suited Tom fine.

The tours were designed to give passengers the impression they had seen much of Cuba in their very short time on the island, but they provided only postcard views of the Caribbean. Passengers were loaded into the tour company's sedans and a guide drove them through pineapple and tobacco fields, past cigar factories and the grand Spanish architecture of downtown Havana. Tom enjoyed it all, the last vestiges of his pneumonia evaporated by the hot Cuban sun. At a jai alai game, a standard tour stop, he won nearly $60. With his winnings, he treated his mother and the women to supper and drinks at the Sans Souci, one of the most famous casino resorts in the world, and the nearby Tropicana's main competition. It was unlike any place Tom had ever seen, even though the club was not operating near capacity—another casualty of the American Depression. The *Morro Castle* provided a respectable share of the casino's customers in 1934.

They had little more than a day in Havana, but Tom didn't mind. He spent much of the voyage back to New York exploring the ship, where, one afternoon, he came across two teenagers in uniform working outside the bridge. Tom was curious how these guys not much older than he had jobs on the ship, so he struck up a conversation. They were deck cadets, the boys said, and had signed on to study under the ship's officers. The company got cheap labor and the chance to groom their own future mates out of the deal; the boys got a job.

The program held positions for engine room cadets as well, where a trainee could learn how to operate the ship's massive turbo electric engines. In their particular program, these boys learned all the jobs that an able-bodied seaman did. At the end of the program, they could take the test to get a third mate's license.

Tom Torresson, just a few months away from high school graduation, was intrigued. He had yet to map out his future, but was strangely drawn to the ship. He didn't want this trip to end, but at the same time was anxious to get back to New York so that he could ask his father about the deck cadet program. The cadets had made a more lasting impression on him than the Sans Souci, the jai alai, or even the unaccompanied young ladies. Perhaps he could sign up for an assignment on the *Morro Castle* in the summer.

Tom spent the rest of the cruise thinking about his future. He attended the requisite functions—the balls, the dance contests, the captain's farewell dinner, where passengers sang "Auld Lang Syne" with a note of regret in their voices. Tom had to assume everybody felt the same as he did. That's just the way it was on the *Morro Castle*—nobody wanted the party to end.

As the ship followed the Gulf Stream north, Tom felt the air begin to cool and the stirrings of malaise that afflicted many passengers. Every minute, they drew closer to their real, and much less glamorous, lives on the mainland. Soon the wind grew too cold for the girls in their sundresses, the old married couples, Father Murphy or the women at the dinner table to go out on deck. But Tom continued to walk around, inspecting the ship very much as Captain Willmott did.

Upon their return, it was still freezing in New York. As the ship made its way into the harbor, passengers watched the city begin to peek over the horizon from the warmth of the enclosed Promenade Deck. Tom stood outside, where the ocean spray had frozen to the ship, and he watched the crew chip icicles from the railing. He knew the ship would look glamorous, perfectly clean, and reveal no hint of the cold by the time it reached Pier 13. It was all part of the illusion.

Before the ship docked, Tom realized that he was already growing nostalgic for Cuba, tropical breezes, and nights at sea. He missed the ship before he walked down the gangplank, longing for just a little more time on board.

That Saturday morning, the sting of cold on his cheeks welcomed

Thomas Torresson Jr. and his mother home. Before they walked over to the Ward Line offices, Tom set his bags down on Pier 13 and looked back at the ship one last time. It had been a week he would never forget, and he didn't want it to become a singular memory.

Tom Torresson knew he had to find a way to sail on the *Morro Castle* again.

CHAPTER TWO

All Aboard

He could not escape the heat. It clung to him like a wet suit and hindered his breathing, slowed his gait as if he were wading in a swimming pool. If he'd known the travel agency brochures boasted that the ship was "Cooled by fresh trade winds!" George White Rogers would not have been able to control his laughter. There was not a cool spot anywhere aboard the *Morro Castle* on July 23, 1934.

The radio reports said that both a heat wave and a drought had settled in over the country, this despite an unusually heavy tropical storm season. Even in the upper reaches of the Ohio Valley, temperatures had reached 113. Rogers knew the fresh trade winds would not bring relief anytime soon.

That afternoon, Rogers sat down to write a letter to a friend back home in New Jersey. It was the second day of his second voyage as the *Morro Castle*'s first assistant wireless operator, and already he felt he had the job down pat. He worked four-hour shifts and then had eight hours off, maybe the easiest work he'd ever had. He listened to the radio, tended to what few messages the officers and the occasional passenger might need sent. It was just a matter of not getting bored. Perhaps that's why, in his letter, Rogers suggested that his friend—another radioman—should join him at sea.

He stepped outside the radio room every few minutes to try and catch a breeze to fan himself. Inside the wireless room, which was at the highest point on the ship, it felt exactly like sitting inside an oven. Even if there was no wind outside, Rogers could at least see the ship and the ocean spread about below him. The *Morro Castle* was following the Florida coast south on schedule, as usual, to arrive in Havana before dawn the next morning. On the afterdeck, he could see that most passengers had learned better than to believe in the soothing powers of July sea breezes. They fought the afternoon sun by splashing around in the seawater pumped on deck by the crew. The Sea Spray still drew a healthy crowd, although it could be assumed that the greater attraction was the huge congregation of women in bathing suits. The spectacle of wet girls, squealing with delight when the water hit them, was infinitely more enticing than watching senior citizens play shuffleboard. All over the top deck, men in white pants and tennis shirts chatted with women in long bathing suits. The scene on the afterdeck looked like a page out of one of those fancy brochures—just another day en route to paradise.

The tropics held no allure for Rogers. In part, it was because he was not built for the weather. He stood well over 6 feet tall and weighed more than 250 pounds. His cheeks retained what some might have called baby fat, but he didn't appear all that youthful. He had gray hair beginning to show on the fringes of his receding hairline. His cheeks were often so flushed that he could have been mistaken for a tourist. The ship's supposedly natural air conditioning notwithstanding, his massive frame sweated almost every moment he was on board.

Many people would have been delighted to work in such a luxurious setting and travel to exotic locales every week, but these fringe benefits were lost on Rogers. He took the job only because his radio business in Bayonne, New Jersey, had been failing and he needed the money. He didn't give a damn about palm trees or sandy beaches, and had not even gone into Havana once on his first cruise.

Rogers was not even enamored with the ship, although he supposed it was an impressive piece of machinery. He didn't find the formal public rooms enchanting and he would not mingle with the passengers. Some of the other officers attended the dances and socialized with the single ladies, but they usually did so only because they were ordered to do it. Rogers didn't think he had a bad attitude; he simply saw all this for what it was: a travel agent's poster come to life. The notions of paradise peddled by the Ward Line were just illusions. And, more to the point, he knew the *Morro Castle*'s fun ship image was a façade as thin as last week's coat of paint.

After all, strife had gotten him his job.

The labor problems plaguing the *Morro Castle* were very much on George Rogers's mind the afternoon of July 23. It had been hard to avoid the tension in the ten days he'd been aboard. Behind the scenes, out of sight of the passengers and the parties, he quickly discovered a crew divided into two camps: those simply happy to have a job, and others outraged by the shabby way they felt the Ward Line treated them. Both sides used the same facts to justify their position. Because jobs were at a premium, the Line could get away with paying notoriously low wages—20 percent below merchant marine scale, or so most unions said. It all depended on how the men chose to look at their situation. They were either grateful to have anything, or mad as hell to be exploited. The Ward Line did little to enhance its image among employees: its ships were understaffed, the crews overworked. The *Morro Castle*'s complement, in fact, had been quietly downsized as profits decreased. The company justified the layoffs as a result of the declining number of passengers.

The high-society image of the company's officers did little to ease tensions. The Ward Line had the reputation of maximizing profits on the backs of its lowest-paid workers. While Franklin D. Mooney, president of AGWI, made a $128,000 annual salary (an amount equal to more than $1.7 million in early twenty-first-century dollars), ordinary seamen on the *Morro Castle* were paid $35 a month, less than $500 in 2006 dollars. That was hardly better than men earned in the Civilian Conservation Corps planting trees, building parks and draining swamps. Most of the sailors on the *Morro Castle* were paid the wages of unskilled laborers, or worse, government charity cases.

The crew's discontent had turned violent on a few occasions. Rumor had it one sailor threw a plate of food at Captain Willmott because he suspected the meal was leftovers, table scraps and stale bread the Ward Line couldn't serve passengers. The captain allegedly had not recovered from the shock and had come to fear an outright mutiny. His officers kept a wary distance from deckhands, and the simmering tension was almost as thick as the humidity. Rogers watched the choreography of this conflict between officers and crew with detached wonder, like a kid studying ants in a bottle. He believed the *Morro Castle* was only one or two minor incidents away from disaster.

But the radioman kept to himself, did his job and went about his business without getting involved in such things. He spent his off time in the bunk reading technical manuals, dime-store mysteries or anything else he could get his hands on. If the working conditions, the food, the cramped living space or the fact that he sometimes was asked to do things outside his job description bothered him, he didn't say so aloud. Still, he could hardly avoid being caught up in the turmoil. The problems on the *Morro Castle* were the only subject his new colleague talked about. George Ignatius Alagna was infuriated by the injustice. He was an agitator.

George Alagna had signed on to the *Morro Castle* as a radio operator in March—before Rogers joined the crew—and within a few months had become the face of the ship's labor problems. Like many college graduates of the day, the twenty-eight-year-old Alagna came armed with idealism and an eye for social injustice, and he saw little else on the *Morro Castle.* He could not stomach the hours, the living quarters and especially the food. He had been on other ships and had not liked how he was treated there either, but in his mind the Ward Line took labor abuse to a new depth. He thought the bread was stale, the silverware so greasy it had not even been washed.

Alagna's style was exactly the opposite of Rogers's. He complained all the time, although at first not to anyone who mattered, because he did not care to lose his job. Alagna was paid $80 a month as second assistant radio operator, the early-twenty-first-century equivalent of about $13,000 a year. It was more than twice as much as many of the able-bodied seamen were paid. It could have been better, but that was a fair amount of money compared to nothing. And no one was raving about freshness on the breadlines.

Soon, Alagna took it upon himself to speak out for the men piled on top of one another in the forecastle. Conditions in the crew quarters were unsanitary and overcrowded. The work schedule of the lowliest workers was nearly slavery, Alagna thought. The stewards and waiters began their day at 5:30 A.M., cleaning the dining room and setting up for breakfast. They served breakfast for three hours and immediately began preparing for lunch. They stopped for a short break after 2 P.M., and then started again for dinner. If there were enough passengers, they had to work two dinner sittings.

When the ship was in port, the company forced deckhands to work without regard to hours or shifts. Most men weren't allowed to go ashore, even to see their families, because the company feared sailing short-handed. The *Morro Castle* had to depart promptly at 4 P.M. to deliver the mail on time. Because the Ward Line lived off its government contract, delays were not tolerated—a missed mail drop could cost hundreds of thousands of dollars. Anyone who left the ship without permission was fired. It was a rule that Alagna found most unreasonable.

He wasn't selfless; Alagna of course had problems with his own job. Radio operators, he believed, were professionals who should not be forced to take on menial chores. When he was supposedly off duty, he was often ordered to polish brass around the ship's radio room with a kerosene solution that ate at his hands. He had been asked to type personal letters for the ship's officers.

The chief radio operator, Stanley Ferson, listened to Alagna's complaints patiently but offered little solace. Ferson had to get up early on Sunday mornings and play music over the ship's public address system, either from records or whatever radio station signal he could pick up. "Try doing that," Ferson said.

Before long, Alagna took his long list of concerns up the chain of command, where he was treated civilly and promptly ignored. He repeated his complaints with a growing frequency. Every time he was dismissed, he grew angrier.

Although handsome in a swarthy way, Alagna was not blessed with amiability, and that only made his demands more grating. He fought with immigration officials who tried to check his papers at the dock, he griped about his quarters to sailors who had no better. Before long, he boiled over. In June, two months after taking his job on the *Morro Castle,* Alagna decided to get up a petition.

He planned to ask everyone on the ship to sign it, and then present it to Ward Line officials. Ferson told him that he supposed that would be an acceptable way to complain, but mostly he did not want to be just another officer who told Alagna "No." Alagna had the first assistant radio officer, Morton Borow, circulate the petition when he was off duty. Reluctantly, Ferson was the first to sign.

The idea was not exactly a hit. While a few of the deckhands agreed to sign, Alagna only found one officer, besides Ferson, to join his cause. And Clarence Hackney, the third officer, told Alagna that if he couldn't get everyone's signature, he had to tear up the petition—or at least the part with his signature. Hackney was not about to lose his job. Ultimately, Alagna could not convince anyone else with stripes to sign and, bowing to Hackney's request, destroyed the petition.

It was too late. Captain Willmott and the Ward Line had already heard about the petition and requested two new wireless operators from the Radio Marine Corporation of America, which supplied radiomen to all merchant ships. When the ship docked in New York City, Alagna and Borow would be fired.

News of their dismissal drew the union's ire. When the *Morro Castle* arrived in New York that Saturday, June 23, a Radio Marine Corporation representative met it at the docks. The union man asked to speak with the captain, but Willmott had gone ashore and did not return until twenty minutes before the ship was due to sail again. By then, the harbor pilot and the passengers were aboard and it was time to cast off. Willmott told the union man there was nothing he could do, it was a company issue— and they wanted two new operators. But the Radio Marine Corporation would not supply any other operators, and Ferson, Borow and Alagna refused to sail.

Alagna, Borow and a reluctant Ferson left the ship but did not reach the bottom of the gangplank before they were met by Thomas Torresson Sr., the company's marine superintendent. The Ward Line faced an unforgiving deadline: by law, the ship could not sail without three wireless operators. And Torresson knew it was too late to find new radiomen, especially any who would go against the union. He asked them to return to work temporarily and said he would try to solve their problems over the next week. Seeing the company's bind as leverage, Alagna picked up his bags and started to walk away. Borow followed. The *Morro Castle* was essentially grounded.

Torresson, not lacking in diplomacy, convinced the men to follow him to the Ward Line offices at the foot of Wall Street. If they could work for just one more cruise, Torresson promised, he'd do what he could. But Alagna wanted a guarantee in writing, something they could get only from Henry Cabaud, the Ward Line's executive vice president.

Cabaud's natural inclination was to fire Alagna on the spot, but he knew something of sneaky diplomacy, too: as he tried to convince the radiomen to get on the ship, Cabaud had Torresson trying to find new operators. No luck; it was too late.

When he found out there were no other radiomen, Cabaud's veil of diplomacy melted quickly. He beat his fists on the desk and threatened to have Alagna and Borow arrested for holding up the U.S. mail. Alagna thought he had the upper hand and little to lose. He asked for private quarters, more sanitary conditions in general and—in an enviable display of chutzpah—a raise. Ward Line officials had no alternative. Cabaud caved.

The agreement Cabaud signed that day was officially a contract between the Ward Line and the American Radio Telegraphists Association. It was a worthless document, guaranteeing the radio operators their jobs, their salaries and the right to "make complaints" with regard to living and working conditions—nothing they didn't already have. They did succeed in adding a clause that forced the company to pay for their uniforms.

Ultimately, it did nothing but cause the radiomen trouble. Before they were back aboard the ship, Cabaud's staff began working on a complaint to the federal Radio Commission. The damage had been done. The *Morro Castle* sailed nearly two hours late that day, and Alagna was finished in the Ward Line.

They got Borow first. Within a few weeks of the ministrike, the junior radioman got into trouble with Cuban police for being drunk in Havana. It was more than enough to legitimately petition the Radio Marine Corporation for a new operator, and this time the union could not protest. Borow was gone. The man sent to replace him impressed the Ward Line greatly. Captain Willmott appointed the new Sparks, George White Rogers, first assistant radio operator. Alagna was denied a promotion, which would have been standard with a new man coming aboard.

Alagna became even more sullen when Rogers arrived. Most of the ship's officers went out of their way to avoid him anyway, but after the strike most people were afraid to be around him. It didn't help that Alagna whined nearly all the time, often without merit. Although he complained about the food, he actually ate with the officers from the same menu as guests. In fact, many of the *Morro Castle*'s officers thought they were treated pretty well, which only reinforced the idea that Alagna was a malcontent. Some even suspected he was a Red.

There almost certainly were Communists on the ship, foreign sailors the company had picked up in Cuba. Some of the others showed some leftist sympathies, and Captain Willmott had run-ins with what he called "radicals" on several occasions. But Alagna was no Communist. On the ship, as in the country, the threat was overblown. If some Americans had come to view socialism more charitably, it was understandable in the cauldron of the Depression. But when real Communists tried to infiltrate labor unions, they were branded, like Alagna, with a scarlet R. And when Alagna tried to organize a strike—a common tool of unions—he only appeared to verify the stereotype.

Compared to all these misfits, George Rogers seemed like a model employee. The same people who suspected that Alagna was a Communist thought this new radioman brought a modicum of professionalism to the wireless room. Certainly, his résumé suggested he was more than qualified. He claimed more than twenty years of experience with radios on land and sea, including posts on "more ships than I can remember." Among those he named was the competing Grace Line's *Santa Luisa,* a ship that sailed a South American route. He said he'd been aboard the USS *President Lincoln,* a troop transport ship sunk by a German U-boat in the waning days of World War I, but rarely spoke of his navy days. Most recently, he said, he'd worked for a radio company in his hometown and, before that, as an engineer at WJZ—one of New York City's first radio stations.

At first, Alagna resented Rogers—the man had taken his promotion, after all. But soon, Rogers deftly soothed Alagna's bruised ego and they became friends. It wasn't too difficult a task, since Alagna didn't have anyone else on his side. Rogers listened sympathetically to Alagna's complaints and said just the right things to put the young radioman at ease. At the same time, he also stoked the fires of conspiracy. During his first trip aboard the *Morro Castle,* Rogers had let Alagna in on a secret.

"Be careful, RCA is watching," Rogers said. "I've been sent to spy on both of you."

Rogers claimed Alagna and Ferson were under surveillance because of the attempted strike. Alagna couldn't tell if he was joking, but was nevertheless pleased when Rogers claimed to have collected nothing incriminating so far.

Rogers liked Alagna and, except for the heat, his new job, too. He was having fun, as much as he ever did, anyway. Perhaps the ads about these ships were right, he thought with some amusement. His opinion of the ship and the Ward Line was high enough on July 23 that he wrote to his friend Preston Dillenbeck in Bayonne suggesting that he apply for a job on the *Morro Castle*.

> *Dear Pres:*
>
> *Was in New York last Saturday but didn't get a chance to see you. Well OM how goes everything in Bayonne? This is my second trip and everything's going along very nicely. How is the code practice getting along? Suppose that service work is keeping you very busy these days. Well, don't forget the fact that you need that 2nd class license.*
>
> *One of our juniors is in a jam with the Federal Radio Commission and I hate to see the fellow get in a lot of trouble. . . .*

Rogers told Dillenbeck that a friend on the ship was under investigation for sending messages to the American Radio Telegraphists Association without authorization. The company had made a lot of static, claiming the transmission was essentially a fraudulent signal. Rogers didn't mention the failed strike, the radio operator who had been dismissed subsequently, or any of Alagna's complaints about the ship. Perhaps Rogers didn't want his friend to have second thoughts about joining the crew. He certainly didn't tell him how hot it was.

Before signing off, Rogers reminded Dillenbeck a second time to make sure he had his licenses in order. With all the things happening on board the *Morro Castle,* Rogers thought there might soon be an opening in the radio room.

There were always jobs to be had on the *Morro Castle.* Invariably, some position needed to be filled an hour before the ship sailed. Passengers never saw this controlled chaos, but it was always the same way. It was worse in the summer, when some sailors got fed up with the no-leave policy and quit to take vacations with their families. Given the ship's labor problems, they weren't taking much of a risk—they could usually get their jobs back. That revolving-door policy, however, did not extend to the deck cadet program. Thomas Torresson Sr., who had scrambled to find a replacement for Alagna, simply laughed at his son's request to join the crew as a cadet. The waiting list was a mile long, he said.

Tom Torresson had toiled through a harsh and tedious winter to get that disappointing news. He hadn't asked his father about the program when he got back from his cruise because he had more pressing matters: he wasn't sure he was going to graduate. By the time he returned from Havana, it was early February 1934 and he had allowed two months of absences to pile up at Xavier High School, the private, all-boy Jesuit school in Manhattan. His bout of pneumonia had hit in December, at a time when he was studying for his midterm exams and, of course, he had missed them all. His teachers suggested that he start his senior year over again, an idea that did not appeal to Tom. Adding a semester to his schooling would cost him a summer on the *Morro Castle* and whatever future lay beyond it.

Tom had begged the Xavier headmaster to let him take his missed exams. After some cajoling, he prevailed, but then wondered why he'd fought for such torture. In two days, he had to take two weeks' worth of tests in algebra, chemistry, trigonometry, Latin, English and Spanish. He studied hard, but still suspected some of his teachers gave him a break. He passed.

After he graduated that spring, Tom asked his father about becoming a deck cadet. He had not considered exactly what he wanted to do with his life, but knew it was time to begin the business of deciding. Those cadets on the *Morro Castle* were actually learning something that might come in handier than algebra, he thought. He wanted to plot a course for his future, and the ship seemed an ideal place to do it. His father did not attempt to sugarcoat the bad news. There were fifty kids on the waiting list and Torresson wouldn't pull any strings for his son. Thomas Torresson Sr. had gotten only one break in his rise through the Ward Line ranks, and he paid dearly for it.

Tobias Torressen, Tom Torresson's grandfather, emigrated from Mandel, a small town in Norway, aboard a sailing ship in the late 1800s. He got a job with the Ward Line in its golden age and sailed its ships up and down the coast. He stayed with the company long enough to apply for and receive his American citizenship. When he did that, his entire family was automatically naturalized. Eudora Torressen—as the family spelled their name then—and her fourteen-year-old son, Thorbald, arrived at Ellis Island on October 9, 1897, aboard the SS *America.* While Tobias plied the seas, they settled in Brooklyn.

Tobias Torressen soon was named captain of the Ward Line's *City of Washington* and spent most of his time at sea. Just a few months after his family arrived in the States, the *City of Washington* got caught in a storm in the Gulf of Mexico. As the ship rocked through the waves, some of the deck cargo broke loose and threatened to fall overboard. Torressen was on deck supervising the sailors struggling to lash down the cargo when he was swept overboard. His body was never found.

In an age devoid of death benefits, Torressen left behind a wife and five children with no means of support. His widow was forced to open their home as a boardinghouse, and the children learned to help out in whatever way they could. In a direct act of charity, the Ward Line gave one of Mrs. Torressen's children a job. He would run errands for company officials and help out in the Wall Street headquarters. Although he would never work for anyone else, Thomas Torresson—as Thorbald Torressen had renamed himself—would never work on a ship.

It should have come as no surprise to Thomas Torresson Sr. that his son wanted to work for the Ward Line. The steamship company had been a part of the family for three generations. In fact, Tom had the company to thank for his existence; his parents met in the Ward Line office. His mother, the former Winifred McNamara, had been the company's first female employee. She couldn't really type and had few secretarial skills, but she answered phones and scheduled appointments for the company president. They had hired her primarily as a calming influence on the hired help. Many passengers came into the company office to pick up their tickets, and management didn't want the customers to hear a lot of salty sea language from sailors while they were there. Thomas Torresson fell in love with the secretary and, in 1912, married her. When Winifred quit the Ward Line to raise her family, the company gave her a lifetime pass to sail on any of its ships. She would take advantage of the offer several times over the years.

By 1934, the Ward Line still employed many Torressons. Two of Tom's uncles were engineers on Ward Line ships, and one of his cousins was a bellboy on the *Morro Castle.* Tom was eager to join their ranks, but it didn't look like it was going to happen. It was a disappointment, but he didn't feel he could complain. Although his family was better off than most, Tom was not spoiled. He knew not to take things for granted and understood the troubles of the country better than most his age. Things were tough everywhere, he knew, and there were probably others who needed the work worse than he did.

At the time, the Torressons lived in Woodcliff, New Jersey. From their home, Tom had watched workers building a massive span across the Hudson that schoolchildren ultimately would name the George Washington Bridge. In the summer, the family spent much of its time in upstate New York, where they had a small house. Tom knew a summer among the farms in Monroe wouldn't be a total waste. The local farmers regularly hired boys to pitch hay. It was a good excuse to goof off with the guys, and it paid 50 cents a day.

While Tom, his three sisters, younger brother and mother spent the summer in Monroe, his father continued to work in New York City. On the weekends, Tom would drive over to Erie Station in Middletown and pick up his father. He'd gotten his driver's license the September before, when he turned seventeen. He enjoyed the freedom of driving, the responsibility of being the one to make the commute. One night as June was fading into July, his father walked out of the train station at such a fast clip it looked like he'd just robbed the place. He got into the car and, without any other greeting, said, "Pack your bag. You're leaving for Havana in the morning."

Tom could not believe what he was hearing. The idea of going from upstate New York farmland to Havana in a matter of days was overwhelming. He could only think of one thing to say.

"You told me there was no deck cadet job."

Thomas Torresson Sr. was matter-of-fact in his response.

"You're not going as a deck cadet. You're going as a third assistant purser."

The *Morro Castle* was, as usual, shorthanded.

* * *

It was only supposed to be one trip.

Torresson explained to his son that one of the pursers had taken ill and the captain radioed ahead on Friday that they needed a replacement. The other pursers had moved up in rank, but they had not been able to find anyone to fill the third assistant purser's spot. The requirements of the job were relatively simple: a purser had to speak Spanish, type and dance. Pursers did the office work on the ship, and the cruise director often drafted them to entertain the ladies at shipboard dances. Tom thought he could handle the job: He'd had two years of high school Spanish—he wasn't fluent, but he could get by. He'd learned to type by doing his schoolwork. And his oldest sister, Rita, had taught him to dance.

Thomas Torresson Jr. did not care if he was in over his head; he would've done anything to get back on that ship and, anyway, he knew better than to argue with his father. The only thing he said was a short "Yes, sir."

Saturday morning was a whirlwind. Tom and his father boarded the train at 7:12 A.M. for the trip into the city. On the ride south, his father had given him marching orders. Go to Apple Uniform, pick up two sets of summer whites with shoes, socks and a cap that said "Asst. Purser." He had to have his photograph made in the quarter machine and then take it to the barge office, where he got his seaman's passport. He had to be on the ship by 11 A.M.

Tom made it to the East River docks early and found the ship right where he'd left it five months earlier. It looked as beautiful as he remembered, but this time he did not have the luxury of gazing at it lovingly. In fact, this time when he saw the ship, Tom Torresson was a little scared.

He trudged up the gangway with his suitcase and uniforms and reported to Bob Tolman, the chief purser. Tolman was considered a fine Ward Line employee and also an organized man: he made crib sheets. He kept little cards listing the third assistant purser's duties in the order they had to be done—a miniature manual that immediately put Tom at ease. He knew that at the very least he could follow instructions. By the time he had gone over his considerable chores, Tolman took him to eat in the First-Class Dining Saloon, where all the officers ate while the ship was in port. He realized it was the first time he'd sat down since getting off the train.

His duties began at 2 P.M., less than nineteen hours after learning he had the job. He would be required to check in passengers at the foreign debarkation office on the docks and make sure everyone's paperwork was filled out correctly. Then he had to address the bon voyage packages that people had sent for passengers.

Before he walked back down the gangway, he donned his new uniform and went to introduce himself to the officer on the bridge. The pursers reported to the chief officer, and it was courtesy to let the officer know who was working for him. Tom found William Warms friendly and, even a few hours before sailing time, not too busy for chitchat. He was a man clearly proud of his position. Tom was thrilled to be back on the ship's bridge, which he remembered very well from his tour. Perhaps Warms could read his thoughts. Gesturing to the grand ship stretching out below them, the chief officer asked the newest *Morro Castle* sailor, "What do you think of her?"

"This is one beautiful boat," Tom said.

The remark aggravated Warms. His gentle demeanor melted away, exposing an old sea dog who had just been rubbed the wrong way.

"Mister, we have twelve boats swinging in the davits out there," Warms said. "Those are boats. This is a ship and I never want you to call it a boat again."

Tom said a quick "yes, sir," left the bridge and made his way back to the docks. The pressed uniform was still a little stiff, he wasn't sure what he was doing, and he'd just had his first dressing-down from a senior officer. But he didn't care.

The *Morro Castle* would sail in two hours, and when it did, he would be on board.

CHAPTER THREE

On to Gay Havana!

The letter came in the ship's mail on July 28, postmarked New York City. No return address. When Stanley Ferson opened the anonymous note, Manhattan several hours in his wake, it seemed to confirm his worst fears: the Ward Line wanted him gone.

Ferson had been chief radio operator on the *Morro Castle* for three years and, until this business with Alagna, he'd had no problems. He did his job, kept his mouth shut and didn't complain when he had to do insipid things such as playing music over the public address system like he was some sort of station announcer.

He had worked commercial and military ships all his life, and thought this job was better than some, worse than others. Ferson had signed Alagna's petition more out of politeness than outrage, walked off the ship because he was a union member and that's what he was supposed to do. The captain had understood that, he thought, but perhaps not.

The letter purported to be from "A Friend" who warned that Ferson was in danger of being fired for his "attitude toward the company." The writer hinted that he was from the Radio Marine Corporation and had handled paperwork related to Ferson's pending dismissal. Ferson never for a minute suspected it might be a hoax, because the person who sent it mentioned things that only an insider could know.

Ferson might have ignored such a warning if he hadn't been summoned to the American consul's office in Havana just ten days earlier. While the *Morro Castle* was in port, he was called in, forced to take an oath and describe the events leading up to the strike attempt. The men in the consul's office told Ferson he was testifying for an ongoing Federal Radio Commission investigation.

Then there was the investigation into the transmission to the American Radio Telegraphists Association, a telegraph message that boasted about the new contract between the Ward Line and its radiomen. Ferson assumed Borow had sent it just before he was fired; the radio room log had been falsified in a feeble attempt by someone to cover his tracks. *Perhaps they thought it was him?* Ferson had initially thought they were investigating Alagna, but could he have been wrong?

The letter seemed to connect all these disparate events, and it made Ferson a nervous man. He hoped his friend was overreacting, because he had done nothing as insidious as the writer implied:

> *As you probably know, there is an action being taken against you by the Ward Line with the Federal Radio Commission. This action is, primarily, to discipline you for your action in the recent Morro Castle disturbance. Reports are received from the Morro Castle every voyage regarding your attitude toward the company and these reports are being compiled in the final summation of your case. . . .*
>
> *Send in your resignation as operator on the Morro Castle and apply to the Radio Corporation of America for an indefinite leave of absence. This will remove you from the jurisdiction of the Ward Line, who then, from what I have learned, will, necessarily drop their action against you.*

Something about the note wasn't quite right. Although this "friend" claimed sympathetic motives—"I don't like to see anyone framed as they are evidently doing to you"—Ferson felt there was something menacing about the letter. After all, didn't the line "As long as you stay clear of Ward Line vessels you will be all right" sound like a threat?

Ferson shared the note with the two Georges, Rogers and Alagna, and asked if anyone had questioned them. Alagna remembered Rogers's claim that he was a spy, but said nothing of it. He did not think the company above just this sort of shenanigans.

Rogers said that perhaps Ferson should get in good stead with the

Radio Commission by writing a letter to explain his part in the strike and reminding them of his record.

"I think you've gotten yourself in a lot of trouble because of the walk-out," Rogers said.

Rogers speculated that whoever wrote the letter was likely telling the truth, and that Ferson should take it seriously. Ferson liked Rogers—he was a brother Mason, after all—but he could not believe Sparks was right. The consul's questions had not been accusatory, and he made the story so boring they did not even suggest a follow-up interview. He could not imagine he had implicated Alagna in anything other than a conspiracy of whining.

The wireless room was abuzz about the note for the entire cruise. The three radiomen had different ideas about what the note meant, but they agreed on one thing. Each cruise on the *Morro Castle* seemed to get a little stranger.

Surely, moving dead bodies qualified as strange. It seemed that Bob Tolman left that little chore off the official list of duties for the third assistant purser.

Tom Torresson had expected to be back in upstate New York after one trip as a purser aboard the *Morro Castle.* But he quickly learned how much the ship's crew fluctuated. One week a purser wanted off, another quit, still another was transferring to the *Oriente*—he couldn't keep up with all the scheduling changes. Shortly before the ship arrived in New York after his first trip, Tolman asked Tom to stay on for another cruise, which spoke well for the way he had performed his duties. After the second extension, it was just assumed he would stay on for the entire summer. Within a few weeks, Tom even found himself briefly promoted to second assistant purser in the midst of all the comings and goings. He still had not turned eighteen.

He settled into his job almost effortlessly—Tolman's list made it impossible to miss a task. But Tom also made a perfect purser. He was personable if a little shy, and if he was unsure of himself, it came off as modesty. He quickly made friends on the ship and found he already had one on board. His first day on the job, while addressing the packages and fruit baskets for passengers, he ran into his cousin the bellboy. George

Dahl took one look at his cousin's hat that read "Asst. Purser" and immediately dubbed Tom the "ass purser," a name that would follow him around
the ship all summer.

Most of his duties were fairly mundane—handling special requests
from guests, fetching Cuban stamps while in Havana. In some ways, Tom
felt as if he were starting out as an office boy, just as his father had with
the Ward Line. But he quickly found that pursers had the luxury, or the
curse, of variety. Or so the ship's doctor, De Witt Van Zile, informed him.

The man had been one of the wealthier passengers, an executive staying in an A Deck suite. A steward had gone into the cabin to make the bed
that morning and found the man dead. Dr. Van Zile diagnosed it as a heart
attack, but cause of death was not the most pressing matter. He had to be
moved. Cadavers do not hold up well in the tropics, and it was time for the
late breakfast sitting.

Russell Du Vinage, the assistant purser, told Tom to find a couple of
crewmen and get the body down to the refrigerated compartments on E
Deck. That meant moving the man's body literally from one end of the ship
to the other. And Du Vinage asked that he keep the body out of view of the
passengers. *This is definitely not in the manual,* Tom thought. At seventeen, he had not seen many dead bodies, and certainly had never handled
one before, but he had been given a job to do and did not argue. It crossed
his mind that this chore was proof of his suspicion that his father had ordered the purser's office to not cut him any slack.

It was a trick to avoid passengers, to be sure, as many of them were
out for their morning strolls along the Promenade Deck. Tom found two
sailors and had them fetch a stretcher from the infirmary. They hoisted the
body onto the gurney and threw a sheet over it. Great, he thought: This
looks *exactly* like a dead body. But there was little way to camouflage it.
Tom knew he couldn't just roll it down the staircase with the folks on their
way to the 8:30 breakfast sitting (Now *there's* something to make your
cruise a memorable one!), so he commandeered the forward elevator from
the operator, a man named Sidney.

Of course, the stretcher wouldn't fit. Standing in the ship's grand
foyer, dead guy on a gurney, Tom was nearly in a panic. He was within sight
of the purser's office and didn't want Tolman or Du Vinage to witness this
scene—not to mention the passengers. After studying the situation for a
moment, he told the sailors to stand the body up and then prop the

stretcher in the elevator. Once they had the dead guy wedged into one corner and the stretcher in another, Tom told the sailors to run down the stairs and meet him on D Deck—as far as the elevator went—and they could carry it from there. He held the body in place with his hand while Sidney operated the controls. But when the car started moving, the sheet slipped off the man's head, leaving his dead maw drooping over Torresson and a horrified Sidney. Eventually, they got the body to the freezer without anyone seeing, but the ship had to carry the corpse for nearly a week, until it returned to New York.

There was never a shortage of drama on the *Morro Castle*. Not long after Tom had to move the dead body, a steward reported that another passenger had not shown up at his assigned table for any meals. The man had missed his Saturday dinner as well as breakfast and lunch on Sunday. Fearing another cadaver in his future, Tom was sent to investigate.

It was one of the cheaper rooms down below, D Deck aft—"propeller suites," the crew derisively called them. Tom knocked and was relieved to hear the man respond, "Come in." Inside, he found an old man who had apparently settled in for the trip—in fact, it looked as if he hadn't left the cabin. Tom asked the man why he hadn't shown up for any meals. Was he sick? Was something wrong?

"No, son, I'm a farmer," the man said. "I always wanted to take a sea trip. I lost my wife about a year ago and decided if I was ever going to take this trip, I better do it now. I had money for the passes, but I can't afford to buy the meals. I brought things with me, sardines, crackers. That's what I've been eating."

An all-inclusive trip was a concept hard to grasp in 1934, particularly for folks who rarely traveled. There weren't many things free in the world anymore. Tom was struck by the man's story and gently explained that his $65 ticket paid for his passage and all the food he could eat.

"You're throwing your money away by not eating."

The farmer was delighted. For the rest of the trip, Tom noticed the man didn't miss a meal—or a chance for seconds.

Aside from the occasional corpse, Tom loved being a purser. Traveling and helping people to have a good time was fine, but mostly he felt as if he were a part of something special. He had no rank, no power, but he ate with the ship's officers, interacted with them daily. Although he was one of the youngest members of the crew, he was thrilled to find that he was treated like an adult. Still, he got nervous around the chief officers, something he noticed the day he was called to Captain Willmott's cabin. Willmott was writing a note to his father, the company's marine superintendent, about plans to cut a canal through the Florida Keys to shorten the trip to the Gulf of Mexico. Willmott told Tom he wanted the dispatch to be perfect.

Tom was quite proud of the letter, which he drafted on an old Underwood typewriter in the purser's office. He showed the note to Tolman and Du Vinage, both of whom nodded approval, before he took it back to the captain. He knocked, entered and saluted—a habit from his military school training. He was the picture of a merchant ship officer in his dress whites. Willmott read the note to himself, and perhaps suppressed a smile as he said, "Young man, that's a fine letter, but there's only one 'r' in 'coral.'" The Ward Line had little call for a corral in Florida.

Such light moments were becoming rare for the captain. The past year had changed Robert Willmott. A combination of things had taken their toll—insubordinate crew, Alagna's strike, trouble in Cuba. On a recent trip, Havana port officials had not allowed them to unload their cargo. Then, during another cruise, Willmott found illegal immigrant stowaways on board shortly after the *Morro Castle* left Havana. It had infuriated him so much that he turned the ship around, schedule be damned, to kick them off in another Cuban province.

Some of Willmott's top officers had noticed the change in him. Eben Abbott, the chief engineer, considered the captain a friend and took his meals with him often. Their conversations were mostly superficial, however. Whenever Abbott asked anything about trouble on the ship, Willmott cut him off abruptly, like he was some deck cadet.

The polite rumor was that the captain was sick and the time he took off with increasing frequency was health-related. No doubt some of it was stress-related. The captain took vacation in early August, and Commodore Joseph Jones left the *Oriente*'s bridge to take his place.

Because of his absence, Willmott missed the August 4 Steamboat Inspection Service checkup. It was a busy Saturday morning, with an oil barge refueling the ship off the starboard gunwales while stevedores loaded and unloaded cargo. The records of the *Morro Castle*'s inspection suggest that on that day all of the ship's lifeboats were tested, lowered to the water and checked out. An Inspector Moffat looked over the ship's hull, its steering gear, gangways, telephones, radio equipment and anchors that morning. The records also said he examined 849 life preservers and 100 fire extinguishers. According to the report, the efficient Inspector Moffat did all of this work in less than two hours.

By the late summer of 1934, the *Morro Castle* was due for a more thorough examination. Since its first inspection at its launch in 1930, the ship had spent 988 of 1,449 days at sea, 425 days at dock, but only 35 hours in dry dock. The Ward Line ran its show horse hard.

That attitude carried over on board as well. On the *Morro Castle,* inspections and drills were terms tossed around loosely. Mostly they consisted of sailors reporting to a duty station. Willmott said he did not want to "perturb" his guests with meaningless drills, so he just didn't conduct them. Although passenger lifeboat drills had been mandated by federal law in the wake of the *Titanic* tragedy, it was a law seldom enforced. The *Morro Castle* violated this requirement perhaps more than most other ships, mainly because of its captain. Willmott thought his ship was safer than walking down a city street, but he considered his crew incapable of handling a drill, much less an emergency. And he had no patience for practice.

Jones was a different kind of skipper. During his four days on the ship, Jones hardly stopped conducting drills. He checked the hold constantly, afraid that someone would tamper with the 125 bags of mail inside. He ran the ship through a litany of tests—opening and closing the watertight doors, launching the lifeboats—as if he were looking for something. It would not have been unprecedented to find contraband, human or otherwise.

In the past year, Cuban generals had stowed away on the *Morro Castle* to escape the dictatorship being run behind the scenes by the new military dictator Fulgencio Batista. Many people, not just military leaders, had attempted to flee the island nation in recent months, and cruise ships were their best bet. These stowaways most often paid crew members to help them sneak away. Illegal immigration from Cuba to the United States had become so rampant that Ernest Hemingway wrote about it in a short story published in *Cosmopolitan* just that spring. In "One Trip Across," Harry Morgan paid dearly for agreeing to smuggle Chinese immigrants across the Florida straits. The story became the first part of a novel Hemingway would release three years later, a book that summed up the effects of the Depression with the eloquent title *To Have and Have Not.*

Much like the *Morro Castle* itself, Cuba was in constant turmoil behind an alluring façade. In 1933, Batista led a band of men to overthrow President Gerardo Machado, then installed a five-man junta to control the island. The United States government feared this was the first step toward Communism and threatened military retaliation if a new president was not elected. Batista relented, but the United States chose not to recognize this new president, either.

In January of 1934, Batista appointed and replaced three different presidents in a three-day span. The last man won U.S. approval, although it was clear who was really in charge. In May, the United States had signed a new Treaty of Relations with Cuba, replacing the 1903 Platt Amendment put into effect after the Spanish-American War. The agreement guaranteed Americans the continued right to a military base at Guantánamo.

This series of minirevolutions and bumbling attempts at a new dictatorship took place right under the noses of the *Morro Castle*'s passengers. Once, in November of 1933, port officials had warned the captain not to let passengers go into the city because of fighting in the streets. A few errant bullets even hit the ship. On board, the band played louder to drown out the sound of gunshots as the pursers and the cruise directors distracted passengers with vague excuses of "immigration problems" to explain canceled tours.

Most people were oblivious to the revolution. Havana was a seductive paradise unlike any other city, a picture-postcard world of cigar factories, sugarcane fields and sugary white beaches. The *Morro Castle*'s passengers visited the President's Palace, the Hotel Nacional, Sloppy Joe's, the Floridita and the Tropicana believing they had found Eden. These *turistas* strolled along one of the most beautiful waterfronts in the world, the Malecon, across the harbor from the stone fort that gave their cruise ship its name, and gasped at the beautiful scene. When they returned from the elaborate dinner show at the Sans Souci, they were mesmerized by the beam of the Morro Castle lighthouse cutting a wide swath across the city.

Havana had become so romanticized that it may have been the most desirable vacation destination in the world. Lately, that had been enhanced in no small part by Hemingway's love letters to the city in the new *Esquire* magazine. On August 7, had passengers on the arriving *Morro Castle* bothered to look out across the harbor, they might have spotted Hemingway's boat, the *Pilar,* slipping quietly past the fort. If not, they may have walked past the author himself that night at the Sans Souci.

Tom had come to love Havana as much as the tourists. He surprised himself by looking forward to seeing the city on his first cruise, but it hadn't worked out as he hoped. After the ship docked, he had to go to the post office and buy more stamps. He went straight there and back in a taxi. When he returned, he planned to take his uniform off and go exploring, but William Warms had other ideas. All new crew members were required to be tested on the lifeboats, and that included Tom. So while Hemingway was fishing for marlin off the Morro, Tom rowed around Havana Harbor. After four hours, his hands were so blistered he couldn't muster the strength to leave the ship.

On subsequent trips, Tom became quite adept at navigating Old Havana. A friend of his father in the building materials business, Bill Haines, lived in the city, and Tom struck up a friendship with his daughter, Margaret. They would go to the beach and sometimes even the Sans Souci, where Sylvia Slidel, a fan dancer who often traveled on the *Morro Castle,* had invited Tom to see her show. Her sexual allure aside, Tom mostly felt pity for the fan dancer, because a new cartoon character named Mickey Mouse got top billing on the marquee, and Sylvia Slidel lost so many feathers during her act that she appeared to be molting.

Tom had been warned about the revolutionaries and violence in the streets, but he soon found that danger lurked in many forms. One night, while standing gangway watch—where he checked people for the little Ward Line buttons that identified them as passengers—he saw a seventeen-year-old girl being escorted across the docks by a Cuban man with slick hair and "Latin lover" looks. She had gone on a Valdez Tour earlier that day with her parents. Later they had dinner and drinks at the Sans Souci, and the girl met her suitor on the dance floor. The Cuban impressed the parents with his air of propriety, asking permission to escort their daughter back to the ship.

Tom was less than impressed. He wouldn't let him aboard, no matter how much the man persisted. He could not believe the girl's parents would entrust her to this joker, and felt the stirrings of anger. The man argued that he only wanted to walk her to her room and say good night. Too bad, Tom told him—it was a company rule that only passengers were allowed aboard. Without further argument, the Cuban escorted the girl back down the gangway, explaining within Tom's earshot that they would say their good-byes on the dock.

The girl did not return. After several minutes, Howard Hansen, the ship's fourth officer, decided something was wrong. He ordered a Cuban guard on the dock to go look for the girl. Twenty minutes later, they heard her cries as she ran back toward the ship followed by the guard, who had her boyfriend in a headlock. The man had tried to rape her on the docks.

The night watch crew had a dilemma. If Hansen called the Cuban police, the ship would be held while witness statements were taken. The island's police officers—not above a little bribery—would have made it difficult for the *Morro Castle* to stay on schedule. Hansen thought about it for a moment and then told the guard to throw the man off the dock. Evidently, there was a language barrier. The guard took him literally and heaved the would-be Latin lover off the landing, where he bounced down three flights of steps. No one bothered to check on the man's injuries.

That incident opened Tom's eyes just a bit. He may have been unaware of much of the turmoil on the *Morro Castle,* but he was beginning to see that not everything was fun and carefree, that Havana was not—despite the claims of the Ward Line brochures—all that gay. The next day, he saw the girl who had almost been raped. She walked up to thank him, but he stopped her. Tom looked at her—his age, but years younger—and told her to forget it.

"Everything is fine," he said. "Enjoy the rest of your cruise."

Before the ship left Havana that morning, Willmott returned to the helm. He had spent a few days off with his wife. The two rarely saw each other except on the ship, although some crew members whispered that was the way the captain preferred it. Some said Willmott was trapped in the marriage. Their proof was how much time he devoted to the ship. In the past year, the newlywed captain had spent less than a month at his Long Island home. Still, the vacation seemed to do him good. Willmott seemed in slightly better spirits than he had been when he left; he had some of his old spark back. It wouldn't last long.

* * *

Stanley Ferson got his second anonymous letter that day.

It was a little more threatening, a little more insistent that Ferson resign. The note claimed that the Ward Line suspected he had written a letter complaining of conditions on the *Morro Castle,* and the company was ready to file charges with the Federal Radio Commission.

> *The Federal Radio Commission has no interest in this matter other than the charges presented by the Ward Line. Should the Ward Line drop their charges the whole matter will die a natural death.*
>
> *With you out of the picture, temporarily, this can be accomplished from this end.*

Ferson suspected a trick. He knew the Ward Line couldn't fire him outright—they could only request a new operator, and the Radio Marine Corporation was not always inclined to make random personnel changes. The burden of proof of wrongdoing was on the Line, wasn't it? Still, Ferson worried. This letter, like the last, had a menacing tone. He was particularly spooked by the shove-him-out-the-door sound of the letter's last line:

"There are jobs much bigger and better than the *Morro Castle* that you can get."

Ultimately, Ferson decided to avoid the threat of trouble. When the *Morro Castle* arrived in New York on August 11, 1934, Stanley Ferson resigned as chief radio operator. He packed his meager belongings and left without much attention, saying a few words to Alagna on the way out. Before he walked off the ship forever, Ferson shook hands with George Rogers, who was disembarking for a week's leave. He said his wife was having pain in her side and he feared it was appendicitis. Rogers was given permission to take a cruise off, something few officers were allowed.

Willmott said nothing when Ferson resigned because little surprised him anymore. The Radio Marine Corporation sent a young Finnish man named Charles Maki to fill the slot, but it was clear he knew very little about radios. Willmott promoted Rogers to chief radio operator, and George Alagna became his first assistant.

That Saturday afternoon, however, with Rogers taking a week off, Willmott had little choice but to temporarily appoint George Alagna chief radio operator of the *Morro Castle*. It had been about six weeks since

Alagna had held up the ship, was fired and rehired. It gave Willmott pause, but he thought that surely they could get through one week without something going wrong.

They couldn't. That week, Alagna managed to start a war with the purser's office. He refused to sign receipts for personal messages the pursers handled for passengers. The office was supposed to collect the fees and pay the wireless room at the end of the voyage, but someone was either pocketing a good bit of the money or trumping up false charges. Alagna didn't know if Maki or one of the pursers was stealing money, but it didn't matter. He didn't trust anyone. And he had other reasons to dislike Maki: the young radioman couldn't spell, and had thrown away a coded message for a passenger that he had been expecting. When he asked about it, Maki said he'd seen the message but didn't think it was important.

Before the end of the week, Alagna asked the Radio Marine Corporation to send him someone else. As usual, his request was denied.

Rogers returned as chief radio operator the next voyage, a promotion he expected but only learned about while in Bayonne. He took to the job effortlessly and seemed to be a natural leader. Alagna and Maki enjoyed working for George Rogers. He ran an easy shop and, as long as everyone pulled their shift, he said little. Rogers continued to read in his bunk when he was off duty and hardly ever ventured into the city. He seemed satisfied by his promotion, and his newfound authority manifested itself in a certain cockiness. Still, he was always fair, always nice to Alagna and Maki. They were a team, a concept he promoted even if he declined to use the term. His men respected him. Alagna even considered him a friend, although he rarely looked comfortable when Rogers would hug him, squeezing the first assistant's slender frame against his considerable girth.

Tom Torresson was not particularly enamored with any of the radiomen. He had been assigned to a table in the officers' mess with Rogers, Maki and Alagna, and he ate with them on most days. From the beginning, he was wary of Rogers and Alagna, and dismissive of Maki. He thought Maki acted like he was from another planet.

The chief purser, Bob Tolman, had told Tom to stay away from Alagna—he was nothing but trouble, and maybe even a Communist. Tom's own observations seemed to bear that out. At one lunch, Alagna complained about the fat globules floating in the broth of his chicken soup. As soon as the bowl was set down in front of him, Alagna jumped up and began cursing at the waiter.

"You let your sweat drip into the bowl," Alagna cried. "You did that on purpose."

Eventually, William Warms, eating at a nearby table, told Alagna to sit down and shut up.

Although Tom considered Alagna a troublemaker, he thought Rogers much creepier. Rogers was jolly and always laughing—the polar opposite of Alagna—but he was strange. And Tom was disgusted by the radioman's thick, pouting lips, grotesque and as dark as a woman's lipstick. He sometimes couldn't help but stare at them. Rogers tried to joke around with him, but Tom wasn't interested.

Most of the time, Tom dreaded eating. When the waiter served their fish course—a piece of broiled mackerel, usually—it came with a slice of lemon or lime. Rogers rarely failed to spear Tom's wedge with his fork, bury it between his oversized lips and smile. He did it in a joking way, but Tom found it threatening. Rogers always had a look on his face that seemed to say, *What are you going to do about it?*

Captain Willmott's vacation did little to rejuvenate him. Throughout August, he showed up less often for dinner, and passengers complained that he rarely told his wonderful stories. He seemed, well, depressed. Behind the scenes, the crew had noticed the same thing. Willmott, who had always been a kind man, became withdrawn and quick-tempered. He was grumpy most of the time, and his health problems had become more apparent.

On the August 25 cruise, Willmott conducted his regular inspection with Bob Tolman in tow. After they finished, the purser said he had to retrieve some paperwork and suggested they ride up together in the elevator. Willmott said he preferred to walk, so Tolman got the papers from his office and made his way to the bridge. A few minutes later, Tolman met Willmott in the chart room, where the captain had just emerged from his cabin in an undershirt, holding himself and gasping.

"My God, my God, I never had such a thing," Willmott said, then fell backward over a davenport.

Tolman called De Witt Van Zile. The ship's doctor gave Willmott bicarbonate of soda and peppermint, and the captain drank four glasses of ice water in quick succession. For a long time, Willmott sat in his cabin without moving.

When Tolman returned later, Willmott feigned recovery, but the chief purser still worried. He would never do anything as inappropriate as ask Dr. Van Zile if there was something about the captain's condition that the officers needed to know. But he certainly wished that he could.

Later that cruise, Willmott had another reason for chest pains. On August 27, just as the *Morro Castle* cleared the Florida coast on its way to Havana, fire broke out in a cargo compartment on E Deck. He had just finished the tedious job of navigating the southern tip of the Florida peninsula and was about to lie down for a nap when word of the blaze reached him. It had spread over sixty bundles of cardboard and tar paper—kindling that could have set the entire ship aflame.

The crew's response was disastrous. It looked like the Three Stooges had come aboard to fight the fire. Only two crews showed up and, when they did, the fire hoses proved useless. One of the hose's couplings broke, and there was no water pressure from the other. Eventually, deckhands put out the fire with handheld extinguishers. The incident only reinforced Willmott's low opinion of his sailors. He filled out the appropriate paperwork to report the fire, but the passengers were not told. No reason to alarm anyone.

On September 1, just before the *Morro Castle* left on its Labor Day cruise, he had the Ward Line deliver the fire report to the Steamboat Inspection Service. Willmott hated to do it—he knew it would trigger an inquiry—but he realized it was the law.

More than he feared a bunch of federal investigators asking questions, Willmott worried what—or *who*—might have caused the fire. Fires on board ships were not unheard of, but they weren't commonplace either.

Willmott was increasingly nervous. In a letter to a friend in England, he recounted the fire incident casually, but his words belied an affected nonchalance. Clearly, the fire had scared Willmott—not because he worried about losing his ship, but because he feared that it had been *set.*

"Due to modern design and efficient equipment we soon had it extinguished," Willmott wrote to his friend. "But something like that gives one a jolt."

CHAPTER FOUR

Summer's End

Pier 13 was busy that afternoon, September 1, 1934. The *Morro Castle*'s Labor Day cruise had attracted more than the usual number of passengers ready to trade the concrete city for tropical breezes. The heat wave had withered, at least in the Northeast. A few hours north of New York, in Boston, there already had been snow flurries. Highs in the city hovered around the low 60s. At night it was as chilly as the deck of a ship at sea.

This fresh group of vacationers was ready to sail away from a depressing world. Despite the New Deal programs, the country was in shambles. Jobs were scarce, crime was on the rise, and Congress had just passed the National Firearms Act in response to the image—and reality—of machine-gun–toting gangsters. In the past few months, J. Edgar Hoover and his Bureau of Investigation agents had killed John Dillinger in Chicago, and Bonnie Parker and Clyde Barrow in Louisiana. Abroad, the militarists in Berlin, Rome and Tokyo darkened the international landscape.

The people who boarded the *Morro Castle* that day would leave the troubled world behind for a few carefree days, and they were celebrating from the moment they reached the pier. A couple from Bangor, Pennsylvania, had a large party of friends there to see them off. On the dock, the group walked past a retired brewer and his wife who had waited years for this vacation. Two sisters had booked a cabin to finally spend some time together; a mother and daughter emerged from a taxi with similar ideas.

As they followed bellhops toting their luggage up the gangway, these new passengers marveled at the huge ship much as Tom Torresson had done months earlier. In the foyer, they admired the inlaid wood paneling and were charmed by pursers who took the time to chat with them. The better officers would remember their names and something special about each guest and bring it up later. Such personal service was standard, but the stories often blurred—there were so many honeymooners, retirees and single women on summer break from a teaching job. On this cruise, there was more variety than usual on the passenger list.

Eva Hoffman, a twenty-six-year-old nursing school graduate and Guggenheim fellowship winner, wanted one final trip before she began a new job and married her fiancé, Max Krauss. She was given Cabin 315, on D Deck, forward near the elevator. A tall, lanky man in a priest's collar, the Reverend Raymond Egan, a young assistant pastor at St. Mary's Church in the Bronx, was traveling alone. He would share Cabin 276, C Deck aft, with another passenger, a stranger to him. The former New York state senator Herman Torborg, accompanied by his niece and nephew, was traveling on the cheap. The politician and the teenagers took propeller suites on lowly E Deck. Next door, in Cabin 603, the Lione family was traveling for free. The Depression had forced Anthony Lione, an architect by trade, to take work as an insurance salesman, and he had proven quite good at it. Recently named salesman of the year by Metropolitan Life, this trip was his reward. Lione's wife, Mary, and their sons, Raymond and Robert, shared the small cabin with two beds. From the moment they walked on board, young Robert—two months shy of his fifth birthday—was entranced by the ship's grand staircase.

Doris Wacker, an eighteen-year-old girl from Roselle Park, New Jersey, was much more impressed with the ship than her father seemed to be. Her parents had allowed her to tag along on their annual cruise as a reward for graduating salutatorian at Benedictine Academy in nearby Elizabeth. The Wackers were traveling with the McArthurs from Philadelphia and the Bodners from Elizabeth, New Jersey. The mayor of Roselle Park, Murray B. Sheldon, had planned to join them but at the last minute had business he could not escape. He would miss all the fun. This was the third year the couples had cruised together, but their first on an American liner. Herbert Wacker, borough engineer for Roselle Park, was skeptical the Ward Line could live up to European standards. His wife, Lillian, somewhat superstitious, was wary of the pier number.

The Wackers had two reasons to celebrate: Doris's graduation and Herbert's forty-second birthday, which would fall during the voyage. Doris had tanned to a dark brown over the summer and could not wait to get on the water. The Wackers took Cabin 228, while their daughter bunked with her friend, Marjorie Budlong, in Cabin 214, just next door to the ship's office.

If Thomas Torresson Jr. noticed pretty Doris Wacker when she boarded the ship that day, he would not remember it later. He was too busy nursing his growing melancholy. When this group of passengers departed the ship, so would he. The summer vacation rotation was ending, and he was out of a job come next Saturday. This was going to be his last cruise aboard the *Morro Castle.*

Tom had come to love his job and the sailing life. He enjoyed traveling up and down the East Coast, visiting Cuba every week. In two months, he thought he'd found a home, and now it was all ending. He wanted to make the most of his last voyage, but also longed to find a way to stay aboard. Those are the thoughts that ran through his mind as he checked in this new group of passengers. For him, this cruise was the end of his last summer vacation.

By the time the ship sailed that afternoon, Tom and the other pursers had welcomed 259 passengers, not quite half what the ship would hold. Others would join the cruise in Havana, including a famous tennis player from Yale and a few wealthy Cubans who had reserved A Deck suites. These additional bookings would add another 59 passengers, for a total of 318. Even if it did not strain the ship's capacity, it was more crowded than normal.

Captain Robert Willmott was not particularly looking forward to this cruise. He was still wary of his crew's low morale and could not help but feel the undercurrent of trouble. He could hardly avoid such thoughts as he turned in his report on the fire from the previous voyage. In it, he did not mention the fire hoses that had failed. If he even knew it happened, he would have supposed his bumbling crew simply did not know how to operate the hoses; he suspected no mechanical failure.

This would be the 174th cruise of the *Morro Castle.* During his regular inspection, Willmott found the ship in fine shape, almost as good as she had been four years earlier. She was still beautiful, still as fast as ever, and if there were problems with the crew, they were too subtle for most passengers to notice. On the surface, at least, everything was running smoothly.

It would be quite a profitable trip. Along with the mail, the ship carried a large cache of ammunition—marked "sporting goods" on the manifest—for delivery to unnamed parties in Cuba. In Havana, they would pick up tobacco, pineapples, avocados and other produce for the importers in New York. The cargo was more profitable, and less trouble, than a few hundred tourists.

The weather was expected to be fine, which pleased Willmott as much as it would the passengers. The tropical storm season had reached its peak, and the Atlantic was even more unpredictable than normal. The hurricane that Willmott had battled the prior September made him wary of this time of year, but the weather reports suggested the run to Havana would be smooth and pleasant. A hurricane had passed the week before and the ship managed to stay out of its way. There was nothing extraordinary percolating in the tropics at the moment except for Willmott's growing sense of dread.

The first night was uneventful. The passengers went through the slow dance of acquainting themselves with their new surroundings. They made a show of exploring the formal rooms, of smoking in the Smoking Room and lounging in the Lounge. The passengers would not be fully comfortable with the ship until Monday, and on Tuesday they would be in Havana. The schedule was perfect to keep everything new, keep people breezing through their vacation. Just as they became familiar with the ship, they were allowed to stretch their legs in Cuba.

In the few hours they'd spent on the ship so far, the cruise compared unfavorably to others that the Wackers, Bodners and McArthurs had taken. Like many passengers, they noted the ship had not held a lifeboat drill. Another passenger, in fact, Arthur Sivation of Philadelphia, asked cruise director Bob Smith why the *Morro Castle* did not conduct lifeboat drills after leaving port. Sivation said he'd done it on other ships and thought it was fun.

"The passengers would get a kick out of it," Sivation said.

Smith said such drills were more for the crew than for passengers and that the captain did not want to trouble his guests.

"As far as safety is concerned, you are safer on this ship than you are at 42nd Street and Broadway in New York," Smith said. It was a line Willmott used often.

On Sunday, it was sunny with highs in the 70s, a pleasant day for everyone but Doris Wacker. She had gotten horribly seasick; it was her first ocean cruise, after all. With the *Morro Castle* undulating beneath her, Doris held her head over the rail while her father steadied her. He told her to look at how beautiful the water was, then to look up at the sky. After a while, her nausea passed. By the late afternoon, she was sunning herself on deck with Marjorie Budlong while other guests splashed about in the Sea Spray. Nearby, Bob Smith and the assistant cruise director, Herman Cluthe, kept guests busy with tennis, shuffleboard and a miniature track, complete with toy horses and real betting.

Early Sunday morning, while most passengers were still adjusting to sleep aboard a rocking ship, George Alagna took his shift in the radio room. He had the predawn watch and was bored as usual. There was little to do except stretch and watch the sun break over the Atlantic. The ship was quiet, and Alagna thought that, despite the hour, it was one of the most pleasant times on board.

At 5:45 A.M. a buzzer signal from the bridge alerted Alagna that someone wanted to use the ship's radio direction finder. The *Morro Castle* was sailing just off the Outer Banks of North Carolina, a hazardous stretch of sea known as the Graveyard of the Atlantic, a place where no fewer than 600 ships had been recorded lost. The receiver picked up signals from beacons, which in turn guided the ship through the tricky waters of the graveyard.

Silence, then the sound of a jazz band. Alagna heard the strains of music squeezing through the ship's tinny speakers and realized what was going on. The men on the bridge were using the direction finder as a radio, and it aggravated him to no end. Not only were they not hunting navigation signals; they were playing with equipment that Alagna considered his. It happened all the time, and usually the bridge crew would give up after a minute, get their readings and turn the radio back over to him. So, at first,

Alagna said nothing. But this morning they kept tuning, as if they were trying to make the signal come in clearer. It went on for nearly eight minutes, and by then Alagna had had enough. A navigation reading usually took less than three minutes. The officers on the bridge had been playing with the equipment three times that long.

Alagna rang two bells, a signal the wireless room used to call a messenger from the bridge. It was supposed to be for emergencies, in case the radioman on duty had gotten an important weather report but could not leave his post. The signal suggested that the wireless operator was indispensable, so Alagna was very fond of it.

Ivan Freeman, the *Morro Castle*'s second officer, had charge of the bridge that morning, and when he got the signal from the wireless room, he sent a quartermaster down to see what Alagna needed. The man got an earful.

"Tell the mate not to use that goddamned compass so much and stop tuning in music on it," Alagna said.

When the quartermaster reported this, Freeman had a fit. He certainly did not believe he had to take such grief from a whiner and a troublemaker over some harmless fun with the radio receiver.

"Watch things," Freeman said, and marched off the bridge.

Freeman stormed into the radio room and told Alagna he was a smart-ass who had no right to talk to him, or any officer, in such a manner.

"I am in command of the ship when I am on that bridge. I will do anything I want with that radio compass," Freeman said. "Those are my orders. You have no business speaking to an officer the way you did."

Alagna was as cocky as any officer on the ship, and perhaps even more headstrong. Freeman's tone offended him, and he would not back down. The bridge, he said, had been misusing equipment, trying to tune in radio stations for six and a half of the previous eight minutes.

"I'll speak to you any way I please if I feel my duties are being interfered with," Alagna said.

Freeman could not believe this arrogant radioman showed such little respect. After all the trouble he'd had, Freeman thought Alagna should be thankful to have a job. So, sounding like a schoolyard tattletale, Freeman said he would report Alagna's outburst to the captain.

"I will see that you are fired when we get into New York."

Freeman kept his promise. At the shift change, he told William Warms that he had been "grossly insulted" and that Alagna was out of control. Warms suggested he go to Captain Willmott about it.

Later that morning, the captain called George Rogers to his cabin to discuss Alagna—a meeting that was never recorded in his log. Until that point, Willmott said, he had been able to overlook the radioman's attitude and, despite his paranoia, even the attempted strike. But it seemed that every cruise, there was another problem with Alagna.

The tiff with Freeman wasn't a serious offense—just another case of clashing egos among the ranks. Of course, he didn't want Alagna to use the buzzer to summon another officer, particularly to cuss him out. But it wasn't just that. There was also the problem with the purser's office, and the trouble with customs. While the ship was in port, immigration officers stood at the gangplank and checked the papers of everyone coming or going. Alagna thought it amounted to harassment and often refused to show his. One time, he nearly started a riot.

"What is the matter with this second operator of yours?" Willmott said. "I think the man is crazy."

Willmott said he had no choice but to fire Alagna. But he was concerned about how the young agitator might react, so he told Rogers not to tell Alagna he was being dismissed until they were back in New York. For the rest of the cruise, Willmott said, he wanted Rogers to handle the most sensitive wireless room duties.

"I want you to take the key to that emergency room and I want you to put it in your pocket," the captain told Rogers. "I do not want that key to the emergency room anywhere that man can get it, because I do not trust him."

Willmott was afraid Alagna might tamper with the radio compass, leaving the ship blind in a fog or rain. Once a week, Rogers was supposed to inspect the radio compass to make sure that everything was working and that the batteries were charged. The compass was stored in a small room off the bridge, where the ship's most sensitive electronic equipment was kept. Sometimes Rogers sent Alagna, but now the captain wanted the equipment checked twice as often as normal, and he wanted Rogers to do it.

If there were other reasons he feared Alagna, neither man said anything of it.

* * *

56

Monday night was the Fancy Dress Ball, one of the more lavish parties of the cruise. Held in the B Deck Ballroom, just off the enclosed promenade, passengers danced into the early morning hours as the band played on a stage decorated like an old sailing ship, complete with sails, bow and sea-horse figurehead. Passengers were invited to the ship's costume room to pick out something for the occasion, and a good number of them played along. The pursers were required to keep the female passengers happy by dancing with them and buying them an occasional drink. Every week, each purser got a $14 bar account that they were supposed to spend buying drinks for passengers. It amounted to a lot of socializing, as drinks cost only 25 cents apiece. Tom Torresson routinely dressed as a gaucho for the Fancy Dress Ball, going so far as to add a black mustache and flat hat. In honor of the ship's décor, Bob Tolman went as Louis XVI, or "Louis the Quince," as the other pursers called him.

Tom didn't particularly care for the dancing or mingling, but he didn't feel too silly. Most people were too drunk to notice his clumsy dance moves, and the rocking ship covered up a lot of missteps. In all, it was a sloppy affair, the most ostentatious of all the parties aboard the *Morro Castle*. Although he wasn't a big fan of dancing or gauchos, Tom thought that he would even miss the Fancy Dress Ball when he left his job behind.

He had little time to sleep off the party. Tom was awake before dawn on Tuesday, September 4, to meet the harbor pilot who came aboard at Havana. The captain always invited the pilot on board to eat breakfast before the ship reached the harbor. It was a perk the pilots appreciated, and it made them prompt—just the way the Ward Line liked them. Tom pulled the same duty with the New York Harbor pilots on Saturdays.

On this morning, Tom escorted the Havana pilot to the officers' mess and then took him to the bridge, where he would steer the ship past its namesake fort and into downtown. The tired young purser went through his work mechanically that morning. It occurred to him that he would not miss getting up before 5 A.M.

Later that morning, George Rogers checked the radio compass. When he got to the bridge, he found someone had locked the door. He had not realized how serious Willmott was about security, and it alarmed him. Rogers had not thought it was a big deal. Somebody was always on the bridge, so who could sneak into the radio compass room without being seen? The locked door meant that the captain had ordered someone else to watch the compass, too. It made Rogers wonder what else from their conversation Willmott had shared with his other officers.

Ivan Freeman saw Rogers trying to open the door and called over to him.

"If you want to go in, I have got the key."

Rogers, perhaps detecting a little power play in Freeman's tone, went along with it. "Yeah, I've got one, too. But why is the door locked?"

"Well, don't you know?" Freeman said.

"What are you going to do, give me ten guesses?" Rogers said.

"One ought to be sufficient."

"What do you mean, something about Alagna?"

"Sure," Freeman said. "The old man told me to lock that and keep the key where I could get it."

Rogers shrugged, unlocked the door and stepped inside the room. There was nothing wrong with the compass—he hadn't expected there to be—and he left quickly. The captain's suspicions and heightened security were interesting. He wondered whether Willmott feared other members of the crew. Obviously, a lot of people knew about Alagna. Did they know something he didn't? Rogers studied his options. He considered telling Alagna what was in store for him in New York, then thought better of it. He decided he would follow Willmott's orders and say nothing. Not yet.

Havana was in turmoil. When the *Morro Castle* arrived that morning, tensions in the Cuban capital were simmering in the aftershock of revolution. Weeks earlier, the Cuban government claimed to have captured three Americans and veterans of earlier attempted coups. Hours before the ship arrived, there had been bombings from other revolutionaries in retaliation, most targeting the homes of high-ranking officials. Rumors that large arms shipments were coming ashore drifted through the city. It's unclear whether anyone connected these rumors to the *Morro Castle*. That night, while the ship was in port, more than a dozen bombs exploded across the town, and the ship's officers could only hope the passengers would think the noise was fireworks. It seemed the city was getting worse every trip. Gay Havana no longer seemed to live up to its billing, and it felt like the end of something. It had gotten so volatile that Hemingway—who had been in town since July—left his boat with friends that very night under the guise of having the *Pilar* scraped and revarnished. He ducked out on the evening ferry to Key West.

Most of the *Morro Castle*'s passengers noticed none of this commotion. Herbert Wacker hired a car and driver to show his family the predictable sights. Like many passengers, Herbert Wacker dressed up to tour the city, wearing a white suit and tie like a Caribbean plantation owner. His wife, Lillian, wore a casual white dress, while Doris and Marjorie Budlong sported sun dresses and also carried their bathing suits. On the streets, the locals teased Doris about the deep tan she had cultivated over the summer.

"You're too dark to be an American," one man called out.

"She must be a Cuban," another said.

Later the four posed for a portrait photographer on the beach beneath a palm tree and the blazing Cuban sun. That afternoon they went to Sloppy Joe's, where Herbert bought his daughter her first drink of alcohol, a crème de menthe frappé. He did not allow her to drink—and did not want her to start—but while in the famous bar, he thought she should at least have a taste.

Doris was thrilled to be in the city, and thought that cruising must be one of the most fun things a person could do. She enjoyed Havana almost as much as she enjoyed the ship. It was a magical day; the Wackers ended it at the Sans Souci, and Doris loved the famous nightclub, too. It was beautiful. She thought the dancers were amazing.

She did not notice later that evening when they drove past a row of houses with red lightbulbs on their porches. The driver pointed them out to her father.

"Those are the drug stores, and they are open all night," the man said.

Tom Torresson did nothing in particular on his final trip into Havana. Perhaps he thought of calling up Margaret Haines or going out to the

Sans Souci, but he did neither. He knew the city was becoming more dangerous. In fact, Havana had taken on ominous tones in the two months since he had first visited. Of course, it was only his perception that had changed. From the deck of the ship he could look out across the Malecon, where tourists and locals strolled along the city's waterfront. He could see the fortress Morro Castle standing at the headwaters of Havana Harbor, with its lighthouse jutting skyward like a proud figurehead. The lighthouse's beam swept across the bay where just two months earlier he'd spent an afternoon rowing a lifeboat. That experience was not so far removed that he could be nostalgic for it, but he certainly would never forget it. If he had thought about it at the time, he might have been nervous. The waters of the harbor were as dangerous as the city. Only weeks before, a shark had attacked a young swimmer within sight of the fort. Fishermen caught the shark and beat it to death. That was justice in Cuba.

That evening, as the ferry left for Key West carrying scores of tourists, their cars and a famous American author, Tom took his last look at Havana from the deck of the *Morro Castle.* If he noticed the ferry, he most likely only thought that soon he too would be leaving this magical and malevolent city.

The next morning, September 5, the *Morro Castle* cleared Havana Harbor and began its return voyage to New York. On board were the 59 additional passengers, many of them Americans who had spent the summer in Havana. A young Cuban girl going to New York for school, Rosario Felipe, took an exquisite A Deck cabin, No. 17, just off the ballroom mezzanine. Renée Méndez Capote, the daughter of a wealthy Cuban politician, planned to meet a man in New York with whom she would travel to Europe. Capote took Cabin 15. So, with 318 passengers and 231 crew members aboard, the *Morro Castle* sailed out of her last port.

That morning, two angry thunderstorms collided over the Atlantic nearly 600 miles east of Miami. Moisture was released into the atmosphere, and the condensation created water vapor. A low-pressure system was born. The weather patterns began to clash, mingling as they drew strength from the warm ocean. Later, the systems coordinated and began a counterclockwise dance that drew them west. Clouds were drawn to this new storm, heat was generated. The wind picked up speed. An eye formed.

By the end of the day, winds around the storm had reached 60 mph, and the pattern became flawlessly circular. The sixth tropical system of the season began to move on a course for Freeport, where the warmer waters of the Gulf Stream would give it even greater strength. As the sun set on September 5, 1934, the storm broke free of inertia and started to move.

Thursday passed at sea. Off the Florida coast, passengers were served a lavish dinner. The typical menu included Boiled Alaska Salmon with Hollandaise sauce, Roast Young Vermont Turkey, dressing and cranberry sauce, or Baked Domestic Ham. Passengers had their choice of an assortment of soups, fruits, pies and ice cream, American and Cuban coffee, and lettuce salads with Roquefort dressing. No one left the *Morro Castle*'s dining room hungry. The service, however, was another matter.

The Wackers had sailed on the Hamburg-American Line's SS *Resolute* the previous year, and the Cunard–White Star's RMS *Berengaria* before that. The *Morro Castle* did not live up to their European expectations and, if possible, the service had gotten worse as the voyage progressed. When Herbert Wacker complained, a steward told him a lot of the crew had gotten drunk in Havana and were in their bunks recovering. He apologized for the inconvenience.

Once again, the captain did not show up for the main dinner sitting. Willmott's absence particularly upset Dolly McTigue and her new husband, Sidney Davidson, who had managed to get seats at the captain's table. They had looked forward to his legendary tales, but the honeymooners would hear of no heroics at this meal. Willmott was "persistently absent from all meals, so that at the captain's table there sat only emptiness and silence," Rosario Comacho, another guest at the table, remembered. "As rumor had it through the entire voyage, this was because of some serious trouble of some kind in relation to the crew." Willmott had told some passengers about trouble on the ship, as if inoculating himself and the Ward Line against later complaints. There could scarcely be any other reason for airing the company's dirty laundry.

The Elimination Dance that evening was marvelous, the party perhaps the best of the cruise. Passengers danced to the big band music for a while and then took breaks outside, where the temperature on the deck was nearly perfect—just cool enough to refresh them after being packed into a ballroom full of people. To Doris Wacker and Marjorie Budlong, it was exhilarating. Doris loved to dance and was good at it, and she enjoyed the chance to dress up formally every night—things she rarely got to do in Roselle Park. She and Marjorie even took a spin with the assistant cruise director, Herman Cluthe. The cruise directors were so nice that evening Doris suspected her father had tipped them. It never occurred to her that perhaps the men enjoyed the company of an attractive young lady with a smile as bright as the Caribbean sun.

As the *Morro Castle* sailed north, the ship rocked through heavy swells, though not heavy enough to upset the party. Even Doris Wacker had her sea legs by now. The dancing and drinking went on into the night as 300 vacationers tried to squeeze as much fun as they could out of their trip. After all, they had only one more night on the ship.

On Friday morning, September 7, George Rogers had another meeting with Captain Willmott. Rogers would not discuss it with Alagna, who was curious, but afterward Willmott told William Warms there was great trouble brewing on the ship. Two bottles of sulfuric acid had been smuggled aboard, and Willmott feared someone planned to sabotage the ship with it. He had been told the acid could disable the engines or, if it were thrown into one of the public rooms, would create a stench that would force an evacuation. Robert Willmott feared that, if nothing else, someone meant to open one of the bottles and hurl the deadly acid at him.

Willmott never said where he learned about the acid, but he clearly believed it existed. It seemed there was something every week. There was the fire during the previous cruise, the constant smuggling, the crewman who had thrown food at him, the strike. It had all built up into more than Willmott could take. He felt the ship was spiraling out of his control, that all the rumors of mutiny and sabotage were true. Rogers later said that Willmott suspected Alagna had gotten the acid in Havana. It seemed to fit a pattern. But Rogers never said where the captain could have gotten such an idea.

Willmott asked Rogers to find the vials of acid and get rid of them. If he could just get through this cruise, the captain thought, he could set everything right. Until then, he would take no chances, because Robert Willmott was not sure whom he could trust.

Later that day, Rogers told Willmott he had found the vial in a locker in the radio room. It wasn't acid, Rogers claimed, but some sort of stinkball fluid. He said it was not nearly so dangerous as they had heard, but he threw it overboard anyway. The captain said little about this news. It appeared that, in a matter of days, he had lost all the confidence he once had. Perhaps that was because he wasn't so sure that someone wasn't out to get him.

Years later, one passenger on that voyage said that he had a conversation with the captain in which Willmott was very frank about his problems with the crew. This passenger said Willmott claimed he was going to fire some of his officers when they got back to New York. As this person recalled the talk, Willmott had said it was George Rogers who had become a problem, not George Alagna.

That morning, William Warms awoke early. He got up at 5:45 after less than seven hours of sleep, much less than he would have liked—he was beat. On Thursday, he had spent the entire day running the ship's operation at the captain's request. He turned in at 11 P.M., knowing that Friday would be a long day, the last at sea before arriving in New York. Seven hours would not be nearly enough.

At 10 A.M., the captain called Warms into his quarters. Willmott looked rough, as if he hadn't slept in days. He seemed scared and spoke in clipped sentences. The things he told his chief officer that morning were even more shocking than his appearance, but Warms tried not to show his surprise.

"I am afraid something is going to happen tonight," Willmott said. "I can feel it."

He told Warms about the sulfuric acid, said he feared sabotage. Willmott related his concerns to many officers, even Arthur Pender, the old night watchman. Still, some thought it was a sign of desperation that Willmott would confide in Warms, who was not the most well-liked man in the Ward Line ranks. Willmott had told his wife that he did not trust his mate.

"Warms is too erratic. . . . He doesn't know what he's doing from one moment to the next." But that wasn't the whole story. On some levels, Willmott considered William Warms his only confidant. He had taken Warms as a first officer when others wouldn't. He knew Warms was a sailor's sailor, a tough guy with a knack for handling cargo—a handy skill indeed aboard the *Morro Castle.* That had become the arrangement between the two men: Warms handled the technical side of the ship, while Willmott hammed it up with the passengers and put a happy face on their business. The two men trusted each other, at least to an extent. But Warms had never heard Willmott talk as he did on that morning.

"You know I keep my doors locked for fear that he may come in here and throw acid on me," Willmott said.

Willmott had always been a strong man, not easily startled or given to superstition or flights of fancy, and Warms was surprised to hear him talk this way. Warms did not care for Alagna, either, but had not suspected he was dangerous. But he thought it best to humor the captain.

"We can search his cabin, Captain, or take him downstairs and lock him up," Warms said.

"No, he is so damned smart that he would not keep anything in his room."

Willmott said he didn't want any trouble. A company man to the end, he preferred to take the risk just to avoid bad publicity. He had written a letter to the Radio Marine Corporation asking for a replacement operator. Now he only needed Warms to keep a watch out again during the final day; he had already told the stewards and pursers to make sure the radioman didn't linger in the public rooms.

"There may be trouble, and you know he held this ship up for an hour and forty-five minutes before, and I don't want that trouble," Willmott said. "When we get to New York, we will discharge him."

Friday was quiet. It was too dreary outside to run the Sea Spray, and most of the guests milled about the public rooms, drank and prepared for the end-of-the-cruise party that night. The Captain's Farewell Dinner and Gala Ball would be held that evening and last well into the morning. Some people, in fact, usually just stayed up until the ship reached port. There was no question it would be the party of the cruise, but some wondered whether the captain would finally show up.

Willmott tried to keep up appearances that afternoon, giving a tour of the bridge to two doctors and their families. He recounted the storm of the previous September once more, describing in grand detail the waves that had been as high as the bridge, which Willmott noted stood 65 feet above the water. He likely showed them the photograph and framed resolution from the passengers of that cruise, thanking him for saving their lives. No doubt the weather was once again weighing on him. The crew had gotten word that Hurricane No. 6 was tracking along the Gulf Stream and was now astern of them by only a few hundred miles. The storm's winds had reached 86 miles per hour and its eye was just south of the Carolinas. Sometime in the night the outer bands of the storm would catch up to the *Morro Castle*. For now, the ocean was calm, murky and dark.

Tom Torresson was busy with the ship's business that afternoon, for he had to have everything in order when the passengers disembarked the next morning. There was a mountain of paperwork to do, a lot of standardized immigration forms for the foreign passengers. At one point, he took a break and wandered out on deck to stretch his legs. The ship hardly seemed like a floating party barge at that particular moment. The *Morro Castle* was plowing through heavy fog off the Outer Banks, a mist cut by the ship's whistle every fifteen seconds. It was otherwise quiet on deck, and he felt alone. It only enhanced the doleful feeling hanging over Tom. He would be off the ship in twenty-four hours, cast adrift in life with no rudder and no set course. He supposed he would apply for college, but he wasn't sure what he wanted to do.

Tom had a funny feeling, although it would have been hard to avoid it with the view he had that afternoon. The weather on the ocean was reminiscent of those popular black-and-white horror pictures, Bela Lugosi movies like *Dracula* or *Island of Lost Souls*. He would later wonder if it was just his pending departure from the ship that had him in a mood, but in retrospect Tom imagined that he had felt like there was something wrong.

By that afternoon, Warms had stirred up half the crew with the captain's wild tales of sabotage. He told the boatswain to watch Alagna and, when the night watchman came on duty at 5 P.M., Warms called him to his personal quarters.

"For God's sake, watch that fellow tonight. The captain thinks he's going to do something tonight, the last night out, and he has bragged that he was going to tie the Ward Line up and they would not run any ships, and he was going to raise hell in general."

Warms was referring to a story that George Rogers had related to Willmott. A few weeks earlier, Rogers said, a sailor from the *President Wilson*, another cruise ship, had come aboard in Havana to visit Alagna. The two men compared conditions on their respective ships and concluded that if something happened, "there is lots of ways to get even on the ship." The *President Wilson* radioman allegedly said he had a friend who was a chemist, a man who had created a solution that would stink up an entire ship so much that it might take an entire week to fumigate it. Such hearsay was all the proof Willmott and Warms needed.

Not to worry—the night watchman told Warms he would take care of this problem. He enlisted another officer to help him set a trap for Alagna, although they never actually explained what the trap was. They never got the chance.

The rain hit late that afternoon, just as the kitchen staff prepared for the early dinner sitting. It was the busiest time of day on the ship as cooks and the waitstaff got ready for the meal while the pursers, cruise directors and stewards decorated for the Ball. Warms took his dinner around 5 P.M. As he was leaving the bridge, he saw the captain in the chart room. Willmott made some small talk, perhaps about the weather, but he seemed preoccupied. Warms spoke to him briefly—later he would not remember what it was about—and went on his way.

Willmott telegraphed the Ward Line offices that afternoon to inform them the ship was passing the Outer Banks. They should be into port early, he said in his brief message. The captain loitered on the bridge that afternoon, making no effort to get ready for the formal dinner because he knew he wasn't going. Willmott had decided to eat in his cabin once again. Perhaps paranoid, he reasoned that his presence in the dining room could be the catalyst for an attack, so he would avoid public appearances for the rest of the cruise. It seemed the safest thing to do.

Willmott summoned Ferdinand Zarb, his personal steward, and ordered dinner. He wanted casaba melon, a filet of beef, mashed potatoes, lima beans, alligator pear salad, Roquefort cheese and coffee.

"Ferdinand, I'm not feeling so well, so will you bring the fruit with the dinner instead of after," Willmott said.

As he left the cabin, Zarb thought Willmott seemed nervous or excited. The steward collected the captain's dinner and returned within minutes. When he went back for Willmott's dishes, he noticed that only the melon had been eaten, and the captain was sipping his coffee.

"I don't want to eat anything else," Willmott said. "Take everything away. And bring me some hot water."

Before Zarb left, he heard Willmott call Dr. Van Zile.

"Will you please come up at once. I have the same trouble that I had last week," Willmott said.

Van Zile brought the captain some medicine, which he mixed with the hot water. When Zarb checked back a half hour later, Willmott and the doctor were still talking. It was about 7 P.M.

The passengers noticed Willmott's absence with a measure of irritation. After he had failed to appear the prior evening, they were more confident he would show up for this meal. After all, it was the *Captain*'s Farewell Dinner. It was the last night of the cruise.

A rumor spread among the passengers that Willmott had promised a close friend on board that he would dine publicly that evening. But as the hours passed and he didn't show, people were not quiet with their displeasure. Some complained to the staff, others whispered among themselves. Soon, Bob Smith announced that Captain Willmott would not be dining with them due to unforeseen circumstances.

A half hour later, a few minutes before 7:30 P.M., the bridge called the purser's office and told them to find the doctor. De Witt Van Zile was having a drink with Smith and Bob Tolman. The message from Howard Hansen, the fourth officer, was short and serious: Come quick, the captain has had another attack.

Warms had just returned from dinner and not heard about the captain, but he knew something was wrong when Van Zile appeared on the bridge with his black bag and a mood to match. He explained that the captain had taken ill, and it appeared to be the same kind of attack he had suffered before. Word among the crew had been that Willmott was going to have to take some time off, and this only seemed proof of the rumor's truth.

"I am giving him some medicine and he is now taking an enema," the doctor said.

Warms decided to check on Willmott under the pretext of ship's business. The rain, already coming down hard, was picking up. The hurricane behind them seemed to be losing strength but also gaining on them. There was another weather system ahead, a nasty one. They would have a hard time squeezing through. The *Morro Castle,* it appeared, was in for a rough night.

Willmott seemed not to care about the weather report. He told Warms that he was taking his enema and would feel all right in a bit. He mentioned that the bridge ought to have a reading on the Diamond Shoals Lightship by now, but the rain and fog was too thick. It was a scary place to be, approaching the Graveyard of the Atlantic completely blind. Warms couldn't decide if he was more worried about the *Morro Castle* or about the captain. Willmott asked him to mind the ship.

"I'll stay on the bridge," Warms said. "Don't worry, everything will be all right."

Warms went back to the wheelhouse and monitored the ship's progress from there. It was rocking well enough that there would most likely be some folks sick at dinner, and it would only get worse as the night went on. If Warms was nervous, he didn't let it show—although he had every reason to be. The *Morro Castle* was sailing through the most treacherous spot on the eastern seaboard, sandwiched between two storms. They didn't know exactly where they were, and the captain was sick. Mr. Freeman offered him no comfort.

"Well, it is getting bad. I cannot see very good, so we will take the nozzles off and slow her down and blow the whistle," Freeman said. "Do you want me to go in and tell the captain, or will you go in?"

"I'll go."

Warms was of little use at the moment and wanted to check on Willmott again anyway. Before walking back to the captain's cabin, he noticed it was 7:30 P.M.

Warms did not find Willmott in his office, so he called out to him. He got no answer, and so Warms stepped into the captain's bedroom, connected to his office. He still did not see him.

He noticed that the door to Willmott's private bath was ajar and a light was on. Warms was uncomfortable with walking in until he called out and got no reply. Then he tentatively stepped into the bathroom. What he saw horrified him.

Robert Willmott was slouched over the bathtub, his knees on the floor, his hands behind his back holding an enema bag. His pants were down and his head was slumped over into the tub. Warms could not see the captain's face, but he didn't need to. Nor did he need Dr. Van Zile for a diagnosis. William Warms knew all too well what he was seeing.

The captain was dead.

PART II

CHAPTER FIVE

Last Dance

A storm was coming. It began with a stirring in the air, a cool breeze out of the north that gathered momentum as the sun set over New Jersey. By dark, the wind roared through the canyons of Manhattan like a runaway train, kicking up paper and dust that belted those people unfortunate enough to be out walking in it. The glancing blow of the nor'easter crawling down the coast forced many New Yorkers to abandon plans to go out for the evening.

Victor M. Seckendorf was among those who preferred to stay in. The traffic passenger manager for the Ward Line was secure in his West 66th Street apartment sometime after 8 P.M. on Friday, September 7, 1934, when bad news arrived at his door. It was a courier with an urgent telegram from one of the company's ships.

Seckendorf wondered why he would receive a message at home from the *Morro Castle*. Wouldn't such a dispatch be better directed to Henry Cabaud? He signed for the telegram and, shocked, had to read it twice before the news sank in.

WILLMOTT DECEASED 7:45 P.M. ACKNOWLEDGE WARMS

Many people at the Ward Line knew Captain Robert Willmott was not in the best shape. Despite his meticulous attention to his ship's condition, Willmott seemed to not particularly monitor his own health. He was overweight, and rumor had it the captain had suffered more than one minor

73

heart attack—if any heart attack could be "minor." Seckendorf didn't have time to think much about it. He dressed, stepped out into the nasty weather and made his way to Henry Cabaud's home.

The executive vice president of the Ward Line was stunned by the news, and also furious over the way he received it. The telegram raised more questions than it answered—in fact, it was downright cryptic. What the hell was Warms thinking, Cabaud wondered, sending such a vague message? This was devastating, but the message was so sketchy he had to wonder if it were even true. He called the office and ordered a response sent immediately. Cabaud wanted answers. Had Willmott passed away from natural causes, he wondered, or something worse? The end result, he knew, was the same. It meant trouble for the Ward Line.

Cabaud went to await an answer in the Ward Line offices, where he would call in other company officials, including Tom Torresson Sr., who had left for his home in Monroe earlier that evening. As Cabaud fought his way through the wind tunnels of lower Manhattan, he most likely realized the storm was moving south. Before the *Morro Castle* made it into port, it would sail right through this storm.

The call from the bridge came into the purser's office at 7:30 P.M. Samuel Hoffman, the quartermaster, wasted no time on pleasantries. His snippy tone of voice suggested an emergency.

"Find Van Zile—quick. Tell him to get up to the captain's cabin."

There was no doubt what the call meant. Already, the purser's office had heard that Willmott would not attend the farewell dinner. Bob Tolman sent two pursers to find the doctor, even though it was not hard to guess where he was.

De Witt Van Zile was in the First-Class Dining Saloon, taking Captain Willmott's place as the ship's host. There wasn't much for a ship's doctor to do on the *Morro Castle*—mostly treat sunburns and hand out seasickness medicine—so he often passed the time entertaining passengers. On this evening, he was able to socialize and do some public relations for the Ward Line simultaneously. He apologized for Captain Willmott's absence, told upset guests that the captain was not feeling well. He could honestly tell them, in fact, that he'd just left the captain.

When the pursers interrupted, it only added intrigue to the story quickly making its way through the ship. There was no mistaking the urgency in the purser's tone, or the look of concern on Dr. Van Zile's face. His hasty departure only confirmed growing suspicions that something must be wrong with the captain.

The bridge was in chaos. The doctor found officers in white suits scurrying around, shuffling back and forth between the chart room, the wheelhouse and the captain's cabin. They seemed more concerned by what was going on in Willmott's quarters than with the weather outside, which was deteriorating quickly. But at the moment it seemed there were more dire circumstances elsewhere. In Willmott's room, Samuel Hoffman and Howard Hansen tried desperately to revive the captain, whose face had turned blue. Hansen pumped Willmott's arms back and forth as if rowing a scull while Hoffman pushed on his chest and smacked his cheeks. They tried for several minutes to resuscitate him, stopping only when Van Zile pushed his way into the room.

The doctor was horrified by both the ghostly face of the captain and the amateurish attempts to revive him. Hoffman and Hansen said that no matter what they tried, they couldn't get a reaction—not even reflexes. Nor could they feel a pulse. They had just about given up and had put the captain in his bunk to await the doctor. Van Zile went to work quickly. First, he pulled a syringe from his medicine bag and gave Willmott an injection. He then felt for a pulse, tried to detect shallow breathing and listened for a heartbeat.

In a few minutes, he confirmed what everyone already knew: it was hopeless.

De Witt Van Zile had not always been an underused ship's physician. He had spent much of his career practicing serious medicine, and had once worked at a hospital in Bayonne, New Jersey, not very far from the home of the ship's chief radio operator, George Rogers. If the easy life on the *Morro Castle* had left his medical skills rusty, it did not show. He spent a half hour examining Willmott's body, taking detailed notes and digging through his black bag for instruments. After he finished, he declared that the captain had died of a heart attack brought on by "acute indigestion." It was the same thing he'd said a month earlier about the passenger found dead in his stateroom—the man Tom Torresson had moved. Not only did the doctor's diagnosis sound suspiciously like his previous one, more than a few of the men on the bridge thought Van Zile was just plain wrong.

William Warms, especially, had to wonder if the captain had really succumbed to natural causes. After all, he had spent much of the cruise worried about his own safety, afraid that there were mutineers, saboteurs—perhaps even a murderer—aboard the *Morro Castle.* And now, just hours from port, Willmott was dead. Perhaps the captain had been right after all, someone had been out to get him, and Warms feared that he hadn't done enough to protect him.

"God bless his soul," Warms said to no one in particular.

With the death of a captain at sea, all officers move up one step in rank. That left William Warms the acting master of the *Morro Castle* and, as soon as the doctor pronounced Willmott dead, Warms made his first executive order. He told a couple of the men to dress Captain Willmott in his uniform and lay him out in his cabin. Then Warms called Eben Abbott, the chief engineer, to lock the door. Warms could not be sure the cabin wasn't a crime scene.

Abbott arrived within minutes, surprised by this turn of events—he had just spoken with the captain earlier that day. He knew Willmott had been under stress but, as usual, the captain did not share his troubles with Abbott. They had simply discussed ship's business and gone on their way.

The captain's death technically left Abbott the ranking officer on the ship, but the engineer said nothing about it. He did not want to fight William Warms for control of the ship, despite the rumors among officers that there was no love lost between the two men. After paying his respects to the captain, Abbott simply shook Warms's hand and wished him luck.

"All right, Chief," Warms said. "We'll make it."

Tom Torresson was filling out immigration paperwork when news of the captain's death reached the purser's office. He had heard talk that the captain was sick, but still could not believe it. It was sad; he liked Willmott a lot, what little time he'd spent around him. The captain had always treated him well. The news extinguished whatever fun Tom could hope to have on his final night aboard the ship. The entire staff in the purser's office seemed to be in mourning, but they kept working. There was still much to do.

Not even the death of its captain could delay the *Morro Castle*'s rigorous schedule. The ship would arrive at Pier 13 before 7 A.M. Saturday and sail again at 4 P.M. that afternoon with a new set of passengers, cargo and, now, a new captain. The company had only two choices: they could bring in a new master or promote Warms. It would be difficult to find a new captain on such short notice, but Warms would not be accused of delaying the call. He wanted to give the company as much notice as possible. Warms wanted the Ward Line to make him captain, but not because they had no other option.

Bob Tolman arrived on the bridge without knowing what had happened. He had missed the call to the purser's office, leaving for the bridge just after he sent his men out to look for the doctor. He remembered how sick the captain had seemed the week before—when he'd fallen over the davenport—but Tolman did not suspect the worst until he stepped onto the bridge and heard Hoffman, the quartermaster with the pencil-thin mustache, telling someone that "we found him in the bathtub. It must have been a stroke—or a heart attack."

Rumblings to the contrary were already circulating among the crew. Willmott had spoken of his suspicions to several of his officers, and many of them took his death as proof that the captain had been right. Hansen, the impressionable fourth officer, could not believe the captain's death was coincidence. More than a few of the other sailors had to agree it seemed unlikely that Willmott would fall to illness just a few hours from port on this particular cruise. The captain had been poisoned, Hansen decided, and he did not keep this suspicion to himself.

"Somebody slipped him a Mickey Finn," Hansen whispered to several members of the crew. The rumor spread quickly among the gossipy *Morro Castle* crew. Before the night's end, a few sailors even repeated the claim to some of the passengers.

The men not involved in that conspiracy chatter had their own parlor game, one nearly as sinister as this talk of poison. Within an hour of Willmott's death, speculation among the ship's officers turned to who would take command of the *Morro Castle*. The captain's death left a controversy in the ranks. Willmott had been one of only two men on the ship with four stripes on his uniform, and the other was Abbott—Warms had only three. Although Warms, the executive officer, assumed command in the captain's absence, many believed the company lacked faith in him. When Willmott was absent, and there had been more than a dozen occasions of that in the past four years, the Ward Line always sent in a substitute—they had never let Warms run the show. A number of men preferred to read that motive into the company's action. These men believed Abbott might be given the ship just on the basis of rank and standing in the company. It wasn't that there was a groundswell of support for the chief engineer; it was simply that Warms was widely disliked by the officers. Perhaps they found him stern, or simply not as personable, as Willmott. Whatever the reason, several members of the crew did not want to serve on a ship commanded by William Warms.

For at least one night, however, that is exactly what they faced. Before Van Zile and Abbott left the bridge, they talked about the chain of command with Warms, Hoffman, Hansen and Tolman in the captain's cabin, Willmott's body stretched out behind them. Few of the officers dared speak against Warms in his presence. They feared him or, more accurately, feared that he would become the permanent captain in less than twenty-four hours. Only one person broached the subject of rank, but Abbott remained silent. He seemed content to let the first officer run the ship, at least for the time being. Warms did not see that it was open for debate.

Still, William Warms could not take any pleasure in his appointment. This was not particularly the way he wanted to secure a promotion. Warms was torn by the circumstances. He had considered Willmott a friend and was genuinely saddened by his death. He felt guilty that the captain's death might advance his career. Perhaps Warms suspected what the other officers thought they knew, that the Ward Line had little faith in him and would never give him command of its flagship. The uncertainty of it all, perhaps coupled with his own insecurity, led Warms to go out of his way to assert himself. He ordered Tolman to send a radiogram to company officials, informing them of Willmott's death, and added, "Sign it 'Warms.'"

"I am in command now, and everyone should obey all orders I give," Warms said.

Tolman found the remark odd, especially since command had just been discussed—and settled—moments before. It made him afraid to question the wording of the radiogram. Tolman knew they should send a more detailed dispatch, but he did not argue. Perhaps, he thought, Warms was just living up to his reputation for being cheap. The purser did as he was told.

* * *

George Rogers knew the captain was dead even before Bob Tolman appeared in the wireless room. Rogers, in fact, had begun his 8 P.M.-to-midnight shift early so he could transmit the radiograms he knew would have to be sent. Although not much escaped his ears anyway, Rogers could hardly have avoided hearing the commotion of people coming and going from the bridge less than 60 feet from the radio room—and his bunk. So when Tolman arrived, Rogers was waiting.

The Ward Line offices in New York had closed for the evening, so Rogers suggested they send telegrams to the homes of company officials. But Tolman could not find Cabaud's address. Only Willmott had that information, and it was locked in the captain's safe. Getting an address for Thomas Torresson, the marine superintendent, had been as easy as calling the third assistant purser, but there was some concern Torresson would not be home. They did not have many choices. Finally, they found the address for Seckendorf.

Once the initial message was sent, the news spread quickly over the airwaves. An operator for the radio station in Tuckerton, New Jersey, called Rogers asking if "the captain in command of the *Morro Castle* was dead?" It was a sure sign the message from the frugal Warms caused more confusion than anything,

Rogers spent an hour relaying the news to various people by telegraph. After answering Tuckerton and thanking the operator for his condolences, he sent word to the *Morro Castle*'s sister ship, the *Oriente*. He thought Commodore Jones, who often substituted for Willmott, should hear this from someone in the company. There was a good chance he would take over the *Morro Castle*, at least temporarily. Rogers knew Jones well enough to send the message, but Alagna—had he known of the dispatch—would have said Rogers was just sucking up.

The rest of the crew was as busy as Rogers; the captain's death altered everyone's work in some way. Shortly after 8 P.M., Tom Torresson was called away from the purser's office to the infirmary to help Dr. Van Zile fill out the report on Willmott's death. He did not know Dr. Van Zile very well, only enough to say hello when they passed each other on deck. On this evening, Tom found the doctor professional and composed, particularly given the chore he had just finished. He took dictation as Van Zile went over his notes, reliving every step of Willmott's examination. Tom was relieved to find the captain had not been moved to the infirmary. He had seen one dead body, and that was enough.

Tom typed the report in the purser's office and then filled out the standardized forms for a shipboard death. He needed a dozen copies, and even though he loaded up the typewriter with forms and carbon papers, he had to type the entire report four times. It took him more than an hour.

While he banged on the typewriter keys, Tolman met with Bob Smith and Henry Speierman, the chief steward, in the purser's office. The men discussed what, if anything, they should tell the passengers. It was almost time for the gala. They did not want to ruin the last night of the trip for passengers by thrusting this tragedy upon them, but neither did they think it was an appropriate time for a party. Certainly, they didn't feel like pretending to have a grand time or singing "Auld Lang Syne" with a crowd of merry drunks.

In truth, they also feared the bad publicity of withholding the news. Willmott's absence had been noticed, and more than a few passengers had complained of not having met him yet. Since he didn't show up for his own farewell dinner, and his death would be reported in the papers, it would look bad—perhaps coldhearted—to pretend nothing had happened. Tolman, Smith and Speierman decided there should be an announcement, and recommended as much to Warms. They asked the acting captain if they should also cancel the gala. Warms did not have to think about his decision more than a moment.

"Of course," he said. "Cancel the party."

By 9 P.M., the passengers were getting restless. The gala was a half-hour late starting, with no sign it would commence anytime soon. This, in addition to the poor dining room service, left many passengers with the impression that the crew could not get its act together. A few people may have heard about the captain's death, but the word had not spread. Most people were stunned when Bob Smith made the announcement—once in the Dining Saloon and again in the Lounge—that Captain Willmott had died. Out of respect for the captain, Smith said, the evening's festivities were canceled.

Smith invited passengers to stay on deck, and promised the bars would remain open. If anyone wanted to have private parties in their room, Smith asked only that they keep the noise down for those guests who wanted to turn in early.

The news snuffed out the excitement that had been building for the last dance. Doris Wacker and her family had just finished dinner when the announcement came, and it made her sadder than she could have imagined. She was sorry to hear about the captain, whom she never met, but was also upset that the trip had to end this way. Doris knew it might be a long time before she got to attend another fancy dress gala. The dances had been among her favorite things on the trip.

Few people would take Smith's suggestion to retire early that night. Most loitered in the Lounge, drinking, smoking and chatting, the reverence that followed the cruise director's announcement soon doused by alcohol. Before long, a dozen impromptu parties were under way around the ship. Some gathered in the public rooms, others retreated to private cabins. Few of the people on board had any intention of retiring early.

The Wackers were among those few exceptions. It had been a disappointing cruise for Herbert and Lillian Wacker, not up to the standards they had enjoyed on other ships, and they chose to turn in early. They would not be sad for their trip on the *Morro Castle* to end. Their daughter, however, had too much energy to go to bed before 10 P.M. So Doris Wacker and Marjorie Budlong were left to stroll through the public rooms in their party dresses, watching everyone else apparently having more fun than they were.

While wandering the decks, Doris and Marjorie met Rosario Felipe, one of the few passengers their own age. They talked for a while on the Promenade Deck with friends of Felipe's family, and then later moved on to Felipe's A Deck suite, No. 17, which opened onto the First-Class Lounge Mezzanine. The girls decided that, since it was the last night of the cruise, they should stay up all night and watch the ship sail into New York Harbor at dawn. They did not want to miss another minute of their vacation. As they talked, they could hear strains of revelry in the lounge below them.

The bridge was like a funeral parlor.

The men spoke in hushed tones, the lighting was low, and the captain's body was laid out in the next room. While Willmott had not made many friends among the deckhands and able-bodied seamen on board, most of the officers had liked—even admired—the captain. His death brought not only sadness, but uncertainty, and some of the somber mood in the wheelhouse most likely reflected the fear of change on the horizon. The *Morro Castle* would be a different ship without Willmott, and no one was sure it would be for the better.

The whispers in dark corners that evening centered on the impending captain controversy and whether the Ward Line would give the ship to Warms. The officers were divided. If the first officer was promoted, many of them might also advance in rank—fourth officer to third, third officer to second, second officer to first. It could mean slightly more money, but for some even that did not make the idea of a Captain Warms palatable. They disliked him because he was so stern, a rigid by-the-book man, and nowhere near as politic or personable as Willmott. He was not, well, *warm*. Some, those few with a view of the larger picture, thought he also lacked the leadership qualities necessary to keep such a bickering, ego-maniacal crew working together.

Warms may have known what his crew thought of him and his chances to succeed Willmott, and in response went out of his way to project an image of control and command. That evening, he worked beyond his usual shift. He would not relinquish the bridge even though he had been on duty since early morning. Shortly after 10 P.M., he told Ivan Freeman, who was now the acting first officer, to take the rest of the night off. Warms said he would handle things.

"You better lay down," Warms said. "You have a long day tomorrow."

More interesting than Warms's work ethic was his protracted conversation with the chief engineer. Eben Abbott rarely loitered on the bridge so much, and seldom had much to say to Warms, but on this evening he spent much of his time doing both. Some officers speculated he was establishing his presence, while others believed he was fishing for information. It was obvious to anyone who saw the two men that they weren't just talking casually. More likely, they discussed what tomorrow held, what the Ward Line might do, and how they would play into it. They spoke quietly, as if sharing a secret. It was in the middle of this conversation that Tom Torresson found the two men in the dim light outside the chart room.

Tom had finished typing Van Zile's report and, after the doctor signed it, he needed the captain's signature. The purser interrupted the men and handed the report to Warms, who seemed mildly surprised. Instead of signing, the acting captain demurred.

"You should sign it because you have four stripes," Warms said to Abbott.

Abbott had to wonder if Warms was just being obsequious, or if he was serious. The engineer made no move to take the report; he said nothing. Finally, Tom spoke up. Although he had great respect for his elders and his senior officers, the seventeen-year-old also knew his duty. He had been ordered to have the captain sign the report and, as far as he was concerned, Warms was now captain of the *Morro Castle.*

"Sir, it says here 'captain,' and you are now the captain," Tom told Warms. "You have to sign it."

Finally, Warms signed the report.

The Ward Line's response arrived at 10:30 P.M. The cable amused George Rogers not only for its clipped brevity and demand for more information, but because it was addressed to Bob Tolman. Perhaps the radiogram was directed to the chief purser because his name had been included in the last dispatch, but the conspiracy-minded radioman took it as yet another sign that the company had little confidence in Warms. It was hard not to notice that the Ward Line, in one sentence, managed to ask the obvious question and criticize the acting captain:

PLEASE CONFIRM QUICKLY MESSAGE SENT BY WARMS TO
SECKENDORF REGARDING WILLMOTT GIVING DETAILS. WARDLINE.

Tolman was horrified that the message was addressed to him. The purser feared such a slight to Warms could mean political problems, especially since Warms had directed that his signature be on the first dispatch. If Warms thought Tolman had tried to undermine his authority, or held other allegiances, it would be hard to remain on the *Morro Castle* should the chief officer be named captain. Such pettiness was not uncommon on the ship and, even though Tolman had not solicited it or wanted any part of it, he was in a jam. The Ward Line was waiting.

The only thing Tolman could do was gamble. He responded to Cabaud himself without telling Warms, and asked Rogers for his discretion. In his reply, Tolman added a few details from Van Zile's diagnosis—not enough to satisfy Cabaud, but perhaps enough to let him know what had happened—and included an unnecessary update about the ship's paperwork.

CONFIRMING MESSAGE FROM WARMS STOP WILLMOTT DECEASED ACUTE
INDIGESTION AND HEART ATTACK SEVEN FORTY-FIVE THIS EVENING
STOP ALL PAPERS FOR ENTRY IN ORDER. TOLMAN PURSER

The last sentence was Tolman's insurance, an attempt to make it look as if he were only responding to the inquiry about Willmott as part of his normal business. If Warms saw it, that's what he would say. But he hoped it would not come to that, because he knew that Warms wouldn't buy it.

The *Morro Castle* passed near the mouth of Delaware Bay sometime around 11 P.M., its rigid bow slicing through the dark Atlantic at nearly 21 knots. It sailed 10 miles off the coast and, to anyone who happened to notice, it looked like a floating city gliding gracefully along the horizon. Four years had done little to diminish its beauty. It still looked like a photograph from a travel agent's brochure come to life. From the shore, it would have been hard to imagine anything in the world could have been wrong on the ship. It looked like an outpost of paradise, an oasis at sea.

It was, quite literally, the calm before the storm. To the south, a hurricane with 85 mph winds was riding the Gulf Stream north. If the ship maintained its current speed, it would reach the safety of New York Harbor before the weakening tropical system caught up. But there was little chance of avoiding the nor'easter ahead, which was churning the sea into fitful waves. Already the wooden decks were sticky with saltwater. The 15-knot wind was kicking up, and every nautical mile the seas became angrier. It was going to be a rough night.

It was late, the ship was close to port, but a good number of passengers refused to sleep. To sleep meant to give up, to wake up in port when it was all over. Most of them didn't want their cruise to end, and even without the gala ball, without the singing of "Auld Lang Syne," the parties limped on into the early morning hours. The atmosphere in the formal rooms was like a hotel lobby filled with conventiongoers, quiet but full of activity. People milled about like scavengers, looking for something to do, anything to avoid bed. They huddled in corners nearest the bars. The Library was empty. Few people, if any, loitered in the Writing Room.

In the Lounge, the banter between young men and women was lightning quick in a complex courtship dance between people who would not give up trying to find someone, if only for one night. Card games covered many of the tables not littered with empty glasses—mostly poker, but at one a group played pinochle. When the game broke up well after midnight, William F. Price walked back to his cabin on D Deck. Along the way, he stepped outside for a breath of salt air to clear his head. He noticed the wind had picked up, enough so that a door between decks was slamming against the bulkhead like a bass drum.

In the purser's office, Tom Torresson had finished his work. He'd been so busy filling out immigration forms and retrieving passengers' valuables from the ship's safe that he barely had time to consider it was his final night as third assistant purser. When he completed the last of the paperwork, it was just after midnight. He felt sad, melancholy—he didn't know exactly how to describe it. It wasn't just the end of his job or the death of the captain. Tomorrow was back to reality, whatever that meant for him. His future was as uncertain as the ship's. It was a scary proposition, but even a few weeks shy of his eighteenth birthday, Tom didn't frighten easily. He might have dwelled on all this more, but he was bone-tired.

Tom left the office with Les Ariessohn, the second assistant purser, and walked down to Cabin 332. It was all the way aft on D Deck, port side, and the room he and Ariessohn slept in most often. Because it was in the back of the ship, the cabin was rarely occupied. It was perfect for the pursers: Twin beds, one at each end of the room, separated by a private bath. The cabin even had two portholes. Tom had bunked down in 332 on nearly every voyage since he took the job in July. In that time, the *Morro Castle* had been booked enough to need 332 for passengers only once or twice.

He would not get much sleep his last night on the ship. Tom had to get up before 6 A.M. to greet the New York harbor pilot and escort him to breakfast. He set his alarm to go off between 5 and 5:30 A.M. It wouldn't take him much time to get ready, less than fifteen minutes to clean up, throw on his uniform and go. He did not yet need to shave every day.

So, in the early minutes of September 8, 1934, he went to bed fearing he would never spend another night aboard the *Morro Castle*. He may have noticed it was a rough night at sea, but he had become accustomed to the fickle weather on the Atlantic—little bothered him anymore. The ship's rocking might even have been comforting. But Thomas Torresson Jr. needed no help falling asleep on this night. He was out immediately.

George Rogers signed off at midnight as well, satisfied with his evening's work. It had been, without a doubt, the most eventful shift in his six weeks on the *Morro Castle*. He had enjoyed the action, the activity of having people in and out of the wireless room all night. Actually, he enjoyed the attention. Between the constant checks for weather updates and all the chatter back and forth about Willmott, it had been almost chaotic. And who knew what the next day might bring?

In the confusion of the night, it would have been easy to forget that his assistant, George Alagna, was supposed to be fired when the ship reached New York, but Rogers remembered all too well. He wondered if Willmott's death had bought the young radio operator a reprieve, but quickly dismissed the idea. Surely the captain had told others of his decision. Alagna seemed to suspect nothing, and Rogers had not yet told him. He liked the kid, thought maybe he could help. Perhaps Rogers even thought he'd just see how things played out and then do what he could for Alagna. Yes, he would just see.

When Charles Maki came to relieve him, Rogers said he was going to turn in. It had been a long night. But first, he wanted to take a walk on deck.

William Warms remained on the bridge of the *Morro Castle* into the night. He was tired, bleary-eyed and anxious. His fatigue, both physical and mental, was apparent to the other men in the wheelhouse. They suggested he get some rest, but he brushed aside their concerns. He seemed mildly like a man possessed, but to his thinking, Warms was just doing his job. He was the captain—temporary though that title may be—and he had a ship to bring in. Although the *Morro Castle* had survived worse weather, the storms lurking out there were not to be taken lightly. Perhaps he realized that his chances of command to an extent depended on how well he managed the ship in the final hours of this voyage. He had never had the chance to prove himself. Every time Willmott took leave, the Ward Line sent in Commodore Jones or one of their other skippers. It might have been company policy, but William Warms was a veteran sailor and he most likely found it a little insulting. Warms was an old salt, as comfortable on the seas as any man who worked for the Atlantic, Gulf & West Indies Steamship Lines. He knew how to do his job.

Thoughts of his duty and his future raced through Warms's mind as the *Morro Castle* plowed north through churning seas at nearly 20 knots. He might have slowed down, ahead of schedule and less than 150 miles from New York, if not for the storm behind him. The latest weather report had said the hurricane, with sustained winds of 80 mph, was gaining. The *Morro Castle* was sandwiched between two storms, and already the sea was bucking in protest of the converging weather systems. Warms hoped he could make the turn at Sandy Hook, the entrance to New York Harbor about 20 miles south of the city, before the worst of this weather collided over the ship.

At 1:35 A.M., the ship passed three miles east of Barnegat Light, midway up the Jersey coast, and Warms found himself fighting sleep. He had to do something to keep himself awake, so he left the bridge for a stroll around the deck. It was quiet, the crew cleaning up, getting the ship ready for the first impression it would make on a new group of passengers. On his walk, Warms greeted a couple of night watchmen, but they had nothing to report. Later, the acting captain would recall that everything had seemed normal that night. Certainly, he had noticed nothing amiss on his ship.

By the time Warms took his walk, the *Morro Castle* had quieted considerably. The parties were winding down, alcohol taking effect, and most people stumbled back to their cabins for a few hours' rest. In that way, it was like any other night on the ship. Herman Cluthe, the assistant cruise director, ordered stewards to escort a dozen drunken passengers to their cabins, while he personally tended to a half-dozen inebriated young women.

There were no more than the usual number of staggering stragglers on this night, but the difficulty was finding them. Without the gala or any other event to concentrate activity, passengers were spread out all over the ship. By 2:30 A.M., only a very few people still lingered in the ship's public rooms—a few at tables in the First-Class Lounge, a couple sitting at the bar. Most of the private parties had died out. In the Smoking Room, one party of four was still going strong, a round of drinks on the table. Daniel Campbell, a steward, thought the people were fairly quiet and well behaved for the time of night. The men wore tuxedos or dinner jackets; the women sported colorful dresses that hung below their knees and heavy high-heeled shoes. While cleaning the room—picking up ornate glasses and wiping out ashtrays, all with the Ward Line logo embossed on them—he hinted that perhaps they should get some sleep. One of the men argued that it was only a quarter till three. Campbell reminded them that was ship's time. It was actually a quarter till four in New York.

"We'll be picking up the harbor pilot soon," Campbell said.

The group made no move to leave, so Campbell went about his business. They weren't bothering anyone enough for him to argue. In a way, it was nice to have someone around—it got boring on the night shift. Campbell was officially the assistant beverage steward, an inane title that wasn't even grounded in reality. In fact, he did all sorts of things on the ship, including late cleanup. Campbell was not a typical member of the *Morro Castle*'s crew and, in fact, shared several things in common with Captain Willmott: he was born in England and had a home on Long Island. But if he felt any special connection with the captain, he said nothing of it, showed no particular emotion at Willmott's passing. Like most of the crew, Campbell was just trying to get through his shift.

It was quiet on board and Campbell could hear the hum of the engines below. The work was always the same—he cleaned by the soft light of the sconces reflected off the dark paneling. Occasionally, he could hear some piano music in the background. He saw few of the passengers—only the drunk ones. He could hear the wind picking up outside and felt the ship rock more than normal, scooting dishes around with a sharp *clink* behind the bar. Just after 2:45 A.M. ship's time, a passenger approached Campbell in the Smoking Room. The man asked if he smelled smoke, which the steward thought odd, given the room. *What else would you smell in here?* But all Campbell said was that he didn't particularly smell anything.

"Well, I think there is a fire somewhere," the passenger said, "because I can smell smoke very strongly."

It was the sort of thing people said all the time, but it never amounted to much. Passengers often thought they heard or smelled something out of the ordinary, but they simply weren't used to being on a ship. Campbell thought the guy may have had too much to drink, given the time of night. There were few people around to report such a thing to. At that time of the night, or morning, there weren't many members of the crew stirring—about eight night watchmen and whatever unfortunate souls had late cleanup. Campbell knew he had to check it out.

The man said the smoke smelled strongest in the First-Class Lounge, and Campbell followed him there. At worst, he expected to find a wastepaper basket on fire. Sometimes passengers made a game of seeing who could flick their cigarette butts into the trash, and the crew was left to extinguish the resulting fire. Cigarettes were a big problem on the ship. A passenger had once thrown a cigarette overboard only to have it blow back into the ship through an open porthole, where it started a fire in one of the cabins. As he followed the passenger to the Lounge, he thought that drunks just don't get it—you don't throw a lighted cigarette into a can of paper.

But there was no wastepaper-basket fire in the Lounge. A group of people were gathered around one table drinking brandy, but they weren't smoking. It seemed they had not smelled anything either, and Campbell decided not to disturb them. He wandered through the Lounge toward the two doors ahead, scanning the room as he went. The door on the right opened into the Library, the one on the left led to the Writing Room. Some sort of movement caught his eye, so Campbell stepped into the Writing Room. He quickly realized that what he had seen was smoke.

It was coming from the storage locker, a little hidden closet in the corner that Campbell had rummaged through once before in search of a vacuum cleaner. There was a Yale lock on the door, but no one ever locked it—there was nothing in the locker worth stealing. It was small, with a narrow white door that blended into the paneling. The biggest thing ever stuffed in there was a steamer blanket. Mostly, it was filled with pens, paper and cleaning supplies. When he reached to open the door, the unlocked handle burned Campbell's hand. And when the door swung open, the heat shoved him backward. All he could see inside were the remains of supplies, and flames.

Campbell, frozen with fear and mesmerized by the fire, could not look away for a moment. When he did, he realized he was alone—the passenger who had alerted him to the smell of smoke had not followed him into the Writing Room.

He didn't know what to do. The fire was out of control, he thought, and there was no way he could extinguish it. Opening the door had only made it worse, supplying more oxygen to fuel the flames. Campbell slammed the locker door and ran out of the room. In the hallway, he ran into one of the night watchmen, the old merchant sailor Arthur Pender.

Pender had spotted smoke a few minutes earlier, while he was patrolling the deck and dodging the spray coming over the rail. He had been just about to wash down the decks, a chore the crew performed every morning around three, when he glimpsed what looked like steam coming from a cargo ventilation shaft. Pender had spent enough nights walking the decks to know it was an uncommon sight. He knew what came out of each vent, and he knew what he saw wasn't right.

Of all the things night watchmen were charged with looking out for, fire was the most serious. Few things are as dangerous as a fire at sea. For all the water that surrounds a ship, there are only so many places to retreat. People on a ship had few places to run from a fire. For that reason, Pender had considered pulling the general alarm when he first saw smoke, but then thought better of it. No need to stir up a ruckus in the middle of the night if he didn't have to. Pender hadn't reported to the bridge because he did not yet know what he would report. He knew if he walked all the way to the wheelhouse to tell someone he saw smoke, they would just tell him to go check it out and then come back.

Pender saw Campbell and the source of his smoke as soon as he stepped into the B Deck lobby. He caught a glimpse of the fire in the Writing Room locker just before Campbell slammed the door shut. What struck him most about the sight were the flames. They were bluish-white. Pender had watched a thousand fires burn exactly the same outside Paris after the war. Those bluish flames were the sure sign of a chemical fire.

The two men spoke only briefly in clipped, nervous sentences. Campbell said he was going for help to fight the fire, and Pender said he would retrieve one of the fire hoses he'd been planning to use to wash down the deck. Pender was going to alert the bridge first, but then he saw Harold Foersch running toward the wheelhouse. It saved him several minutes because he realized the junior night watchman knew exactly what was going on.

The *Morro Castle* was on fire.

CHAPTER SIX

This Evening's Entertainment

By a quarter of three, Doris Wacker had given up her plans to watch the *Morro Castle* sail into New York Harbor at dawn. She only wanted her cabin, her bed and sleep.

As much as she wished the cruise would never end, Doris was finally exhausted. For a week, she had drifted through an endless procession of sunbathing, afternoon teas, big dinners and formal dances. It took a lot to wear out an eighteen-year-old girl, but the *Morro Castle* had managed to do it. She had never had so much fun, and, unlike her father, her only complaint was that the trip just wasn't long enough. But now she was forced to admit she needed at least a few hours of rest. The long night had taken its toll.

Doris and her friend Marjorie Budlong had met Rosario Felipe after the gala was canceled, and for two hours they sat on the Promenade Deck talking with some of the Cuban passengers—Renée Méndez Capote, Dr. Emilio Giró, Dr. Francisco Busquet, his wife and daughter. Dr. Busquet knew Rosario Felipe's family, so there was a lot of talk about Havana society, an entirely different world from Roselle Park. Shortly after 11:30, the girls had followed Rosario back to her cabin on A Deck, Suite 17.

At 1 A.M., Doris shed her party dress while she and Marjorie packed, and then the girls went back upstairs to help Rosario Felipe with her things. After two more hours of talking, the plan to stay up all night no longer seemed so wise. In the morning, Doris's beau, Jimmy Churchill, planned to meet them at the docks with her younger brother, Kenneth.

She figured the least she could do was get a few hours of sleep before seeing them. Doris and Marjorie said their good-byes to Rosario, made plans to stay in touch, and then got up to return to their considerably less spacious cabin on C Deck.

The door of Suite 17 opened onto the First-Class Lounge and Ballroom Mezzanine. It was a gorgeous view of the grand room, its wood-paneled walls and elegant drapery, and seeing it only reminded Doris how much she had enjoyed dressing up fancy every night, how she loved the ship, and how she would be sad to see it all end. Then she glimpsed a flash of light out of the corner of her eye.

Across the Lounge, the Writing Room was a bright orange shroud of flames. Men in white coats were rushing to the doorway and hurling buckets of water onto the fire. Doris realized it had been burning for several minutes, and they had not heard a thing. If they didn't know about the fire just 25 yards from them, certainly no one on the lower decks knew.

Doris realized she had been sitting just outside that room a few hours earlier, and now it was lost—all the beautiful furniture, the rugs, the white wood paneling. And she could tell the men were wasting their time. Already the flames licked the door frame leading into the Lounge, and the paneling closest to the door was blackened. This was not some little fire that could be extinguished one bucket at a time. When one of the men threw his water into the Writing Room, a huge plume of smoke shot out the door.

Doris and Marjorie called Rosario, and she joined them on the Mezzanine. The three girls watched, both scared and curious, like a gathering crowd at the scene of an accident. It was a strange sight, men in white uniforms and black bowties throwing buckets of water from the safety of a room filled with upholstered chairs and linen tablecloths: formal firefighting. To Doris, it seemed unreal. Finally, she called out to the men.

"Should I call for help?"

Her voice startled the men. They looked more panicked by the sight of three teenage girls than the fire.

"No, no, no! Don't do anything," one of them called out, waving his arms wildly. "Everything is all right. Don't alarm anyone."

For another minute, they watched the fire grow. There was a wicked crackling in the air, the sound of flame devouring wood, and the fire was winning this battle. Rosario Felipe ducked into her room to get her money and jewelry, aware she might not be able to do so later. By then, Doris had seen enough. She knew this was no minor fire and that the entire ship was in danger. She didn't care what the crew said.

"I'm going to get my parents," Doris said.

As they turned to leave, flames erupted from the Writing Room and into the First-Class Lounge, and Doris Wacker, Marjorie Budlong and Rosario Felipe ran as fast as they could.

Clarence Hackney was technically the officer on duty for the midnight-to-4 A.M. shift. He stood in the soft glow of the instrument lights monitoring the *Morro Castle*'s progress up the coast, fighting the bucking ship to keep her on course. The ship was about 38 miles northeast of Barnegat, sailing into a 20-knot headwind. The seas were getting rougher, but it wasn't anything they couldn't handle. Quartermaster Samuel Hoffman was at the wheel and seemed to be holding the ship steady. They were still on schedule and, if the weather didn't get any worse, they might even make the harbor early. More unnerving than the weather was William Warms, who paced back and forth on the covered wings of the bridge, refusing to sleep. Hackney didn't feel like he was in command, he felt like he was being watched.

When he first heard the commotion outside, a few minutes before 3 A.M., Hackney thought it was Warms. But then the night watchman Harold Foersch ran into the wheelhouse, out of breath.

"There's a fire!"

Foersch pointed to smoke coming from around the ventilator for the No. 3 hold, which they could barely see for the rain. Hackney had not noticed the smoke, and at first figured it must be another fire down below. Foersch had not talked to Pender, so he did not know about the scene in the Writing Room. He was just reporting smoke without knowing the cause—something Pender had refrained from doing minutes earlier. No one on the bridge knew what to do because they didn't know what they were dealing with.

Hackney first called the engine room to find out if they smelled anything, or had a fire in one of the holds. No one there had smelled, or heard, anything. Hackney turned his attention back to Foersch.

"What exactly did you see?"

Warms stepped into the wheelhouse in time to hear Foersch say "smoke," and it seemed to wake him up. Though he didn't seem particularly alarmed, he saw the danger right away. Ignoring the watchman, Warms told Hackney to find out if there was a problem.

"That ventilator runs through the public rooms," Warms said. "Get down there and see if there's a fire."

Hackney did not point out that he was the officer on duty at the moment or that he should not leave the bridge, he didn't argue or say another word. As he rushed out of the wheelhouse, Clarence Hackney grabbed a fire extinguisher.

George Alagna woke to the sound of men running and yelling on the deck. He was annoyed, his shift didn't start for another hour and he only wanted to go back to sleep. For a moment, he rolled over and tried to ignore the noise, but as his mind clawed its way into consciousness, he realized something wasn't right. *Who was talking so loud at this time of night?* He could see their shadows dancing on the wall and wondered how that could be in the dead of night? When Alagna got up and looked out of the port, he saw a shimmering glow from somewhere below.

Alagna snapped awake and, for reasons he could not explain, whipped around to make sure no one else was in the room. He had to alert somebody. Alagna pulled on his pants as he stepped around the corner into George Rogers's quarters. Rogers was lying in his bunk, apparently asleep, because he did not answer when Alagna called to him.

"Get up, Rogers, something's happening."

Again, nothing. Alagna started to speak again when he noticed Charles Maki standing in the other doorway, the one leading to the radio room. The junior radio operator shouted, too, but got no response. Rogers seemed to be in a deep sleep. Alagna moved toward the bed, thinking he would pull the covers off Rogers to rouse him. But as he got near the bed, Maki spoke again.

"Get up, Chief. The ship's on fire."

Rogers suddenly came alive, jumped out of bed and reached for his pants in one swift motion. It startled Alagna and Maki, who were sure he had been sound asleep moments before. Alagna thought, *I didn't know George could move so fast.*

As Rogers dressed, Alagna brushed past Maki into the radio room, where he looked at the clock, as he had been trained to do. It was almost 3 A.M. Alagna fiddled with the radio dials, unhappy with what he heard, and then reached for the phone to the bridge. Just then Rogers burst into the room like a bear, pushed him aside and sat down at the radio. He put on the earphones and started tuning the transmitter to the distress frequencies.

Alagna said the emergency system did not seem to be working, but Rogers ignored him and tried the phone to the bridge. There was a roar in the earpiece that made it impossible to hear anything. Dead. Just then, Rogers and Alagna saw smoke seeping into the room. Maki said he'd noticed it a few minutes earlier—it seemed to be coming from behind the wastebasket.

Rogers tuned the radio as Alagna searched for the source of the smoke. He opened the closet, sifted through a sleeping chair, mattress and some other junk. Rogers joined Alagna in his digging, and they both saw it at the same time: the homemade polish they used for cleaning brass. It was a nasty mix of polish and kerosene, the stuff Alagna complained ate at his hands. It was highly combustible, not the kind of thing to leave lying around in a fire, but they had nowhere else to put it. They couldn't figure out where the smoke was coming from. All they knew was that it came from somewhere below. After a minute, they decided there was no fire in the closet, so Rogers went back to the radio and Alagna stepped outside to find someone who knew what was going on.

"I'm going to see what's happening," Alagna said.

Rogers glanced up from the radio and called out to Alagna. "George, go up to the bridge and see what orders the mate has to give you."

But Alagna was already gone.

The crew of the *Morro Castle* began to stir about ten minutes after the fire was discovered. There was no organized effort to fight the fire or alert the passengers, at least not at first, but the sound of panic woke the crew and sparked them into a semblance of action. Most were left to their own decisions about what to do, but they could not move as quickly, or as efficiently, as the flames. Only the deck officers, the ones with cabins near the bridge, got their orders from the captain. William Warms woke Howard Hansen and his acting first officer, Ivan Freeman, with orders to go below and get the fire under control.

"Get up. Fire in the Lounge," Warms told Freeman. "Go down there and take charge."

Freeman leapt from his bed, threw on some clothes and took off for B Deck. He didn't know what to expect when he got there. Warms had not sounded excited, so for all Freeman knew a rug or chair had caught fire. In fact, Warms could not have prepared Freeman for what he was walking into, because he didn't know much more than he had told his first officer.

Hackney had returned to the bridge screaming at Warms about a fire out of control in the Lounge. He had stumbled onto the scene in the Writing Room only after another night watchman pointed him in that direction. He found the stewards throwing buckets of water—this was only moments after Doris Wacker had run from the Mezzanine—and Hackney stepped in front of them and emptied his extinguisher on the flames. It did about as much good as spitting on it. He threw down the extinguisher and ran to tell Warms they needed more help. A lot more help.

No one realized how quickly the fire was spreading. It had moved from the Writing Room to the Lounge, and then spread onto the Promenade Deck, creeping closer to the lifeboats. In less than fifteen minutes, the fire had gone from one room to a half dozen on several different decks. It seemed to be everywhere, growing exponentially. The few men on board who had any experience with that sort of thing said they had never seen a fire move so fast.

Warms could not believe it was as bad as Hackney said, but he would not go see for himself. Captain Willmott's death left them short-staffed on the bridge, and he did not feel he could leave. His top officers had to be his eyes and ears and, for the most part, he trusted them. He figured with so many men fighting it, the fire would soon be under control. When he saw smoke pouring out of a doorway on A Deck, he took it as a good sign. He told himself, *The boys are dousing the fire. Everything will be all right.* It did not occur to him initially that the ship should not be sailing into the wind, fanning the flames, making it nearly impossible to combat. Likewise, Warms never thought to close the fire door between the Writing

Room and the Lounge. But by the time he could have sent the order, it was too late.

Bob Tolman and Russell Du Vinage were bunking in Suite 4 on A Deck when the commotion roused them. From the window, Tolman was horrified to see two lifeboats burning in the davits they hung on. The pursers feared they had been surrounded by fire—Du Vinage could feel the heat in the room. Not knowing what was on the other side of the cabin door, they busted the porthole, climbed out and ran to their office. The fire had spread from B Deck to A in less than fifteen minutes.

The smoke woke Eben Abbott, the *Morro Castle*'s chief engineer. From his cabin on the top deck near the navigation room, he caught much of the back draft that the wind blew aft. He smelled the smoke and thought he heard a ringing. *Fire alarm?* Abbott put on his slippers before going to wake Anthony Bujia, his first assistant. He told Bujia that perhaps he should check on the engine room. Bujia put on his boiler room coveralls and left the cabin.

Abbott went back to his room and dressed in his formal uniform, spotlessly white and pressed, even gathering his hat before he called Bujia for a report. Smoke was seeping into the engine room, Bujia said, but he saw no flames. Three pumps were supplying water to the fire lines, which were obviously in use. Something big was burning.

Abbott supposed he should go to the engine room to take control, and so ducked into the crew stairway that led to E Deck. On C, he met a group of women passengers who were lost and had wandered into the crew-only stairwell. Abbott escorted them to A Deck, where the lifeboats loaded. He told the women not to panic. If the situation was dire, that's where they would need to go eventually.

Abbott met Bujia in the stairwell. The assistant engineer said smoke had begun pouring into the engine room more heavily, and he didn't know how much longer the men could hold out. Bujia could not get the bridge on the phone.

Ten years earlier, Abbott had been chief engineer on the Ward Line's *Esperanza* when she foundered off Tampico, Mexico. His efforts to save the ship had won him praise in several newspapers, but he felt he had done nothing but stand around in the engine room giving orders. He remembered that scene and thought the men didn't need another officer in the way. He sent Bujia back down and said he'd go to the bridge.

"When it gets impossible to tolerate the smoke, have the turbines tripped, shut off the fuel oil system and leave the fire pumps running," Abbott said. Then, as an afterthought, he added, "Don't let anyone leave until they have to."

By 3:05 A.M., Warms realized that his boys, in fact, did not have things under control. There were conflicting reports, but it was clear that there was a growing fire forward on the port side, and it was spreading. He could only tell them to keep hitting it with the hoses, and called out "Left wheel" to Hoffman to get the wind off the ship's nose. But that's all he said. And then Warms sounded the general alarm. He was reluctant to do it, because he hated to wake the passengers if they could get the fire under control, but there wasn't much to worry about. Most people would never hear it.

Fire is the most destructive force in nature, a simple chemical reaction that is technically only the by-product of oxygen and any sort of fuel at ignition temperature. Those temperatures vary depending on the material. Combustion of wood, for instance, begins at about 300 degrees Fahrenheit. Cellulose material in the wood begins to decompose and, as it does, it becomes airborne as a gas, or smoke. At 500 degrees, the atoms that make up an elemental compound begin to break down; they recombine with oxygen and change form. They burn.

Perhaps the most dangerous thing about fire is that it is self-sustaining. It feeds on itself, growing exponentially as it burns. Heat generates more combustion. Fire breeds more fire. A ship at sea made a very small cage for such an uncontrollable force.

When fire broke out on the excursion steamer *General Slocum* in June 1902, more than 1,000 people died in New York's East River within sight of the city. The *Morro Castle*, sailing more than five miles offshore, was completely isolated. Although its hull was made of steel, the ship's interior façade was constructed almost entirely of the one material fire consumes most quickly: wood. And on a weekly basis, that wood was lathered in a toxic polish to keep it looking shiny and new. Even small traces of the concoction, a mixture of various chemicals, made the perfect accelerant. It was nearly as bad as lighting a can of gasoline.

More than anything else, fire needs oxygen. Had it been a normal night, the breeze might have been welcomed. The sea-cooled air would have flowed through the ship's intricate venting system, circulating through ducts built behind the cabin walls very much like modern air conditioning. But in the early hours of September 8, 1934, the wind simply provided an abundance of oxygen for a hungry fire. The ducts behind the cabin walls allowed that wind to move effortlessly through the ship, supplying the fire with more fuel. The *Morro Castle*'s ventilation system acted much like a flue, and the entire ship was becoming a fireplace.

In the years following the *General Slocum* disaster, Congress capitalized on the tragedy by ordering ships to be better equipped to handle fire. The *Morro Castle* was built with fire doors, which theoretically would contain any blaze, stop flames from moving from one room to the next. When the fire began to spread from the Writing Room to the Lounge, from B Deck to A, no one thought to close the fire doors, and no one gave an order to do so in the short time that it might have mattered. Instead, with the ship making 20 knots into a 20-knot headwind, the fire was essentially being pushed, and fueled, by tropical-storm-force winds. Every minute it grew exponentially. There was no stopping it.

In many ways, the Writing Room was the worst place a fire could have started. It was close to the elevators and main stairwells, and so the growing fire effectively cut off escape routes in minutes. Within twenty minutes, it had reached A Deck. By the time the first passengers escaped their cabins, they found their route to the lifeboats or between decks blocked.

The fire soon found its way into the vent that ran behind the Writing Room locker. The vent led to the room's ceiling, an unfortunate course. The ship's Lyle gun was stored just above the Writing Room. The gun was used to shoot the line for a breeches buoy—a bucket that carried passengers on a taut cable to shore in case of an emergency evacuation. The firepower for that shot was 100 pounds of gunpowder, all of it stored atop the Writing Room.

Howard Hansen and Ivan Freeman were near the Lyle gun when the flames reached the gunpowder. The explosion knocked them backward, rocked the ship and blew out several portholes. The shattered windows allowed more precious air to fuel the flames inside. The fire spread out, stretching from one side of the ship to another—a wall of flames now nearly 70 feet wide.

Freeman and Hansen watched as the fire incinerated the grand ship around them, melting tables and the deck-chair-rental desk before serious efforts to douse it had even begun. The fire had spread to every public area on the ship in minutes. If the wind had been blowing from the stern, it would have contained the fire, perhaps even have bought enough time for the ship to get close to shore. By staying on a northern course for New York, they were fanning the flames, and speeding along the possibility of death for everyone on board.

"We've got to stop this ship," Hansen told Freeman. "This fire is all out of control."

When Alagna returned to the radio room, he found Rogers listening to chatter on the emergency station.

"The ship is on fire, there are people standing around, and there's a great deal of confusion," Alagna said breathlessly. He patted Rogers on the back, a gesture meant to say all is not lost yet.

He'd tried to make it to the bridge, but Alagna said he could not get there. There was a wall of smoke between the wireless room and the wheelhouse, and he was afraid to walk into it because he didn't know what was on the other side. Although they were barely more than 50 feet apart, he'd felt like it was another ship. Through the smoke, he could hear men screaming at each other, and on the way back he tripped over a fire hose.

Rogers sent Alagna back to try again. He could not send out a distress signal without an order from the captain or, at the very least, the officer on duty. Even though he knew the ship was on fire, Rogers said he must play it by the rules—he would not transmit an SOS. He told Alagna to find a way to reach Warms: "Go to the bridge."

Rogers continued to fiddle with the radios and asked Maki—standing around with nothing to do—to wet some towels for them to breathe through. When Maki finished that, Rogers sent him away.

"Go up to the bridge and find out what's detaining Alagna."

While Rogers was alone in the wireless room, the lights went out. Sitting at the operator's desk, listening to the radio, he was bathed in the orange glow of approaching fire. A stray flame occasionally shot through the room's aft porthole, where it licked the wall. Paint on the wall began to bubble.

Outside, Alagna circled the top deck and reached the bridge from the starboard side. From the high perch of the wheelhouse, he could see flames creeping up the hull, making their way toward him. On the bridge, he saw one of the officers standing at the wheel, spinning it frantically. They had just realized that the ship's steering had been knocked out, presumably by the fire. The *Morro Castle* was speeding through rough seas without anyone in control. In the chaos, Alagna found Warms in the dark.

"Rogers sent me to find out what we should do," he said.

Warms looked at him, said "All right," and then something that Alagna could not understand. He disappeared into the smoke, and seemed to be mumbling as he walked away. The wheelhouse was chaotic, dark, crowded and smoky, and it took Alagna a moment to realize that Warms had not given him any orders. He caught up to the captain, tried to get his attention for several more minutes, but finally gave up and went back to the wireless room.

Rogers was alone, listening to the radio, when Alagna returned. Someone from another ship was talking to WSC, the Radio Marine Corporation station at Tuckerton, New Jersey. The operator, from the freighter *Andrea Luckenbach*, asked if anyone out there had information concerning "a ship aflame in the vicinity of the Jersey coast." The WSC operator responded: "Haven't heard of any." Rogers listened without responding. Alagna could not believe Rogers had not taken the opportunity to say anything—mention it was the *Morro Castle* and the radio room was awaiting orders. He could have said any number of things, Alagna knew, but Rogers maintained radio silence. Alagna said nothing of it, instead told him about the confusion on the bridge.

"They're a bunch of madmen up there," Alagna said.

Rogers looked up from the equipment and smiled.

"Cheer up. It'll turn out all right."

By 3:10 A.M., there were few people still asleep on the *Morro Castle*. The noise should have been enough to wake all but the most inebriated passengers, but some of the crewmen were doing anything they could to get people up and out of their cabins. One stewardess ran down the hallways shouting, "Get your life jacket and get on deck." One man, presumably a cook, ran down the hall banging pots and pans together. A member of the ship's orchestra blasted out reveille on his trumpet.

The hallways and open stern decks were filling with people in various states of dress. Some wore pajamas or bathrobes, others had on their street clothes. A few were very nearly naked. The Bodners had been awake since hearing Doris Wacker beat on the door to her parents' cabin just before 3 A.M. She had called out, "Mother, Mother, the ship's on fire!" And that's all the Bodners—and a number of other passengers—had needed to hear.

The Wackers had a head start on the evacuation. Herbert Wacker had spotted the glow of flames from his cabin window and went looking for his daughter. Doris met her father in the hallway wearing his striped pajamas and a dark belt, and he told her to get a life jacket from her cabin and come back. She and Marjorie did as they were told, and then the four of them took turns tying each other's life jackets. Doris was scared, but her father tried to calm her, just as he had when she was sick the first day of the cruise.

"Don't worry, the crew will tell us what to do," he said.

Herbert Wacker decided they should go to the stern, just a short walk down the hall. If nothing else, they could escape the smoke and get a better look at what was happening. If she had had time to think on her way to the covered stern deck, Doris might have thought that perhaps her father had been right about the ship all along. It was run like hell.

The haphazard efforts to fight the fire were spread out over three decks in the forward half of the ship. While some crew members had reported to their appointed fire stations, other didn't even know where they were supposed to be posted—a result of Willmott's reluctance to even attempt drills. These ragtag firefighting teams, which included some passengers, were having little success. One hydrant had been capped on Willmott's orders after it leaked and caused a passenger to slip on an earlier voyage. A hose could easily have been attached to the hydrant if anyone had known how to take off the cap, but that was a skill most of the crew did not possess. Not that the hoses were doing much good anyway. The crew in the Lounge had been forced to retreat, the flames pushing them backward. Harold Foersch, the watchman who had first reported the fire to the bridge, stayed and fought as the flames closed in all around him. Even when the others left, Foersch didn't give up. Soon, the fire surrounded him.

Bob Tolman and Russell Du Vinage led the group fighting the fire in the main foyer. The elevator shaft was a chimney of flames and the chief purser wondered briefly how a fire that had started on B Deck had gotten below them. He didn't have long to think about it, because the fire was spreading too quickly to analyze anything. The only luck the pursers had was the arrival of some professional help. John Kempf, a New York City firefighter, was staying in Cabin 208 just behind the ship's office and had been awakened by a familiar smell. When he mentioned the ship was on fire, the man who had been sharing the cabin jumped up and ran out of the room. Kempf calmly put on his trousers and stepped out of the cabin, where a man he did not know called out to him, put him to work.

"Hey there, big fellow, you can turn on that valve."

Kempf at first assumed the fire was no big deal. He imagined that someone lit a rug on fire with a cigarette, that it could be rolled up and tossed overboard. But as he adjusted the hydrant, Kempf noticed the smoke coming out of the elevator shaft. Before he had the water pressure turned up all the way, someone grabbed the hose and began shooting the stream of water down the shaft. Kempf knew they were wasting their time. Water is only effective when it hits the seat or body of the fire. From his vantage point, he couldn't see flames. But he knew there were a lot of them on the ship, somewhere.

The *Morro Castle* had 42 fire hydrants, 2,100 feet of hoses and two systems to deliver water to them. The regular steam fire-pump system could deliver 1,000 gallons of water per minute at 100 pounds of pressure. Two other electric pumps provided another 300 gallons a minute. The mathematics of this engineering assumed no more than six hydrants would be opened at once. With teams using hoses from nearly two dozen hydrants around the ship, water pressure was down to a trickle. Not one of these teams had more than enough water pressure to douse a campfire.

William Warms got this news twenty minutes after the fire was discovered. By that time, the ship's steering had stopped responding, and he could not reach the engine room on the phone. Then Freeman and Hansen burst into the wheelhouse.

"The fire is getting away from us—the hoses are useless," Freeman said.

Warms could not believe how quickly events had gotten out of control. *How could a fire move so quickly through the ship?* Surely they were exaggerating the situation. And then, as if to prove him wrong, alarms on the bridge indicated the fire had reached a few of the staterooms on A Deck. Warms looked out the wheelhouse door, trying to spot something—he didn't know what. Perhaps something to reassure him all was not lost. He saw the fire creeping malevolently toward the forward lifeboats on the port side, No. 2 and No. 4. He watched as the boats withered from the heat. When the flames overtook them, the metal boats buckled and fell into the sea.

The burning lifeboats finally convinced Warms that the *Morro Castle* could not make it to New York. He had misjudged the situation and now must take drastic measures. He could not believe this had happened. All he had to do was sail the ship twelve hours and it would have reached the Wall Street docks and now, well, it was unimaginable. He seemed dazed by the realization and later Hansen would say that he had to yell at Warms, even strike him, to get it out of his head that he could make it to New York.

Warms simply couldn't fathom the thought that the *Morro Castle* was not going to make its schedule, or might not make it at all. Someone heard Warms say, to himself mostly, that "there's nothing to be done."

Flustered as he was, Warms began to make decisions. He knew he couldn't do anything about the water pressure, but he could do something about the wind. Fighting his natural inclination to keep pushing for Sandy Hook, he ordered the crew to turn the ship directly toward shore. Bringing the *Morro Castle* closer to the beach would make it easier to abandon ship, give passengers and crew a greater chance of survival.

Without steering, it was nearly impossible to maneuver the ship, but they could imitate a rudder by manipulating the ship's two propellers against one another. With the portside prop turning full reverse while the starboard went full ahead, the ship would turn to port. It was a rudimentary way of steering and would not give the bridge perfect control, but it was better than nothing. Such a turn would also get the wind off the ship's nose, and perhaps keep the fire from spreading back through the ship faster than it already was.

Abbott appeared in the smoke at that moment, choking and coughing, and reported the engine room almost lost. The chief engineer seemed dazed and confused, and Warms could barely make out what he said. It occurred to Warms that if there was still crew in the engine room, he could turn the ship. But Abbott did not appear to be much help.

"What are we going to do?" Abbott pleaded with him. "What are we going to do?"

Alagna had arrived back on the bridge. He glared disdainfully at the chief engineer, who looked as if he were dressed for the captain's ball. Alagna wondered if Abbott thought this is what one wore to a fire. While the radioman tried to get Warms's attention, he looked at Abbott and gave him a pithy, "Buck up." After a few more minutes of unsuccessfully trying to get the captain's attention, Alagna left. He felt he needed to check on Rogers.

Thirty minutes after the fire was discovered, the *Morro Castle* was a bright flare on the Atlantic, attracting the attention of most traffic in the shipping lanes. Rogers could hear the radio operators speculating about what was burning so brightly off New Jersey. He was listening to the increasing radio chatter on emergency power when Alagna returned. Smoke had overtaken the room and Rogers was alone, which Alagna found odd. Maki had not been there for several minutes, and Alagna asked what had happened to the kid.

"Hackney told me that he ordered Maki to go on a boat," Rogers said.

Hackney was on the bridge, and Alagna knew Rogers had had no contact with him. Surely, he would have passed Hackney if he'd come to the radio room. Alagna realized suddenly that he did not believe Rogers.

"Are you sure?"

"Why, Hackney told me himself."

He was certain Rogers was lying. He knew the chief radioman was weird, and sometimes said things that made no sense, but there seemed no purpose to this lie. Alagna wanted to ask again—he could not leave it alone—but Rogers was clearly perturbed by the questions. Before Alagna could say anything else, Rogers changed the subject.

"I'm going to send out a CQ."

That was the signal for anyone listening that there was an emergency broadcast forthcoming. It was quickly approaching the time in the hour when all radio chatter ceased to hear any distress signals that might be floating weakly over the airwaves. It was 3:13 A.M.

Rogers sent the message with Alagna standing over his shoulder. The Tuckerton station responded immediately, the operator telling him to "get off the air, it was the silent period." Neither radioman could believe what they were hearing. Rogers had broken protocol, signaling a coming SOS and, for his trouble, had been told to stop transmissions.

"Go ask them if we should send the distress signal now," Rogers said.
Alagna turned to leave, amazed at what he was hearing.

"Silent period nothing," Alagna said. "This *is* an emergency."

In the hallways of the *Morro Castle,* people were running in and out of their cabins, fleeing and then returning for their life jackets, their suitcases, or just trying to find their way to the stern or the lifeboat deck. It seemed that once the fire broke out, people who had had a week to learn their way around the ship suddenly forgot where they were. Bob Smith, the cruise director, made it his job to try to corral passengers on the back of the ship.

Smith had been sleeping in Cabin 213 just across from the purser's office. When Herman Cluthe woke him, Smith ran into the hall, where he found Tolman leading efforts to douse the fire on the main staircase. Still groggy, Smith had grabbed a hose.

"Don't bother with the fire, we'll handle that," Tolman said. "Get the passengers out and get them aft."

Before Smith ran off, Tolman asked to borrow some shoes from the cruise director's cabin. Tolman had escaped the A Deck suite barefooted and couldn't make it back now. Smith ducked into his cabin and reluctantly handed Tolman a pair of dress whites.

"I'm going to get these back, right?" Smith said.

At about the time Smith began rounding up passengers, an electrician from the engine room beat on the door of Cabin 332, startling Tom Torresson and Les Ariessohn awake. Tom couldn't imagine there was a serious fire on the *Morro Castle.* From listening to Willmott, he knew all about the sprinkler system, the alarms and the fire doors. There had to be some mistake. As a result, he didn't take the electrician very seriously—he didn't hurry. Tom put on his uniform and even stopped to comb his hair. But he and Ariessohn did put on their life jackets before reporting to the purser's office—they knew the regulations. Unlike many members of the crew, they followed the rules.

On C Deck, Tom spotted Tolman manhandling a flaccid fire hose. The scene had made him slightly nervous, now aware that perhaps the electrician had been right about the fire being serious.

"How bad is it, Bob?"

"Take a look for yourself," Tolman said, gesturing to the stairwell.

Tom looked up the forward staircase leading to B Deck and saw only flames where the deck had been. Every notion of security he had felt melted on the spot, but Tolman didn't allow him time to get scared.

"Tom, you take the port side of the ship and make sure everybody is out of their rooms. Les, you take the starboard side."

The young purser began knocking on doors, following in the wake of Smith and Cluthe. Few people remained in their rooms, but Tom did not know that. There was no passkey, so he had to beat on the door as long as he thought it might take to wake someone. If no one answered, eventually he moved on. Walking away from an unanswered door was a scary thing. *What if someone was in there? I'm leaving them to die,* he thought. There was nothing he could do but go on. Tom woke one elderly woman and sent her to the stern, and another one tried to run into her cabin to get her fur coat, but he turned her back.

When he finished checking all the cabins he was assigned to, Tom made his way outside to see what else he could do to help. As he waded through smoke-filled halls, he hoped that he had not left anyone behind.

Abbott called the engine room from the bridge to see if the captain's orders to manipulate the propellers had been received. Somehow he got through to Bujia, who said that he was keeping the water pressure dialed up as high as it would go and mentioned that the fire doors were operable if the order came to close them. Bujia said the smoke was getting worse, his men were choking. But so far, the ship had not lost power.

"Everything is running good," Bujia said.

Abbott reported this to Warms, but the captain was more annoyed by the news than anything else, and he wondered why Abbott was hanging so close to him. The engineer coughed as he spoke, his eyes watered from the smoke, and he seemed mildly dazed. He complained that he had "smoke in his lungs."

It never occurred to Warms to ask why the chief engineer was not in the engine room, but he thought Abbott was wasting space on the bridge, and he needed fewer people in the wheelhouse breathing what little air was left. Looking for an excuse to rid himself of Abbott, Warms told the engineer to get down on deck to supervise the lifeboat launching.

"Go on board one of the boats and take charge," Warms said, dismissing him.

For all the air circulating through the ship, Warms could find none to breathe at that moment. He felt like he had been sucker-punched. Nothing he had done helped, and now he must resign himself to losing the ship. It had been just moments, barely more than thirty minutes, since the fire was first reported. *How could it get so bad in such a short time?* Warms had resisted calling for help, hoping his men could get things under control, avoid an incident on the very night he alone was responsible for bringing the *Morro Castle* into port. Now he had no choice—he would have to send the distress signal. And, as if on cue, George Alagna walked onto the wing of the bridge at that moment.

This time, the radioman was determined to get the order to send a distress signal. In nearly a half-dozen trips, he had had no luck getting Warms's attention. The man seemed not even to recognize him. Everything was so bizarre—the way Warms acted, Maki's disappearance, Rogers lying about it.

If Alagna had realized that he was scheduled to be fired the next day—or that Captain Willmott had suspected him of being a saboteur— then he might have understood Warms's wariness. He would have thought that Warms did not trust him.

But, in truth, Warms had not *recognized* him. He believed Alagna was just another panicked sailor, another person trying to talk to him at the worst possible time. Part of the problem was Alagna's interpretation of rules. He did not think that he was supposed to suggest a distress signal and he foolishly had not mentioned the radio in any of his brief exchanges with the captain. Every time he spoke to Warms, he had simply asked if there was "something we can do."

Warms had not understood the question before. On this trip, however, Alagna had worn his uniform hat, identifying him as a radio operator, and he mistook the recognition on Warms's face as a flash of inspiration.

"Can you send an SOS?" the captain asked.

"Why certainly, that's what I have been coming up here for," Alagna said. "That is what we are waiting for, that is what we are here for."

"All right, send an SOS," Warms said. As quickly as he said it, the captain disappeared into the smoke.

Alagna followed him, calling out, "What position?"

"We are off Sea Girt," Hackney said, "about fifty miles south of New York."

Alagna ignored him, and continued to follow Warms. He felt he was following the rules, going by the book, that he should get the particulars of the distress signal from the captain. He found Warms in the smoke, grabbed him by the arm and said, "What position shall we send?"

"Tell them twenty miles south of Ambrose," Warms said.

Alagna repeated the order once and left the bridge. Immediately, he was enveloped in smoke. Now that he had the order, he wasn't sure he could find his way back to the radio room, and the silent period was quickly ticking away. If he did not make it, there was a chance no one would hear the distress call.

In the radio room, even the backup lights were out. George Rogers had to feel around in the semidark to find his flashlight—he would not have been able to see his hands in front of his face if not for the glow of the burning curtains. He had switched the radio to auxiliary power and the antenna to the auxiliary transmitter. The radio caught snippets of a dispatch from Tuckerton: "No, we have no information at all about any ship on fire."

Maritime law of the day required two silent periods an hour to listen for distress calls. The first lasted from 15 minutes past the hour till 18 past. The second one commenced at 45 minutes and also lasted 3 minutes. Rogers would not send out the SOS without a direct order, but as the silent period began, he sent another "CQ" followed by a little more information. This time, he added "DE," which meant "from" and "KGOV," the *Morro Castle*'s call sign.

Tuckerton didn't understand the message and again told Rogers to wait three minutes before transmitting again. He sent the code again, using the radio code for "stand by."

"QRX, may have emergency call."

Time passed, Rogers could not keep track. The smoke grew thicker and the floor was hot enough that he could feel it through his shoes. The curtains behind him were almost completely burned. Using the flashlight, he saw the clock tick off 3:18. The silent period was over. If he sent a signal now, would anyone hear it?

Suddenly, Alagna burst into the room.

"OK, Chief, send out an SOS," Alagna said. "We are twenty miles south of the Scotland Lightship."

Rogers went to work, typing in "SOS" and "DE" and the *Morro Castle*'s call sign. It was as if he couldn't get the distress call out quick enough. He continued to type, interrupted by fits of coughing. He looked up at the clock, and noted it was 3:24 A.M.

Just as George Rogers was finishing the distress call, there was an explosion in the room, a puff of smoke different from the haze already clouding the air. Rogers and Alagna both recognized the problem immediately. Some of the radio's batteries had exploded. They looked at each other, their eyes asking the same question: *Did the SOS go out?*

CHAPTER SEVEN

Dead in the Water

Fear ignites heroism in some people, ignominy in others. On the *Morro Castle,* the fire sparked both extremes of human reaction. While most people moved quickly to the stern, away from the smoke, others pushed and shoved their way through the cloudy hallways—a few even stole life jackets from other passengers. One man burst onto the bridge screaming and grabbed William Warms from behind, as if trying to carry him off like a hostage.

"You've got to save my girlfriend," he cried. "You've got to save her."

Two men in the wheelhouse pulled the frenzied man off Warms, but the captain barely seemed to notice. He had many other things on his mind at that moment—salvaging a ship, evacuating passengers, his soon-to-be-lost command.

"Take him down and put him in a boat," he said.

Warms did not realize that was impossible.

Bob Tolman and Bob Smith had herded everyone they could find to the open stern on B Deck with the idea that they could be moved to the lifeboats from there, but the flames had cut off every route forward. The fire stretched aft of amidships and was inching toward the stern. The passengers huddled there had no idea whether the lifeboats were being readied, and there seemed few people around to ask. So they awaited orders without realizing they were trapped, prisoners on a moving Alcatraz, a floating inferno surrounded by tempestuous black water.

Smith waded through the crowd, unable to comprehend such a pitiful sight. Some people stood shivering in their underwear, while others still wore party dresses. They were drenched by the rain, and coughed and gagged as waves of smoke washed over them. When the cruise director discovered that access to the lifeboats had been cut off by the fire, he did not have the heart—or the courage—to tell these poor souls. *What are we going to do?* he wondered.

Smith realized that he had neglected to get his own life jacket. Funny, after all the preaching he'd done for the last half hour. Now, faced with the prospect that he would not leave the ship on a lifeboat, he ducked back inside to find a vest. He found one lying in the hall near a cabin door on B Deck. Amazed by his luck, Smith slipped it on and returned to the stern. But when he stepped outside, Smith met a young woman who told him she had no life jacket. She was scared, cold and wet. The chivalrous cruise director did not hesitate; he took off the vest and handed it to her. Moments later, he felt a tug at his shirt from a young boy.

"I don't have one either, Mr. Smith."

Smith recognized the boy as the son of Dr. Joseph Bregstein; his name was Marvin or something like that—he couldn't remember. It was hard to hear the boy. People all around them were screaming and shouting because flames were suddenly visible in the hallway. Smith looked down at the boy and did something he had hoped to avoid. He lied.

"You stick to your daddy, sonny, and you will be OK."

The cruise director knew there was no guarantee anyone would be OK. Already, the fire had claimed its first victim. Two waiters had pulled a young Cuban boy named Braulio Saenz from a burning cabin minutes earlier. As they had carried him to the stern, his burning flesh came off in their hands. The boy lay limp in their arms, mumbling, *"Mi madre, mi madre."*

The waiters recognized a doctor among the passengers, Gouverneur Phelps, and asked him for help.

"Dr. Phelps, for God's sake come over here," one of them said. "There is a boy that is burned."

Phelps complied, but could hardly examine the boy on the dark deck with the wind and rain whipping around his face. When he reached out to feel for a pulse, the boy cried, "Don't touch me. It hurts." Phelps turned to check on his wife and his own son, who were standing at the railing. When he looked back, Braulio Saenz had died. The waiters could only push the boy's body to the edge of the deck so it would not be trampled.

* * *

The people on the stern were scared and felt abandoned. The death of the little boy, witnessed by dozens of passengers, made the unfolding disaster more real, and they were near frenzy. For anyone who had not spoken to Smith or Tolman, it seemed there were no officers evacuating passengers, or even around to answer questions. The only official person some had seen did little to instill confidence. An officer with two gold stripes on his chevrons pushed his way through the crowd as if he were annoyed, asking people to be quiet.

"Silence, I am waiting for orders from the bridge," the man said.

The officer was flooded with questions, his order notwithstanding: *Are there more life vests? Are they going to put out the fire?* One woman asked the man, "When are they going to lower the boats?"

The man's reply was chilling to the dozens who heard it.

"Lady, God knows."

The people who left their cabins without shoes could now feel the deck growing hotter. It affected them in different ways. Some stood around placidly, while others screamed and cried. More than a few prayed. Despite the substantial wind and rain, it was growing hotter by the minute, and the sensation of being trapped grew more apparent. With nowhere else to go, that fear finally drove people over the rail. All they needed was the slightest nudge, and they soon got it. In the confusion, someone yelled "Jump!"

The word sent a chill down Bob Smith's neck. The engines were running, the ship still moving—and that meant the propellers were turning. Anyone who leaped from the stern would most likely be sucked into the *Morro Castle*'s giant twin screws. He urged people around him to not listen to the man, to not jump. But he couldn't stop everyone. He could not compete with the urgency in the unseen man's voice.

"Jump, jump. For God's sake, jump. I am being burned."

It was Smith's nightmare come to life. One person jumped, then another. Soon dozens were climbing over one another to reach the railing. A man and a woman with life jackets around their necks embraced, climbed over the rail and fell into the abyss. Smith watched in horror, certain that the couple was already dead. Henry Speierman, the chief steward, found the cruise director in the crowd. He said what Smith was already thinking.

"For God's sake, this is terrible. They will be churned to pieces."

But there was nothing they could do.

The one thing that could save these desperate souls was so close, yet impossibly out of reach. Less than fifty yards from the passengers gathered on the stern swung twelve lifeboats. Together, these metal launches could carry more than 800 people—250 more than were on the ship. Between passengers and crew, there were only 548 people aboard the *Morro Castle* that night. There should have been more than enough boats to rescue everyone on board.

The abundance of lifeboats was the legacy of the RMS *Titanic.* Outfitted at a time when maritime laws had not caught up to the size of the White Star Line's great ship, the liner had carried just twenty lifeboats. That was enough to save only half the 2,201 on board—even though it was more than British law of the day required. The failings of the law had only become apparent when the ship began to sink and there was no room in most of the escaping lifeboats. On that April night in 1912, about 1,500 people died—most of them passengers who had not gotten a seat in one of the lifeboats. They succumbed to exposure or drowned in the frigid North Atlantic waters.

In the wake of that accident, the United States government adopted more stringent laws concerning lifeboats. Ten of the *Morro Castle*'s lifeboats were oversized rowboats that could carry 70 people each and supposedly withstand moderately rough seas. Two of the 30-foot boats had motors on them in addition to oars. Those could carry 58 passengers each. There were also a number of collapsible rafts stored on board. Although the ship had a maximum rating to carry only 500 passengers and 250 crew members, there were lifeboats and rafts to save 2,000—nearly enough to have rescued everyone on the *Titanic.*

William Warms ordered Clarence Hackney to supervise the launch of these lifeboats. The thought of losing the Ward Line flagship was bad enough to make him sick to his stomach—he could not stand to suffer casualties as well. From his vantage point, Warms could not see that access to the boats had been cut off; he just told Hackney to make sure everyone got off the ship. He did not know the fire had blocked all access to A and B decks, the only places to board the lifeboats.

Safety cards in every cabin on the *Morro Castle* informed passengers that lifeboats were on A Deck, and that was where they should go in the event of an emergency. The boats could also be lowered to allow people to board from the Promenade on B Deck. Few realized this contingency because there had been no formal lifeboat drill. As it was, it didn't matter. Only the people on A Deck, the wealthiest passengers, had any chance of reaching a boat. Fire on the stairs blocked everyone else from rescue.

Still, most of the A Deck occupants fared no better. Few of the boats on the port side—where the fire began—would even launch. Warms had watched boats Nos. 2 and 4 catch fire and fall into the sea. The Nos. 6, 8 and 12 boats burned in their davits. Only one boat from the port side would launch. William Torres, another of the night watchmen, saw someone lower No. 10 before the *Morro Castle* had even stopped moving. The boat was dragged through the swells for several minutes before it finally broke free and floated away. When the boat hit the water, there were only two people in it.

Torres tried to lower No. 12, the aft boat on the port side, but could not manage it alone. Like several of the other lifeboats, it was stuck in its davits because the tackle to lower it had been painted solid by the fresh coats of whitewash the ship received regularly. Torres tried to loosen the rigging, but flames got to the boat before he could work it free.

Pushed by headwinds from the nor'easter, the fire was still racing astern. Warms had had no luck getting the ship turned away from the wind and toward the beach. He couldn't make contact with the engine room—the telephone, telegraph, and even the speaking tube would not work. While he repeated the order to set the propellers against each other, the ship continued to sail into the wind. Then, suddenly, the engines stopped. The ship was three miles off Sea Girt, but the smoke, wind, and rain made it impossible for Warms to see the lighthouse beacon onshore. *All hope is lost for sure now,* he thought. The *Morro Castle* was dead in the water.

Below, the engine room crew had fled. A circuit had blown and the lights went out just after the captain's orders to set the screws in opposite directions. They could not carry out the order. The smoke was so thick they couldn't see, and they could not speak to one another for hacking and coughing. Anthony Bujia, the assistant engineer, made the decision to abandon the engine room. He had one man cut off the fuel oil pumps, and then turned off the main engines. That stopped the boilers from generating steam. Fatefully, it also killed all the water pressure on the ship. There was no choice, the engines might explode if left running without anyone to monitor them. But turning them off had about the same effect: it took away the one means the crew had of fighting the fire. Bujia felt there was nothing more they could do.

"Let's get out of here," he said.

After a few minutes, Warms gave up trying to call the engine room. The *Morro Castle* was floundering and he had no control over it. There was only one thing he could do to keep the ship from drifting any farther from the shore. He summoned Ivan Freeman, his second-in-command.

"Well, I lost control of the steering gear and the engines and the telegraph is broken," Warms said. "You better get the starboard anchor ready."

George Rogers believed the SOS had gone out. The blast from the radio apparently was caused by the acid in the batteries boiling, but the explosion seemed only to have affected the receiver. The transmitter still worked. Rogers continued to send distress signals, but he had no way to know if anyone heard them. For all he knew, he would have done just as well to go to the rail and scream "Help!"

He sent Alagna back to the bridge to see if Warms had more orders. Rogers preferred to work alone, without someone standing over his shoulder. In the empty wireless room, he worked to restore power to his receiver. Pawing his way through the smoke, he staggered over to the generator and checked the four or five connections on its back. He found one of them loose, reattached it and heard the generator restart.

The conditions in the wireless room were becoming unbearable. Rogers could hardly breathe even with a wet towel held over his face. The rag was saturated with smoke, and eventually he threw it down in disgust. He wasn't sure he could make it much longer, and he thought to himself that it wasn't supposed to end this way. It was almost funny—it wasn't all bad. *If this is what it feels like to die,* George Rogers thought, *it doesn't hurt very much.* He felt himself getting sleepy.

Then Alagna burst into the room. He had been to the bridge, told Warms the SOS had been sent, and then asked the captain to order Rogers out of the radio room. Warms paid him no mind, muttering, "There's nothing to be done." Alagna left in disgust.

He found Rogers sitting with one hand on the key, listening to the receiver, trying in vain to hear whether anyone had gotten the distress call.

The room was glowing dull orange, the color of the flames muted by the smoke. Some of the furniture was on fire and the floor was hot. Alagna was scared, but not so much that he couldn't think or act clearly. He tugged at Rogers's shoulders, but the burly radioman wouldn't move.

"If we don't get out of here—if you don't get out of here—you are going to die like a rat."

"No," Rogers said. "I am going to stand by and stick to my post."

Burning skin causes one of the most intense forms of pain a person can experience. There are three degrees of burns to human skin. Sunburn is a first-degree burn. A second-degree burn damages the dermis, one layer beyond the epidermis. A third-degree burn reaches the hypodermis and causes extensive tissue damage; it can even melt fingers together. As skin burns, it turns either pure white or is charred black. The effects are devastating, the pain misleading. Fire singes nerve endings, deadening all feeling, sometimes tricking a person into thinking they are not hurt as badly as they are. But until that moment, a burn brings a piercing, unrelenting pain that can send a person into shock. One of the worst things a person with third-degree burns can do is immerse themselves in cold water.

If there is anything more frightening than burning, it may be the fear of it. By 3:30 A.M., only a handful of people had been burned by the flames racing through the *Morro Castle,* but everyone could feel the heat drawing closer. The metal hull had begun to heat up like the inside of an oven. The need to escape this rising heat, no matter what the consequences, became overwhelming. Doris Wacker felt smothered. Even as short as she was, and jammed in between so many other people on the stern, she could see flames shooting out of the hull. If this was the safest place on the ship, Doris thought, she didn't want to be on board any longer. As she stood with her parents, wondering what they should do next, Bob Smith appeared in the haze and told them.

"Go down another deck," Smith said. "The smoke isn't as bad there."

But conditions were only slightly better on D Deck. Lillian Wacker put her hand on the deck to test the temperature, and could feel the heat through the wood. It was just as crowded on D, and even though it was the

117

closest open deck to the water, everyone around them held handkerchiefs to their faces to block the smoke. As it grew thicker, the panic that had permeated the higher decks soon filtered down. Around Doris, people yelled, "Jump! Jump!" She briefly considered the possibility, but realized the engines were still running. Doris knew that leaping over the rail would be suicidal. And then, as if her thoughts had suggested it, the engines stopped.

When it became apparent the ship was no longer moving, that the propellers were not turning, more and more people abandoned ship. Soon a steady stream of passengers poured over the rail, stopping only long enough to remove their shoes. It was nearly a 30-foot drop depending on where a jumper struck the swells, easily a fall long enough to injure anyone who landed wrong. Some crew members tied lines to the rail, and told people to shimmy down the ropes to shorten their fall. A line formed; the deck was clearing out. As people disappeared into the blackness, Doris felt anxious, as if her time was running out, and she only wanted off the ship. Finally, she could take it no longer.

"I'm going to jump," she said.

Herbert and Lillian Wacker seemed petrified by the possibility. They argued with their daughter, told her to wait. They didn't want to become separated from her, and neither of them could swim. Even wearing life jackets, they were afraid of the water. Doris, however, was a good swimmer. She knew her life jacket would keep her afloat and felt it was the only way they would get off the ship. And most important, she was scared.

"I'd rather go in the water than burn," she said.

Finally, her parents agreed. They would go together, and one by one climbed down the stern with the rope tied to the railing. The end of the line dangled ten feet above the water. It was a short fall, but because they had put their life preservers on backward, the cork backing slammed into their chins when they hit the water, knocking them out as soon as they dropped into the unforgiving sea.

Help was slow coming to the *Morro Castle.* Although the ship's distress call had been received, the response was almost casual among the merchant marine. The radio station at Tuckerton, which hours earlier had relayed news of Captain Willmott's death, intercepted the SOS from Rogers and sent it out to all ships in the area. The operator there also called the Coast Guard station in New York. Word of the fire at sea surprised officials there; the only Coast Guard ship that had heard the distress signal was the *Cayuga* in the Boston Navy Yard 200 miles to the north—too far away to help. Coast Guard dispatch ordered the cutter *Tampa,* lying at Pier 18, Staten Island, to the scene. But it would take more than an hour to get the crew recalled, on board and launched. In the meantime, a 75-foot patrol boat in New York Harbor was ordered south, but in the deteriorating weather it would take them nearly as long as the *Tampa* to reach the burning ship.

Anyone who caught a glimpse of the ocean that night could tell something was terribly wrong. The *Morro Castle* was close enough to the coastline—and burning hard enough—that it was visible from the Jersey shore, even through the awful weather beginning to blow onshore. At the Belmar Fishing Club, a group of men and women suffered through a night too hot to sleep by playing poker in a room overlooking the sea. It was so muggy they barely talked, but as a bolt of lightning and rumbling thunder caught their attention, Fred Buck, a watchman at the club, pointed out a bright spot on the horizon.

"There's something the matter out there."

Happy for the distraction, the group gathered at the window to watch this curious sight. As the light grew brighter, it became clear something out there was on fire. One of the men ran to call the Coast Guard.

The *Andrea Luckenbach* was only seven miles away from the *Morro Castle,* and she turned immediately on hearing the distress signal. Several nearby ships had received Rogers's first SOS at 3:24, but two of them had ignored the call. For nearly an hour after the first call for help, the freighter *City of Savannah* and the Furness Line's *Monarch of Bermuda*—just 20 miles north of the *Morro Castle*—continued on their normal courses, which took them farther away from the ship.

At 3:34 A.M., the *Monarch of Bermuda*'s radio operator intercepted a message that the *Andrea Luckenbach* would reach the *Morro Castle* within a half hour, a bit of information he wrote down and delivered to the captain. As the distress signals continued and radio chatter about the accident increased, the *Monarch*'s captain grew more concerned. About 45 minutes later, the *Monarch*'s operator would send the *Luckenbach* a message asking if it had reached the burning ship. He wouldn't get an answer. Five minutes later, Albert R. Francis, the captain of the *Monarch of Bermuda,* tried again, this time asking if his ship could be of any assistance.

By that time, the *Andrea Luckenbach* had arrived on the scene and would only send Francis a short, but urgent, response: "Yes. Hurry."

Clarence Hackney was losing the battle to launch the lifeboats. Even after conceding all the portside boats to the fire, he could not seem to focus the efforts of his men. Some of them seemed to not know how to lower the boats, and those who did could barely do it anyway, the davits and winches were so caked with paint. It was hard to believe the lifeboats had been tested during the regular inspection only a few weeks earlier. If Hackney had not known before that the inspectors often looked the other way, or skimped on their jobs, he did now.

Warms had put Hackney in charge of the boats, but some of the sailors did not wait for orders, or passengers, to launch. A few men had already departed in No. 11, helped by William Torres, the man who had tried to salvage some of the portside boats. After Torres saw that lifeboat hit the water, he joined a small group of seamen in the No. 9 boat. But they didn't realize it took more than a few people to control a 30-foot launch in rough seas. Soon they were stranded, drifting wherever the ocean chose to take them. Hackney could see the men through the rain but could not identify them because of their rain gear. Even from a distance, even through the storm, he could tell they were helpless. He understood the feeling all too well.

Hackney realized quickly there was no way to get passengers from the stern to the lifeboats. No one who wasn't already on A Deck could reach the boats, and he could not see if there was anyone waiting on B Deck if he lowered the lifeboats there. He tried to direct the boats already launched to go astern and pick up passengers in the water, but he knew the men on board them had not heard him. Even if they had, there is little chance the undermanned boats could navigate the rough seas. They were adrift, at the mercy of the waves. And with half the lifeboats lost already, Hackney knew it would take a miracle to rescue any of the people already in the water.

As Hackney struggled to coordinate the ragtag group of men on A Deck, he also fought the flames spreading around him. He tried first to launch the No. 7 boat—the one closest to the encroaching flames—but its winch was stuck. And before he could untangle the cables, flames attacked the boat. Hackney surrendered it to the fire and moved on to the next lifeboat. His job felt like one steady retreat.

Hackney lowered the No. 5 without too much trouble, but lifeboat No. 3 was stuck. Apparently, the pelican hook holding the boat to the deck had jammed and, when the acting second officer came on the scene, he found Eben Abbott already aboard the lifeboat and barking out orders to a crewman.

"Kick it! Kick it!" the chief engineer cried.

Just then, one of the lowering cables got snagged, further entangling the boat. While Hackney tried to help a couple of sailors free it, Abbott gave up, climbed out of the boat and jumped into the next one, No. 1.

"We better get away from here or we'll all be burned alive," he said.

The starboard lifeboats that got away carried few, if any, passengers—a pattern that continued as the rest of the boats were launched. There were only two people who weren't crewmen aboard No. 1. Renée Méndez Capote, the daughter of Cuba's vice president, had been rescued from Suite 15 on A Deck just moments earlier. Three crewmen smashed the oversized porthole in her stateroom and found her standing on the bed. They plucked her out, careful not to cut her on the broken glass, and put her in the boat only a few steps from her window.

William Warms stepped out on the starboard wing of the bridge and surveyed the scene. He was horrified to see one boat lowered with only eight people aboard. Hundreds of people stood on the stern awaiting rescue and these boats were leaving nearly empty. He screamed out to Hackney, to the crew, but no one seemed to hear him. He did not notice Renée Méndez Capote in the No. 1 lifeboat and, if he had, he would have realized the rescue of a single passenger—no matter who her father might be—did not make up for this unfolding fiasco.

"Don't lower that boat," Warms yelled. "Keep it at the rail for passengers."

Warms could see that many people were already in the water, and he called out to Hackney, telling him to order the boats to pick up passengers after they launched. Through the wind and rain, the men on A Deck only caught snippets of what the captain said, and to them it seemed contradictory to the orders from the other officers. Richard Kopf, a steward who was in No. 1, heard the order to not lower the boat. Then he heard Abbott override it.

"Lower the boat," Abbott called out. "Lower the boat."

Things were happening too quickly. The confusion, smoke and storm made it nearly impossible to know what to do. The men, quite simply, had not been trained to manage this sort of catastrophe. Hackney was disoriented, contradicting himself every few minutes. Clarence "Red" Monroe, an able-bodied seaman who had helped Hackney launch the other boats, had been ordered into No. 1. While Monroe sat along with Capote and Abbott waiting for the boat to be lowered, he heard Warms call out again.

"Soon as you hit the water row aft and try to get the passengers," Warms said.

Abbott, who had been huddled in the stern of the lifeboat, saw the captain and jumped up. He yelled out to Warms, waving at him even as Hackney sent the boat plunging toward the black water below.

"Captain, the ship's on fire—all on fire—you'd better get in this boat," Abbott said. Warms apparently didn't hear him or, if he did, paid no attention to the engineer. He watched as No. 1 was lowered toward the hungry sea.

The lifeboat almost flipped the moment it hit the water. The swells pitched the boat away from the *Morro Castle,* several crewmen dropping their oars over the side during the rollercoaster ride. Many of the swells topped eight feet and were growing larger every minute. The boat bucked in protest, tossing its passengers around like they were dolls, slamming them into the wooden gunnels. For a moment, it seemed that the lifeboat was no escape at all, only a quicker death.

Although the No. 1 was one of two *Morro Castle* lifeboats with an engine, no one had yet attempted to crank it. Some of the sailors on board argued it might not be a good idea to start the gas motor so close to the fire, and others said there was no use trying to motor through these seas. Near the lifeboat's stern, Abbott was curled up as if he were sick. Somehow he had cut his hand, and he lay there holding a handkerchief to it. To some of the people on the boat, it seemed that the chief engineer did not know where he was. Later, Morris Weisberger, an able-bodied seaman, would argue otherwise. He claimed to have heard Abbott talking with the electrician, Percy Mille, as soon as the boat was launched.

"Percy, you know how to start the motor, don't you?"

"Yes."

"Then start it," the engineer had said.

At 3:40 A.M. ship's time, less than an hour after Daniel Campbell had discovered fire in a Writing Room locker, flames reached the *Morro Castle*'s bridge. The smoke had become so thick the men in the wheelhouse could not see, their eyes watering uncontrollably. The heat intensified as flames licked the grating outside and threatened to move into the wings of the bridge. If they did not leave, they would be trapped, burned alive.

William Warms knew what he must do and, in one final action, felt his way over to the controls to make sure the engine was set to STOP—just in case. He ordered the remaining men on the bridge to go to the forecastle, ahead of the fire and smoke, a place the passengers could not reach. It was the only relatively safe place left on the ship. William Warms, captain of the *Morro Castle* for little more than eight hours, had no time to consider the symbolism of the act. He was giving up the ship, conceding defeat. The flagship of the Ward Line was lost.

The fire had also overtaken the radio room. When George Alagna returned from the bridge, he found George Rogers slumped over the table, a wet towel wrapped around his head. He shook the chief operator, but it did no good. Rogers seemed barely conscious.

"Chief, the mate says we are going to abandon ship, so get out of here—right away." Alagna hoisted Rogers out of the chair, and that seemed to wake him a little. The scrawny junior wireless operator struggled to move the heavy Rogers as the flames crept toward them. When they made it to the doorway, the outside air seemed to revive Rogers. He tripped over the door coaming and fell onto the outside deck, skinning his leg, but barely felt it. Rogers stood up and made a few tentative steps forward, helped by Alagna, as they struggled to reach the bridge. Alagna told Rogers he thought the ship was lost and that he had heard Warms talking about abandoning the bridge. He didn't think to ask if Rogers had heard of any rescue ships on the way. But then, Rogers wasn't saying much.

When they made it to the starboard wing of the bridge, Alagna saw

Warms through the smoke. The captain, wearing a raincoat and hat, was below them, climbing over the railing.

"Look at that yellow rat," Alagna said. "They are leaving us behind here. They are deserting us."

Thomas Torresson had watched the No. 1 lifeboat lowered into the fitful sea. He had been helping the other pursers and stewards move passengers to the lower decks and stopped for air. He sucked in a fresh breath while leaning over the starboard rail of B Deck near the Ballroom. He briefly thought about all the fun he'd had making a fool of himself on that dance floor. *Not anymore.* He let the rain hit his face and tried to inhale the fresh salt air when he saw the lifeboat's stern kick up on a wave. The boat was tossed around like it was just another passenger in a cork life vest, completely at the mercy of the sea. *Oh my God,* he thought, *those people are dead.*

Despite the chaos around him, Tom was remarkably calm. It was almost funny. Here he was, just weeks away from his eighteenth birthday, on a burning ocean liner several miles off the coast of New Jersey. He could very well die, but he was not afraid. He didn't have time to think beyond doing his duty. The rest, he figured, would work itself out. Tom watched as passengers climbed over the rail and leapt into the water, urged on by Hyman Koch, the *Morro Castle*'s orchestra leader. Koch had decided he was going to jump and encouraged everyone else to do the same. Dozens of people took his advice. Before they jumped, many threw off their coats and kicked off their shoes in a macabre striptease. The clothes lay on the deck where they fell in rumpled piles, like dead bodies that had lost their souls.

The Reverend Raymond Egan had a more calming effect on the crowd. The priest wandered around the deck, offering absolution to Catholics. Tom, himself Catholic, suggested the priest cut a wider swath.

"Father, you should give general absolution."

Egan did, and Tom was glad to see that this seemed to calm some of the people, certainly more than the hysterical bandleader had. But when the priest finished, Tom pulled him aside and asked for his own absolution. Tom feared he hadn't been close enough to Egan for the general absolution to work.

For some time after that—and he didn't know how long because the concept of minutes seemed as nebulous and formless as the smoke—Tom helped Tolman and Smith move everyone from B Deck down to C. Before he left B Deck, Tom picked up a loose fire hose and tried to douse some of the flames. The water pressure had been diminished, and what stream leaked out of the hose did him no good. He thought he'd have better luck peeing on the flames. When he reached the stairs, he closed the door behind him, hoping it would slow the fire's advance.

On C Deck, Tom watched the crowd thin out as more and more people climbed down to D Deck or over the rail. As crazy as he thought the bandleader was, Tom realized that he, too, would eventually have to jump. As he stood there mulling his options, a man walked up and shoved a young boy at him. *Who the heck is this guy?* he thought. The man was wearing a white shirt and, for all Tom knew, he could have been a passenger or a member of the crew—he couldn't tell through the smoke. The man said something like, "Take this kid," but Tom wasn't sure.

The boy was young—not yet a teenager—and he had been burned badly, mainly on his back. Tom asked his name, but didn't understand the answer—Bobby or Roberto, something like that. It was too noisy on the deck to hear the boy's soft voice.

Tom didn't know what to do. The boy was hurt, but there was no way to care for him on the ship. He knew they both would ultimately end up in the water, so Tom took off his life jacket and tried to put it on him. But the boy's skin was burned so badly that he yelped in pain when the rough canvas vest touched him. Tom gave up and took his life jacket back. As he put it on again, he looked down at the boy and asked, "Can you swim?"

The boy nodded. Tom thought for a moment that it had come down to one choice, which was no choice at all. He tried to explain it to the boy as best he could. "Bobby, you are going to have to jump very quickly. When I tell you to jump, you jump, then I'll jump after you. You can get around my neck and that way we can stay together."

Tom didn't have time to consider the danger. He was on C Deck portside, more than 30 feet above the water, but didn't think to climb down to D Deck, where they might shimmy down the lines and have a shorter drop. Tom only knew they had to get off the ship fast; he had to save this boy, who was really just a few years younger than himself. Together they climbed over the C Deck rail. It seemed to be 100 feet down but, with a little nudge, the boy jumped.

Tom Torresson knew the danger of jumping while wearing one of these life vests, how the impact with the water could send a block of cork slamming into your chin. It was something they were supposed to tell passengers during drills: hold on to the life jacket when you jump to keep it from hitting your face. But Tom didn't stop to think about those instructions; he was trying to keep his eye on the boy in the waves below and keep himself oriented. He tried to keep his mind off the fact that he was jumping from a burning ship in the middle of a storm at sea. He didn't know where they were, which direction was land, or what might happen to him when he jumped. He didn't think about the dangers of the cork life vest until he felt the ship flying past, just before he hit the water.

And then Tom Torresson's world went black.

CHAPTER EIGHT

Adrift in the Sea of Fire

George Rogers felt as if he were looking out across the pits of hell. An ocean of fire spread out below him, and against the background of the black ocean, the orange glow was mesmerizing. The heat coming off the blaze was unbearable, almost palpable enough to hold him up. He had never imagined anything like it before in his life. It was, in a way, impressive.

George Alagna had dragged him out of the wireless room and onto the walkway that led to the bridge. They had seen Warms climbing over the rail, headed for the forecastle, but Alagna wanted to make sure no one else was in the wheelhouse before they followed. Rogers volunteered to look— he was curious—so he stuck his head inside the doorway and saw that the chart room was on fire and flames had spread across the entire bridge. The great ship's wheel, the compass stand, the polished instrument panel—all of it was burning. For a moment, he was frozen, as if hypnotized by the sight of the ship being destroyed. And then he heard Alagna beckoning.

"Come on this way, Chief. This is the way down."

He followed without being conscious of it. Alagna led Rogers down a flight of steps that led to the crew deck just below the bridge. Rogers stopped to gaze at the fire once again and, through the flames, saw three crewmen with something big in their hands. He did not know what it was, but it looked as if they were trying to throw it overboard. *Was it a rug? A body?* He found that he could not look away.

In the smoke, they could not find the ladder that led to the forecastle, and they were running out of time. Behind them, they could hear glass from the portholes cracking from the heat. The flames were advancing, eating away at the command deck above them, and it seemed as if the whole ship might collapse in the next minute. Sensing they were almost out of luck, the two radiomen could think of nothing else to do but shake hands.

"We may not see each other again," Rogers said.

"I am going to jump," Alagna said. "I will probably break a leg, but I am going to take a chance. I'm not going to roast up here."

If Rogers was going to try to talk Alagna out of it, he had no chance. There was a lull in the wind and the direction of the smoke shifted, revealing the nearby ladder. The top rung was broken, which made the first step awkward, but still they could climb down. As they descended the ladder, Alagna noticed that Rogers seemed to have shaken off his earlier daze quickly.

On the forecastle, the radiomen met more than a dozen officers who had gathered there, including William Warms, Ivan Freeman and Clarence Hackney. Warms seemed horrified by the clear view he had of the ship burning behind him, his first real look at the fire. The upper decks of the *Morro Castle* were now consumed in smoke and flame, the inky water below littered with bodies. Lights twinkled in the distance like stars— lanterns in lifeboats a quarter mile off the bow. They were the only traces now of the ones who got away.

If Warms was glad to see his radiomen, it did not show. There was no slap on the back, no congratulations for making it out of the fire, or thanks for sending the distress signal. Despite what he'd been through, Warms was still all business, still the old sea dog. They weren't out of this yet, he said. When Rogers and Alagna walked up, Warms handed Rogers a flashlight.

"Sparks, there is a ship off out there. See if you can raise that fellow."

Rogers aimed the light at the silent hulk in the distance and blinked out a short SOS in Morse code. When he finished, the ship answered. As it did, Rogers deciphered the flashes from the bow of the ship, which was the *Andrea Luckenbach.* The message asked, "Do you need assistance?"

Rogers flashed out a succinct response: Immediately, 540 passengers.

* * *

He awoke before a great black wall.

It stretched as high as he could see, to the heavens, blocking every-thing else from his vision. It was beautiful and imposing, and seemed al-most like a gate close enough that he could reach out and touch it. For a brief moment, Thomas Torresson Jr. was entranced by the sight. *What is this?* he thought.

The sting of saltwater slapped him into consciousness and Tom spat. He squinted once, his eyes adjusting to a new level of darkness, and then he realized what he was seeing. It was the *Morro Castle*. It came back to him quickly. He had jumped off the ship, jumped with the boy. He whipped his head around—a reflex—looking for the child and then felt him there. The boy was clinging to his back, clutching the life jacket that had mo-mentarily knocked Tom out cold.

They were near the ship's flank, just below the propeller suites, riding swells that lifted them up and dropped them nearly sixteen feet in a few seconds. It did not concern him to float so close to the ship, he was fairly certain the engines had stopped, so they had nothing to fear from the pro-pellers. Still, the ship was imposing, like a giant sea monster hovering over him. It would not have mattered if he wanted to get away from it, because it was impossible to swim in the life jacket with the boy clinging to his back.

He felt that if he could hang on for a bit, hold on to the boy, everything would be all right. One of the lifeboats would come along and pick them up. He wondered if anyone else had been rescued. The waves around him were so high that he couldn't tell if anyone else in the water was nearby. All he could see was the ship's dark hull, rising out of the water like a great New York City skyscraper. Tom knew if he had to try and swim for land, he was in big trouble. The Jersey shore was somewhere out there a few miles away, but he had no idea which direction.

He heard a noise and it took him a second to recognize it as the soft voice of the child. The boy was awake and trying to speak to him. He told Tom that his name was Roberto González, and he was on his way to school in New York. Tom had to strain to hear the boy, but he thought it might calm both of their nerves to talk. Casual conversation was difficult as they awkwardly tried to ignore the situation. They were two boys—one not yet a teenager, the other barely a man—clinging to a single life jacket in the middle of the ocean. There was little for them to talk about, and before long they could no longer avoid the thing that weighed most heavily on them. They were scared. Perhaps he remembered Father Egan on the ship, for Tom suggested he and Roberto say a Hail Mary. They floated together in the darkness, barely able to hear each other over the shrieking wind, as they repeated the words.

"Hail Mary, full of grace, the Lord is with you . . ."

Less than 100 yards away from Tom Torresson and Roberto González, the end of a long string of *Morro Castle* passengers drifted away from the ship. These were the people who had leapt from the stern, and some were already a half-mile away from the ship, carried south by the current and pushed west by the wind. They tried to hang on to one another, feeling safer in numbers. The water was cold, but the more immediate concern was the pitching waves that made them sick, strangling them with saltwater. Doris Wacker and her parents had found one such group after briefly being separated. The water splashing in their faces had not allowed them to remain unconscious for long. Doris worried about her parents, whose fear of the water led them to fight harder than they should. They would wear out quickly.

The Wackers had joined a chain of about sixteen people. Doris didn't recognize any of them—and she had no idea what had happened to Marjorie Budlong or the couples her parents were traveling with—but she was glad at least that somebody was nearby. Some of the people panicked, a few yelled "Shark," but they could have just as easily been bumping each other's leg. They were scared and imagining things, Doris believed.

Occasionally, they saw a lifeboat drift by just out of reach. It was hard to swim in the life jackets, and the boats seemed under no more control than they were. The sea tossed them around as if they were kelp, and it was all Doris could do not to drown on the seawater that gushed into her mouth once, even twice, before she could catch a breath. Even holding on to her parents and the other people around her, it was difficult not to get lost in the swells.

All around Doris, people were thrown together or separated at the whim of a particular wave. Lucille Robinson was torn from her mother shortly after they floated away from the ship, and Eva Hoffman found herself alone, carried off into the darkness. If possible, it was more terrifying than watching the flames approach.

By 4 A.M. ship's time, Bob Tolman had given up fighting the fire. The flames had consumed the barber shop on C Deck and were now only seven cabin lengths away from the stern. The purser knew it was only a matter of time before the fire reached the remaining passengers. There were still dozens of them on the stern, maybe as many as 100, waiting for some sort of rescue. Tolman didn't know the bridge had already been abandoned, that the ship had been given up as lost. Nor did he know if anyone was coming to rescue them. Tolman, Russell Du Vinage and Bob Smith decided they should get the remaining passengers off the ship. Smith, who had spoken for the crew so far, gave the order that less than an hour earlier had made him cringe.

"Jump. Everybody with life preservers jump," he called out.

Most of the passengers took Smith at his word and, believing this was the order they had been awaiting, immediately began climbing over the rails. Tolman and Du Vinage helped some people, but most didn't need more than a nudge. A husband threw his wife over the rail, a mother and daughter jumped together. For an hour, they had been counting on a miracle. Now they knew none was coming.

In the final stampede to escape the ship, many people were injured. One man, James Petri, fell and broke his hip. Another passenger callously took Petri's life jacket while he was down, and so two crewmen tried to lower him to a lifeboat on a rope. But Petri slipped out of the harness and fell into the water. One elderly woman got the stern rope twisted around her neck as she tried to slide down it. She was stuck; if she let go of the rope to free herself, she would have hung. Trygue Johnson, one of the ship's carpenters, climbed down the rope to free her. When he reached the woman, he pulled out his knife and cut the rope above his hands, dropping them both into the waves below. The crowd watched this rescue until the two popped up from below the surface, Johnson swimming along with the woman in his arms.

Anthony Lione's free dream trip had turned to nightmare, and he had no choice but to split up his family. He took nine-year-old Raymond under his arm, climbed over the railing, and told his wife to follow with Robert. Then he jumped.

But Mary Lione could not follow. She could not bear to wake Robert, who somehow was managing to sleep through the chaos on deck. After her husband and oldest son disappeared into the blackness, a crewman came along and offered to lower Mary and Robert to the water so that they wouldn't have to fall so far. Together they hung there, dangling over the water, listening to the howl of the wind, hoping to hear the call of Anthony below. But they heard nothing. Anthony and Raymond Lione were gone.

Howard Hansen, the acting third officer, met Dr. De Witt Van Zile near the stern. Van Zile carried a bottle of rum, and said he was about to jump but, "I've got to have a drink first." After taking a swig of Havana rum, the doctor jumped over the rail. But Van Zile forgot to hold on to his life vest, and Hansen watched him smack the water with great force. When the doctor rolled over, Hansen could see blood smeared on his face. Van Zile rolled over again, facedown in the water, and floated away. Hansen hoped that a lifeboat would find the doctor.

Tolman and Smith could see lifeboats in the distance, just beyond the reach—or sight—of the passengers in the water. They spotted some of the boats by their white hulls and others by small lights on them. There were three or four close by, near enough and empty enough to rescue all the people floating near the *Morro Castle*'s stern. Tolman and Smith waved and yelled to the boats and pointed at the people in the water, but the crews in the lifeboats could not hear them, or ignored the orders. Eventually, the wind drowned out their words. The boats faded into the darkness.

One lifeboat drifted very near Rafael Mestre. Mestre found himself in the water through the unlikeliest of circumstances. He had been afraid to jump and climbed all the way up to A Deck, where he saw a woman scared and crying. She wanted off the ship, but did not have a life jacket. He gave her his vest both because he was a gentleman and he didn't plan to use it anyway. But even with this gift, the woman was afraid to jump. So Mestre hoisted the woman up onto the railing and threw her overboard, watching as she emerged between two waves. Mestre, a native of Santiago, Cuba, believed he had just thrown away his own chance to live. But he did not want to die before helping as many others as he could. He had heard someone say a person was trapped in one of the A Deck suites, so he charged into the burning hallway and kicked open the door to the cabin. The room was empty, but inside he found a life jacket. He took it as a sign, put on the vest and jumped from A deck, much higher than B deck, where he had been afraid to jump minutes before.

When he surfaced, spitting saltwater and disoriented, he saw a lifeboat. He recognized one of the passengers, Rosario Comacho. He spoke to her as if they were passing on the Promenade Deck.

"Hello, Rosalie, how are you? Where am I?"

"You are in the water."

"I think I am in a boat."

Comacho urged him to swim toward her, but soon the boat was out of his reach and he was left alone in the water.

Not all the people in the lifeboats were callous to those in the water. Few of them, however, had any control over their boats. William Torres, the watchman who had left the ship in the No. 9 boat, tried to help several people. He had tried to paddle to one woman floating alone, but with only one other sailor to help him maneuver the lifeboat, he could not reach her. Torres thought it was ironic. He had launched the boat to save it from burning, but now found that with no one aboard to row, it was worthless. A boat built to rescue seventy people saved only two lives.

Most of the lifeboats got nowhere near the passengers. The current pulled some of them away from the passengers at the *Morro Castle*'s stern and toward the ship's bow. The No. 9 boat with Torres in it passed between the anchor chain and the ship's bow at one point.

By 4:30 ship's time, most of the ship's 318 passengers had left the ship, as had nearly all of the 231 crew members. There were fewer than two dozen people on the bow, and only a couple of those were passengers. If there was anyone left inside, they were dead or soon would be. At the stern, the few remaining officers had given up. Tolman and Du Vinage jumped into the water shortly after they made sure no passengers remained.

Bob Smith had gotten lost in a fog of smoke on B Deck while searching for stragglers. Soon he was overcome with a feeling of solitude, as if he were the last man in the world. Fire blocked the stairs, so he climbed over the rail onto C Deck, but didn't find anyone there, either. He could not find Tolman or the other pursers, nor did he see Speierman. He assumed the chief steward and the ship's photographer, who had also helped with the passengers, were long gone. Most everyone had abandoned ship, and if there was anyone left, Smith knew he could not reach them. He could not go back inside, either. The fire was beginning to creep onto the stern, the hallways all but incinerated. He realized that once again he had no life jacket, and perhaps the irony made Bob Smith smile. He was alone and without a choice. After telling hundreds of others what to do, Smith could do nothing but follow his own orders. He climbed over the C Deck railing and dropped into the ocean.

When the *Andrea Luckenbach* drew close enough to lower its lifeboats, the freighter's crew was struck by the sight of the burning ocean liner. It was a scene out of Dante's *Inferno*—the ship was almost completely ablaze, people were jumping from the rails of all decks while others hung out portholes, waving their arms furiously. The freighter's crew wondered if there was anyone left to save.

The *Andrea Luckenbach* had received the original SOS while ten miles farther out to sea, heading north, but had closed the distance in an hour's time, fighting the waves as it went. After receiving George Rogers's Morse code message, the freighter put four lifeboats in the water, each crewed by 35 sailors. It was the law of the sea they had to help, but they did so at great peril. A 60-person lifeboat was little protection in a storm at sea.

By the time the *Luckenbach* began its rescue operations, a small armada of ships was steaming toward the *Morro Castle*. The *Monarch of Bermuda* had turned around just before picking up its New York harbor pilot. The *City of Savannah* was closer, and the Dollar Line's *President Cleveland* had diverted to the scene, although its captain would not risk any of his lifeboats in the vicious seas. The Coast Guard had several other boats en route, including a motor surfboat from the Shark River Station eight miles northwest of the *Morro Castle*.

The officers of the *Morro Castle* could only watch these rescue efforts from the bow; the fire had trapped them on the forecastle. As the *Andrea Luckenbach* lifeboats fought their way toward the passengers in the water, William Warms—the color drained out of his face—shook his head in disbelief and said to George Rogers, "My God, am I dreaming or is this true?"

Rogers watched the bridge burn above him, sparks from the flames shooting into the sky and whisked away by the wind. It hurt to look up for long as the rain pelted his face, but he could barely turn away. He walked over to Alagna, who was watching the same scene.

"Well, George, it looks like we were the only two who kept our heads," Rogers said. "We have nothing to be ashamed of. We did our part."

As Alagna scanned the faces on the bow, a random thought popped into his head. "I wonder what happened to Maki."

"If he deserted, he will be taken care of," Rogers said.

Alagna remembered how odd Rogers had acted when he'd brought up Maki earlier, but did not want to have the conversation again. Not now, anyway.

Some of the officers stood at the rail, directing lifeboats toward passengers and crew in the water. The heavy seas swamped the people, and it was clear some of them would not last much longer. But the sailors in the boats had a difficult time spotting them. Alagna suggested that one of them should jump in to help, but Warms would not allow it.

"No, we can't do anything. We will let these boats rescue them," Warms said.

Alagna argued that it wasn't very far and, thinking of an earlier boast by Rogers, added, "We have some good swimmers here—one at least," Alagna said.

Warms wouldn't have any of it, and Alagna stalked off in disgust. He complained to Rogers. It was a damnable state of affairs.

"People are drowning less than a hundred feet away while we do nothing but stand around and watch the flames," he said.

Alagna felt helpless, but George Rogers seemed content to let it all unfold around him. He took it all in without emotion.

The tide carried the *Morro Castle* refugees toward the Jersey shore in a southwesterly arc, the survivors riding increasingly high swells that did not abate as the first strains of light crept into the sky. The hurricane that had followed the ship along the coast was moving into the area. It had been downgraded to a tropical storm, but it still had more than enough power to throw the ship's survivors off course, sending them up or down the coast at a whim. Most of the people would reach land near Manasquan Inlet or Sea Girt, if they made it that far.

Many of the *Morro Castle* passengers and crew survived the fire only to drown or succumb to shock in the water. A person loses body heat more than twenty-five times faster in water than on land. The ocean temperature off the New Jersey coast that morning was just above 70 degrees Fahrenheit, on the cusp of what some scientists consider "cold." While people have survived up to forty-eight hours in water that temperature, the effects of hypothermia can set in quickly—especially if they are exacerbated by serious burns, exhaustion, fatigue or alcohol. Some people from the *Morro Castle* were suffering all four.

Marjorie Budlong had not had anything to drink, but she was extremely tired. She had been separated from Doris Wacker during the confusion and, in the water, Marjorie drifted alone. At one point, a young Cuban man swam up to her, suffering from exhaustion and, most likely, the early stages of hypothermia. Marjorie could see the terror in his eyes.

"I can't swim any more," he told her.

Marjorie was hardly in a position to offer encouragement, but she told the man to grab on to her and fight it. They would be rescued soon enough. The man clung to her for what seemed like hours. He said little, until she heard him say a quiet prayer before letting go.

"Give my love to my mother," he said, and disappeared into the darkness.

Bob Smith had better luck without a life vest. After a half hour of treading water, the cruise director found his assistant, Herman Cluthe, in a cluster of people that included Tolman and Du Vinage. The men held on to Smith, allowing him to relax until a giant wave crashed into the group, separating them. Somehow, Smith managed to hang on to Du Vinage, and the two men floated away from the pack on a single life jacket.

Nearby, Tom Torresson ached so badly that he didn't know how long he could take it. It hurt to carry the boy on his back and made it hard to keep his head above water. But he knew letting go would be a death sentence for Roberto González. For more than an hour, he had not seen another person in the water until finally, just as the sky was beginning to lighten, he saw a woman—remarkable only for her girth—float by. Tom hated to say anything to the woman, who was obviously a passenger, but he felt he was at the limit of his endurance.

"Would you help me with this boy," he called out. "I'm having difficulty keeping him on my back."

The woman looked at him as if he were crazy. She refused, and continued to paddle by without stopping.

"Let him go and save yourself," she said.

Nice, Tom thought. He shifted his weight, boosting Roberto higher onto his back and continued to wonder if anyone was going to find them in the middle of the ocean.

The rescue boats were out there, supplied not only by the *Andrea Luckenbach* but also by the *City of Savannah* and the *Monarch of Bermuda,* both of which had arrived on the scene just before dawn. Captain J. N. Diehl of the *City of Savannah* ordered his lifeboats dropped shortly after 5 A.M. as he watched the last people leap from the *Morro Castle*'s stern. Captain Albert R. Francis, who turned the *Monarch of Bermuda* around when he learned the Coast Guard would not make the scene for two hours, sailed within 100 yards of the *Morro Castle,* and later described what he saw as anarchy. He had seen maritime disasters before, but nothing like this. His previous command, the *Fort Victoria,* had been rammed by another ship once near New York and that day he had stayed aboard until all 400 passengers were rescued. That accident seemed like a pleasure cruise compared to the horrible spectacle he saw on this morning. Shaken by the death around him, Francis ordered all his lifeboats in the water, told the band to warm up and sent out an appeal to his passengers to donate clothes to the survivors he hoped his men could retrieve.

When the *Monarch of Bermuda* passed within a few hundred feet of the *Morro Castle*'s bow, Francis called out to Warms and offered to get him and his men off the ship. But just the presence of the Furness liner seemed to give the *Morro Castle* officers hope. They finally felt their sense of urgency subside and thought that perhaps they weren't going to die. Warms waved off his would-be rescuers, told them to get the passengers.

"We are OK up here," he said. "Take them off aft first."

Within minutes, one of the *Monarch*'s boats had come alongside the bow and Warms told the men there were two passengers on the bow, a man and a woman. They would lower them with a Jacob's ladder. The woman was scared, afraid to climb down the rope ladder. George Rogers took her hand and told her it would be all right. Alagna thought, for a moment, the radioman was a different person.

Just as the lifeboat moved away from the bow, Warms and Rogers heard a scream in the darkness. A naked woman was hanging half out of a porthole, waving her arms frantically, screaming, "Help me!"

Warms, Rogers and Alagna yelled for her to jump, but she was stuck. For several minutes, they tried to coach the panicked woman. When she finally wiggled free, she fell twenty-five feet to the water and landed stomach first. She floated on the water, unconscious, toward the stern. Rogers kicked off his shoes, making a production out of saving her, but Warms stopped him before he could get on the ladder.

"Don't jump, Sparks, there is some other fellow going after her," the captain said.

Soon both the woman and the sailor who dived in to save her disappeared into the waves. The men on the bow wondered if they would be found by one of the lifeboats.

The lifeboats from the *Andrea Luckenbach,* the *City of Savannah* and the *Monarch of Bermuda* had no trouble finding people to rescue. One *Monarch* lifeboat found Mary Lione and her son, Robert, still dangling from a rope off the *Morro Castle* stern, and quickly pulled them aboard. The boats reached their capacity within an hour and returned to their ships. The surfboat from the Shark River Coast Guard Station let off survivors on the *City of Savannah* and went back for more. The crews on these lifeboats would never forget the range of emotions they encountered among the passengers. Some of them were terrified and would remain in shock for days. For others, this dip in the ocean seemed like nothing more than a continuation of the party.

Frank S. O'Day, a seaman from the *Andrea F. Luckenbach,* was unnerved by the screams he heard coming from the *Morro Castle.* He saw a woman hanging from a porthole with her hair on fire and a sailor lower a boy into the water before jumping after him. But O'Day was most impressed with a girl—he guessed she was nineteen—who barked out orders to other passengers, urging them to keep one another afloat. When the lifeboat got within shouting distance, O'Day threw a line to the girl, but it fell short. Instead of looking dejected or scared, she called out, "Hey, sailor, you're a bum shot."

With his next throw, O'Day got the rope to her. He pulled the girl aboard the lifeboat, where she asked for a shot of rum. She drank it down straight, in one gulp, and promptly fell asleep.

The *Morro Castle* during its construction at the Newport News Shipbuilding & Dry Dock Co. in Virginia, winter of 1930. (COURTESY OF MICHAEL ALDERSON /WWW.WARDLINE.COM)

A Spring 1934 Ward Line travel brochure advertising one of the *Morro Castle*'s rare excursions to the Bahamas and Miami. Despite advertising it as an Easter special, the ship only diverted from its normal course because it had cargo to deliver. (COURTESY OF MICHAEL ALDERSON /WWW.WARDLINE.COM)

The *Oriente* First-Class Lounge, identical to the *Morro Castle*'s. Doors off this popular gathering spot on the ship led to the Library, the Smoking Room and the Writing Room. (COURTESY MICHAEL ALDERSON / WWW.WARDLINE.COM)

Captain Robert Willmott on the *Morro Castle*'s bow, September 1933. The ship was missing for two days in a hurricane off the Outer Banks and feared lost. Willmott returned her to the docks in New York with no more damage than a couple of wet towels. (COPYRIGHT BETTMANN/CORBIS)

Morro Castle officers Ivan Freeman, George White Rogers, William Warms and Clarence Hackney (from left) during the Department of Commerce Steamboat Inspectors hearings in New York, September 1934. (COPYRIGHT BETTMANN/CORBIS)

George Alagna, as he appeared in newspapers across the country during the Department of Commerce's *Morro Castle* inquiry. The photograph accompanied his first-person account of the disaster published in New York newspapers. (COPYRIGHT BETTMANN/CORBIS)

Thomas Torresson Jr. in a 1930s photograph taken around the time of his *Morro Castle* experience. (COURTESY THOMAS TORRESSON JR.)

Doris Wacker (bottom right) and her friend Marjorie Budlong pose with her parents, Lillian and Herbert Wacker, on a Cuban beach during the *Morro Castle*'s Labor Day 1934 cruise. (COURTESY OF DORIS MANSKE)

The *Oriente* Writing Room, identical to the *Morro Castle*'s. The Writing Room locker, where the fire allegedly began, is behind a hidden panel beneath the fan mounted in the corner. (COURTESY THE MARINERS' MUSEUM, NEWPORT NEWS, VA.)

The fire at sea, September 8, 1934. The *Morro Castle*'s officers are huddled on the bow, trying to saw through the anchor chain. (COURTESY MICHAEL ALDERSON / WWW.WARDLINE.COM)

This photograph taken from the deck of the *Monarch of Bermuda* shows a partially loaded lifeboat on the morning of September 8, 1934. (COURTESY THE MARINERS' MUSEUM, NEWPORT NEWS, VA.)

The *Morro Castle* beached at Asbury Park, probably on the morning of September 9, 1934. While thousands stood on the shore watching the Ward liner burn, Coast Guard district commander R. W. Hodge went aboard to survey the damage. (COURTESY OF THE COLLECTION OF THE NORTH JERSEY CHAPTER OF THE NATIONAL RAILWAY HISTORICAL SOCIETY)

The attraction that saved Asbury Park's season. Local officials said between 100,000 and 300,000 flocked to the resort town in the days after the *Morro Castle* washed ashore there. A 25-cent ticket bought tourists a view from the grand Convention Hall's deck. (COURTESY OF THE COLLECTION OF THE NORTH JERSEY CHAPTER OF THE NATIONAL RAILWAY HISTORICAL SOCIETY)

One of the eeriest photos from the *Morro Castle* disaster. A rescue worker examines clothes, coats and shoes on C Deck that were discarded by passengers just before they jumped from the stern into the ocean. (COURTESY THE MARINERS' MUSEUM, NEWPORT NEWS, VA.)

The *Morro Castle's* First-Class Lounge. The door on the left leads to the Writing Room. Heat from the fire warped the balcony supports in the foreground. (COURTESY INDEPENDENCE SEAPORT MUSEUM)

Looking forward from starboard, what remains of the *Morro Castle's* Deck Veranda and Tea Room on the Promenade Deck. (COURTESY INDEPENDENCE SEAPORT MUSEUM)

The port side of the *Morro Castle*, as seen from the roof of the Convention Hall. Notice the hull's discoloration from burning and the portside lifeboats, most of which were never launched. (COURTESY MICHAEL ALDERSON / WWW.WARDLINE.COM)

Bayonne police captain Vincent J. Doyle, years after his encounter with George Rogers. (COURTESY MONSIGNOR VINCENT J. DOYLE)

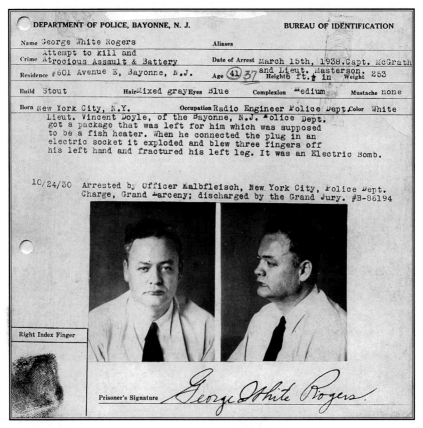

The Bayonne Police Department's booking card for George Rogers after his arrest for the attempted murder of Vincent Doyle. The card includes his signature and fingerprint. (COURTESY MONSIGNOR VINCENT J. DOYLE)

George Rogers in 1930 mug shots after his arrest in New York City for stealing electronics equipment from a store where he worked. (COURTESY MONSIGNOR VINCENT J. DOYLE)

* * *

The sea was doing its best to drown Doris Wacker.

Every wave sprayed saltwater in her face, down her throat, up her nostrils. She could barely catch her breath between blasts. Doris and her mother were sick, constantly vomiting the seawater in their lungs. Doris had never felt so miserable in her life, but she was fighting it, trying to reach a point where she could gulp down some fresh air and stop the pattern. Once, she saw a lifeboat nearby. She waved frantically but was too sick to call out. It passed by them, leaving all their hope in its wake.

If it was possible, Herbert Wacker was doing worse than either his wife or daughter. He had swallowed so much seawater he couldn't breathe, even as Doris begged him to spit it up. When he caught a breath, he told Doris he couldn't take it anymore. The shock and the stress were too much for him. He could not swim and, even in the life jacket, it was hard for him to keep his head above water in these seas. He swallowed so much ocean water that finally his lungs were filled.

"I give up, I give up," Herbert Wacker said. Then he stopped speaking.

Doris realized what had happened before her mother did. She was only an eighteen-year-old girl from Roselle Park, but she was tougher than most of the sailors on the water that morning. She didn't cry, not so her mother could see her, anyway. Perhaps it was because she didn't think any of them would survive, or she just didn't want to upset her mother any worse than she was, but Doris turned her father's face away from her mother to hide his death. She held her father in her arms as she lied to her mother.

"He's sleeping."

The storms were lashing the Jersey shore. In Brielle, where fisherman John Bogan and his sons lived, the trees were bent over by the wind, the rain coming down so hard they could barely see. It didn't look like fishing weather. Still, they drove to the docks a little after 6:30 A.M. There was work to be done whether they went out or not.

The Bogans' ship, the *Paramount*, was a 60-foot monster well known on the New Jersey coast. The boat had been a rumrunner during Prohibition, and the Bogans bought it from the U.S. government in one of those auctions where they sell confiscated contraband. She'd been a good boat, but they were wary of taking her out in this weather.

On the docks, all the talk was about the ship on fire. Some of the fishermen who had just come in said they had seen it but didn't stick around because the water was so rough. James Bogan and his brother, John Jr., wanted to see for themselves, so they drove to the beach, where they spotted the smoking hull and the glow of flames in the distance.

Back at the dock, John Bogan called the Shark River Station and asked if they could help. The Coast Guard dispatch said there were several boats assisting with rescue efforts already, but they could help find survivors in the water if they could get out. The Coast Guard didn't give private boats much of a chance in the vicious seas that morning.

The *Paramount* had a crew of five, and John Bogan asked if any of the men on the docks wanted to go along. Four fishermen volunteered. It took this crew only a minute to load the gear they needed for rescue operations and, with James Bogan at the wheel, the *Paramount* motored out of Manasquan Inlet.

Barely away from the dock, the *Paramount* barreled into a wall of water. So much sea swept over the bow that the decks were awash. The storm was overwhelming, much worse than they had anticipated. In the pilothouse, the elder John Bogan told his son to head for the docks.

"It's suicide to go out there," he said. "We'll never stand it."

As Jim wheeled the boat around, John Jr.—the *Paramount*'s captain—rushed up from the downstairs cabin, asking what they were doing. When his father said it was too rough to go out, John Jr. argued with him. If there were other people out in it, he said, they needed to be there, too.

"We've got to go out there, there's something doing," John Bogan Jr. said.

After a second, his father agreed and Jim Bogan turned the boat back into the weather and pushed the throttle. The fishing boat sliced into an oncoming swell and topped it, engines whining in protest. In the cabin, the volunteers held on tight.

The *Paramount* was headed out to sea.

CHAPTER NINE

A Parade of Lost Souls

They could make out dark shapes along the Jersey shore: Victorian beach cottages with imposing turrets, looming radio towers, a great domed hotel. The details were harder to see in the murk. There was no dawn, only vague suggestions of the night sky fading to dull gray. The weather was growing worse, the wind and seas angrier, the rain falling intermittently for the moment. It seemed darker than it had been when Clarence Monroe, one of the sailors in the boat, noticed the burning cruise ship on the horizon like a sunrise. Now the only thing the people in the lifeboat could see clearly were the rocks they were about to hit.

Aboard the *Morro Castle* lifeboat No. 1, a man the others called "Chief" ordered the crew to row harder. They were drifting near the mouth of the Shark River Inlet, in danger of being slammed against rocks that marked the channel. The men reacted slowly to the order. The boat had been smacked around in the frenzied Atlantic for hours, and nearly everyone on board was seasick. They barely had the strength to hold an oar.

There were thirty people in the lifeboat, all but three of whom were members of the ship's crew. The lone female passenger, Renée Méndez Capote, rested her head on a man next to her, and the two men who were passengers watched nervously as the sailors tried to avoid the rocks. Dr. Charles Cochrane did not know the man the others called Chief. Despite his formal uniform, there was no way to identify the officer except that he had a cut across his palm. All insignias and indications of rank had been stripped from his uniform, and even from his hat. One sailor would later claim that, as the boat approached the shore, the man had defaced his uniform in an attempt to conceal his identity. According to that sailor, the man realized that coming ashore in a lifeboat filled with crewmen and only the barest sampling of passengers did not look very good at all. The sailor claimed that the man had said to no one in particular, "I'll be jailed for this."

The crew rowed seaward and slowly the boat drew away from the rocks. Currents caught it and carried the boat south. When they finally made landfall, they were at the southern end of Spring Lake, not too far from the town's boardwalk. They were the first survivors of the *Morro Castle* fire to reach land. Dr. Cochrane was led to a bathhouse on the boardwalk, while Eben Abbott, the *Morro Castle*'s chief engineer, got out of the boat unassisted, but was then led up the beach by Monroe and another sailor. Surveying the growing crowds, he ordered the men not to talk to reporters. He was put into a private car on the beach and driven away. Abbott didn't look back.

The No. 1 lifeboat made it to shore first, but it was only one of several dozen launches spread over miles of ocean that morning. The rescue efforts had reached their peak. The lifeboats of three ships fought the ocean off New Jersey, tiny white smudges on the ugly gray water. Between the burning liner and the shore, a few small Coast Guard cutters ran search patterns, occasionally finding someone to pull from the ocean. Several miles away, workers from lifesaving stations plucked dozens of people— and a few dead bodies—out of the rolling surf.

These efforts had a growing audience along the shore. From Manasquan to Belmar, hundreds of people had gathered along the beach, at the marinas, watching as survivors came ashore like long-lost castaways. Reporters who were tipped off by a Coast Guard dispatcher lurked among the spectators by sunrise, which was 6:29 that morning at Sea Girt.

The *City of Savannah*, the *Andrea Luckenbach* and the *Monarch of Bermuda* had launched a dozen lifeboats before realizing how dangerous the water actually was. Several of them were very nearly swamped before they could reach the first survivors. By the end of the morning, a few of the rescuers would find themselves in need of rescue. Some sailors estimated the seas reached 25 feet at one point.

On the *Morro Castle*'s bow, the ship's officers had a front-row seat to these operations, but could do little to help. They couldn't even rescue screaming passengers trapped in cabins just yards away—the stairs were impassable, the only way off the bow a 50-foot jump. A couple of the men did just that, desperate as they were to save others, or get off the ship themselves. When an engineer dived into the water to save a drowning woman, George Rogers turned to George Alagna and said, "I was just about to jump in after her."

Rogers seemed quite spry for all the smoke inhalation and the "near-coma" he had suffered less than two hours earlier. When he noticed the bulkhead glowing red, the radioman told Warms they should get all the flammable materials out of the forecastle below them, and then led the scavenger hunt. He ran into the burning hallways a few times looking for a pair of shoes after he lost his in the confusion. On one trip, he came out carrying a canary that belonged to one of the boatswains. He pulled the bird from its cage, wrapped it in a towel and released it on deck. The bird briefly lighted on one of the ship's lines.

Finally, Rogers made a harness to lower two passengers who had found their way onto the bow. Rogers was going out of his way to keep busy, Alagna thought, to save the day. Funny how a crisis affected some people. As he worked, Rogers echoed—or mocked—sentiments Alagna had expressed over much more minor things only weeks earlier.

"It's a darn shame that the radio operators not only had to do what they did on the vessel but still had to be depended on to do important things," Rogers said.

Just before 8 A.M., a tugboat offered to tow the *Morro Castle* to shore. Earlier, Warms had dismissed a suggestion from Alagna that they request a tow from a passing tanker, saying they were in no danger on the bow and the Ward Line would take care of them. (In fact, company officials told the Coast Guard they had hired tugs to go get their flagship, but no boats ever showed.) Now, Warms seemed desperate and tried to barter with the tug's captain. He asked what it would cost, and acted as if he didn't believe the man when he said the tug company wouldn't charge anything, they were just trying to help.

"Do you hear that, boys? This man—they won't charge us anything for pulling us in," Warms said. "You know sometimes these fellows forget what they say."

There was no way that this little tug could tow a ship that displaced 17,500 tons when fully loaded, as it was, and every man on the forecastle knew it. *Why is Warms making such a big deal out of this?* Alagna wondered. Others thought it an odd thing for the captain to say, too, but some probably suspected it was because Warms had been awake now for more than twenty-four hours. Although he appeared to handle himself well most of the time, occasionally the weary skipper acted as if he'd lost his mind. No one dared question his negotiations with the tugboat, which were interrupted when the Coast Guard cutter *Tampa* steamed alongside.

The cutter had been on two-hour standby at Staten Island when the distress call came in from Coast Guard dispatch. It took just over an hour to get all personnel on board and enough steam built up to leave port. The *Tampa* pulled away from the docks at 5:40 A.M. and immediately ran into force six winds—gusts of up to 27 knots, or 31 miles per hour. It was enough to qualify as a tropical storm and, in fact, was the outer band of the storm moving up the coast.

Lieutenant Commander Earl G. Rose, captain of the *Tampa,* did not know what kind of mess he was sailing into. He would later complain that the *Morro Castle*'s SOS had been uncharacteristically vague. But when he arrived at the coordinates twenty miles south of the Scotland Lightship, he had no trouble picking his target out of the gathered ships. A huge plume of smoke rose from the liner, visible even through the horrible weather. Pushed by the wind, the stark white flume snaked away from the *Morro Castle* like one of Sylvia Slidel's feather boas.

The *Tampa* anchored 200 yards seaward of the *Morro Castle.* Rose noted the position was 2 miles off Sea Girt and recorded in his log that the ship had 12 fathoms under its keel. They were close to shore. Rose used a megaphone to call to the officers on the bow, which he spotted with his binoculars.

"Do you want to be taken off or taken in tow?"

Rogers replied for Warms using the flashlight and Morse code. They wanted a tow, but for now they would be fine on the forecastle.

"Any of you fellows want to go ashore, now is your chance," Warms told his men.

None of them did. It was Rogers, acting the hero, who answered for all of them when he said, "We will stick by you, Captain."

In response, Warms could only manage a weak "Thanks."

Surprisingly, the two captains would not speak again for hours. Rose did not ask about survivors in the water or on the ship, and Warms did not ask the cutter to launch its lifeboats. The two men were most interested in getting the cruise ship under tow before the weather got worse. The logistics of stringing a towline between the two ships made that goal nearly insurmountable. It took more than an hour for a dory crew from the *Tampa* and a power lifeboat crew from the Sandy Hook Lifesaving Station to string a 12-inch hawser from the Coast Guard ship to the *Morro Castle*. The two small boats fought mountainous, 12-foot waves as they attempted to run the thick line the 600 feet between the two ships.

Warms suddenly realized the *Morro Castle* could not be towed anywhere—she had been anchored. The anchor could only be raised with a motor, and that is one of many things they did not have use of anymore. They were stuck unless they could cut the chain, and each link was 3 inches thick per side. After tense moments of debating their situation, the men found a small hacksaw and Warms put them to work in shifts. It was slow work, like trying to chop down a tree with a nail file. Rogers and Alagna watched in disbelief as the men broke one blade after another trying to cut the giant chain.

"It's a damnable thing to resort to a five-and-ten-cent saw to cut through both sides of this huge link," Rogers told Warms. "Why don't you see if the *Tampa* has anything better to cut with?"

Warms ignored the suggestion, and soon Rogers was back to what Alagna later called his "heroics act." The radioman tried to help saw the chain but seemed tipsy on his feet. Eventually, Warms stepped in and told him to give it a rest.

Tom Torresson could not tell how long he had been in the water, only that the sky was growing lighter. His back ached under the weight of the boy, and he was very nearly numb from holding Roberto's arms around his neck. They had talked for a long time, or it had felt that way, but the boy had not said anything for a while. *How long? An hour, perhaps longer.* Tom did not know. He spoke the boy's name, got no answer, so he tried again. Nothing.

Tom reached behind his back as best he could in the awkward life vest, and pulled the boy to him. His face was blue, rubbery and he wasn't breathing. Tom could not tell if it had been the burns, the shock or the hypothermia that had finished off Roberto González, but it did not matter now. The boy had been dead for some time, and Tom hadn't even realized it.

He shifted the boy's weight to his back again, and held on to the body as he rose up and down swells, a swing high enough to take his stomach. When an oar drifted by, probably lost from one of the *Morro Castle* lifeboats, Tom tied the boy's body to it. He would not let go, nor could he just leave him out there. But he didn't know that it would do any good. He had not seen another passenger for a long while, and had not even noticed any lifeboats in the distance. Occasionally, he could still see the ship, marked by the great plume of smoke. *What a mess,* Tom thought. He wondered if he would soon be just another body littering the sea.

Tom Torresson was scared, to be sure. He was two weeks shy of his eighteenth birthday, and he desperately wanted to live to see it. So much he had not done, had not seen. His time on the *Morro Castle* had given him a little taste of the world, and he liked it. And now, because of some stupid fire that for all he knew was caused by an idiot's cigarette, he might not experience all that he wanted to do. It made him angry, perhaps even more so than frightened. But for all those fears, for all the reasons in the world that he had to worry, Tom did not panic. He wondered if he would be rescued, but he knew he wouldn't give up either way. His resolve to hang on and find out was as tight as his lips blocking the saltwater that splashed into his face.

The water chilled him, or was it his nerves that made him shake? He wasn't sure, but whichever it was, Tom accepted his fate stoically. Silently, he floated through the ocean clutching the body of the boy he had met only a few hours earlier. More time passed; he did not know how much. Hours, he guessed, but in truth he had only discovered the boy's death a few minutes before his rescuers appeared in the drizzle. It was a *City of Savannah* lifeboat, and in it Tom saw his boss, chief purser Bob Tolman, along with Russell Du Vinage and Bob Smith. Tom thought to himself, *Now there's a sight for sore eyes.* Tolman had a similar thought, quite pleased he would not have to tell the Ward Line's marine superintendent that he had lost his son during this fiasco.

A sailor from the *City of Savannah* reached over to pull Tom aboard, but the young purser tried first to hand up the boy's body. "There's only room for the living," the sailor said. The seas were getting so bad that there was no guarantee they could even get the young purser aboard. In fact, the lifeboat was so crowded already that the men couldn't properly row. They were packed in, weary, their fatigue clinging to them like their wet clothes.

Tom was in no shape to argue, but it pained him to let go of the boy. With some work, a couple of the lifeboat's crew pulled him aboard and dumped him on deck. As the boat drifted away, Tom watched the body until it disappeared behind a swell. He wondered whether he had done enough to save Roberto. And then Tom sadly slumped into the boat.

Arthur Harry Moore had just sat down to breakfast when his phone rang. The governor of New Jersey was vacationing at Sea Girt, a brief rest before beginning what would eventually be a successful campaign for the U.S. Senate. On the line, an aide told him there was trouble just outside his back door—a national disaster was about to wash ashore. Moore quickly forgot about his breakfast and his vacation.

The governor called for a plane and a pilot, and within an hour they took off from the local National Guard encampment. The tropical-storm-force winds did not make for ideal flying conditions, and Moore's plane barely cleared the sand dunes as it banked over the surf. The plane flew low—less than thirty feet above the waves—with Moore strapped in the backseat, door open, waving to survivors. Moore, a politician with a flair for the dramatic, had his pilot signal the rescue boat crews so he could point out survivors to them.

Moore was shocked by the sight of the burning liner, and the people littering the sea deeply moved the man who would become the state's only governor to serve three nonconsecutive terms. At one point, he shook his head and said to his pilot, "Those poor people."

For most of the morning, Moore pushed the pilot to keep the plane flying, despite worsening conditions, so that they could find more survivors. His political opponents could have called such grandstanding a cheap campaign gimmick, but it was no token gesture from Moore. When the pilot argued they were running low on fuel, the governor ordered him to keep the plane up so they could continue searching. The pilot only convinced Moore to give up when the plane's fuel gauge hit "empty." When they returned to the National Guard base, the governor jumped out of the plane and ordered soldiers to get on the beach and pull the survivors out of the surf. The pilot noted that there was less than a half-pint of fuel left in the plane.

Doris Wacker was one of the dozens of people whom Moore spotted that morning. She and her mother had drifted away from the larger group, but Doris did not feel alone. She still clung to her father's body, and when she rose up on the swells, the entire catastrophe was spread out before her. In the distance, she could see the burning *Morro Castle,* the *Monarch of Bermuda* and a dozen little lifeboats sprinkled across the water. None of these rescue boats were close enough to signal, however, and she knew they could not see her. Occasionally, someone would drift or swim by her, and it seemed to Doris that everyone except her was making progress toward the beach. When she turned toward shore, she could see the Monmouth Hotel in Spring Lake looming over the boardwalk. Beautiful in its ornate architecture and sleek domed roof, the hotel seemed so close that she could swim to it. But every time she tried, the waves smacked her back.

Doris and her mother continued to vomit seawater throughout the morning, and they were quickly dehydrated. Every time they opened their mouths, it seemed they swallowed more. When there was a break in the swells, enough so that they could speak, Doris told her mother that Herbert was still asleep. Doris feared that she and her mother would drown before anyone got to them. Still, she clung to her father, wishing for a miracle.

The plane provided some hope. Doris could see the man waving as he flew over, offering encouragement with a smile she could see from nearly 100 feet away. She did not realize it was the governor; she only knew that someone had seen her. Perhaps the man would send someone for them, she thought.

Despite their best efforts, the Bogans had missed some people on the way out and had to backtrack to pick them up. There were so many people who needed help, the Bogans were overwhelmed. Even some of the other rescue boats were having trouble. Near the *Morro Castle,* the *City of Savannah* blew its own distress signal. When Jim Bogan pulled up alongside in the *Paramount,* its captain came out on deck with a megaphone.

"We put a lifeboat overboard and it apparently can't make its way back," the captain said. "Will you look out for it?"

The *Paramount* was more efficient at rescue than nearly any other boat on the water that morning. The men on board fell into an efficient assembly line. Captain John Bogan Jr. stood with one leg over the rail, hoisting people on deck—even after a few nearly pulled him into the water. Once on board, the fishermen on the *Paramount* tended to the survivors with blankets, coats, coffee and whiskey. Soon after they started fishing passengers out of the water, they'd caught their limit.

That morning, the *Paramount* picked up the Prinze sisters, Agnes and Ruth, as well as Mrs. Alexander McArthur, who clung to the body of her drowned husband. When Bogan told Mrs. McArthur they could not take her husband—there's not enough room, he told her—she came aboard reluctantly. At the wheel, Jim Bogan followed the low-flying plane to several people, never knowing who was directing him. The plane led the *Paramount* to a young boy in the water and then a huge group of people holding on to one another. Finally, Governor Moore's plane brought the Bogans to Doris Wacker.

Doris saw the fishing boat coming toward her, unsure if she had actually been spotted until the men on board waved to her. When the boat cut its engines and drifted near her, Captain Bogan reached over the transom for her. Doris offered her father's body up. But, as he had told Mrs. McArthur, Bogan would not take it.

"We're only taking the living," Bogan said. "There'll be another boat along for the dead."

Doris cried, pleading with Bogan not to leave her father in the ocean. Perhaps it was then that Herbert Wacker's death hit her hardest. She couldn't bear the thought of leaving him, but Bogan said the boat was already overcrowded. They had picked up nearly 60 people. Finally, Doris relented and let go of her father's body. It drifted away quickly, but she could not watch. It was hard enough just to climb aboard, which she did only after they had pulled Lillian Wacker aboard. Her mother fell several times, bruising herself badly before they got her into the boat. Then, John Bogan took Doris's hand and hoisted her over the stern like she was just another fish. As she landed on the deck of the *Paramount,* Doris Wacker passed out.

Better that she did not see the scene on the Atlantic that day from a higher vantage point. Many people who witnessed the final hours of the

Morro Castle's last cruise had nightmares about it for the rest of their lives. The ship burned on the horizon like a funeral pyre, bodies littering the ocean, held afloat by the bulky—and sometimes lethal—life vests. No one would ever know how many people died because they were knocked unconscious by the hard cork life jackets and then drowned. The accident scene stretched for miles, the ocean parading its dead along the Jersey shore until fishermen with grappling hooks came along, snaring the bodies as if they were the catch of the day.

The *Paramount*'s crew, which almost didn't leave shore that turbulent morning, rescued 67 people from the water before they returned to Brielle, two more than all the lifeboats from the *City of Savannah* retrieved together. The *Monarch of Bermuda* saved 72 others, and the scene aboard the luxury liner was the one that made all the newsreels. Staterooms were filled with hysterical survivors begging to know if their husbands, their wives, sons or daughters had survived. In the *Monarch*'s playroom, a rescued four-year-old—almost certainly Robert Lione—browsed through the toys without any idea what he had just been through, unaware that his father and brother were dead. When he asked for a wooden boat, one of the ship's stewardesses broke into tears.

The *City of Savannah* lifeboat carrying Tom Torresson, Bob Tolman and Bob Smith drifted aimlessly throughout the morning, unable to fight the currents. The boat's crew had intended to return to the *City of Savannah*, but it soon became clear that would be impossible. A small Coast Guard boat came along and tried to tow it, but its engine quit. The lifeboat was batted around in the waves until a fishing boat came along and tossed another towline.

It was not until 10 A.M. that Earl Rose, captain of the *Tampa*, realized there were still people in the water. He had been waiting for the *Morro Castle*'s officers to cut the anchor chain when a radio dispatcher mentioned that several Coast Guard boats were still trolling the waters from Brielle to north of Asbury Park. The *Tampa* was on the far side of the *Morro Castle*, so Rose could not see all that was happening. When he heard, he was horrified. He had been on the scene for nearly two hours— two hours that his men, who were loitering on deck, could have saved lives. He ordered all the *Tampa*'s lifeboats into the water.

* * *

Survivors made landfall throughout the rainy morning, from Point Pleasant to Allenhurst. Locals crowded the boardwalks, the marinas and the oceanfront roads as people appeared in the surf and came straggling onto the beach. Mrs. Howard Panamo was one of those who emerged from the breakers after swimming nearly six miles. She had lost her husband in the water and thought it too dangerous to stay near the burning ship. She told her story to reporters at a local hospital, not knowing if her Howard was alive.

Ambulances and police paddy wagons lined the roads near the docks. The sound of fat raindrops hitting piers and distant sirens drowned out the moaning of the injured, as the rescued were led ashore by an endless stream of fishermen, shop owners and local residents. Many people along the shore were so horrified by this spectacle that they opened their homes to the survivors, offering dry clothes, hot meals and warm beds. This charity did little to ease the burden on local hospitals, which soon ran out of supplies. The New York Red Cross chapter rushed blankets and robes to lifesaving stations. Trenton hospitals sent down extra oxygen.

It was too late for some survivors—they had been rescued only to succumb to the trauma. At Point Pleasant, a *City of Savannah* lifeboat landed with seventeen survivors, but one died as soon as they reached the beach. A Coast Guard picketboat brought five people ashore but one of them, a seventy-two-year-old woman, passed away before she could be carried ashore. The dead were laid out on the docks covered in white or gray blankets. The wind rustled the blankets enough that it appeared the bodies were moving.

News of the *Morro Castle* disaster spread on the newswires, making the Saturday evening papers in most cities across the country. The newsreel crews and reporters were there when the *Monarch of Bermuda* docked in Manhattan at 1:15 that afternoon and later when the *Andrea Luckenbach* arrived. New York police officers helped the survivors off the ships, some still in their robes, others wrapped in blankets. One woman stopped to talk to reporters wearing a hat that did a poor job of hiding her wet hair. She could not look at the camera as she tried to explain what had happened, how a *Morro Castle* steward had knocked on her cabin door, told her to get on deck because there was a "small fire." When a reporter asked her how long she had drifted before being rescued, she thought for a moment before matter-of-factly answering, "Six hours." Another woman,

Augusta Pusrin, had been pulled from the water unconscious and so blue that she was mistaken for a corpse. She awoke among a long line of dead bodies on the deck of the *City of Savannah.*

The Ward Line sent most of its employees to the accident scene, which left the Wall Street offices unprepared to deal with the 300 people who had planned to greet their friends and family when the ship landed at 7 A.M. Henry Cabaud's office made reservations for 150 survivors at the swanky new Hotel New Yorker on Eighth Avenue. If Cabaud was trying to bribe his customers with the first-class treatment, it would not work.

The Bogans' *Paramount* led the convoy of fishing boats into Brielle that afternoon. A good number of the people they had rescued were still unconscious. They were a ragged-looking lot, most of them soaking wet, many in pajamas or nothing more than lingerie. Some of the women wore shawls or had their hair in curlers. One woman, noticing the audience on the dock, began to scream out, "There were no lifeboats, no lifeboats," she cried. "We had to jump into the sea." As Jim Bogan docked the *Paramount,* a fisherman tried to calm the woman.

Doris Wacker woke up in a fire station at Spring Lake. Her heavy cotton, dark brown eyelet dress had been shredded in the water, and she looked as if she had been shipwrecked on a desert island for a year. First-aid workers cut the dress off her, wrapped her in a blanket and poured brown liquor down her throat. It was hardly a cocktail from Sloppy Joe's, but Doris was not strong enough to protest. She could barely speak.

The young woman had no idea where she was, and her throat hurt too much to ask. She had gotten separated from her mother, and soon realized Lillian Wacker was not even at the same fire station. A woman tending to survivors, Mrs. Cavanaugh, took Doris home with her, thinking she was an orphaned twelve-year-old. The woman gave Doris clothes, fed her and put her to bed in an oceanfront mansion. When Doris finally explained what had happened, Mrs. Cavanaugh called the fire halls and first-aid stations, trying to find Lillian Wacker. Doris could not hold out long enough to hear the outcome of those phone calls. She had been through enough to last a lifetime and as soon as she settled into a warm, dry bed, she could not fight consciousness any longer. Doris passed out again.

A trawler towed the *City of Savannah* lifeboat into Manasquan Inlet later that afternoon. By then, Tom Torresson had recovered enough that he was standing up as they passed the breakwater. A film crew onshore recorded that pose, which made the young purser look like Washington crossing the Delaware. As soon as the lifeboat touched the dock, the trawler turned around and went back out for more people.

Tom stepped out onto the pier, passed a gasoline sign advertising 18-cent fuel and walked toward a waiting ambulance. Before he reached it, someone peeled his wet uniform jacket off and wrapped him in a coat taken from a kid standing nearby. Behind him, a barely conscious Bob Tolman was whisked away to a Point Pleasant hospital. Tom was taken to a first-aid station, where they took his wet clothes and gave him Levi's and a work shirt. He was barely aware of all the activity around him, work carried out mostly by a bunch of well-meaning volunteers, Boy Scouts and Junior Leaguers. Tom was met by a young woman who handed him a glass of dark liquid.

"Drink this," she said.

Tom obeyed without thinking, taking the whole glass in one swallow. His throat was scorched from the fire and smoke, deadened by the salt water, so what he was drinking didn't register until it hit his empty stomach.

"Wow. That's rye."

Tom sat in the first-aid station for what seemed like hours. He was exhausted, hungry and a little sick. He was uncomfortable, too, being barefoot. They had found him pants and a shirt, but had no socks or shoes to offer him. While he stood outside the building, watching the flurry of activity, his father walked up.

Thomas Torresson Sr. had not gotten the telegram concerning Captain Willmott's death because he had been at the family home in Monroe. But Cabaud called him there to tell him about the fire, and Torresson and his wife left their other children with the maid and drove through the morning to reach the Jersey Shore. The marine superintendent had no shortage of work to do, but not before he found his son. As worried as he was, the stoic

Torresson patriarch showed no emotion when he saw his son standing outside the first-aid station.

"Did you do your duty?" he asked.

"Yes, sir," Tom told his father.

"Fine." Torresson shook his son's hand and walked off, ready to attend to the unfolding disaster. The exchange lasted less than ten seconds.

A few moments later, someone grabbed Tom by the back of his neck and bear-hugged him. James McDonald, a friend of the family, was so happy to see him that he cried. McDonald put Tom in his car and they drove to the Essex-Sussex Hotel in Spring Lake, where Winifred Torresson was sitting in a rocking chair on the front porch, praying. Her husband would not allow her to see the scene at the beach, perhaps for fear that their son would be one of the bodies on the docks. When she saw Tom, she showed considerably more emotion than her husband had.

McDonald treated them to dinner at the hotel, which was one of the finest on the coast. Tom was hungry but more than a little self-conscious about going into a nice restaurant, dirty as he was. He tried to talk them out of it, but McDonald insisted. Throughout the meal, Tom felt bad about his good fortune. From the restaurant's windows, they could look out on the ocean. Out there, he knew, there were people cold and hungry—and God only knew how many dead—and here he was eating in a fancy restaurant. Everyone was nice to him, treated him like a hero, but Tom Torresson only felt odd and uncomfortable. He kept thinking that he shouldn't be there, that he was barefoot.

The last of the *Morro Castle*'s crew finished cutting the anchor loose at noon, the heavy chain finally breaking free and pouring into the sea with a clamor. When the towline was secure, the anchor gone, Rose ordered everyone off the ship. A Jacob's ladder was lowered from the bow to a Coast Guard powerboat, one that had been pulling people from the water all morning. When George Alagna looked over the forecastle rail at the scene below, he was sickened by the sight of dead bodies lying on the boat's deck like some grotesque game fish.

One by one, the men climbed down until only William Warms was left on deck. He had been acting captain of the *Morro Castle* for seventeen hours, and in that time he had watched his chance of a command quite literally go up in smoke. He had adhered to one of the oldest laws of the sea, that a captain is the last to leave his ship, but it did not feel like enough. When everyone else had gone, Warms stood on the forecastle and declared, "I will stay."

Years later, people would say that Coast Guard officers got William Warms off the *Morro Castle*'s bow only by pointing a .45 pistol at him. In truth, it didn't matter—he was going against his will, at gunpoint or not. As he climbed down the rope ladder, perhaps he had a thought that made him more uneasy. The *real captain,* Robert Willmott, was still aboard. Willmott, who had once joked he wouldn't go unless he could take the *Morro Castle* with him, would get his wish.

From the deck of the *Tampa,* the *Morro Castle*'s officers could finally see the full extent of the damage. The smoke was so thick it obscured the top half of the hull, and the ship's two black smokestacks barely peeked above the plume. They noticed, with some twisted amusement, that smoke now poured from both of them—even the fake one.

It was, above all else, a sad sight. Her flawless white topsides had been consumed, and her shiny black hull had dulled to a dead color. Cancerous splotches were beginning to appear on her flanks. She would not impress anyone at the docks today, and would no longer sparkle as the crown jewel of the New York coastal liners. Even if she were repaired, no matter how many new coats of paint were applied, who would sail on her now? She was a wreck, a coffin, and her name soon would become synonymous with maritime disaster.

Towing the cruise ship, the *Tampa* set sail shortly after 1 P.M. A Coast Guard pilot boat had tied on to the *Morro Castle*'s stern and acted as rudder for the shaky convoy. The *Tampa* needed all the help it could get. The tropical storm had arrived, and the liner bucked in protest against its towline, drawing it taut enough that water sprang from it. Rose watched nervously from the bridge of the *Tampa,* hoping he could keep both ships off the Sea Girt beach. He figured that if he could make the turn at Sandy Hook 40 miles to the north, fireboats from New York Harbor could put out the fire and get the *Morro Castle* to a shipyard. But it wouldn't be easy. At

2:30, he heard over the radio that the search-and-rescue operations had been abandoned. The seas were too rough even for the Coast Guard.

That afternoon, the *Morro Castle* convoy passed within sight of the beach, a scene thousands of onlookers would never forget. Even with the *Tampa* at full throttle, it was hard to tow the much larger cruise ship, particularly sailing into the wind and against the sea. The strain on the *Tampa* became worse when the fire burned through the line that connected the pilot boat to the cruise ship's stern. The train was down to two ships.

By 3:45 P.M., conditions were so bad that the *Tampa* had to use its foghorn, even as slow as it was moving. Other ships in the area monitored the struggle, including the Pennsylvania-class battleship USS *Arizona*. The battleship likely could have towed the ship easily and its captain offered, but Rose shuddered to think of the fallout from dragging a warship into harm's way. The water was way too shallow for the *Arizona*. Rose thanked the navy, but declined the invitation.

On board the *Tampa*, the *Morro Castle* officers accepted food, water and dry clothes. Some watched their ship burn from the cutter's deck. George Alagna busied himself with finding a doctor to tend to George Rogers. When they finally took the radioman to the ship's infirmary, Alagna went to eat. He had many things on his mind, not the least of which was Rogers's revelation on the bow. Rogers had told him the Ward Line meant to fire him when the ship reached New York, and that they had to stick together. Alagna was surprised, but wondered why Rogers had waited until then to tell him.

Sometime later, the *Tampa*'s doctor found Alagna. Rogers, he said, was delirious and not making much sense. He'd been out of it for some time, and it seemed he was very nearly in a coma. The only thing he said that they could understand was that he wanted to speak to Alagna. It seemed odd to the junior radioman. *How could Rogers drift in and out of consciousness?* He was out of it in the radio room, then fine on the bow. Now this. Alagna thought it strange.

Rogers was quiet, but stirred when Alagna walked into the room. He seemed to be talking out loud, to himself. Alagna was struck by the vindictiveness in George Rogers's voice.

"Those darn murderers are waiting until the last minute before they do anything. They are leaving everything up to George and me to take care of and I am going to tell the truth when I get back and show how yellow these men were. So George was the only one that stood by me and Maki deserted."

After that, Rogers appeared to pass out, and Alagna, perplexed, left the room.

Outside, the nor'easter and tropical system conspired to push the ships even closer to shore. By the time the *Tampa* and the *Morro Castle* passed Asbury Park, Rose could make out the resort's Midway through the mist. By 5:20, they were 4 miles off Long Branch. They had gone about halfway between Sea Girt and the mouth of New York Harbor, but it had taken nearly five hours. The tow was not working—the *Tampa* could not pull the cruise ship seaward against the current, the swells and the wind. Rose reluctantly radioed the New York Coast Guard commander with the news that the *Morro Castle* was becoming unmanageable.

To control the cruise ship, the *Tampa* needed to pull her farther out to sea, something the Coast Guard ship could hardly do while lugging the *Morro Castle*'s weight and fighting the tide. At 5:30, they were within 2 miles of the beach, and the water was so shallow that it was hard to navigate. Rose ordered his men to increase power, first from 60 rpms to 100 rpms. It did little good, so Rose pushed the engine to 110 rpms. Still, the *Morro Castle* resisted. The ship seemed to pull back, straining the 12-inch hawser until, at 6:12 P.M., the towline snapped.

The force of the break sent the line hurling toward the *Tampa*'s stern, where it fouled the ship's propeller. If a man had been in its way, he would have been killed. As it was, the cutter was dead in the water. And immediately, the swells began pushing it toward the beach. Rose had no choice: he ordered the anchor dropped. Once the ship swung to a stop at anchor, Rose, William Warms and his men watched as the *Morro Castle* drifted off, a runaway ship.

For the entire day, WCAP in Asbury Park had broadcast news of the ship disaster. Thomas F. Burley Jr. interrupted programming every time there was a new update—a lifeboat ashore at Spring Lake, a fishing boat rescues more than 60 survivors—to the point that listeners barely heard anything else. Burley offered the most up-to-date bulletins, and the people wanted to know it all. The final edition of the *Asbury Park Press* that evening declared the ship had been "gutted" by the fire. The headline read "199 RESCUED, 359 FEARED LOST WHEN LINER BURNS OFF BELMAR." Another headline added, "Cause Not Determined."

Burley was the station manager for WCAP—the call letters stood for City of Asbury Park—and for three years, his Chamber of Commerce–owned radio station had broadcast from the shore town's grand Convention Hall on the north end of the boardwalk. Burley, a Chamber officer himself, had been working all day and was about ready for a break. Before he took one, though, he interrupted for one more update: "The *Morro Castle* is adrift and heading for the shore," Burley said, and then paused for a station break. It was 7:34 P.M.

As he got up, Burley glanced out the station window overlooking the Atlantic and gasped—a reaction that went out over the air.

"My God," he said.

There, just a few hundred yards away, the blackened hulk of the *Morro Castle* appeared to be steaming toward shore, smoke billowing from her stacks. It was coming straight for him.

PART III

PART III

CHAPTER TEN

Greetings from Asbury Park, New Jersey

On Sunday, the boardwalk came alive at daybreak as if the season had never ended, as if it were the Fourth of July all over again. The calliope sounds of carnival drifted out of the casino, providing an easy soundtrack for the hawkers and hustlers selling saltwater taffy, popcorn and—in a concession to the hour—hot coffee. For a moment, the smell of sugar and corn oil and cocoa drowned out the stench of the burning wreck.

When R. W. Hodge stepped out of his car at the corner of Ocean Avenue and Sunset, he was amazed to see the Palace Ferris Wheel, the Merry-Go-Round and the Steeple Chase running, selling thrills in the shadow of disaster. It was not yet 8 A.M., but restaurants already had begun to advertise their views of the ship. It had taken little time for the town, just a week past the end of the summer season, to spring back to life. But then, these were desperate times.

Hodge, the acting commander of the Coast Guard district, had watched the crowds gather the night before as the hull burned and crackled like a giant beach bonfire. The great cruise ship had run aground just a hundred yards in front of the Convention Hall moments after it was spotted by Tom Burley, the local radio announcer. Some had feared it would hit the Art Deco building—which sat on pilings over the surf—but tides pushed the ship broadside to the beach. From a business point of view, it had come to rest at a most advantageous spot.

A crowd had accumulated throughout the night until there were thousands watching the flames dance on the ship's funnels. On the beach, they could feel the heat radiating from the steel hull, still so red-hot that it cast a glow on the sand. At one point, a white bird flew out of the smoke like a phoenix and circled the ship several times before turning and flying into the wind. As it arced seaward, a flock of birds emerged from the flames and followed, as if the spirits of the dead were debarking at the end of their voyage. The local paper called the story a "superstitious horror," but hundreds of people on the beach that night swore they saw the same vision.

Hodge thought this a cold place, a town that would profit from such misery. But it was more complicated than that. Asbury Park was one of the most popular destinations along the Jersey shore, but the town built sixty years earlier as a religious amusement park was enduring the Depression badly. There were few options for the local economy. Now the tide had brought them another chance, and no one needed an appointment at Madame Marie Castello's Temple of Knowledge to figure out that this was a way to make up for a lackluster summer. Lured by signs hanging at the city limits that read "Two Miles to the *Morro Castle* Wreck," thousands were flocking into town, and the hordes needed food, beds and something to entertain them while waiting to see the main attraction.

The beautiful Convention Hall—like the casino down the boardwalk—had been designed by Warren and Wetmore, the men who planned Grand Central Terminal in New York, but Hodge took no notice of the grand architecture. He pushed his way through the crowd, folks dressed in suits and Sunday dresses as if they had just walked out of the Berkeley-Carteret Hotel across the street, and passed the entrance to the Paramount Theater, which Ginger Rogers and the Marx Brothers had helped open just a few years earlier. He bypassed the man selling tickets to see the wreck from the balcony, joining hundreds of spectators who watched firemen shoot streams of water at the smoking hull. More than a day after it had started, the fire was still burning. The Coast Guard man knew no one on the ship could still be alive.

Getting aboard the *Morro Castle* was a problem that took hours to solve. One fireman took a canoe out to the ship's stern, where lines still hung from the D Deck railing. The ropes that had helped many escape the ship now provided the only access to it. Once the first man climbed aboard, he was able to pass lines back and forth with others at the Convention Hall until they had rigged a breeches buoy, a bucket that traveled on cables to carry people between the ship and the shore much like the sky rides at the amusement park.

The sound of the crackling fire greeted R. W. Hodge when he reached the deck nearly an hour later. It was the only sound he heard, the wind drowning out the noise of the boardwalk. He could feel the heat through the soles of his shoes, and the smoke pouring from the portholes was so thick he could barely breathe. He spent much of his tour with a handkerchief held to his face.

For nearly five hours, the Coast Guard man walked the warped, blackened decks of the ship, looking for survivors, for clues to what had started the fire, for any answers he could find. He left horrified by what he saw.

Shoes and purses littered the decks, where they had been discarded by escaping passengers. Some were charred black, others strangely unmarred. Hodge stopped to look at a pair of high-heeled shoes and wondered if the woman who had worn them was safe in a shelter or buried in the sand somewhere along the shore.

Near the stern rail, Hodge found the scorched body of a young boy, his clothes burned off his back. There was little left to identify the mass as human save for the sad shape it made in the ashes. The body had melted into the deck, and Hodge suddenly felt his stomach turn. When he grabbed the rail to steady himself, he burned his hand, angry blisters rising on his palm.

The Promenade Deck was littered with scorched debris and the skeletal frames of burned-out deck chairs. Black lumps along Hodge's path may have been clothes or human remains—he did not care to know which. Above his head, he could see withered lifeboats still hanging in their davits. *How many people could have been saved by these boats?*

If any clue to the fire's origin had been left behind, it likely had been destroyed—none of the ship's interior was spared. Electrical wiring and conduits hung from the ceiling like Spanish moss, and the ashes of furniture covered the deck. In the ship's playroom, the walls still showed traces of the happy scenes painted on them. The cavernous lounge, its paneled walls burned completely away, was now a huge hole in the middle of the ship. Hodge found the Lyle gun that had fallen through the ceiling, one of the few identifiable objects he saw anywhere. He found nothing of substance in any of the cabins—only small, charred clumps of material that he speculated might be molten pieces of jewelry.

Oddly enough, the Writing Room seemed the cleanest place on the ship, as if the fire had burned so intensely there that it consumed even the ashes. The pilothouse had been gutted by the flames, and even the bulkhead wall had buckled. In the wireless room, an empty metal box lay on the floor—all that remained of the *Morro Castle*'s complex electronic radios. No one, Hodge thought, could have destroyed the ship more thoroughly if they had tried.

Hodge left the ship that afternoon sickened by what he'd seen. When he got on the breeches buoy, he was astonished by how fresh the air seemed after being aboard the ship. As he stepped off the *Morro Castle*, he noticed the soles of his shoes had melted.

By the time Hodge finished his inspection, there were more than 100,000 tourists in the tiny town, an influx of traffic that forced city fathers to experiment with a novel solution: one-way streets. These day-trippers crowded the beach or played miniature golf and rode paddleboats on Wesley Lake behind the casino while waiting for a closer look at the wreck. Hodge thought Asbury Park should have more sympathy. Less than twenty years earlier, a catastrophic fire had destroyed more than fifty buildings in a few square blocks. The town that stretched out before him had risen out of that city of ruins in a 1920s building boom.

Notorious for its corruption, the town was living up to its reputation that day. Perhaps it was the poor economy that spurred them to take advantage of the situation, to make a dollar at the first opportunity. No one in town stopped to think about how callous it all appeared, how disrespectful it was. Not even the accident scene was sacred. City officials allowed anyone with enough money to climb aboard the *Morro Castle* as it smoldered on the beach. When the reporters arrived, someone on the beach charged them $5 to tour the wreck. Once aboard, they were told they could not look inside without a gas mask, which they could rent for another $5. Raphael Avellar, a writer for the *New York World-Telegram*, paid his $10 and then asked for a flashlight. He was charged another dollar. The man collecting the money disappeared that afternoon, and city officials swore later they had no idea who he was.

These scams took place in the shadow of a surreal beach scene, where children played in the sand near temporary morgues and shallow graves dug to hide the stench of corpses. It did little good, the smell of death mingling with the aroma of sweet carnival food.

Among the gawkers on the shore that day were the families of the dead. Theodore Distler found his parents, Ernest and Adelaide, on cots in one of the temporary morgues a few miles down the beach. Ernest, a retired brewer, had quit his job just weeks earlier, declaring he wanted to spend more time with his wife. Their son noted grimly that they had achieved but one goal: they spent the rest of their lives together. As the sounds of the calliope drifted through the streets of Asbury Park, as people laughed and marveled at the spectacle of the beached ship, Theodore Distler wept for his parents.

The Coast Guard cutter *Tampa* arrived at Staten Island on Sunday carrying the officers of the *Morro Castle*. It had taken more than twelve hours to repair the *Tampa* after the cruise ship's towline fouled its propeller, and the delay made the arrival of the doomed liner's crew even more anticipated. The newspapers already were calling it one of the worst maritime disasters in history, and reporters were hungry for follow-up stories.

A weary and gaunt William Warms led his officers down the gangplank, looking as if he had left the burned *Morro Castle* only moments before. What remained of his thinning hair was mussed; he wore a blue turtleneck, white pants, and galoshes, along with a bandage that covered most of his left hand. He had broken his knuckles, but could not explain exactly how. Warms held a vacant stare as reporters hurled one question after another: What caused the fire? Why had so many of the crew abandoned ship? Why were the passengers left to fend for themselves? Why weren't more lifeboats launched with passengers on board? Why couldn't the crew contain the fire? Warms offered no answers.

"I don't know nothing. I ain't got nothing to say," Warms said. "It was a day in hell. I'll make my report to the steamboat inspectors."

Katherine Warms gave the reporters more than her husband would. She had met Warms along with their eleven-year-old son, Donald, in Captain Rose's cabin when the *Tampa* docked. On Saturday, before she even knew if her husband was still alive, Katherine Warms had told some of these same reporters that William Warms would not leave his post. Now, she followed him off the *Tampa* and boasted that she had been right.

"I wouldn't have my husband do other than he did. He remained with the ship until the plates buckled under his feet."

Donald hugged his father for the cameras. When he looked up to ask, "How do you feel?" the old sea dog hugged his son and cried.

Rose described the Coast Guard rescue mission for the reporters, the horrors he'd seen on the water, and answered the questions that the *Morro Castle* crew would not. Had he read the papers, and known where public opinion was, Rose may not have endorsed the *Morro Castle* crew as readily as he did. In his opinion, Rose declared, the cruise ship's officers were heroes.

"They stuck with the ship. They elected to stay. The others elected to go—though I don't blame them."

As is often the case when disaster strikes, the press corps needed a hero and it quickly found one: George White Rogers. The only member of the crew to not walk off the *Tampa,* Rogers was carried down the gangplank on a stretcher. Before he was put in the ambulance and taken to Marine Hospital, he smiled and waved to the cameras. Rose told reporters that Rogers collapsed shortly after being rescued from the *Morro Castle* and that he was the one who sent the SOS. The reporters had their man.

No writer bestowed accolades on George Alagna, who followed Rogers off the *Tampa.* He was seething, which the reporters mistook for sullenness, and he would not respond to the questions hurled at him. Alagna remained quiet, even though he had a lot he wanted to say.

Earlier that morning, before the *Tampa* docked, Ivan Freeman had ordered Alagna to the ship's lounge. "Someone from the office wants to speak to you." There, he joined Freeman and the other *Morro Castle* officers—Clarence Hackney, Samuel Hoffman, William Warms—who were seated at a table with two men he didn't recognize. The men called one of them "Captain Hall," evidently the port captain. The other was Stanley Wright, and Alagna soon deduced that Wright was a lawyer for the Ward Line. The men had met the *Tampa* on the outskirts of the harbor in one of the pilot boats. *Jesus,* Alagna thought, *this must be pretty important, if they couldn't wait for us to make port.*

Very important, as it turned out. Wright told the men what to expect when they reached the docks—the herd of reporters, the questions. For his part, Wright did not ask what happened—he told them.

"Now, boys, this is a terrible thing that has occurred, most unexpected, and it was entirely an Act of God, and I want to advise you on a few important matters. The majority of you have not been involved in anything like this before, so I consider it very prudent to make a few statements for your benefit, for the benefit of the Ward Line and for the benefit of everybody concerned."

Wright told them not to speak to the reporters—let the photographers take their pictures, but say nothing. He advised the men to do the same with any government investigators that approached them.

"The U.S. attorney may come aboard and he will want to get testimonies from you, and I urge you to ignore him completely. You know those fellows, if you are not careful, they will garble everything up and you will be saying things that you never would have said, and you will make it hard for yourselves and everybody else," Wright said. "All I ask is that you boys cooperate with me and the Ward Line, and we will take good care of you."

To Alagna, it seemed that the Ward Line was trying to buy their silence or threaten their jobs, and he knew his was gone anyway. Still full of the passion that had led to his strike attempt, he could not sit by quietly. Alagna challenged Wright.

"Under whose authority have you come to this boat and made these remarks?"

Wright said he was merely offering tips for how to handle the press, nothing more. Then he lowered his voice and looked at Alagna with piercing eyes.

"Now you know I do represent the Ward Line, but of course I do not want anyone to know it. Of course, I have heard that you and Rogers did fine work. . . . How is he?"

Alagna could not believe what he was hearing. "Excuse me," he said as he stood and walked out of the room. He went to the infirmary to see Rogers. The rest of the crew and the entire company, Alagna decided, were a bunch of crooks. Rogers might have an idea about how to handle the situation. In fact, the visit put him at ease, as Rogers complimented him on not buckling to pressure from the Ward Line.

"We've got to stick together, George," Rogers said. "We've got to expose this affair."

Rogers did not tell Alagna that Wright had been to see him already or that, moments before he told Alagna to ignore the Ward Line's heavy-handed orders, he had agreed to play along. Alagna had not considered that George Rogers's idea of what needed to be exposed might differ greatly from his.

Just before the *Tampa* docked, Wright cornered Alagna in a hallway. Without other witnesses, he was much more menacing. Whether the other men had told him Alagna would be trouble or he had figured it out on his own, the lawyer tried once more to quiet the radioman. Wright suggested it would be better for Alagna to not say anything—for everyone's sake.

"I've done more than my share, and so has Rogers," Alagna said. "We're both irritated by the lack of coordination on the bridge. It's too bad Captain Willmott died. Fewer people would have died. Warms walked around in a daze, muttering about how he 'must be dreaming.' He left it up to the stewards to help people. He's incompetent. I consider him a murderer."

"You go ashore and make statements of this kind you are making to me—in the first place you are employed by the Ward Line and secondly, you have had a lot of trouble with the Ward Line," Wright said. "These two events will convince the public that you are not telling the truth. That you are merely trying to disparage the Ward Line, getting the enmity, and you will only get yourself into deep water. Keep your mouth shut and don't say anything and . . . this will soon blow over."

For the first time since he left the *Morro Castle,* Alagna was afraid. A conspiracy-minded man, he believed there was no limit to what the company might do to maintain its reputation. So when George Alagna walked down the *Tampa* gangplank, he looked at the reporters blankly and said nothing. He played along. But that would soon change.

The Ward Line was not as successful in quieting most of its employees. While the top officers of the *Morro Castle* were quarantined for more than a day aboard the *Tampa,* reporters had reached nearly every other survivor. The Saturday evening edition of the *New York World-Telegram* included more than a dozen first-person accounts of the fire under the bylines of passengers and several members of the crew, including Joseph

Markov, a steward; Carl Jackson, an able-bodied seaman; and even Chief Engineer Eben Abbott.

"I ran to the lower deck, trying to warn as many passengers as I could, but the fire was so intense I couldn't stand it. I jumped from the rail into the water and was picked up by one of the lifeboats," Abbott wrote.

A much different story would come within the week.

The family of the late captain also caused the Ward Line stress, stoking the fires of malfeasance. Willmott's first cousin, a Camden photographer named Theodore Read, told some newspapers that the captain had not been sick a day in his life—certainly not with any heart trouble. By insinuation, Read said there was more to the story than had been revealed.

"He was strong, heavyset and healthy and never was troubled with indigestion," Read said. "He led a healthy life at sea and used to be a great athlete. I never knew him to be even slightly ill. We are going to find out more about this later on."

The captain's death had warranted several stories. Mathilda Willmott collapsed when she learned her husband had died, and the family summoned a doctor to her Long Island home on two occasions. Now she complained to the papers that she did not even have his body to bury. On Sunday afternoon, several Asbury Park and Coast Guard officials had gone aboard the ship under the pretense of locating the captain's body, but none of them knew the layout of the ship and they came back empty-handed. Mrs. Willmott spoke frankly about the tragedy when reporters called on her at home.

"It is terrible," she cried. "I hoped, at least, that my husband's body would be brought back to me. As it is, his ashes are probably scattered throughout the wreckage."

Mrs. Willmott wanted more than a body to bury. She wanted an autopsy. And soon, some important people would agree that seemed like a very good idea.

Captain Willmott was just one of dozens of bodies unaccounted for a day after the disaster. Some newspapers estimated the death toll at 229 or higher, and others predicted dozens of passengers might never be found. The Ward Line had kept a detailed list of passengers and crew, down to the cabin they slept in, but the accounting was still difficult. Survivors and the dead were spread from Sea Girt to New York City. And there was no way of knowing how many people had come ashore and walked away, how many had burned to death on the ship, and how many were still float-ing in the sea.

These unanswered questions fed the press frenzy. Reporters wanted to know what caused the fire and why the crew could not extinguish it. They got a variety of answers. Passengers and even some crew blamed it on a lack of water pressure, poor training and sailors who abandoned ship in the early minutes of the disaster. The Ward Line could not douse the firestorm that followed. By Sunday afternoon, it was clear the press was looking for a villain. In absence of one man, the whole crew, even the en-tire Ward Line, might take the blame.

Meanwhile, the photographers shot George Rogers's picture while re-porters fawned over him and speculated on the amazing story he had to tell. All they could do was guess, because Rogers kept his word to the Ward Line—he said nothing. But he let the newspapermen take his picture, lying in his hospital bed, beaming like a little boy as his wife, Edith, sat at his bedside. In the photos, which appeared in dozens of papers the next day, more than a few people no doubt noticed how much older than Rogers his wife appeared to be.

That day, Tom Torresson and his mother drove home to Woodcliff. The ride was interminable for a still exhausted Tom. After a long dinner at the hotel, James McDonald had taken Tom to his apartment near Spring Lake, where Bob Tolman and Russell Du Vinage were recuperating. Tom as-sumed his father had sent all the pursers there. Winifred Torresson in-sisted her son take a bath before going to bed. After all the hours he'd spent in the ocean, the last thing Tom wanted to do was get wet, but he did not argue. He knew that when he finished, he could sleep.

On the drive home, Tom adjusted to a world seen through a single eye. He had hurt his right eye somehow—he supposed it had been jabbed by something—so the doctors made him wear a patch over it. It only made him look more like a hero to the crowd at his house.

Sunday afternoon, while the *Morro Castle*'s officers tried to avoid re-porters, Tom sat in the family library embellishing his adventure for friends. Reporters hovered outside, but Winifred Torresson—loyal to the Ward Line and her family—refused to allow them to interview her son. It did not keep his name out of the papers. One small newspaper, in fact, published a story that credited the young third assistant purser with rescuing cruise director Bob Smith. The report claimed Tom had held Smith's head above water all night to keep him alive. When his friends asked about that story, however, Tom did not exaggerate. "Baloney," he said.

Later that week, Tom would wander into the city and drop by his alma mater, Xavier High School. He ran into a fellow in the hall who had been a grade behind him, and the kid looked at Tom like he was seeing a ghost. In a way, he was. The school had just held a memorial service for its lost alumnus. Conflicting newspaper reports led school officials to believe Tom had died in the fire.

"What the heck are you doing here?" the boy said. "We were just in there praying for you."

Tom could do little but hang around the city. His plans to go off to college were on hold because, by the end of the week, he and the rest of the *Morro Castle*'s final crew would be under grand jury subpoena, under court order to stay in New York for more than a year.

Late Sunday, the first of more than a hundred funerals for victims of the *Morro Castle* began in Brooklyn. The family of Charles Filtzer rushed to have his services just ten days after they had seen him married, barely a week after he left for his honeymoon aboard the Ward Line flagship. The stress of all that had happened was too much for his young widow. Selma Filtzer fainted several times during the ceremony until finally she was carried out of the chapel.

Selma at least had the memory of her wedding, something Max Krauss never would. He found his fiancée, Eva Hoffman, among the bodies in a New Jersey armory Sunday afternoon. At the same time, Dr. Braulio Saenz of Havana spent all day looking for the bodies of his wife and four children. When he found his daughter Martha on a cot, Saenz's huge frame shook. He dropped to his knees and caressed her hair, sobbing. More than a dozen families on the Jersey shore offered the sad man a place to rest, sleep and tend to his grief as he continued the search for his wife. There was no shortage of compassion among the people who had witnessed the disaster firsthand.

As the families of the dead sorted through the remains of the disaster, a tugboat carried William Warms, George Alagna and the *Morro Castle* officers across New York Harbor. When it reached Manhattan, the tug docked at Pier 13, where the *Morro Castle* had moored for four years. From there, taxis carried the men the short distance to the Ward Line offices. They were not allowed to go home, or even to a hotel in the city, to rest. The men were weary, getting by on whatever pitiful amount of sleep they had gotten on the *Tampa,* but company officials gave it little thought—or just didn't care. The health of the crew mattered little; the men of the Ward Line had more important things on their minds. Dickerson Hoover would begin the Steamboat Inspection Service inquiry the next day, and company officials wanted to know what was going to be said beforehand. They didn't want any surprises.

Dozens of people, many of them disheveled or wearing ill-fitting clothes, were scattered throughout the cavernous Ward Line offices. They were a distressed lot, and Alagna realized these people were passengers and the families of the missing. He thought to himself with more than a little apprehension, *They're herding them all in here.*

The company announced it would launch its own investigation to run concurrently with the Steamboat Inspectors' hearings, which had been organized and announced with surprising swiftness, and Ward Line lawyers busied themselves taking statements from crew and passengers. One newspaper photographer snapped a candid photo of William Warms sitting alone beside a desk in an empty room of the Ward Line offices. The man who was briefly captain of the *Morro Castle* had a dead look in his eyes, as if he were another casualty of the lost ship. The gaze would remain frozen on his face for months.

Meanwhile, Alagna felt trapped. He believed the Ward Line meant to keep him in its custody until the hearings started, and he did not like it. He tried to be polite and seem cooperative to Wright, asking if he could go to his home in Connecticut for a bath and fresh clothes. Wright told him to sit tight, that he would soon be taken care of. Alagna didn't believe the lawyer and could not keep himself from saying so.

"It's extremely strange that the Ward Line thinks more of my testimony and these other men's testimony and is very, very negligent of our immediate wishes," Alagna said.

Wright allowed Alagna to phone his mother, but asked him to stay in the office. For the rest of the afternoon, Ward Line officials probably wished they had let George Alagna leave. As the fall sun sank into the western sky, casting strange shadows on the walls, Alagna wandered through the office telling everyone he saw to not cooperate with the company's investigation. The Ward Line, he said, was trying to find a way to absolve itself of any blame in the disaster. He was so convincing that one of the *Morro Castle*'s bellhops walked out of the office without giving any statement. Alagna soon followed suit but did not leave before saying goodbye to Wright.

"What! Aren't you going to give us any testimony?" Wright asked.

"No. I am sorry, I don't see why I should," Alagna said.

Wright begged Alagna to stay, offered him money and then reminded him he couldn't buy clothes in the city on Sunday. The lawyer seemed desperate, and Alagna suddenly knew why. He had witnessed what really happened, and the company did not want a hostile witness when the Steamboat Inspectors hearings began. But the company had poor diplomacy skills. Instead of treating him well, the Ward Line had tried to bully him. Realizing that the company had no authority over him, Alagna quit.

"I regret that the Ward Line seems so selfish under the circumstances and, as a result, I feel justified in not having any further relations with the Line," he said.

As dusk fell on the city, George Alagna walked out of the Ward Line offices for the last time, promising he would see Wright again—at the hearings that would begin the next day, Monday.

Martin Conboy, the U.S. attorney in New York, spent Sunday in his Manhattan office planning his own *Morro Castle* investigation. There was little doubt in the prosecutor's mind that a crime had been committed, perhaps even two hundred counts of murder. Not exactly a publicity seeker, Conboy did not shy away from it, either. He knew this case might earn barrels of ink. Already, the story had covered the front pages of newspapers across the country for two days running. And when the press paid this much attention to a potential crime, he knew his office could not ignore it. Conboy instead chose to do the opposite. He made the *Morro Castle* his highest priority. That afternoon, Conboy called in staff to interview New York and

New Jersey port officials about the ship and the Ward Line. Late that afternoon, a man in a dark suit walked into the office. Conboy immediately recognized him as one of J. Edgar Hoover's men.

Francis Xavier Fay carried himself with the calm and confident air of most Bureau of Investigation agents. Barely thirty-six, Fay had been an investigator with the Bureau for twelve years. Before that, he worked in his uncle's detective agency. His dad was a veteran New York City cop. In short, he knew his business well. He had been involved in any number of high-profile cases, including the kidnapping of the Lindbergh baby, and he spoke with the authority that the Bureau increasingly had. He told Conboy he was there to offer his help.

Although Conboy may have been wary of the Bureau of Investigation, he outlined his plans to subpoena every crewman and interview every passenger who had been aboard the ship. It would be a monumental task, one that he conceded his small staff could not handle alone. Conboy asked Fay if the Bureau could help, perhaps lend some manpower to the case. Conboy made clear that it was *his* investigation. Fay said he had three men, but promised to ask for more. Saying he would do all he could, Fay smiled.

Fay's orders had come straight from Washington, and he did not dally. He sent his agents out that very evening to find survivors, most of whom were still in hospitals or private homes along the Jersey shore. He sent another man to the Ward Line to get a list of passengers and crew, and by that evening Fay joined in the hunt. He found dozens of survivors in New York City, a few in the New Jersey suburbs. They were short, cursory interviews—a chance to hit the high spots, get a first impression and contact information. The Bureau, he promised, would be back around. Hoover's men were casting a wide net.

Fay had been in the Bureau of Investigation long enough to know how to save a good deal of legwork. He kept in touch with a large network of newspaper and radio reporters, men more than eager to trade information for the promise of a later scoop. Fay worked these reporters skillfully, leaking them information he wanted publicized and holding back everything else. On Sunday night, he spoke with an Associated Press reporter to get an idea what people were saying about the disaster. The reporter related all the whispers of mutiny, sabotage, arson and murder swirling around the beached ship. All the things that made a good Bureau man listen carefully.

Sunday night, Fay spoke by telephone with his supervisor, E. A. Tamm.

He related what he'd learned, what Conboy's office had said, and how many survivors his men had tracked down. Tamm said to work it hard—the boss was interested in this one. He also told Fay to be selective with the information he turned over to Conboy. The Bureau did not do grunt work for anyone, especially someone who had the makings of a publicity hound. Tamm told Fay what he certainly already knew.

J. Edgar Hoover was in charge of this case.

CHAPTER ELEVEN

An Agitator Among Us

The train arrived in Jersey City early Monday, the low rumble of its approach echoing through the streets like distant thunder. Nearly half of the recovered dead of the *Morro Castle* rode silently in one car, followed by a Pullman filled with reporters and Ward Line officials. Per the orders of M. L. McElhenny, superintendent of the New York & Long Branch Railroad, it had been a slow funeral procession from Sea Girt. McElhenny told his engineer not to exceed 20 mph, that the bodies "must not be jostled or further bruised." They had suffered enough indignity.

His sympathy for the *Morro Castle* casualties went beyond respect; he also had been a passenger on the cruise. McElhenny had jumped from the ship into the ocean just as many of these people had, but he'd been luckier. A lifeboat picked him up. On shore, McElhenny ignored his own broken leg to direct efforts to move the dead. Perhaps he felt he owed it to them.

At the station, men in dark suits and ties awaited the train's arrival with a small, makeshift fleet of hearses and ambulances. The bodies, which had been arranged on army cots, were carried off the train one at a time by engineers in bib overalls and the funeral-home workers. A reporter noted, "The dead were handled gently in death." The 47 bodies were then placed in the waiting cars and, with few witnesses other than photographers, carried to the mortuary of B. A. Waters on Brinkerhoff Street.

By Monday, the official death count of the disaster had been amended to 116 confirmed dead: 85 passengers and 31 crew. As the *Morro Castle* continued to burn on the beach at Asbury Park, nearly 100 people were still unaccounted for, and many of the bodies had yet to be identified, including 17 of those in Waters's care. That morning, police lines were set up around the three-story, black frame building to control the expected crowd.

Waters arranged the bodies as neatly and tightly as he could and still leave room for people to walk through. The funeral-home director had experience with sizable tragedies. Two decades earlier, he had handled arrangements for many of the workers who perished in the Manhattan Triangle Shirtwaist Factory, a fire with similar statistics. More than 500 people had been in the factory; about 150 of them were killed. This time, Waters felt a bond with the dead much as McElhenny did. The undertaker had been aboard the *Morro Castle* on its maiden voyage.

The police lines proved unnecessary. Fewer than 100 people milled about the mortuary at any time that morning, and none of them caused a ruckus. Inside, funeral-home workers led visitors through this sea of sheets, saw them recoil at the faces of death and finally break down when they saw what they most feared. The wife of Samuel Petty, a *Morro Castle* waiter, found her husband on one cot. She knelt beside his body and prayed before cutting off a lock of his hair. On the way out, she fainted and had to be carried to Waters's home. Later, another young woman walked through the rows of corpses several times but could not find her husband, a *Morro Castle* steward named Carlos Alvarez. She left Jersey City that morning wondering if she would ever see him again.

Across the Hudson, no less than four investigations were under way with varying degrees of interest in answering that question. The Ward Line and its insurers had promised separate inquiries, and the U.S. Attorney's Office would announce its own investigation by the end of the day. But most attention was focused on the very public, very grand proceedings of the Department of Commerce's Bureau of Navigation and Steamboat Inspection.

Dickerson Hoover, chairman of the inquiry board, opened the hearings in the Customs House, an imposing, ornate seven-story building near the Battery at the lower tip of Manhattan. That Monday, the first of fifteen days of hearings, the room was packed with Commerce Department bureaucrats, newspaper and radio reporters, and a ragged gallery of survivors and homeless sailors from the *Morro Castle,* many of whom were staying at the nearby Seamen's Institute. Martin Conboy stood in one corner listening closely. The U.S. attorney wanted to hear more about this alleged accident before talking with the two men he would meet that afternoon.

That morning, the three surviving top officers of the *Morro Castle* gave their version of events, a groundwork from which the panel would then question all other witnesses. William Warms, Ivan Freeman and Clarence Hackney had been affected very differently by events. Hackney seemed relaxed, nonplussed, while Freeman appeared so confident as to be cocky. Warms wore a blue suit that highlighted the tired lines in his craggy face. He seemed unsteady on his feet, and had to be helped into the room by his wife. He looked as if he were still in shock.

Despite his appearance, Warms maintained his composure as he recounted the events of the long day that stretched from September 7 into the next morning. He said that he had stayed at his post after Captain Willmott's death because he was determined to get the ship into port safely. When the fire began, he said, he sent some of his ranking officers to extinguish it and others to wake the passengers. He recalled ordering them to run through the halls banging pots and pans if necessary. Warms said that many of the passengers panicked when they were cut off from the lifeboats by the flames, and some even refused rescue. A steward had to force one female passenger into a lifeboat, he claimed. Perhaps, Warms suggested, the problem was all the alcohol flowing among the passengers that night.

"I understood there had been several drinking parties and also that they carried six or seven girls into their rooms who were very drunk."

Warms attempted to inoculate himself against the criticism already making its way into news stories, arguing that beaching the ship would have resulted in more deaths. He said that he did not send an SOS earlier because he wrongly believed the fire could be brought under control. But within minutes, William Warms conceded, it became clear there was no saving the ship.

He told this emotional story with few signs of distress except when talking about his friend, the late captain. As he recounted the final minutes of Robert Renison Willmott, Warms wept openly.

"God bless his soul," he said.

The sight of Warms shedding tears in the middle of the crowded room was forgotten when he delivered his most shocking revelation. He said the fire on the *Morro Castle* had probably started in two separate places, the hold and the Writing Room. The fire was so strong and spread so quickly, Warms claimed, that it had to have been fueled by gasoline, kerosene or some kind of oil. It was, he said, the work of an arsonist.

"I believe the fire was set by someone," Warms said. "I think somebody put something in that locker."

The audience gasped in surprise, but Dickerson Hoover had expected it. Already, the story was spreading through New York. That morning, Cuban officials and a New York detective had claimed that Communist radicals started the fire. Harry V. Dougherty, a private investigator who often traveled to Cuba on the *Morro Castle,* told reporters that the fire was a "deliberate Red plot" started by a mechanical pencil filled with chemicals. And Captain Oscar Hernández, chief of Havana's port police, blamed terrorists. Hernández claimed his informants predicted more disasters. Such fantastic theories might have been dismissed if the Grace liner *Santa Rita* had not caught fire near the Panama Canal that very day. While the *Santa Rita*'s captain blamed spontaneous combustion for the fire in the hold, several of the ship's officers told news services in Balboa that it was arson, the work of "an international radical organization." The next day, the British freighter *Bradburn* would also catch fire in the Caribbean.

Dickerson Hoover, officially the assistant director of the Department of Commerce's Bureau of Navigation and Steamboat Inspection, had heard such things before—but he was not so enamored with conspiracies as his brother, J. Edgar. A stout man with close-cropped hair and a bureaucrat's soul, Hoover had seen his share of controversial shipwrecks at Commerce. Six years earlier, he had led the investigation into the sinking of the Lamport & Holt liner *Vestris,* an accident that claimed 110 lives. But the *Morro Castle* disaster promised to be more deadly, more controversial, than anything he had faced, and he did not want other ship fires to muddy his investigation. With the press in a feeding frenzy, he had enough sensationalism on his hands.

It would only get worse. Freeman and Hackney expanded on Warms's allegation that day, contradicting the acting captain's claims that everyone on board the *Morro Castle* was "a good sailor." Freeman speculated that the Ward Line might have been the target of an attack, and that he expected "more fires aboard other ships very soon."

Freeman and Hackney echoed and complemented Warms so well it was almost as if they had been coached. Hackney spoke of the unnatural speed of the fire and his efforts to extinguish it, while Freeman dismissed the idea that a cigarette from a careless passenger had caused the blaze. Freeman said it was no coincidence that fire had broken out on the *Morro Castle* during two consecutive voyages. He said the ship's own investigation of the August 27 fire suggested it was no accident.

"It would have been necessary for the cigarette to take two right-angle turns and jump two screens if someone had carelessly thrown it down into the hold," Freeman said. "Besides that, a section of charred paper was found where the fire started."

That afternoon, the New York newspapers were filled with wreck photographs and survivor stories. Editors could not get enough of the *Morro Castle*. Even the stoic *New York Times* decided to run nearly complete transcripts of the day's testimony. If it had been just a shipwreck, the headlines might have abated after a few days. But this inquiry—only a few hours old—was beginning to look very much like a murder investigation. The evening edition of the *Daily News* carried the headline: "Line Arson Clue Sought. 163 Liner Blast 'Murders' Probed."

In Asbury Park, firemen, rescue workers and a few anonymous federal investigators spent Monday searching the *Morro Castle* for survivors. Their efforts were restricted to the outer cabins because the fire continued to burn so intensely that no one could stand the heat deep inside the ship. In the rooms that rescue workers could reach, they found little. The fire seemed to have consumed nearly everything. Every so often, another explosion rocked the ship, sending embers shooting out of the aft smokestack nearly 100 feet into the air.

As smoke drifted through the streets of Asbury Park, town leaders considered how to best profit from it. Cries of murder and arson in the New York papers sounded as sweet as the call of a carnival barker to commerce-minded politicians. Such insidious claims would only make their new tourist attraction that much more popular. A shipwreck was one thing—a crime scene something entirely different.

At long last, business was booming in the old shore resort. More than a quarter-million people had visited the town since Saturday night, and nearly every one of them had bought something. People filled the restaurants and hotels and spent money freely. They paid to see the wreck and then gave money to hustlers who took their picture in front of it. Soon, the arcades would have machines to flatten pennies, stamping them with the profile of the burned liner, and the Boardwalk Taffy Shop would send out picture postcards of the wreck with the slogan "We Mail Salt Water Taffy to Any Part of the United States" printed over the burning hull.

That afternoon, a plump man pink with sunburn watched workers pile into the breeches buoy as if it were just another ride on the Midway. He remarked to a reporter, "Maybe the city will keep her here and charge admission to go aboard." He must have been a tourist, because a local would most likely have realized such plans were already in the works.

Fifty years earlier, in the summer of 1884, Asbury Park's *Daily Spray* had opined that a real first-class shipwreck would put the town on the map. William K. Devereaux had written, "We need a first-class shipwreck. Why? To make Asbury Park a famous winter resort. She should strike head-on, and we could accommodate her all winter. A pontoon or suspension bridge could be built from the pier so the ship could be used as a casino. Atlantic City would then yield place to Asbury as a peerless winter resort. We need a shipwreck."

The glut of tourism that this ship had sparked in just a few days convinced city leaders that Devereaux's speculation had been prescient. Why not become known for a shipwreck? The *Morro Castle* would be front-page news for months. If they kept the ship, it would be like free advertising every day. The season would never end.

Martin Conboy must have thought them an odd pair—an enormous goof in ratty sneakers and a tie too short to cover his belly, and his skinny, stylish friend. A seagoing Laurel and Hardy, that's what they were. When the U.S. attorney met the radio operators at the Federal Building on Monday, he may have worried briefly about his case. Certainly, he could not relish the idea of facing the grand jury with only a vagrant and a dandy. But after talking to the two men, Conboy realized that George Rogers and George Alagna were key to any criminal investigation into the *Morro Castle* incident.

The radiomen seemed eager to share their story. Rogers puffed on his pipe with great affection and apologized for his clothes, explaining that he'd lost everything he owned in the fire. Alagna was in an upbeat mood, as his first-person account of the disaster had just been published on the front page of the *New York American*. Alagna posed for a picture in the paper wearing a sailor's hat, smiling as if satisfied the truth was out at last.

Conboy was so interested in Alagna's version of events that the attorney spent several hours talking with him. The junior radioman detailed how many trips he made to the bridge the night of the fire, how most of the officers ran around dazed and did little to help the passengers. He said Warms had refused to give an SOS order, or even allow him to jump into the water to save a woman. Alagna told Conboy just what he'd told the Ward Line lawyers the day before: William Warms was a murderer.

Rogers criticized no one in his self-serving interview, instead outlining the timeline of events in the radio room: Alagna woke him just before 3 A.M. He sent out a "stand-by" message around 3:15 A.M. and another at 3:19. Then the SOS at 3:25. Conboy's staff sketched a timeline from his memory. In all, the two radiomen spent more than five hours giving what would be the first of many depositions. When Rogers finished with Conboy, he walked to the Ward Line offices and met with attorneys there. He did not tell Alagna where he was going.

That evening, a reporter from the *Bayonne Times* met Rogers on the sidewalk outside his home. Rogers declined to be interviewed, then continued talking. He apologized for his dress and his ratty shoes. Due to the fire, Rogers said, he didn't even have a decent pair. Rogers was more than happy to poor-mouth to the reporter. He said he was broke but had gotten offers from two London newspapers that would pay top dollar for exclusive European rights to his story. Rogers said he could not accept such offers yet, and groused that such opportunities would likely evaporate before long. "The whole world will get it for nothing soon," he said, a reference to his pending testimony. In the article that resulted from the conversation, Rogers sounded overly bitter about his failed radio shop in Bayonne. He came across almost as if he were two different people—cheerful one minute, nasty the next. Before the reporter left the radioman, he asked why Rogers was not burned like so many of the crewmen. Rogers smiled and said that perhaps he was just better prepared.

"Say, those men went through something. They earned those burned faces so many of them had—they didn't deliberately put their faces up to portholes," Rogers said. "The only reason I didn't get burned myself was because I kept a wet towel over my face."

There was one interesting fact revealed in the story, but no investigator ever followed up on what, if any, meaning it had. The *Bayonne Times* reported that Rogers's wife, Edith, and her mother had planned to take the Labor Day cruise aboard the *Morro Castle,* but had been told it was sold out.

The next day, September 11, George Rogers arrived at the Federal Building in the same tattered clothes he had worn the day before. He testified before the grand jury for nearly four hours—sealed remarks that were supposed to be confidential. But because of what happened next, most folks could guess what the radioman had said. That afternoon, a judge ordered federal marshals to arrest George Alagna.

At least publicly, Alagna took it well. Outside the courthouse, he laughed as photographers shot pictures of him handcuffed to a U.S. marshal. He even joked about his predicament, trying gently to get across the message that he had not done anything wrong.

"They consider me of great importance. They're taking no chance of my getting out."

Almost as soon as he was in custody, Conboy's office leaked word that Alagna would not remain behind bars for long. Reporters were told his arrest was not a question of contempt of court or even a grand jury order. The U.S. attorney, it was explained, simply wanted to make sure Alagna would be available "for further questioning if that is deemed desirable." Conboy's office said there was a rumor the Ward Line planned to give Alagna a job on the *Siboney,* which was scheduled to leave the country the next day. The message: somebody wanted him out of the picture.

The leak had less to do with clearing Alagna's name than it did Conboy's growing concerns about the Ward Line. It seemed attorneys for the company were manipulating the testimony of every sailor who went before the Commerce committee or the grand jury. On several occasions, marshals had to boot Ward Line attorneys from the grand jury room. When Chauncey Clark and William Dean said they were merely trying to "advise" their clients, Conboy had the lawyers subpoenaed and hauled before the court themselves. And when the U.S. attorney learned that several *Morro Castle* sailors were due to leave on other ships throughout the week, the district attorney subpoenaed every person who had worked on the ship, barely bothering to sort out the dead ones. Big business, Conboy declared, could not run roughshod over government. But reporters noted that none of the other sailors or Ward Line lawyers had been arrested. A few even mentioned in print that it was perhaps "significant" that George Rogers was not treated the same as Alagna.

The arrest of George Alagna might have been bigger news had Eben Abbott not overshadowed it. The testimony of the chief engineer, and the survivors who followed him, on that day established the legacy of the *Morro Castle* disaster that would linger for more than seventy years. Because Abbott—bags under his eyes, Ward Line attorneys by his side—admitted that he left the burning ship within a half hour after the fire was discovered.

During his testimony, Abbott seemed nervous, gesturing wildly with his hands. He explained that he was overcome by smoke; that he spoke several times with his assistant in the engine room, who had things under control as well as they could be. Finally, he said, Captain Warms had ordered him to supervise the launch of the lifeboats. The cameras that day captured a look of disgust on Hoover's face. At one point, he dismissively told Abbott that his "company attorneys have no standing in court" and asked why, if he were in charge of lifeboats, he did not make sure more passengers got on the boats.

"What efforts did you make to find passengers to put in these boats?"

"I saw no passengers," Abbott said.

Abbott became the personification of the disaster's most repulsive statistics: Only 6 passengers escaped in the first five lifeboats, compared to about 100 members of the *Morro Castle*'s crew. There were nearly 200 empty seats in the first six lifeboats launched, enough to have saved everyone who died that night. The Ward Line was forced to concede the casualty rate among passengers was greater than 30 percent but less than 18 percent among the crew. Anthony Bujia, Abbott's assistant, admitted that the lifeboat he escaped in had carried only 1 passenger and 19 crewmen. Hoover asked why the lifeboat did not pick up survivors in the water, and Bujia's answer sealed the reputation of the *Morro Castle* crew.

"The majority of the crew wanted to get to shore quickly," Bujia said.

Many passengers could attest to that. Gouverneur M. Phelps said that a lifeboat carrying a dozen *Morro Castle* sailors floated past his family, but they did not offer to stop. It seemed there was no end to the crew's callousness; most offered no evidence of doing anything for passengers. Ship's electrician William Floyd Justis speculated that "spite" among the crew may even have led to the fire. Hoover said a separate investigation into the Ward Line's employment practices might be warranted.

By the end of the day, even the president of the United States had something to say about the disaster. FDR told reporters in Hyde Park that he wanted Congress to "encourage" metal shipbuilding. The days of wooden interiors on passenger ships were almost over.

George Rogers made it easy to vilify Eben Abbott. When the *Morro Castle*'s chief radio operator testified for the Steamboat Inspectors the next day, he proved to be the perfect foil to the engineer. Rogers not only remained at his post as the fire closed in around him, he had risked his life to send the SOS that saved hundreds of lives. With his deft storytelling abilities, Rogers made sure that point was lost on no one.

The heroic tale that reporters had anticipated for nearly a week exceeded their expectations. Rogers recounted his time in the wireless room to the minute, peppering his testimony with details of exploding batteries and loyally awaiting orders as the room burned. He explained how he remained conscious by breathing into a wet towel and that he repaired the radio while nearly blinded by smoke. Rogers recalled that even after he was ordered to escape, he remained at the radio retransmitting the distress signal to make sure someone heard it.

The news stories of the day would call his story gripping and graphic, and claim that Rogers had faced death "without fear." The committee listened to his testimony without comment, and their subsequent questions seemed less concerned with what he did right than what had gone wrong. Hoover in particular was more interested in what the radioman could tell him about the consternation behind the scenes on the *Morro Castle*. Hoover did not want to hear about heroics, he wanted to know what had caused the fire.

"Have you ever had any trouble on that ship in regard to radio operators?" Hoover asked.

The question brought the hearing to a halt. Rogers fell silent, staring ahead as if he had been cornered. If it was an act, it was a good one. For nearly ten minutes, Rogers shifted in his seat, started to speak several times and then stopped. He consulted with his attorney—Stanley Wright from the Ward Line—and caught himself before speaking again. He held his head in his hands and wiped sweat from his brow. One newspaper later ran a series of photographs of Rogers taken during these silent minutes. In one, he holds a finger to his chin; in another, he looks down at the ground. In a third, he has his hand on his head.

"Sir," Rogers began, "I am afraid if I answer that question that the whole question is going to be misconstrued."

At least "99 percent" of people would take such information out of context, Rogers said, if he talked about it in open court. He did not think the two things were related. If he was trying to protect Alagna, he failed miserably. In fact, he planted the idea Alagna was guilty of something the moment Hoover demanded he answer the question.

"There was a strike. . . ."

For more than an hour, Rogers told the Steamboat Inspectors about Alagna's problems on the ship. He recounted the fight with Ivan Freeman over the compass. Rogers said that Captain Willmott had planned to fire Alagna at the end of the voyage; that he was ordered to check the radio equipment and electronic compass constantly to make sure that it had not been sabotaged. At the end of his story, Hoover asked Rogers if the chief officers of the *Morro Castle* had been afraid of George Alagna.

"They were afraid of almost everything," Rogers said. "The captain . . . was afraid that something was going to happen. He understood that Mr. Alagna was a very vengeful sort of a person and he would not trust him any further than he could throw a safe."

Rogers gave the disaster its villain. While Eben Abbott might have been a coward who ignored drowning passengers, Alagna was "an agitator"—just the sort of sailor that William Warms, Ivan Freeman and Clarence Hackney had suggested might be responsible for the fire. If he hadn't already been in custody, it would not have surprised anyone to see the radioman arrested that very afternoon. As it was, headlines that claimed "Dead Captain Feared Alagna" all but convicted him. The *New York Journal* that evening focused on a different angle of the story, however, one that most other reports either ignored or glossed over. The *Journal*'s headline read, "Rogers Turns on Man Who Saved Him."

* * *

In Asbury Park that day, an undertaker named Harry Bodine walked out of the Convention Hall carrying a suitcase that he said contained the remains of Captain Robert Renison Willmott. Fire Chief William F. Taggart told reporters he had found the body the night before while he and other firemen searched the ship. Although Taggart had not previously been aboard the *Morro Castle,* and did not carry any blueprints, he claimed he was fairly certain he'd found the captain's cabin.

"There was a safe and a radio and a bunch of keys on a ring," he said. "The legs of the bed had melted off."

More important, there was what appeared to be human remains on the floor—but only enough to fill two shoeboxes. The body effectively had been cremated. Although they could barely stand the heat, Taggart said he and the other firemen stayed long enough to recover the body.

Taggart had spent nearly every waking hour at the wreck site over the past few days, eventually closing the Boardwalk around the Convention Hall on Monday because he feared someone would be hurt by the continuing explosions. He told reporters the fire would eventually burn itself out, but boasted that his men were ready to pump 10,000 gallons a minute on the fire if it didn't. Taggart did not tell the press that he was also keeping up with his expenses and, by the end of the week, would send the Ward Line an amazingly large bill for these services.

Perhaps city officials hoped to barter with the Ward Line for the wreck. The New York papers reported that Asbury Park had offered cash for the *Morro Castle,* and the city council had even passed a resolution authorizing city manager Carl H. Bischoff to negotiate for the purchase or rental of the ship as a permanent museum piece. The city council denied making such a resolution after one of its members, Max Silverstein, attacked his fellow councilmen for such a "shocking, revolting, base and vicious attempt to exploit a horrifying misfortune." But soon, Bischoff publicly admitted he had been given those exact orders, forcing Councilmen Louis Croce and James J. Digney to claim they had only wanted to see if the lower part of the hull could be salvaged as a jetty. If most people took that explanation with a grain of incredulity, it was only because Asbury Park residents seemed unable to stop huckstering for even a minute. Days after Willmott's body was recovered, some shops were selling postcards that featured his alleged remains dangling in the breeches buoy between the *Morro Castle* and Convention Hall. Asbury Park merchants would do any unholy thing for an almighty buck.

Despite Taggart's find, the Willmott family still would not get their funeral. Martin Conboy seized the remains from Asbury Park that afternoon and ordered an autopsy to search for traces of poison. In one newspaper article on the pending exam, a man named Francis Xavier Fay—identified only as a Justice Department investigator—was quoted as saying some poisons could be detected, while others could not.

Tom Torresson arrived in Asbury Park shortly after the captain's alleged ashes were recovered. His father was directing the team of Ward Line workers at the wreck site, and he went there to help. There was still talk of hauling the luxury liner off the beach and salvaging it, even refitting her. Mostly, young Tom did paperwork and ran errands, much to his irritation. Tourists had the entire town jammed up, particularly around the entrance to the Berkeley-Carteret, where he and the other Ward Line employees were staying.

Although he could see the *Morro Castle* from his hotel room, Tom had no desire to go aboard the ship. The sight of the beached liner, which he had admired so much, saddened him, and he didn't care to see it any closer. He left that to Frank Crocco, who over the course of two months would go from cabin to cabin aboard the *Morro Castle,* taking an inventory of what he found inside the charred hull. In some rooms, he found only one thing he could identify. A typical entry in his log read, "Stateroom #18, Mr. Robert González. One key. One belt buckle."

With the resilience of a teenager, Tom suffered little stress over his near-death experience. He stood in the shadow of the burned hull several times without even noticing it or casting a glance back to what might have been. As he did on the ship, Tom focused on his duties. Still, he had a little fun. He fought the reporters who pounded on his hotel room door at all hours. When Dickerson Hoover brought his investigation to town, Tom followed them up and down the Jersey shore, serving as his father's eyes. The committee went to Sea Girt to see one of the *Morro Castle* lifeboats. They found the boat behind a fire station, and Hoover inspected it with reporters and Tom looking on. Finally, he took a ball-peen hammer and hit the boat's watertight tanks without making a hole in it.

"Gentlemen, this lifeboat is 100 percent seaworthy," Hoover said.

One reporter in the crowd pushed his way up to Hoover and handed him a sledgehammer. Tom, shocked, heard a reporter say, "Give it a whack with this, Mr. Hoover." Hoover refused.

After a week, Asbury Park seemed more trouble than fun. Tom was not upset when he finally went back to Woodcliff. He had other things to occupy his time at home. A friend of his father's had offered him a job in Manhattan.

Sometime after Tom Torresson left town, Frank Crocco, by then the ranking Ward Line official in town, got a bill for $2,783.47 from Asbury Park for fire services, which included firemen sitting on the Boardwalk watching the *Morro Castle* burn. Crocco apologized, but said that neither he nor the company's insurance could pay the bill.

"It rather looks to me as if the only way to offset this expense would be the benefits the City received from the many visitors who came to view the steamer on the beach there after the tragedy."

George Rogers returned to Bayonne a hero. After his testimony, after his picture appeared on the front pages of newspapers around the country, accolades washed over him like a great wave. That week the Veteran Wireless Operators Association publicly "rejoiced" in his safety and the *Bayonne Times* lauded his actions in an editorial that declared him a "new name" for the roster "in the thrilling saga of the sea which bears the names of those who put their own welfare last when danger threatened."

"When there was no further possibility of helping others, Rogers bethought himself of his own safety," the *Times* said.

There was a rumor the city council would pass a resolution honoring him, fueled in part by Mayor L. F. Donohoe's public declaration that "George Rogers stuck to his job. No man could do more."

That Sunday, Rev. Frank Artley at the Christ Presbyterian Church delivered an entire sermon on Rogers, and the next week, a local club held an appreciation dinner for the radioman at Rosie's Restaurant. Among the invited guests were Charles Singer and Lieutenant Vincent J. Doyle of the Bayonne Police Department, themselves survivors of ship disasters. Singer had sent the SOS when the liner *Comanche* burned off Jacksonville in 1925, and Doyle had been a seventeen-year-old wireless man aboard a

British tanker, the *Tacoma,* when it ran aground in 1921. Enjoying the attention, Rogers made quite a show of being the concerned, levelheaded seaman.

"I certainly had no intention of giving the inference, when I testified about the trouble between Alagna and Captain Willmott, that Alagna had anything to do with the fire," Rogers told people that night. "Of course, whatever inference unthinking people may draw from what I said . . . I cannot help."

Most people found Rogers charming, but Vincent Doyle found something about Rogers a bit unsettling. Doyle heard Rogers claim it was so hot in the *Morro Castle* radio room that "solder was melting from the connections on the transmitter." Doyle knew that was impossible, and considered Rogers a poor liar.

When the two were introduced, Rogers insulted Doyle, asking, "What ship did *you* ever sail on?"

No doubt Rogers was jealous of Doyle. He had seen the story about Doyle's heroics in the *Bayonne Times* the same day his actions on the *Morro Castle* were recounted. Constantly worried that someone might outshine him, Rogers did not like to share the spotlight and often elevated himself by denigrating others.

Unaware of the exchange, the police commissioner asked Doyle to say something about Rogers during the dinner. Doyle, insulted and perhaps feeling a bit self-righteous, could not bring himself to say, "Welcome home, hero" and sit down. Instead, he stood before the crowd and asked Rogers if it was true that the solder melted off the *Morro Castle* radios? The room was quiet for a full fifteen seconds, Rogers glaring at Doyle.

"I am sure that, in your position as a radio operator, you have used a soldering iron many times," Doyle said. "I am sure, also, that you had to wait many times for your iron to get hot enough to melt the solder. . . . Do you know or have any idea how hot your iron must be before solder will be melted by its heat?"

Rogers said nothing, but Doyle felt that if looks could kill, he would be dead. He didn't care. Rogers was making outlandish, even ridiculous, claims of being a hero. With the audience stunned silent, Doyle continued to talk. He could not make himself be polite, or even quiet.

"I was invited here tonight to meet you and to welcome you home as the hero of the *Morro Castle,* " Doyle said. "I met you and I welcome you home. You have had a trying experience. My conscience, however, will not allow me to call you a hero. A hero, in my humble opinion, should be modest and truthful. You are neither and I feel sorry for you."

Vincent Doyle was not the only person who questioned Rogers's heroism. The *Morro Castle* investigation was turning up all manner of information. Among the tips coming in to the Bureau of Investigation's New York office, Francis Xavier Fay got one about Rogers that prompted him to telegram J. Edgar Hoover.

> KINDLY EXPEDITE ADVICE WHETHER CRIMINAL RECORD OR PHOTO-
> GRAPH AVAILABLE ON ONE GEORGE W. ROGERS, ABOUT 39 YEARS, 6
> FEET 1 TALL, 293 POUNDS, BROWN HAIR, BLUE EYES, FAIR COMPLEX-
> ION, SLIGHTLY BALD, MARRIED, OCCUPATION RADIO OPERATOR. SAID TO
> HAVE BEEN ARRESTED NEW YORK BETWEEN 1927 AND PRESENT TIME,
> CHARGE GRAND LARCENY.

The report he got back was bigger than Fay had expected. It seemed Rogers had been busy in the years before he joined the *Morro Castle* crew. As he skimmed the report on Rogers, Fay found it all very interesting, even though he knew none of it meant anything. Well, most of it meant nothing.

Fay had little time to devote to such minor leads, as he received new intelligence on the *Morro Castle* nearly every day. His office got anonymous letters that outlined insurance scams, the plots of radical "Reds" and elaborate tales of espionage and bombs aboard the Ward liner. At the same time, Fay had to keep Washington happy. J. Edgar Hoover had taken an interest because of the allegations involving Communists, with whom the Bureau chief was increasingly obsessed. He sent a plane filled with agents to Havana to investigate, and ordered a full background check and investigation of Renée Méndez Capote. Capote, the daughter of Cuba's former vice president, was a suspected Communist. One of Hoover's men, posing as an Associated Press reporter, eventually interviewed the vice president about the disaster and his daughter.

Hoover told Fay to concentrate on the autopsy of Captain Willmott and afterward to do a background check on the doctor who made the report. He thought Willmott's death hours before the fire could not be a coincidence. Hoover also told Fay he did not want Conboy talking to the press about this case.

Fay could do nothing to hush the U.S. attorney, but he had plans to convey the Bureau's perspective publicly through Walter Winchell. The influential newspaper and radio commentator had taken an interest in the Ward Line, and Fay had his ear. Hoover was more than happy to let his agent craft the story that Winchell put forth, but refused to let Fay leak information about George Rogers's criminal past—either to Winchell or Conboy. Fay wanted to quell the "hero" stories about Rogers, but Hoover would not allow it. Not yet, the director said.

With a formal apology, George Alagna was released from custody little more than a day after he was arrested. A federal judge ordered Alagna freed at the request of Louis Mead Treadwell, an assistant U.S. attorney. Martin Conboy either decided Alagna would not be useful as a hostile witness, or that it had been wrong to hold him. The man hated the Ward Line, Conboy thought, so how bad could he be? Conboy's office made sure Alagna got as much publicity when he left the jail as when he had arrived. United States Marshal Raymond J. Mulligan said that it had been a mistake to handcuff the radioman. The government was backpedaling.

"A civil prisoner held solely as a government witness should never be handcuffed," Mulligan said to reporters. "I gave orders that the incident should not be repeated."

Not even his very public release could clear Alagna's name. He still carried the label of agitator, and public opinion seemed very much against him. Never mind the potential legal problems, Alagna could not stand for people to think him guilty, so he went to work repairing his reputation. He called reporters to his attorney's office, declared that he was no troublemaker and certainly not a Communist. Alagna explained his arrest and offered a preview of his own testimony, which he said he looked forward to delivering next week.

"I refused to be guided by the Ward Line attorneys when the *Tampa* docked," Alagna said. "I believe it was because of that they brought out my part in the strike of three months ago and attempted, in a vindictive mood, to brand me an agitator. That is a smoke screen to discredit me in order to shift the responsibility from the shoulders of those upon whom it rightfully belongs."

Thanks to Rogers's testimony, Alagna was still the government's best arson suspect, but he refused to look guilty. He took the offense, criticizing the Ward Line at every opportunity. And by the end of the week, he had his reunion with Rogers.

Rogers had been invited to the American Radio Telegraphists Association on Friday. When he arrived that morning, he looked preoccupied, not his usual jovial self, even a bit nervous. Rogers told reporters that he hoped to see Alagna so that he could explain.

"I meant nothing against him personally," Rogers said. "I had to testify as I did. My remarks have been misconstrued. I admire Alagna. He is an able man."

If Rogers was worried how Alagna would react, the suspense did not last long. As if it had been timed, Alagna showed up moments later. He walked in, smiled at Rogers and stuck out his hand. The relief was evident on Rogers's round face. Soon, he had turned the whole thing into one big joke.

"I don't mind shaking hands," Rogers said, "But I refuse to kiss him. Kiss that homely mug? Never."

Alagna played along, noting that "when I pose with him, I look like a toothpick alongside a great big oak."

Both men swore they were never going back to sea again—"One big swim was enough," Alagna said.

If Alagna had misgivings about Rogers, he didn't let them show. He just looked up at his former boss and smiled for the cameras. The two men at least had something in common. The third radioman, Charles Maki, had just testified for Dickerson Hoover and told the Steamboat Inspectors that he had been the last person in the wireless room.

Alagna and Rogers at first tried to laugh off questions about Maki's claims. Rogers said, "What ship was he on? Certainly not ours. I never saw him again after I sent him up to see the captain. I'm sure he never came back."

Soon, Rogers's remarks would become more vicious. He said that Maki's hair color—yellow—suited him just fine.

* * *

The *Morro Castle* crewmen were becoming characters in a melodrama that played out across the United States. It was hard to avoid the hearings, even outside of New York. Dickerson Hoover's committee hearings were broadcast around the country, a serial that thousands tuned in to hear every day. Some of the crew and a few passengers got fan mail or hate letters from listeners. Hoover got dozens of telegraphs suggesting questions to ask, opinions on who was lying, who should be arrested, and who should be commended. Every day, the witnesses introduced new elements to the story. While few matched the intensity of George Rogers, Samuel Hoffman provided frightening details of Willmott's death and the final moments on the bridge. Looking every bit as dapper as a movie star, cruise director Bob Smith recounted the horror of watching passengers jump into the great ship's twin propellers. And Daniel Campbell, the beverage steward who first discovered the fire, was particularly eloquent, telling listeners that the entire ship "burned like celluloid."

"All hope was lost within five minutes," Campbell said.

After a week, the hearings became repetitious, not even enlivened by the testimony of Ralph Mestre, a passenger who claimed a bomb had started the fire, or Robert E. Carey, captain of the *President Cleveland,* who was criticized for doing nothing to help, of sailing past the ship and holding his lifeboats "as people died."

On Wednesday, September 19—the eighth day of testimony—the first person to testify was a striking young woman wearing a dark dress and fashionable hat. She was escorted into the room by a friend of the family, the mayor of Roselle Park, New Jersey. Doris Wacker, perhaps the first passenger to see the fire, had a story that would prove especially damning to the crew of the *Morro Castle.*

Doris looked confident that morning, but in fact she had had a rough week. She was reunited with her mother the day after the disaster and together they stayed at her grandparents' house. Lillian Wacker would not go back to her own home down the street without her husband, Herbert. The family worried that the shock and trauma of the accident and the loss of her husband had left Lillian with mental problems. She could not even attend her husband's funeral.

Doris had to grow up fast. She moved back to the house alone while other family members took in her younger brother. She had planned to attend college in Pennsylvania but now refused to leave her mother. While her grandparents urged her to enroll in a secretarial school in East Orange, Doris—still harboring dreams of those endless balls aboard the *Morro Castle*—had ideas of opening a dance studio.

In her testimony, Doris explained how she and Marjorie Budlong and Rosario Felipe had come to find themselves on the balcony as the Writing Room burned below them. She described a scene of panic, incompetence and poor decision making at a moment when the crew could have made a difference, when they still had a chance to stop the fire. In response to questions from the Steamboat Inspectors, Doris said that she did not notice anyone using hoses on the fire, nor did she see anyone try to close the fire doors between the Writing Room and the Lounge.

"They were throwing buckets on the fire," Doris said. "I asked the steward what to do. He raised his hand and told me to be quiet and not to awaken any passengers."

Later that day, George White Rogers put on a freshly pressed white uniform and new patent leather shoes, then rehearsed his lines as he waited to go onstage. He was not nervous, not one bit.

He had been hired by a promoter to do a week-long engagement at the Rialto theater at 42nd Street and Broadway in Times Square. This was the big time—Broadway—and Rogers felt he was finally getting his due. When he announced the deal in the *Bayonne Times*, it seemed that celebrity had already gone to his head. He smugly said that all the praise he'd received was nice, but accolades weren't putting food on his table.

"It's not acting, though," Rogers said. "All I have to do is appear on the stage and tell what happened."

He hinted that he was making big money for this limited engagement, which he was: $1,000 for the week (almost $15,000 in twenty-first-century money). He did not mention that the Ward Line had tried to stop the show and would not supply him a new uniform. The promoter supplied a generic ship officer's uniform that Rogers could squeeze into.

He would appear onstage before screenings of the motion picture *Million Dollar Ransom*, about a former bootlegger who emerges from prison in a world where booze is once again legal and falls into a fake kidnapping scheme to earn a few bucks. Rogers did not recognize any of the stars in the picture—Phillips Holmes, Edward Arnold, Mary Carlisle or Andy Devine—but he knew his name appeared bigger than any of those Hollywood people in the advertisements. They said:

In Person! All Shows! Radio Hero "Sparks" Rogers. Sensational,
Startling Inside Story of the Morro Castle Disaster.

It was only supposed to be for a week, but Rogers had hopes that his run might be extended. Didn't that sort of thing happen all the time with these Broadway shows? He felt like this was only the beginning, that he was destined for great things.

Certainly, the tragic end of the *Morro Castle* had helped no one else. In lower Manhattan, the hearings continued with the testimony becoming so confused and contradictory that it would likely never be sorted out. More than 130 people had died, the Ward Line would likely go bankrupt, and George Alagna might be charged with arson. But for George Rogers, things were looking up.

Apparently, his ship had just come in.

CHAPTER TWELVE

Breaking Point

Your name in full?"

"George I. Alagna."

"Speak up louder, please."

"George I. Alagna."

"Your place of residence?"

"Wallingford, Connecticut."

"Your name in *full*."

"George Ignatius Alagna."

"Mr. Alagna, will you talk just as distinctly as you can and loud enough so that we can all of us hear you," Dickerson Hoover said. "Take your time in answering and put yourself at ease. We simply want to get some information about this fire. Will you state what position you held on this steamer at the time of this fire?"

"I was first assistant radio officer. I joined the ship about four months ago as third assistant."

"A little bit louder."

"I remained third assistant until Mr. Rogers, who had been promoted . . ."

"Will you speak up just a little bit louder, we can't hear you."

"I am sorry, I don't ordinarily speak very loud."

"I know that you don't, but just try to speak just as distinctly as you can and then even if you don't speak louder, we will understand better," Hoover said.

George Alagna could not stop trembling. Through the dark wisp of hair that hung down over his forehead, he stared at the men and wondered if he was being set up. For more than a week before he testified on September 20, Alagna had suspected the Ward Line had some measure of influence over the Steamboat Inspectors' proceedings. He feared it was going to be an inquisition, and he might become the scapegoat for the entire disaster. He believed the inspectors had waited so long to call him because they were *preparing* for him. Hoover's next question only convinced Alagna that he had been right to worry.

"Have you ever had any trouble on that ship, any difficulty?" Hoover said. "The reason I ask you that question is because it certainly might be inferred from the testimony of Mr. Rogers. Had you ever had any difficulty on the ship?"

Alagna paused for a moment before he began. "Yes, I did have difficulty . . ."

For more than an hour, Alagna explained his many troubles aboard the *Morro Castle*—the working conditions, the unprofessional duties he performed, the strike, the fight with Freeman. Hoover interrupted frequently—Who signed the petition? Did you delay the vessel? But with every answer, every detailed description of what Alagna had seen and heard on the ship, the questions became less accusatory. Hoover slowly became much more interested in the unflattering portrait of the ship's top officers that Alagna painted.

By the time his testimony turned to the night of the fire, Alagna had found his voice, and his fears of being cast as the bad guy subsided. When the ninth day of the Department of Commerce hearings was over, all anyone would remember was Alagna's harsh depiction of William Warms and his officers on the night the *Morro Castle* was lost. His testimony rivaled George Rogers's for pure sensationalism. More than 100 people died, Alagna said, because the ship's top officers were incompetent, because William Warms was in a daze.

"The captain kept staring at the fire and muttering about dreaming or just saying 'It's out of our hands,'" he said.

Warms did not appear to understand the gravity of the situation, Alagna told the Steamboat Inspectors, and did not try to coordinate the movement of passengers when he had a chance to send them to the side of the ship that was not yet on fire. Most damning, Alagna said he went to the bridge six times—stumbling through smoke and fire all the while—before Warms ordered him to send an SOS.

"It seemed to me finally as if inspiration came to him and he asked if we could still send a message. I told him that was what I had been trying to tell him all along. Then he said, 'All right, send the SOS.'"

Alagna also managed to make Eben Abbott look even worse than the engineer himself had done. Alagna claimed Abbott was in tears on the bridge, running around in the smoke and screaming, "What are we going to do? What are we going to do?"

But Alagna saved most of his harshest criticism for Warms. He noted that the acting captain had dismissed the idea of taking Willmott's body when the crew abandoned the bridge. He claimed Warms told a tugboat captain that everything was "under control" when hundreds of people were still in the water. And finally, the Ward Line had tried to coerce his testimony and buy his silence, Alagna said, because he knew the truth: That more than 100 passengers died because of the crew's incompetence.

"I am sure if the dead captain were alive the fire would have been handled differently."

Alagna proved every bit as dangerous as the Ward Line had feared. He put the company on the defensive and squelched their attempts to avoid blame for the delayed SOS. But Alagna did not realize how much he had helped himself. Calm but not cocky, Alagna seemed more sensible, more educated, than many of the sailors grilled by the Steamboat Inspectors. And it did not go unnoticed. After the hearing, Dickerson Hoover made a statement to reporters that chilled Henry Cabaud's blood when it appeared the next day in the *New York Times.*

"He seems a very intelligent witness, and he gives a very plain picture of the captain being in a state of mental paralysis."

The big man walked onstage wearing white, carrying a portable microphone.

He set the stand down, took off his cap and bowed. There was no applause. George Rogers looked out at the crowd and, in what the papers later called a "stout and gruff" manner, began to speak.

"This is a job that is actually not to my liking," Rogers said, turning his hat in his hand. "You people have made a hero out of me, but it was just a job."

For thirty minutes he described the *Morro Castle* fire, in that time praising Alagna and accusing Charles Maki of being one of the men who ran. He did not engender warmth, and the applause for him at the end was merely polite, even after his selfless closing.

"I hope such a condition will grow out of this inquiry that ocean liners will be built safe and sound, so that people can spend their good money and go out and enjoy themselves without fear of being burned up."

Two days after he testified for the Steamboat Inspectors, Alagna visited George Rogers at the theater, his lawyer in tow. Alagna was irritated by the sign out front—"In Person! Radio Hero 'Sparks' Rogers!"—and the sight of Rogers backstage in his new uniform. It was an awkward meeting. On the surface, Rogers was kind to Alagna, talked incessantly of being glad to see him. Alagna found Rogers more boisterous than usual, even more of a braggart than he had been. Fame, it appeared, did not agree with him.

Whatever the reason for the visit, Alagna learned that Rogers was still in close contact with the Ward Line. Rogers said that Stanley Wright, the attorney who had threatened Alagna, had been asking questions about the acid that was purportedly found on the ship. Rogers claimed he had taken care of the problem, however.

"I told him this would be another attempt to make you the scapegoat, and I would not tolerate it," Rogers said. "'I stand behind George 100 percent.'"

Rogers said Wright had promised no one from the Ward Line would bring up the acid after he threatened to "reveal new things" about the incident. Alagna found the information useful mainly because it showed that Rogers was still talking to the Ward Line. He also had to wonder whether Rogers was helping him—or threatening him.

Just before Rogers's next show, Alagna left the theater. He was even less certain than before as to whom he could trust—certainly not the officials at the Ward Line and, increasingly, he felt the same way about George Rogers.

Moreover, Rogers was wrong. The Ward Line revealed the story of the acid bottles on Monday, September 24, when William Warms appeared before the Steamboat Inspectors for the second time. Warms had been recalled to answer lingering questions and provide a more detailed testimony of his actions. Mostly though, Warms used the occasion to talk about the trouble with Alagna.

Sounding very much like he had been coached by Ward Line attorneys, Warms refuted everything Alagna had said the week before, denied there was any panic among the crew. He claimed the SOS was delayed ten minutes, in fact, because of Alagna's incompetence. Warms even proclaimed that it had been he—and not Alagna—who tried to save Willmott's body. He found Alagna's contention particularly odd, Warms said, because the captain had been so frightened by the radioman.

"He had this friction with the man. He said (Alagna) was very resentful and could not be trusted and he would not trust him. He went so far that he locked up the direction finder, and that is the first time it has ever been locked up in four years, for he was fearful that he might do something to the direction finder at the time we needed it most, say in a fog or heavy rain."

The sinister allegations would not work this time—the Steamboat Inspectors were on to the Ward Line's tactics. Hoover said it was strange that Warms suddenly remembered all these horrible things after Alagna came forward and told a story extremely critical of the *Morro Castle*'s officers.

"Now, on your direct testimony, when the inquiry opened, I don't recall your making any reference to these fears the captain had of Alagna."

"I was not asked and I was in such a state of mind . . ."

"At the time, however, you were sworn not only to tell the truth, but the whole truth, were you not?" Hoover asked.

"Yes, sir."

"Did it occur to you that a thing such as you have now told was very important and that it ought at that time to have been told?"

"I realized it the second day, when I came to myself."

"Now, how did you come to tell it to us now?"

"I thought now would be my opportunity to let you gentlemen know what the friction really was and what fears my captain had against this man and for this man."

Hoover was annoyed and growing increasingly tired of these hearings. For every new detail, there were hours of redundant testimony. Hoover felt he had gathered all the facts the committee would get, and he didn't want to see the proceedings descend into name-calling and character assassination. This serial had run its course, with newspapers devoting less and less space to it every day. The longer it went on, the greater chance it would reflect poorly on the Department of Commerce. After interviewing Ward Line officials later that week, Hoover would declare the hearings closed. But before he dismissed William Warms that day, he asked one more question. He asked if Alagna had been right.

"Did the captain's death cause any panic among you?"

"Not among my men or the whole crew," Warms said.

Just as Dickerson Hoover's inquiry came to an end, the other investigations into the *Morro Castle* disaster stalled. The Bureau of Investigation had turned up no evidence of a Communist conspiracy; Conboy had found no proof of a plot by or against the Ward Line. And in recent days, the *Morro Castle* had been overshadowed in the newspapers by an arrest in the Lindbergh baby kidnapping. Bruno Richard Hauptmann swore he was innocent, but New Jersey was about to become the focus of a second, even more disturbing, press frenzy. A month after the fire, the *Morro Castle* was old news.

Nothing new or sensational came along to keep the disaster anchored to the front pages. The toxicology tests on the supposed ashes of Captain Robert Willmott had found no traces of poison. Even though the findings meant little—some poisons would not show up in burned remains and no one had verified that the body was even Willmott's—it didn't matter. Only the hint of murder could have kept the story alive.

Still, Martin Conboy released the findings to the press almost as soon as he got them, much to the consternation of J. Edgar Hoover. The U.S. attorney was asserting his authority in the case because he felt it had been threatened. In recent weeks, Conboy had complained to the Justice Department that the Bureau of Investigation duplicated all his work and told him nothing. Relations between the U.S. Attorney's Office and the Bureau had devolved to outright surliness.

One afternoon, Conboy called Francis Xavier Fay to his office to discuss this problem, only to find it was worse than he thought. Conboy said he was tired of subpoenaing witnesses, interviewing them and then watching Bureau agents escort them out of the building and question them again. He suggested that perhaps the Bureau should back off, but

Fay suggested the U.S. attorney might be the one taken off the investigation.

"I take exception to the fact that the Assistant United States Attorneys are going out and actually conducting investigations," Fay said. "If you want it investigated properly, we will of course be very glad to do it, but it's necessary for us to do it in our own manner. This is our policy, the policy throughout the country. I don't see any reason to make an exception in New York. I can't remember a case in which the District Attorney conducted his own investigation."

Conboy complained to the Justice Department about the conversation, but J. Edgar Hoover jumped to Fay's defense. Hoover told Justice there was no friction between Conboy and the Bureau, but there was a need for a clear policy. Then Hoover called his agent. He told Fay to either take all his men off the case, or take it over completely. Internal politics threatened to shut down the *Morro Castle* investigation.

Fay was not ready to give up because his investigation was just gearing up, and going in a different direction. A reporter had called with an interesting tip, a tidbit that led Fay on a chase across New York City. He had spoken with a half-dozen people who related a chapter of George Rogers's life that had not appeared in any of the glowing newspaper stories about the radioman. When Fay finished chasing down this story, he had a string of circumstantial evidence that made him believe the hero of the *Morro Castle* was nothing of the sort.

A man named William Egart claimed that he met George Rogers in 1929, when Egart owned and operated a retail radio shop on Manhattan's Greenwich Street. Rogers would come into the shop often, always with another unbelievable story about his radio work. Despite his bravado, Egart could tell that Rogers was not just talking, that he had "unusual ability" as an electrician and radio operator. Egart eventually hired Rogers.

Rogers did not stay employed long, Fay learned. Not only did he have "unusual" ability, Egart thought Rogers was just plain unusual. Things kept disappearing from the store, and Rogers could not get along with Sam, Egart's son. After the business burned in September of 1929, Egart told Rogers he didn't need him anymore.

At the time of the fire, only Sam and George Rogers had keys to the shop. But another tenant in the building, Mrs. Patrick Pierce, had been working the newsstand on the corner that morning, and she swore the shop's door was standing wide open just before the fire began. No one was ever charged, but Egart secretly suspected the fire was set to cover up the theft of his equipment.

Rogers next went to work for Lucien A. Dussol, who owned another electronics store in the city. Dussol also told Fay that Rogers was a "gifted" electrician, but he too suspected something was wrong with him. Things went missing almost from Rogers's first day on the job and once, while Dussol was out of town, Rogers called to say there'd been a break-in at the store. Some equipment was missing, and he'd called the police. Ultimately, the police told Dussol the theft looked like an inside job, a suspicion that was confirmed when they found one of the stolen oscillators at William Egart's new store. Egart said he'd bought the oscillator from George Rogers.

Rogers broke down immediately under questioning. He cried, pleaded for leniency, and told the police he had feared Dussol would not pay him what he was worth, so he wanted to "get his." Recounting the incident for Fay, Dussol said that Rogers could "elaborate on any incident to an extent far beyond any sense of adherence to facts."

Despite Rogers's confession, Dussol chose not to press charges. He felt Rogers might come after him if he did.

"He's mentally unbalanced."

F. X. Fay took all this down in his notebook, feeling the chill down his spine that told him he was on to something. Just because somebody was a thief did not mean they were an arsonist or a murderer, but William Egart and Lucien Dussol were describing an unstable man—a dangerous man. And they both swore the George Rogers they knew was the same one that had been in the papers. The one everybody now called a hero.

Fay reported his findings to Washington but said nothing about it to his usual sources. He would not tell the *Daily News* reporter, or even Winchell. He certainly wouldn't give this report to Martin Conboy. Quietly, Fay began to make other inquiries about George Rogers, and he asked agents in other cities to start background checks. None of this meant anything, he knew, but there was one word in his notes he could not forget. It was what had happened to Egart's shop near Greenwich Village. Fay looked back at his notes, at the word that bothered him: *fire.*

* * *

Tom Torresson had to report to the U.S. Attorney's Office once a week to get his subpoena card punched—proof that he had not taken off, that he was within reach of the prosecutor. It was an annoyance, but Tom figured there were two good things about it. The courthouse was only a couple of blocks from the Murray Street factory where James McDonald had given him a job, so Tom could walk there on his lunch break. And better still, they paid him $1.50 every time he showed up. But the three times he was actually interrogated by attorneys in Conboy's office, he earned that money and more.

Torresson was never interviewed in a courtroom, never put on the witness stand. But on several occasions, attorneys asked him about Dr. De Witt Van Zile's death report for Willmott. The doctor had been found dead in the water, and Torresson—who had typed Van Zile's report that night—was as close to that diagnosis as anyone could get. Torresson felt they were just looking for somebody to charge with a crime, and on a couple of occasions believed they were attempting to bully him. Once, when he told one of Conboy's young assistants about fighting the fire with one of the shipboard hoses, the lawyer accused Torresson of making up the story.

"You're a liar, there's no fire station there," the attorney said, pointing to a diagram of the ship.

Tom stared at him for a moment, reached down and grabbed the right diagram.

"There's the fire hose, that's the right location," Tom said.

The attorney had been looking at the wrong blueprints, but simply moved on to another line of questioning without bothering to apologize. Torresson thought, *These guys are just out to hang somebody.*

Because he was under subpoena, Tom could not go off to college, and he felt like his life was never going to begin. The accident haunted him. Every day, he went to work at the Goodall Rubber Company, but it seemed everything reminded him of the disaster. The rubber company mostly made firefighting equipment.

Doris Wacker delayed her plans for college as well. Months after the disaster, her mother still had not recovered from the shock, and Doris wanted to stay nearby for her. Eventually, Doris opened the dance studio she had dreamed about. Her notoriety as one of the witnesses in the *Morro Castle* investigation lured customers, sometimes as many as 100 students in a week. Like Torresson, her new job ensured that she would never forget about the *Morro Castle*—she was dancing, just as she had on the ship. She tried to remember the good times, and not the night the dancing stopped.

Few people who had been on the *Morro Castle* could escape the memory of that cruise. Neither Doris Wacker nor Tom Torresson would become active in the survivors organizations, but many others would. Some of the liner's final passengers would band together to file lawsuits against the Ward Line and lobby for Senate hearings into the disaster. They would be successful on both fronts. But the survivors were turned back in their attempts to secure a separate grand jury indictment for Ward Line lawyers who meddled in the Steamboat Inspectors hearings.

George Alagna and the man who briefly went on strike with him, Morton Borow, also sued the Ward Line. They wanted $50,000 each from their former employer because they couldn't get work after the Ward Line made what they called "unjustified" complaints against them to the Federal Radio Commission.

For the Ward Line, the trouble was just beginning.

On October 26, 1934, the Department of Commerce's Bureau of Navigation and Steamboat Inspection released its report on the *Morro Castle* fire. Dickerson Hoover said "laxness" on the part of the crew led to the ship's complete destruction. Had the fire been discovered earlier, he wrote, perhaps it could have been stopped. Hoover's committee commented on several possible causes of the fire—electrical shorts, spontaneous combustion in the cargo spaces, carelessness of passengers, and the idea that the blaze was set in the Writing Room locker—but refused to take a position. As for arson, the report said that "nothing definite was revealed."

Playing it safe, Hoover put the burden of investigating arson on Conboy, writing that the Steamboat Inspectors would only examine matters "pertaining to our responsibilities." But he noted that if an arsonist was responsible, it made little sense. The firebug would have been jeopardizing his life as well as the lives of the other 547 people on board the ship. In other words, if there was an arsonist on the *Morro Castle,* he would have to be a psychopath.

The newspapers called the report a "whitewash" and accused Hoover of skirting the serious questions of the Ward Line's culpability and the cause of the tragedy. Hoover said criminal investigations were not his job, although he privately had his own suspicions, suspicions that would remain secret for more than seventy years.

The cause of fire would barely come up in the U.S. Coast Guard license revocation hearings that began in November. A panel of judges was called in to hear evidence on whether five officers of the *Morro Castle* should lose their licenses due to negligence on the job: Eben Abbott, Clarence Hackney, Howard Hansen, Anthony Bujia and William Warms.

Warms appeared in the court wearing a black armband, a symbol of mourning for his mother, who had passed away recently. Flanked by Ward Line attorneys Chauncey J. Clark and Eugene Underwood, Warms spoke firmly and with authority, a much sterner and imposing figure than he had been in September. Warms and his attorneys made it clear where they thought the blame for the disaster belonged. They said the radiomen delayed sending the SOS for seven minutes after Warms had given the order. The issue was brought up during the first day of testimony, with George Rogers on the stand. Clark claimed that precious minutes were lost between the time the order was given and the distress call was sent.

"How do you account for that?"

"Alagna told me he got lost on his way back from the bridge to the radio room," Rogers said. "He told me that at first he was unable to make his way through the smoke and went to the deck below to try to come up a passageway to bring me the message. He was driven back and then returned to the upper deck and tried to climb over the roof of the radio shack, but found he couldn't do that. The wind shifted and he found the passageway, but that time he overshot the shack and had to make his way back."

Clark asked it a different way: Wasn't the passageway between the wireless room and the bridge wide enough for two people and weren't the two rooms less than 60 feet apart? Rogers admitted that they were.

George Rogers had claimed he would defend Alagna against any attempts by the Ward Line to blame him for the disaster. But now, for the second time, Rogers had delivered testimony that made Alagna seem a bumbling incompetent at best, and possibly even a saboteur. Many people, Alagna included, found it hard to believe this was coincidental.

The hearings would last throughout November, as one witness after another paraded into the courtroom to defend Warms and try to repair Abbott's reputation. The witnesses said Abbott did not panic, Warms was not in a daze. They refuted every claim George Alagna made, yet the court did not call him. Although mentioned by nearly every witness, the court refused to subpoena Alagna, even when one New York newspaper editorialized to that effect with the simple headline: "Call Alagna."

Alagna did everything he could to make sure his side of the story was heard. He wrote a letter about Rogers's conduct to Dickerson Hoover, a cry for help to the one man who had believed him. With the Ward Line's new effort to blame the deaths of the passengers on him, he felt as if everyone had turned against him. If he was subpoenaed for the license revocation hearing, Alagna decided, he would refuse to testify. Only one person, Alagna thought, could help. On November 8, he sent a telegram to President Roosevelt:

> MORRO CASTLE INVESTIGATION COMPLETELY CORRUPTED BY WARD
> LINE INFLUENCE AND CONSPIRACIES STOP REALIZING THAT THE VIC-
> TIMS OF THIS CATASTROPHE WILL HAVE DIED IN VAIN UNLESS THE
> COURSE OF THIS INVESTIGATION IS CHANGED I URGE YOU TO PERSON-
> ALLY ASSUME SUPERVISION STOP SHOULD YOU FEEL THAT THE OFFI-
> CIALS NOW IN CHARGE ARE SUFFICIENTLY CAPABLE OF EFFECTIVELY
> HANDLING THIS AFFAIR I WILL PROTEST BY REFUSING TO TESTIFY BE-
> FORE THE FEDERAL BOARD AND SHOULD I BE PLACED UNDER ARREST
> WILL COMMENCE A HUNGER STRIKE THAT SHALL NOT TERMINATE
> UNTIL YOU INTERCEDE GEORGE I. ALAGNA FORMER 1ST ASST RADIO
> OPERATOR TEL MORRO CASTLE

Apparently, FDR never replied.

The Coast Guard hearing ended without resolution, and without calling Alagna, in late November. The Ward Line had hoped the hearings would salvage its reputation, but things were only going to get much worse. On November 30, a grand jury indicted Warms, Abbott and Ward Line vice president Henry Cabaud, the man who had ultimate control over the *Morro Castle.* The charges included "misconduct, negligence and inattention to duty." It was the first time the government had taken criminal action against merchant marine officers for negligence since the *General Slocum* burned in 1904. When William Warms was taken into custody, he was heard muttering much the way George Alagna had described him on the night the *Morro Castle* burned.

He kept saying, "What's it all about?"

The publicity only got worse for the Ward Line. At Warms and Abbott's arraignment, Assistant U.S. Attorney Francis W. H. Adams humiliated the men, shouting and pointing at them as he charged them with ruining the lives of hundreds of people.

"These men are accused of a crime of the most nefarious character— conduct which caused the loss of life of upward of one hundred passengers, and as a result of this misconduct, negligence and inattention to duties the lives of upward of fifty persons were destroyed."

They faced ten-year prison terms and $10,000 fines each if convicted, and Martin Conboy noted with thinly concealed glee that the Ward Line could be fined $300,000. All three men pleaded not guilty, though Cabaud would not appear in court until after Ward Line attorneys negotiated his surrender. Each was released on $2,500 bail. Photographers caught Cabaud standing before the judge, his head bowed—either to avoid the cameras or in shame.

Over the next week, the Ward Line took a public beating. Conboy revealed that the Line had collected $3 million in insurance for the accident after poor-mouthing itself to the families of victims. The *New York Post* reported the company actually made a $263,000 profit on the disaster because the *Morro Castle* was insured for more than she was worth. Then the Navy scrapped plans to salvage the ship for a troop transport, but there was no way for the Ward Line to refurbish it, either. The charred hull had cracked under pressure from an incessant pounding by the tides and the wind.

If that weren't enough, newspapers reported that the Ward Line had overcharged the government on its mail contracts by $500,000 in the four years the *Morro Castle* sailed. If the company was found guilty of negligence, Post Office officials announced, the Ward Line would lose its contract to carry the mail between New York and Havana. The fate of the entire shipping line rode on the outcome of the trial.

The winter brought even worse news. In January, the SS *Mohawk*—a Clyde Line steamship the Ward Line had leased to take the place of the *Morro Castle*—collided with a freighter 4 miles off the coast of Sea Girt, in almost the exact spot where the *Morro Castle* had burned. All 163 people on board were rescued, but the company's reputation was beyond saving. Coupled with the loss of the *Havana* to shoals along the Florida coast, it was the third ship the Ward Line had seen wrecked in five months. The company that four years earlier boasted it had never lost a passenger had now lost more than 100, and stranded hundreds of others in the Atlantic Ocean.

To add insult, in February the federal government revoked William Warms's license and ordered the *Oriente,* the *Morro Castle*'s sister ship, into dry dock after reports that the ship had a leak. Congress announced it would investigate the *Morro Castle* and *Mohawk* disasters. It appeared the Ward Line's long cruise was almost over.

Francis Xavier Fay was growing bored with the Bureau of Investigation's *Morro Castle* investigation. Washington had insisted he follow leads that he knew would take him nowhere. He spent months studying the chemical composition of cleaning solutions used on the ship after crew members blamed the toxic, homemade—and potentially illegal—substances of fueling the fire. There was no proof they had been anything more than accidental accelerants. Then, because someone found an unidentified piece of brass tubing near the ship's engine room, Fay spent a month only to conclude that the pipe was not part of a bomb.

Nothing the Bureau did turned up a lead, even the background checks on Alagna. He had been a malcontent on other ships, but never did anything more than whine and wear out his welcome wherever he went. Alagna had no criminal record. Fay continued to believe they were looking at the wrong radioman.

In the early hours of March 14, 1935, Asbury Park lost its most popular tourist attraction. After four months, the winter tides and the Merritt-Chapman tugboats *Willet* and *Resolute* had dislodged the *Morro Castle* from the sand. It was a 2 A.M. departure that most Asbury Park residents and merchants missed, but few were sorry it was gone. In six months, the great salvation of the Midway had overstayed its welcome.

The ship remained a popular attraction throughout the fall and winter, despite the rotting smell of animal hides in its hold. Two weeks earlier, on March 4, a sunny day brought unseasonable 46-degree temperatures and so many people to the boardwalk that the paper noted, "Every available foot of space was taken." Although merchants conceded the *Morro Castle* had pulled their year out of the red, it had become a nuisance. The city was forced to pour lime on the hides to drown the stench, and the courts were jammed with people who, in one way or another, got into trouble because of the *Morro Castle*: two boys were arrested after swimming out and trying to board the vessel; a man was fined for selling photographs of the ship without a license.

The economic boom transcended mere tourism, as the Ward Line had housed a half-dozen or more employees in the city at any time, and the Merritt-Chapman workers filled oceanfront hotels that normally would have been empty through the fall. Their work on the ship became an attraction in itself, people watching from the Convention Hall's promenade for hours at a time. The homesick workers caused their own bit of controversy when they put a Christmas tree on the ship's bow. Some thought it an inappropriate display of good cheer at the site of so many deaths.

Perhaps that show of festivity was meant to ward off the ship's curse, because some superstitious workers believed the *Morro Castle* was jinxed. In November, Captain Harry Cole was killed when he fell through an open hatch on board. The next week, a boat filled with workers flipped on its way to the ship. They said later it was only luck that kept their names off the *Morro Castle*'s growing list of victims.

On March 7, 1935, six months after she had beached herself in Asbury Park, the ship moved nearly 60 feet. Merritt-Chapman tugs worked primarily during the flood tide to take advantage of the ocean's power to lift and move the hull, and that evening the *Morro Castle* rocked like a ship at sea for the first time since the night it was lost.

For the next week, the *Asbury Park Evening Press* noted the workers' progress every day. On March 9, the cables that supplied power to workers on the ship were disconnected in anticipation it would break free of the sand. The bow was 260 feet from Convention Hall, three times the distance it had been just two weeks earlier. The stern now floated at high tide, and the ship no longer lay broadside along the beach; it pointed bow-on at the Berkeley-Carteret.

Calm seas held the ship in place until the early hours of March 14, when the *Willet* and the *Resolute* broke the beach's hold. In an impressive display of the tugs' strength, they dragged the hull through 300 feet of sand and clay to reach deep water. What few people gathered to watch it leave could only see the faint outline of the *Morro Castle* disappear into the night like a ghost.

By noon the next day, the ship was at Gravesend Bay, Brooklyn, where ownership of the hulk reverted to the government. Two days later, the Navy put it up for sale. A week later, the Union Shipbuilding Company of Baltimore bought what was left of the Ward Line's once luxurious flagship for $33,605. The *Morro Castle* would sail out of New York Harbor one more time, when she was taken to Baltimore to be scrapped.

The *Morro Castle*'s arrival in New York dredged up painful memories for George Alagna. Already, it had been a bad month. His lawsuit against the Ward Line was thrown out of court, he had no prospects for a job, and he was forced to share an apartment in Queens with two friends just to survive. And many people still considered him a suspect in the death of Captain Willmott and the loss of the cruise ship.

He could not read the newspaper without getting upset. One day, he saw a notice that George Rogers had been given another award. During the Veteran Wireless Operators Association dinner at the Hotel Montclair, Bayonne mayor L. F. Donohoe presented Rogers with a gold medal from the city commission.

On Wednesday, March 27, Alagna dropped by the offices of the American Radio Telegraphists Association hoping to hear of a job opening. Willard Cliff, secretary and treasurer of the organization, gave him a strange, anonymous message found in the association's mail. The note contained only two sentences: *"Suggest Alagna leave town for his own good. He knows why."*

Alagna tried to shrug it off. He looked at Cliff and nonchalantly said, "I wonder who could have sent that." But it was clear that Alagna was scared. Cliff felt sorry for him, and later said, "That boy got a terrible deal."

Two days later, on March 29, George Alagna sat down at the kitchen table in his Jackson Heights apartment, closed all the doors and windows, and turned on the gas stove. As he sat inhaling the fumes, he wrote a long, rambling letter that jumped from one subject to the next but was mostly about the *Morro Castle*. In the note, he asked one of his roommates, Ernest Wilmshurst, to give his love to his girlfriend and his bankroll to survivors of the *Morro Castle* disaster. He apologized more than once. But he was also fed up. People blamed him for the disaster, he could not find work, and he suspected the Ward Line had blacklisted him. He felt there was no alternative.

"This is the easiest way out and comfort my folks as this is the best way out," he wrote. "Thank Conboy for handcuffing me. Do not think me cowardly."

As Alagna grew more light-headed, the note made less sense. The last rambling lines said, "I smell the gas now. I'm getting a dry taste in my mouth. I am getter weaker."

John Hamrath, the building superintendent, smelled the gas from downstairs and went to investigate. When no one answered his knock, he used his passkey to open the door. There, he found George Alagna lying on the floor, passed out and barely breathing. Hamrath ran to the windows, threw them open, turned off the stove and called for help.

Alagna was taken to Bellevue Hospital, where inhalators and doctors revived him. Soon, he was up and around and not very happy that he had been saved. As usual, he was making everyone around him miserable. When newspaper photographers tried to sneak into his hospital room, he screamed, "You reporters make me sick!"

While he was at Bellevue, Alagna wrote to New York mayor Fiorello La Guardia that the doctors were trying to get him to talk about personal issues, and he asked the mayor to make them stop.

Francis Xavier Fay followed the sad fate of George Alagna from a distance. While some saw his suicide attempt as an admission of guilt, Fay recognized Alagna as a man who had simply reached the limits of endurance, the end of his rope. What most interested Fay was Alagna's unfinished suicide note.

In the letter, he addressed one specific request to Hoyt S. Haddock, president of the Telegraphists Association. George Alagna had asked Haddock that, whatever else he might do, to please "expose George W. Rogers."

PART IV

CHAPTER THIRTEEN

A Short Fuse

By January of 1936, the world's attention had moved on to other news. The Depression continued to plague the nation, and now the headlines were filled with talk of war in Europe, Bruno Hauptmann's death sentence for kidnapping the Lindbergh baby, and FDR's plans for a new program called Social Security. Even the first anniversary of the cruise ship disaster was overshadowed by the shooting of Louisiana senator Huey Long on September 8, 1935.

But the trial of the *Morro Castle* officers was still front-page news in New York.

Editors could not resist the lambasting Francis W. H. Adams gave the Ward Line in the courtroom on a daily basis. Adams proved more theatrical, more vengeful, than his old boss Martin Conboy, who had stepped down as U.S. attorney. Adams ridiculed William Warms as incompetent and Eben Abbott as a coward who ripped the insignias off his uniforms to hide his identity. He said the Ward Line overworked and underpaid its men, and failed to train its crews to handle emergencies. This dereliction of duty, he said, had cost at least 134 lives.

Life on the *Morro Castle* was a "taxing grind all the way through," Adams claimed. "The men were so tired that they actually hid rather than to participate in the few and halfhearted fire and lifeboat drills that were held."

For weeks, survivors told sad tales of the ship burning around them while they received no direction, had no idea whether they would be rescued. They described how their sons, daughters, husbands and wives drowned as an apathetic crew passed them in lifeboats. It was a portrait of lives lost needlessly through callousness.

The *Morro Castle* officers offered a pitiful defense. Warms, looking even more worn than he had during the Department of Commerce hearings, said simply, "I did all I could." Abbott weakly answered "I can't remember" to many questions. The Ward Line attorneys flailed aimlessly for a defense, alternately blaming Communists, arsonists and, finally—as Dickerson Hoover's report had speculated—an act of God. Henry Cabaud said nearly all decisions regarding the *Morro Castle* had been left to Captain Robert Willmott. The Ward Line and its officers had sunk to their lowest point: they blamed the dead man.

On January 23, 1936, a federal jury convicted William Warms, Eben Abbott and Henry Cabaud on charges of negligence in the *Morro Castle* fire. After more than two months of contentious, contradictory testimony, it took jurors less than a day to return the verdict. Judge Murray Hulbert needed no more time to make up his mind than the jury had. The next day, he said that the "essence of the case was the failure of the steamship company to provide life preservers that preserved anything." Hulbert sentenced Warms to two years in prison, Abbott to four. Cabaud got a year, but the sentence was suspended upon his payment of a $5,000 fine. All three appealed and were out on bail the same day.

The prosecutors, editorial writers and *Morro Castle* survivors declared that justice had been served, but they overlooked one detail highlighted by the trial: the cause of the fire remained a mystery. No one had even attempted to speculate on the spark that led to this madness. But, increasingly, fewer people cared.

Those who had been closest to the case a year earlier largely ignored the convictions. Many of them had vastly different lives now. Conboy had stepped down as U.S. attorney, and although Dickerson Hoover was still with the Commerce Department, he said nothing publicly of the verdict. Bob Tolman had taken over as chief purser on the *Morro Castle* sister ship, *Oriente,* and Bob Smith was with another steamship line. Thomas Torresson, Jr., was enrolled at Notre Dame, and George Alagna—released from Bellevue after weeks of therapy—still harbored feelings of injustice. In September 1935, he had joined a strike against the Grace Line, standing on the New York docks holding a sign that read, "Remember the *Dixie, Morro Castle, Mohawk* and *Titanic.*"

Francis Xavier Fay had moved on as well. Months before the verdict, the Bureau of Investigation's New York special agent in charge had accepted a job as head of security for Macy's department store. He had not lost interest in the *Morro Castle,* however, and most likely read the accounts of the negligence trial closely. What he had to notice most was the name conspicuously absent from the list of the convicted.

In his final months with the Bureau, Fay had spent as much time on the *Morro Castle* case as he had the Lindbergh kidnapping. When he left, he turned over all his files and notes on the case, his reports on the leads he had chased. He just assumed the Bureau would finish the case he felt he had come so close to cracking. Fay believed he had found the culprit, and that man had not stood trial with Warms, Abbott and Cabaud.

Throughout the fall of 1934 and the spring of 1935—while Fay had been forced to waste his time examining singed brass and studying the flammability of cleaning solutions—he had agents around the country checking into the background of the man he considered the most likely suspect in the *Morro Castle* case: George White Rogers.

The radioman had proven a much more complicated and troubled man than even Fay had suspected. The theft of a few radios was child's play compared to the trail of suspicion, misery and criminal activity in Rogers's wake. Using information compiled by agents in New York and San Francisco, Fay built a circumstantial, yet damning, report on Rogers that he submitted to the Bureau in the months before he resigned. He had not proved Rogers set the fire, but he showed the man was more than capable. These reports never reached the public and, for a while, even Bureau officials ignored them.

According to Fay, George White Rogers was born in New York City in June of 1896 or 1901—Rogers changed the year to suit his needs, but it seemed most likely that 1901 was the true date. His parents died when he was young, and he was sent to live with his grandmother in Oakland. In 1913, Mary J. Rogers enrolled George in Durant Elementary School, listing his birthday as June 9, 1901. The school placed him in the fourth grade but by the middle of the year promoted him to the fifth. He was a bright student, but his behavior was so poor that two decades later Durant principal E. W. Kottinger still remembered him. Before the end of that year, Kottinger told agents, Rogers was kicked out of the school for discipline problems—he couldn't remember the details—and sent to a reform school more than 100 miles away in Ione, California. Some said Rogers had been expelled for repeated thefts.

Rogers moved from one school to the next over the following year, prompted sometimes by his grandmother and other times by the courts. At the Good Templars' Home in Vallejo—on the north shore of San Pablo Bay—school officials asked the state juvenile court to intervene. The principal there called Rogers "an irresponsible thief, liar and moral pervert." At his next stop, the Boys and Girls Aid Society, Rogers would not do his schoolwork unless a teacher or supervisor watched him. What work he did showed signs of above-average intelligence, but he wanted little to do with serious study. He was eventually expelled, before he turned fifteen, when staff caught him in the act of sodomizing a younger—and, they noted, much smaller—boy.

Left without options in California public schools, Rogers enrolled in a college course on radios (after amending his birth date to 1896). When he completed the course, showing an unusually high aptitude for the work, he took work on the SS *Costa Rica.* Records indicated Rogers got his job by presenting a first-class radio operator's license, but Bureau agents found no evidence of anyone issuing him such a document. The résumé he provided when applying for the job on the *Costa Rica* included the names of Bay Area businesses that no longer existed and schools that never had.

In 1919, Rogers moved back to the New York area, settling in New Jersey. That September he joined the United States Navy—more than a year after Germany sank the USS *President Lincoln,* which Rogers later told the Ward Line he'd served aboard. On his Navy enlistment papers, Rogers claimed to be twenty-three years old, with six years of experience working for various radio companies. He was rated an electrician, third-class, but the navy had no time to find out how proficient at radio work he was. Four months into a three-year tour of duty, Rogers was discharged.

Rogers had been sent to Newport, Rhode Island, for training. Less than a month after he arrived, he reported to the base infirmary with the flu and stayed for seventeen days. Three weeks after returning to duty, Rogers was back in the infirmary, this time claiming he had burned his right eye when a battery exploded and doused him with sulfuric acid. Bureau agents in Rhode Island interviewed the base doctor, who was dubious. If Rogers had gotten acid in his eye, he would have lost it. Nevertheless, he had stayed in the hospital from December 8 until he was discharged on

January 24, 1920. He was in the navy for four months, and more than half that time he'd spent in a hospital bed. He was discharged, but denied disability. F. X. Fay, a military veteran and radio buff, could read between the lines. The navy had just wanted rid of him.

In the nine years leading up to his trouble at William Egart's electronics store, Rogers couldn't hold on to a job. His name appeared on the roster of a number of ships sailing out of New York, but most companies said once they hired him, he didn't show up for work. He took jobs in a number of electronics shops, and Fay interviewed some people who remembered him fondly—there was no doubt Rogers had a talent for radio work bordering on genius. Most everyone, however, could recall at least one strange occurrence: He often got into spats with coworkers and could be disagreeable. He was fired from one company after being accused of stealing from a customer's home.

Even if Rogers was a troublemaker, Fay knew that didn't particularly make him a killer. The Bureau had no evidence linking Rogers to the fire—except, perhaps, for a series of threatening letters sent to the Ward Line headquarters in the summer of 1934. The letters were unremarkable save for the fact they had arrived on company stationery and had been composed, almost certainly, on the typewriter in the *Morro Castle*'s radio room. Fay knew his kind well. Rogers was smart, but he made mistakes. He would crack under questioning. But no one had bothered to ask the right questions.

When the former Bureau man read about the conviction of the *Morro Castle* officers, he most likely wondered why Rogers had not been questioned, why had no one looked at him more closely? Fay had been an agent for more than a dozen years, and he knew when something wasn't quite right. The trouble at William Egart's electronics store fit a pattern. When Rogers was cornered and confronted with his crime, Egart's store had conveniently caught fire. The evidence had been destroyed and there was no case—much the same as had happened with the *Morro Castle*. It was coincidental, perhaps nothing more. But Fay had a feeling. Still, he said nothing—he was no longer a Bureau man and it wasn't his place to meddle in J. Edgar Hoover's business. But as he read the papers on January 24, 1936, Fay probably could not have helped but wonder: where is Rogers?

* * *

George Rogers was going broke.

He had spent most of 1935 at his new radio shop tinkering with electric gadgets and waiting for customers who never arrived. Rogers had taken the money he made in his two weeks on Broadway and invested it in a new business in Bayonne. The Radio Service Laboratory was not so different from the last shop, the one that had failed, but Rogers hoped his fortunes had changed. His new store was at 796 Broadway, and he believed it was a good sign that he was going from one Broadway to another.

But Rogers soon learned that celebrity is transitory, and his hero status did not generate business. People stopped in to talk often at first, and the mayor had even given him another medal, but none of it translated into profit. There was a lot of competition in the radio business, and despite his advertisements in the *Bayonne Times* that his store was the "best equipped in the county," Rogers made no money. He did not take it well, and felt another of his bad spells coming on. He languished in self-pity every time an old-timer said to him, "If only I was in your boots, I'd have made a million dollars."

Now the briefly famous radioman sat around reading dime-store science fiction and El Haren's column in the *Bayonne Times.* The "internationally known" astrologer provided answers to life's toughest problems and was popular in the Bayonne area, but Rogers didn't feel that this wizard could help him. He needed something more.

In September 1935, a reporter from the *Times* had come around to interview him for a *Morro Castle* anniversary story. Rogers bragged that he refused to profit from the disaster and would not put the ship's name in his advertisements (although he reserved the largest font in the ad for his own name). He claimed several offers to go to sea and travel abroad, but said he preferred to stay in Bayonne. Rogers said he was still tending to his fragile bride, who had just lost her mother the previous December. The old woman had lived with them on Avenue E, and died shortly after a trip to Asbury Park to see the shipwreck. Rogers told friends his poor mother-in-law expired from shock, that she was yet another victim of the *Morro Castle.* Now he claimed his wife would not let him go back to sea to earn his living. In truth, he didn't care what she said, but it sounded good for the papers.

The reporter asked Rogers the requisite questions about the wreck, the guilt of the other officers, but the radioman refused to criticize anyone. "No man in the world knows how he would act under similar circumstances. Let sleeping dogs lie." In that spirit, Rogers said, he would not attend the upcoming meeting of the *Morro Castle* Survivors' Association.

"I've been through a disaster, so why should I want to be reminded of it?"

Why would he want to see those people, the dead look in their eyes, the hollow, vacant stares of great loss? It was out of character, for surely he would have enjoyed the attention. It was one of the rare times in his life that Rogers chose to avoid the spotlight. If there were other reasons he did not attend, he never mentioned them.

Nothing had worked out the way Rogers hoped. He had been famous for a brief time, but now he struggled to pay his bills. The only publicity he received was for a stupid shipwreck anniversary story. And when that was published, Rogers was furious with the headline over a picture of him grinning like an idiot. It read: "Didn't Get a Million."

Bayonne, New Jersey, sits across the Hudson from New York City in the shadow of the Statue of Liberty. In the 1930s, it was a busy little town with a Navy base, a large port and an impressive new bridge across the Kill van Kull to Staten Island. It might have looked like any number of towns orbiting New York, but locals—especially those in the town's active high society—took pride in its uniqueness. There was not another town in the country named Bayonne, they liked to say.

Of all things, the town may have been best known at the time for radios. In June 1933, the city had become the first in America to put two-way radios in its police cars. It was a fact the city promoted shamelessly, conveniently omitting the political controversy it had generated initially. The system dramatically accelerated emergency response times, and police departments around the country enviously copied it. This advance in public safety was a great source of pride in Bayonne. Rogers could barely turn a corner without seeing the advertisements:

If you see a crime—
If danger threatens—
If suspicious—phone the police!
Bayonne RADIO police will bring help in a hurry.

The man who built this revolutionary system was a local radio engineer named Vincent J. Doyle. He had been hired by former police commissioner Jerome Brady before he turned thirty—a story famous in Bayonne. The two met by chance at a shoeshine stand when Doyle was an engineer for the New York radio station WOR. Talking shop with the young radioman, Brady lamented that the city could not afford the one-way systems many departments had installed in their cars. Doyle told him about new experiments with high-frequency signals to communicate with airplanes and suggested it might work for patrol cars. An idea was born.

Doyle built nine portable transmitters for squad cars, while engineers erected a 71-foot tower atop the police station. Most folks derisively called the system "Brady's toy" until the department dispatched its first officers via radio and saved a life. The cops had been parked in their Dodge cruiser at Avenue E and 34th Street—not far from George Rogers's home—when the call came in to check a domestic disturbance at 696 Broadway. It took only a minute and a half for police to arrive and arrest Michael Sedas, who they said was so angry he might have killed his estranged wife. The response time was miraculous, the two-way radio a hit, and Doyle became something of a local celebrity.

Rogers remembered Doyle all too well. He was the man who had embarrassed him during the appreciation dinner at Rosie's a year earlier, the one who discredited his story about melting solder on the *Morro Castle* radios. Rogers had not forgotten the slight. Although he considered himself the superior radioman, Rogers still felt threatened by Doyle—someone more famous than he was in his own hometown.

As much as Rogers pitied his lot and thought that people avoided him, a good number of folks still thought highly of him, still considered him a local celebrity. After all, he was the hero of one of the worst maritime disasters in history. One of those admirers was Horace K. Roberson, the new police commissioner, who in June 1936 offered Rogers a job. No one was sure whether Roberson had the idea himself or whether Rogers suggested it, but Roberson said the Bayonne police needed a second radio man, and who knew better about emergency radio broadcasts than the *Morro Castle* hero? The official position was radio technician, and he would report directly to Lieutenant Doyle. The salary was not great—only $2,100 a year, not as much as Rogers had made with the Ward Line—but it was a steady paycheck. Certainly, it was more than the Radio Service Laboratory's annual profits.

Gratefully, Rogers accepted the job. He saw it as an opportunity, nearly as much as his Broadway show. It certainly brought him more notoriety—the news of his appointment even made the newspapers in New York. The idea of working for Doyle had given him pause, but Rogers believed he could manage. The bad spell passed and soon he was feeling his jovial self. By the end of the month, the Bayonne Police Department issued him a uniform, a nightstick, a gun and a badge.

And just like that, George Rogers was a cop.

He insinuated himself into the fraternity of police officers well, understood their humor, their ways. Rogers was a blue-collar guy, just like them. Most of all, and much to his surprise, Rogers got along famously with Vincent Doyle. The two men quickly found they had several things in common, mostly an insatiable need to tinker, to invent things. Secretly, they both enjoyed being police officers, were proud to carry badges (although Rogers noted his was silver while Doyle's was gold). They could talk shop for hours on end, and the more they did, the better the police radio system became. They added the newest technology as soon as it became available, tearing into crates of new equipment like kids on Christmas morning. In their spare time, the two broadcast signals farther and farther from Bayonne, contacting amateur radio stations, ham operators and even other police departments just for the heck of it.

They became close friends, Doyle soon deciding he had been too harsh in his first impression of Rogers. The story about the solder was probably just part of his exuberance at having survived such an ordeal. In truth, Doyle was impressed with Rogers's knowledge of radios, and he found his new sidekick charismatic, telling his aw-shucks stories with a pipe sticking out of his mouth. Within months, the men were spending their weekends together, visiting each other's houses, even riding to work together. Their wives, Estelle and Edith, became friends. The two men were together nearly more than they were apart. When Doyle went fishing at his mother's house in Toms River, he always saved the biggest catch for his friend.

"This is for George," he would say, prompting his mother to ask playfully if he was nicer to his friend than to his own family.

Doyle came to be protective of Rogers, for the man certainly could be insecure—even needy—at times. When Roberson was replaced as commissioner, Rogers worried that he had lost his political protection, as if even he thought that were the only reason he had the job. He feared others in the department did not like him, that someone might fire him to save money in the increasingly taxed police budget. "I guess I'll have to go out and swing a stick," he sighed. Rogers almost pleaded with Doyle for reassurance.

"Suppose you were called in and asked if you need me in the radio bureau, what would you say?" he once asked.

"I'd say I needed you now more than ever," Doyle answered, perplexed and touched at how his friend worried. He seemed almost like a child.

There were occasions when Rogers had tantrums, and these moments often led to spats with Doyle. There was one disagreement, around Christmas 1936, so bad that they did not speak for days. Later, both claimed to not remember what it was about, but it was serious enough that Rogers had asked for a transfer. The chief turned down the request, but later reprimanded Doyle for "bawling out" Rogers.

As disagreeable as he could be, Rogers also was kindhearted, and his generosity touched Doyle. Rogers once made Doyle a fishing pole out of a pickax handle, and he used it on his fishing trips to Toms River. Doyle never said anything when he noticed a similar handle charged to the police department's tab at a local hardware store.

Doyle liked Rogers so much that he pretended not to notice that radio equipment often seemed to get up and walk away. Doyle gave his friend the benefit of the doubt, never asking why samples and catalogues from certain distributors disappeared, why he sometimes received answers to letters that he could not recall writing in the first place.

Only once did Doyle mention these odd events. Rogers had ordered a part for his lathe and charged it to the department's account, and Doyle confronted him with the bill. Rogers apologized, promised not to do it again, and Doyle said nothing of it to anyone. He knew that his friend was not wealthy. And even though what Rogers had done was wrong, Doyle was no snitch.

Rogers talked about the *Morro Castle* intermittently, whenever something reminded him of it. In April 1937, it was news that a U.S. circuit court of appeals had thrown out the verdicts against Warms, Abbott and Cabaud. Judge Augustus N. Hand wrote the opinion that spared the men from prison, declaring the fire spread too quickly for the crew to have done anything else and that Warms had "maintained the best tradition of the sea by staying on his ship until the bridge burned under him and no one else was aboard."

Rogers talked about the fire often in the days following Warms's acquittal, reminding Doyle that he had been on that bridge long after the captain and other officers had gone. He could still see that valley of fire spread out before him as the ship burned like a torch. Careful not to say anything so outlandish that Doyle might call him on it, Rogers bragged about his heroics. Doyle could hardly blame him for reliving his glory days. The disaster had brought Rogers a modicum of fame, and he had a right to be proud. More than most, Doyle could understand. But soon, he noticed that the story was changing.

George Rogers's account of the *Morro Castle* fire and its origin got increasingly specific. Doyle thought perhaps he was exaggerating, as his friend was prone to do, but he eventually claimed to have insider knowledge of the fire. He said that he knew things no one else did.

Rogers told Doyle that an explosion set the fire on the *Morro Castle.* The bomb was an incendiary fountain pen filled with acid and combustible powder, the two separated by a thin sheet of copper. The copper served as a timer—the acid would eat through the metal, but it took a while. The thicker the copper, the longer it took for the acid to reach the powder. The pen had been put into the breast pocket of a waiter's jacket, which was then hung in the Writing Room locker. Rogers said it made the perfect crime—no one had to risk detection while starting the fire, and if the bomb was found, anybody would just think it was a pen. That's why no one was spotted messing around the locker, he said, the explosives had been put there hours earlier. When it exploded, it ignited the turpentine and paint stored in the locker.

Doyle knew such a device was possible to construct. Rogers, in fact, had talked about building one just months earlier. What he couldn't understand was how George knew all this. If this was the cause of the fire, Doyle wondered, why had he not heard about it, seen it in the papers?

"How do you know all this?" Doyle asked.

Rogers would not say. He acted as if he had said too much, but Doyle suspected he was playing coy, trying to amplify his importance. Or perhaps he was afraid of being caught in another lie. Rogers demurred, said it was only a guess.

"I just know a lot about explosives," Rogers shrugged.

When Doyle pressed, however, Rogers began to talk about the bomb in even greater detail. Unless he was lying, Rogers said things that he could only know if he had set the fire. Doyle finally asked the question looming over the conversation, although he feared the answer.

"Why did you do it?"

For a second, Rogers said nothing, then spewed vitriol with his answer: "The Ward Line stinks and the skipper was lousy."

Doyle was horrified. His friend often bragged, but this was different. There was vindictiveness in his voice, and Doyle feared it was true. He didn't know what to do. Even if it was the truth, what could he do? His word was no better than Rogers's and, technically, he wasn't sure Rogers had admitted to anything. But it certainly sounded that way.

After that day, Rogers spoke of the *Morro Castle* rarely. He never again delved into the details, even when Doyle casually brought it up. Doyle listened closely, like a detective, waiting to hear anything new. He decided to keep his suspicions, if that's what they were, to himself.

On March 4, 1938, Vincent J. Doyle was busy at work. It was a Friday, and he had several things to finish before the weekend. He had a meeting with the chief that afternoon, after spending most of his morning in the radio room working alongside a chatty George Rogers. After lunch, he and Rogers were strolling through the department garage when they saw some of the guys standing around a table. John Shallow, a patrolman, was showing off a bunch of .45-caliber machine-gun bullets to the others. Doyle reached down and picked one up off the table.

"What would happen if I hit this with a hammer?" Doyle said, teasing Shallow.

"It would blow your head off."

Rogers acted as if he didn't believe him, like he was the only one who was supposed to know such things. Ever the know-it-all, Rogers seemed almost defensive.

"How do you know, did you study ordnance?"

"Yes," Shallow said, "in the navy."

"Oh, you know then."

When he finished talking with Shallow, Rogers caught up to Doyle and told him someone had left a package for him in the garage. Doyle thanked him and went on with what he was doing, soon forgetting all about it. Rogers reminded him again at 3 P.M.

"There's a package for you in the office of the garage."

Doyle said he'd get it later, and then left. He met with Cornelius J. O'Neill for only a few minutes before returning to the repair shop over the garage. The room was beneath the radio system tower but on the opposite side of the building from where he and Rogers normally worked. By the time Doyle got back, it was 3:40—nearly quitting time. Rogers met Doyle in front of the stairs and handed him a package wrapped in brown paper. Someone had written "Lt. Doyle" on the outside, but he didn't recognize the handwriting. Rogers handed him a note that had apparently come with the package.

"I opened it. You don't mind, do you?" Rogers said.

Doyle took the box and looked around the garage. He saw a few of the motorcycle cops—John Tierney, Edward Jonas, Owen Olsen—and asked them where the package had come from.

"Who left this for me?"

No one had seen it arrive. It had no markings that suggested it had been mailed, but that didn't mean anything. "It wasn't here this morning," Tierney said.

It wasn't that unusual. A lot of officers left broken gadgets for Doyle and Rogers to fix. He shrugged and carried the box up the stairs to the repair room, Rogers following a few steps behind.

Doyle sat down at the workbench and opened the package. Inside, he found a curious contraption. It was a pipe about 6 inches long, 3/4 inch in diameter, with a bore of about 1/2 inch, threaded as if it were an insulator. Inside were several wires, one of which ended in an electrical cord a little more than a foot long. He turned the thing over in his hand, examining it for a moment before he found the note inside the box.

Lieutenant Doyle,
> *This is a fish tank heater. Please install this switch in the*

line cord and see if the unit will work. It should get slightly
warm.

Doyle looked at the thing again and tossed the note on the bench. He showed it to Rogers, who was watching from across the room.

"What is this? Do you think this is a joke?"

Rogers gave it a cursory look, handed it back to him and shook his head.

"It's a fish bowl heater, like the note says."

Doyle inspected the gadget another minute, but could find no markings on it, no instructions that might have come with it. He looked at the note again and then reached for the cord hanging out of it. He heard Rogers mumble something behind him, something about the mail. He looked around to respond, but Rogers was gone.

Doyle turned his attention back to the heater. He wondered if it was a homemade device—in an age when money was scarce, many people had taken up electronics as a hobby. Perhaps that's what it was, because it didn't look as if it were something from a store, something mass-produced. Doyle unraveled the cord with his right hand while holding the device in his left. He reached across the workbench and plugged the cord into the wall socket. And that was the last thing he remembered.

The explosion blew out the repair room window, sending shards of glass flying into the parking lot. The crack of shrapnel ripping through the wall was like gunshot.

Tierney, Olsen and the other officers in the garage heard the explosion and ran toward the noise. When they reached the stairs to the repair room, they saw George Rogers bounding up the steps ahead of them.

The blast had thrown Doyle off the stool and across the room, the force so strong it broke his left leg—the bone jutted out of the tattered remnants of his pants. Rogers could barely see through the smoke, which reminded him of the conditions in the *Morro Castle*'s wireless room just before he had escaped. Behind him, he could hear the other officers come into the room as he bent down over Doyle.

"Bud, what happened?"

Doyle could barely speak, but he looked up through squinted eyes, and weakly said, "George, somebody slipped me . . ." And he passed out.

Olsen and Tierney were struck by the smell of gunpowder in the room and sickened by the sight: pieces of skin and blood covered the floor; scraps of metal from the bomb had ripped through the walls. The two motorcycle cops asked Rogers what happened but received no answer.

Doyle was bleeding all over the room, bad enough that every man there knew he could die, if he wasn't dead already. They moved quickly to save him. Olsen grabbed an electrical cord to make a tourniquet while Tierney helped move Doyle off the debris in the floor.

"Give us a hand, Rogers," Olsen said.

But George Rogers just stood there, staring at the unconscious Vincent Doyle. Blood gushed from his left hand, which had taken the brunt of the blast. As the smoke cleared, Rogers could see the extent of the injury and was stunned by it. The explosion had blown off Doyle's thumb and two other fingers nearly all the way to the knuckle. Even if he lived, Rogers knew, Doyle would be crippled.

His hand was mangled.

CHAPTER FOURTEEN

The Mind of a Fiend

George Rogers didn't watch as the ambulance pulled away, a half-dozen police cars following, sirens wailing. He lingered outside the shop, where he had stood motionless for several minutes as the other cops moved Vincent Doyle onto a stretcher, telling him to hold on, that everything would be all right.

Rogers was more interested in the wreckage. The blast had splintered the heavy drawers below the bench and sent shrapnel flying through the plaster wall. The stool had been blown into the closet, its legs lying in a pool of blood on the wood plank floor. A dusting of soot and smoke covered the workbench and boxes filled with electrical gadgets he and Doyle had saved for parts. Rogers threw away almost nothing.

The dark stain of blood on the floor fascinated Rogers, and he wondered if Doyle would live. The bomb had exploded with enough force to pierce Doyle's heart if the casing had blown in the right direction. Certainly, the blast had carried enough force. Before the motorcycle cops had covered Doyle with a blanket, Rogers noticed pieces of metal lodged in his friend's foot.

Rogers found the paper lying on the bench. It was amazing that the explosion had thrown Doyle and his stool across the room but had not disturbed a single sheet of stationery. Recognizing it was a link to the bomber, Rogers picked up the paper, turned it over in his thick hands. There was a bloody fingerprint on the corner and he realized that it was his, not Doyle's. His hand was covered in blood from touching Doyle.

He stuffed the note into his pocket, and then thought better of it. If Doyle lived, he would remember the note, tell others about it. It would not look good if it were found on him, Rogers knew, and there was a very real chance he would be searched. He had seen the way they looked at him. Doyle was one of them in a way that Rogers would never be, and cops did not take lightly to attacks on other policemen. There would be an investigation, and they would look at everyone—including him. He put the note in a box filled with advertisements for the police radio system—"In 2 minutes police are THERE!"—shuffled the blotters and shoved the box between the workbench and the half-painted wall. Someone was coming up the stairs.

Thomas J. McGrath, captain of detectives, and an investigator named Thomas Masterson walked into the shop. McGrath was old-school, a tough guy with a badge who could sometimes scare a confession out of suspects with a long, hard stare. It was the look he gave Rogers as he stopped in the doorway, and the radioman recognized it.

"What did you do," Rogers said, "come to arrest me?"

"No, not yet," McGrath said.

Rogers said nothing, let the remark hang in silence, hoping that McGrath had been kidding. As Rogers waited for a laugh that did not come, Masterson told him the investigation had begun.

"You know, George, you are under suspicion."

"I'm way ahead of you," Rogers said.

The two detectives cut a look at each other, and Rogers noticed. There was more small talk, and then Rogers followed them out of the room. To hang around would only invite more suspicion.

Later that day, McGrath had the shop sealed. They confiscated all keys to the room, including the one carried by Rogers, and ordered officers in the garage to keep everyone out. The shop was officially a crime scene.

The department dispatched a car to 43rd Street to pick up Estelle Doyle, seven months pregnant and perplexed by the insistence of the officers, who would not say where they were taking her. When the car stopped at Bayonne Hospital, she felt a catch of fear. A nurse in Emergency told her that Mr. Doyle was in serious condition and was not expected to live through the night.

Before she could react, Dr. John Madaras took Estelle by the arm and led her into the emergency room, where her husband lay half-conscious on a table. Madaras reached into the hole in Doyle's leg and felt the splintered bones. He was more optimistic than the nurse had been.

"The artery has not been cut. He's lost a lot of blood, but he'll be OK."

The doctor left the Doyles alone, but Estelle did not know what to say. It had been a tough year for the family. The previous June their six-year-old daughter Patsy had died after a long fight with congenital hip dislocation that kept her in a plaster cast for much of her abbreviated life. Now this. Questions filled Estelle Doyle's head, but the only one that came out was, "How are you?"

Still in shock, Doyle could not feel any pain. He said he felt fine, but his wife—Stell, he called her—did not believe him.

"A nurse told me you were going to die."

"Yes, sometime, as you well know. We all do. Only God can predict when," he said. "God never delegated any nurse, or doctor either, to be His spokesman to carry a message such as she just gave you. Just forget she ever said it. She could not possibly know."

As Doyle tried to ease his wife's fears, Masterson arrived in the emergency room. He had a sympathetic look in his eye and a notebook in his hand. He was working, the radioman knew, and before Doyle was put under anesthesia the detective wanted a statement.

"What happened?"

"I would guess that somebody doesn't like me, Lieutenant. Someone tried to kill me, but I can't imagine who it is."

"What makes you think it was a planned murder?"

"The planting of a bomb in the hands of a fellow human being, Lieutenant, is not done accidentally," Doyle said, adding that the note made it premeditated. "Whoever built that fish-tank heater and asked me to put a switch in the line cord was out to blow my head off."

"A note, you say. Where is the note?"

Doyle was getting groggy. He told Masterson what the note said, how he had followed the instructions. He could not believe no one had told him about it—Doyle remembered reading it aloud just before the explosion. But the detective said everyone in the shop had been questioned about what happened, and none of them mentioned a note.

"Was Rogers there?"

"He most certainly was. In fact, Rogers was the *only* one there when we first entered the shop."

Masterson continued to talk, but Doyle soon slipped into unconsciousness. Later, Mayor L. F. Donohoe and Chief Cornelius J. O'Neill paid a visit to the radioman in the emergency room. Doctors told them Doyle had lost the thumb and two fingers of his left hand and had punctured his skull when the blast threw him into the radiator. His leg was fractured so badly there was a chance he would lose it. Doyle woke long enough to speak with the men briefly.

"Who would want to do a thing like that to me? I did not think I had an enemy in the world. It's a lucky thing that Rogers wasn't there. He would have been blown to bits."

O'Neill agreed—Rogers had made a fortuitous exit.

That night, George Rogers visited Vincent Doyle's hospital room. Doyle was asleep, still drugged from the surgery. The hospital staff had kept a watchful eye on the lieutenant's room and police hovered nearby, on guard. No one was supposed to get in, so the nurse was surprised to find Rogers in the room, standing near Doyle's bed. He must have come up the back stairs, because no one could have missed a 300-pound man sauntering down the hall. When Rogers saw the nurse, he turned and quickly left.

The *Bayonne Times* kept the mysterious bombing on its front page for nearly two weeks, with new reports about McGrath and Masterson's investigation every day. They interviewed every cop on the force, talked to bomb and chemical experts. They dug through sales slips for the materials used to build the bomb. Surprisingly, large portions of the "fish-tank heater" had survived the blast. The parts led them across the Hudson to New York and, ultimately, back to police headquarters. There were no solid leads, McGrath told reporters; the department was stumped. It was another old police trick—pretend to be clueless and hope the suspect relaxes, maybe even gets sloppy.

The bomber, in fact, had been almost inept. The note, which had been found stuffed in an old box with pieces of the bomb, was full of jargon that only someone familiar with electronics would have used: "line" instead of "cord." Obviously, the bomber understood electronics, and the fact that the note and pieces of the device were hidden in the room suggested he had been there since the blast.

Even the delivery of the package spoke volumes—who else would have known where to leave something for Doyle to find? It was, police suspected, a significant clue. More telling, it appeared the note had been typed on a police department typewriter, the one in the radio room. On March 12, the *Bayonne Times* quoted the police chief saying that, more and more, the bombing appeared to be an inside job. He declined to give details, other than to reveal that his men had scoured the country, talking to people from New York to California.

Every cop in the police department was questioned, but detectives narrowed their focus quickly. While McGrath and Masterson interviewed most officers twice, they talked to George Rogers nearly every day. Most of the time, it was informal, at the station, but on Saturday, March 12, the detectives showed up at his home on Avenue E.

Rogers seemed terribly distraught, saying he wished that he had opened the package instead of Doyle. As he talked, the detectives searched the house, which Rogers allowed even without a warrant—he just wanted to help. But when they found a note Rogers had written to Edith while aboard the *Morro Castle,* his demeanor changed quickly. He threatened to hit them if they released the note to reporters. McGrath and Masterson weren't sure what it was about the note that upset him, but they dropped it. Rogers apologized only after Edith scolded him, telling him that was no way to talk to a police officer. As if he weren't another member of the force.

On Tuesday, McGrath questioned Rogers again. The detective asked him to recount the day of March 4, a story that the radioman was clearly tired of repeating. McGrath interrupted often, asking questions and pointing out inconsistencies: "Well, did you open the note and read it or not?" Rogers kept saying that he wished it had been him and that he couldn't understand why anyone would hurt his friend. But the detectives said they weren't buying it. They had a lot of evidence, said they knew who built the bomb, and who left it for Doyle to find. They knew everything. When Rogers had nothing to say about all that, it was Masterson who pulled out an old interrogation trick.

"George, I know you fellows do a little fooling around—it happens in all places. I know you did this, so why don't you tell me and get it all over with."

Rogers sat quiet for a moment, and then asked a question.

"If I told you I did it as a joke, would you charge me with manslaughter?"

He was arrested that afternoon.

Police Chief O'Neill stripped George Rogers of his badge shortly after 3 P.M. on March 15, and then led him to booking. The official charge was "attempt to kill and atrocious assault and battery." With dozens of police officers watching, Rogers stood before the desk lieutenant, Patrick Donovan, crying.

"So help me God, Lieutenant, I didn't do it."

In the middle of police headquarters, a reporter from the *Bayonne Times* took notes as officers searched Rogers, removed his belt and necktie, and took his keys. Rogers kept mumbling about his innocence, his pipe dangling from his lips.

"You've got the wrong guy. I didn't do it."

Some of the cops undoubtedly liked Rogers, even if they thought him strange, but they all considered this a solid case. The evidence, though circumstantial, was overwhelming. His fellow officers pitied Rogers only enough to grant his one plea before he was sent to a dank cell.

"Do me a special favor, Lieutenant, please let me keep my pipe."

That evening, Rogers watched the light fade out of the day from a jail cell as the *Times* carried a headline announcing that the "Hero of the *Morro Castle* Fire" had been arrested in the bomb blast. Once praised for saving hundreds of lives, he now stood accused of trying to take one.

Doyle surely had known it was coming. For two weeks, McGrath and Masterson repeatedly returned to him for more information. The sketchiest part of the case was motive. The best they could come up with was that Rogers had wanted Doyle's job. They had evidence that Rogers had tried to get rid of superiors before to advance his own career, but Doyle told the investigators that career advancement was not Rogers's motive.

"No, Captain, Rogers had a better reason to kill me. George knows that I know he set fire to the *Morro Castle*."

For two weeks, Doyle had been stuck in a hospital bed, in his mind going over the minutes before the blast. It seemed impossible that he had ignored the warning signs. Rogers had been jumpy that day, anxious for Doyle to open the package. He had seemed curious about the package, but then left the room moments before Doyle plugged in the "fish-tank heater." The more he thought about it, the more Doyle became convinced that George Rogers simply considered him a loose end. He knew too much.

McGrath didn't know what to make of Doyle's claim, but he knew that dragging the *Morro Castle* into the case would only muddy the water. He thanked Doyle, humored him by promising to try and soften Rogers up on the arson theory, but stuck to his original motive. He had no desire to re-open a four-year-old case. It didn't matter anyway. McGrath thought he had enough evidence to put Rogers away for life.

At his arraignment the next day, Rogers stood before the judge with his new attorney, former state senator Alexander Simpson. No doubt Simpson, a high-profile criminal attorney, had been supplied by Horace K. Roberson, the old police commissioner who appointed Rogers to the force. People on both sides suspected politics was at play, and Rogers's friends assumed Simpson could sort it out. But Simpson was at a loss to argue against all the evidence the police hauled out.

McGrath skimmed the long list of evidence that had led to Rogers's arrest: The wires in the bomb were identical to the wiring in a tube-testing machine Rogers owned; Rogers had been the last one in the police garage office where the package was found; he gave the package to Doyle; earlier in the day, a clerk had seen Rogers handling the box. For the time being, he would not mention the best evidence, that the note accompanying the bomb had been typed in the radio shop on police paper. Nor did he mention motive—his or Doyle's.

The evidence was circumstantial, Simpson argued, not nearly enough to hold Rogers. But Recorder Raymond J. Cuddy saw it differently. He ordered Rogers to remain jailed until a grand jury could decide whether to indict him. Bail was set at $7,500—an enormous sum in those days, and one that Simpson persuaded Judge Thomas F. Meaney to reduce by one-third. Charles Phillips, a friend of Rogers's, posted the $5,000 to free him, and Simpson told reporters that the case was so flimsy the grand jury would throw it out.

"Rogers is a high-type man. What better proof could you ask than that he turned down contracts that would have amounted to $16,000 after his heroic work on the *Morro Castle.* He turned them down just because he didn't want to exploit the disaster."

Doyle said little publicly about Rogers, and nothing about his suspicions regarding the *Morro Castle* fire. Speaking with reporters from his hospital bed, Doyle feigned surprise. "If the detectives arrested George for this terrible thing, they must have what they consider sufficient evidence," he said.

His bad acting did not fool the reporters, who certainly recognized that Doyle was taking a stab at his former friend when he added a seemingly lighthearted remark, "If George is guilty then he must be a crackpot."

Doyle's injuries had been traumatic and life-threatening, and he considered it a miracle he had not lost his leg. As it was, he would walk with a cane for years, a limp perhaps forever. His hand was another matter entirely. Wrapped in a massive bandage, he would not see the nub that remained of his left hand for weeks. It was a frail skeleton of its former self, a wound that would never heal. Doyle supposed he should have been afraid Rogers might try again, but he could not resist the jab. He was mad.

Doyle was still in the hospital on May 2 when Estelle gave birth to their new baby, a son who would be named after his father. For the first time since the bombing, Doyle seemed in good spirits, receiving visitors and congratulatory cigars from a long blue line of police officers and hundreds of other well-wishers. His son was born two floors above him, but it was several days before he was allowed to see Stell or his namesake boy. He joked that the only Doyle not in the hospital was his nine-year-old daughter, Mary Jane.

Visitors paraded through his hospital room constantly, but there was one whom Doyle would never forget. He introduced himself as John Doe and said he'd been aboard the *Morro Castle* on its final cruise, in fact claimed he was still listed among the missing. Doyle assumed "John Doe" was code; that perhaps the man was in law enforcement—maybe even a federal agent. The man said that on the night before the fire he had dined at the captain's table, and Robert Willmott confided to him that when they reached port, he would fire Rogers. Willmott allegedly said Rogers "was the root of all trouble" on the ship. "John Doe" told Doyle he could not come forward to testify, or even let police know he was on the ship. He merely offered the information in hope that it would help.

Doyle never saw the man again or learned his identity, but the incident strengthened his belief that Rogers had burned the *Morro Castle.* The visit, however, was more mysterious than Doyle would ever realize. For as long as he lived, Vincent Doyle would never know that, on the night before the fire, Willmott did not dine publicly.

Vincent Doyle was released from Bayonne Hospital on June 28, although his recuperation would keep him out of work for the rest of the year. The grand jury had indicted Rogers, but Doyle had nothing to do except wait for the trial, which was scheduled for the fall. He passed the time helping with the investigation, and spent afternoons playing with his new son, whom he had previously only seen from the hospital window—babies weren't allowed in his room.

On pleasant days, Doyle would sit in the sun on the stone steps of his porch, where he could extend his left leg over the wall. The weight of his foot and lower leg helped bend his knee, which had grown stiff during four months of recovery. One afternoon, Doyle saw a car stop a few doors down in front of the home of Dennis Smalley, a lineman in the police and fire signal system. Doyle bent to see under a tree in the yard, wondering if it was someone looking for him. He froze when he saw the man behind the wheel. George Rogers sped away when he realized he'd been spotted.

As the trial approached, Doyle grew more apprehensive. Once he could drive again, he often thought he was being followed. One evening, driving home from police headquarters, he noticed a car tailing him. He sped up and slowed down, made several turns, leading his pursuer halfway across Bayonne, but he could not shake the car. Doyle finally pulled into someone's driveway, forcing his pursuer to drive past. When he arrived at his house a few minutes later, he heard footsteps on his gravel driveway. Doyle ducked behind his open car door.

"Who are you?" he yelled. . . . "All right, you asked for it, now stop right where you are."

"It's me, Joe McCarthy, hold your fire."

Doyle berated McCarthy for not answering the first time. "I could've blown your head off. I thought you were Rogers."

"We have been tailing you for weeks, protecting you as the captain ordered."

Doyle didn't want to admit he needed police protection, but there was little denying it. Too many strange things were happening. A few weeks later, someone in a passing car tossed a Molotov cocktail at his home. The soda bottle, filled with gasoline, hit the porch of the house next door and caught it on fire. The fire chief said there was no doubt about it. Arson.

A week later, Dennis Smalley, the cop down the street, got an anonymous note in the mail advising him to turn himself in as the Doyle bomber. Smalley showed it to Doyle, who in turn gave it to McGrath. Within days, the investigators and prosecutors met to discuss this new development. They had gotten a half-dozen anonymous letters that claimed Rogers had been set up by the police. The only way he would get a "square deal" was if the district attorney searched Smalley's cellar. Near the furnace, the letter said, there was a pile of wood. And beneath the wood was the evidence they needed to convict Smalley.

It was a juvenile attempt by Rogers to frame Smalley, the detectives decided, nothing more. It wasn't Rogers's handwriting on the note, but that was only a technicality. It just seemed like something he would do. Still, they had to check it out. And at Smalley's house, they in fact found a brown paper bag under some wooden chairs in the basement. It appeared to have been thrown in through the cellar window—the writer could not tell the "pile of wood" was actually a stack of folding chairs. Inside the bag, they found an empty machine-gun clip and nine loaded cartridges. The ammunition had been stolen from the Bayonne Police Department.

McGrath kept the incident out of the papers. He feared that, either way, it could help Rogers. No matter how crazy the story seemed, it could cast a shadow of doubt on the whole case. And if the police accused Rogers of planting evidence, it would look like they were out to get him—just as he claimed they were. They certainly did not want to generate any sympathy for Rogers, so they didn't take the bait. As many times as Rogers's attorney asked if police had investigated Smalley, McGrath did the best thing he could to keep his case on track. He said nothing.

George Rogers seemed almost cheerful when he arrived at the Hudson County Courthouse in Jersey City on November 21, 1938. Wearing a blue suit with a matching tie and a gray shirt, Rogers looked thinner than he had in years. He stopped to shake hands with friends outside and spoke to reporters in the rotunda. The courthouse was busy that morning, with dozens of police officers milling about beneath wall paintings that depicted the founding of the New World and the mural of angels that circled the stained-glass dome. The artist Francis D. Millet, director of decoration at the 1893 Columbian Exposition in Chicago, had designed the courthouse décor two years before he was lost on the *Titanic*—one of the few maritime disasters in the same league as that of the *Morro Castle.* Rogers paid little notice to the beautiful interior and ignored his former coworkers from the Bayonne Police Department.

If he seemed confident, it may have been because of his attorney's new strategy. When Judge Thomas H. Brown ordered juror selection to begin, Alexander Simpson announced that Rogers would waive his right to a jury trial. Although it was a fairly unusual request, Brown did not have to think long before granting the motion. Because of all the publicity surrounding the case, jury selection could have taken two days or more, and the trial already threatened to last several weeks. The judge saw Rogers's request as a way to save time.

It was a calculated gamble. Most of the evidence against Rogers was circumstantial, a distinction Simpson hoped to exploit with a trained judge. While prosecutors might spin a good yarn for jurors, a judge should know the difference between proof and the mere appearance of it.

In fact, Assistant Prosecutor William H. Cahill had concocted an elaborate tale of jealousy and greed. In his opening statement, he described how Rogers believed he should be in charge of the police department's radio division. There was not only ego involved, Cahill said, but also the difference in the two men's salaries. Rogers made about $2,200 a year; Doyle, $3,200 (the 2006 difference between $28,000 and $41,000). Cahill promised to outline a pattern of similar behavior on Rogers's part going all the way back to his days on the *Morro Castle.* The remark caught the attention of at least one person in the audience. George Alagna had been subpoenaed by the district attorney's office and forced to attend the trial. Even though they had not told him why he was there, Alagna had a pretty good idea.

The opposing sides were a study in contrasts, the differences between prosecution and defense so pronounced that no one in the courtroom could fail to see it. While Cahill's team of lawyers worked behind a mountainous stack of file folders, thick envelopes and oversized law books, Simpson and Rogers's table was bare save for a single law book and a small notebook that Rogers wrote on during testimony.

To be sure, the prosecution's strategy was overkill, an attempt to show everything bad Rogers had done in his life. They paraded dozens of witnesses before the judge, including several police officers who told stories of missing equipment they believed Rogers had stolen. One said that even if Rogers was acquitted, he would be fired for all the things he was merely suspected of doing. Indeed, Cahill said, it appeared the bomb had been assembled from parts either stolen from or charged to the Bayonne Police Department.

The prosecutors attempted to link Rogers to the bomb on the first day of the trial. Technical experts described its construction, and Cahill produced receipts and bills that showed Rogers had bought or used such equipment. A chemist noted the bomb had been painted with gray paint exactly like some found in Rogers's home. And an expert on typewritten documents from the New York Police Department said that "without a doubt" the note that accompanied the bomb had been composed on the twelve-year-old typewriter in the Bayonne Police Department radio room. Joseph Orshefsky, a department telephone operator who worked out of the radio room, testified that Rogers had been the last man to use the machine. After the bombing, he said, someone had tried to damage the typewriter so it couldn't be used.

Cahill traced possession of the bomb to an almost monotonous level. One patrolman testified that he saw Rogers hand the package to Doyle; another, Sergeant John J. Tierney, said that when he found the package and tried to give it to Rogers, the radio man recoiled.

"He said, 'That's for Lieutenant Doyle, don't touch it,'" Tierney testified.

Vincent J. Doyle sat on the front row throughout the trial, his walking cane resting against the bench. Rogers would not look at him, but Doyle could hardly avoid staring at his former friend. When he was called to testify, Doyle related his story to the judge quickly and methodically. Men in the Bayonne Police Department's shop had supplied a replica of the bomb, and Doyle used the prop to re-create the scene leading up to the explosion. He had difficulty holding the device in his maimed hand, underscoring the injury he had suffered. When he got up for a break,

Doyle walked away with a noticeable limp, another souvenir from the blast.

Doyle speculated that the parts for the bomb had come from a man he and Rogers met at a radio exhibit in Elizabeth. The man sold electrical plugs, much like the one used in the bomb, and Doyle had asked for samples. They never arrived—at least Doyle was not aware that they had.

He could not help but mention the *Morro Castle,* even after Cahill asked him not to. Doyle said Rogers had often bragged about his knowledge of explosives. In fact, Doyle said, Rogers had once described how to make an incendiary fountain pen such as the one he claimed started the fire on the *Morro Castle.* Even though it was the first public link ever made between Rogers and the cruise ship fire, neither the prosecution nor the defense asked him to elaborate on the fantastic claim. Some reporters included the quote in their stories, but they never asked Doyle any more about it. The cruise ship was old news. Alagna would not say a word during the trial.

While Simpson cross-examined Doyle, he was constantly interrupted by Rogers, who kept passing notes with questions he wanted to ask. After Simpson was stopped several times by his client, Doyle chuckled at him.

"What do you find so funny?"

"Nothing is funny, sir," Doyle said. "It is pathetic."

"Explain your answer, Mr. Doyle," Simpson said.

"I sympathize with you, Senator, for having to put up with your client. His arrogance has caused him to lose every friend he has ever had."

Later, during a break in the trial, Doyle watched Cahill needle Simpson in the rotunda to confirm a suspicion he had about Rogers's legal defense fund.

"I'm sorry, Alex," Cahill said. "It's too bad your client wouldn't let you earn all that dough he paid you."

"What do you mean?"

Cahill showed Simpson a signed statement from George Brown that said he and other friends of George Rogers had collected $1,250 for his legal bills. In the note, Brown said he had given all the money to Rogers with instructions to pass it on to Simpson.

"That lying son of a bitch," Simpson muttered. "He told me all he had was $400."

Doyle spotted Simpson and Rogers in the rotunda a little while later. The lawyer had his finger in his client's face, cursing at him.

There was one thing that Simpson and Rogers had not counted on: Judge Brown asked a lot of questions. If he knew what circumstantial evidence was, he also knew what was important, what had a bearing on the case. Also, he paid attention. When the judge got confused by the layout of the Bayonne Police Department, he simply moved the trial there—another advantage of not having a jury, mobility.

Rogers seemed completely at ease during his return to police headquarters, greeting Masterson and several other police officers while he was there. When the reporter from the *Bayonne Times* asked how he was, Rogers said that he was "Fine."

"Keep your chin up," Rogers told the reporter.

"Keep *my* chin up?"

But Rogers was not in such good spirits the next day when Cahill called two surprise witnesses. Preston Dillenbeck and his wife, Anita, were good friends with Rogers, but were too frightened not to cooperate with the district attorney's office. They had been subpoenaed to recount two stories—one anecdote that could have been interpreted as a veiled threat to Doyle, and another that tainted Rogers's heroic stint as chief radio operator of the *Morro Castle.*

Four years earlier, Rogers had tried to get Dillenbeck a job aboard the Ward Line flagship. On a July afternoon aboard the *Morro Castle,* just a week after he was hired, Rogers had written two letters—one to Dillenbeck, and another for him to transcribe and mail. Rogers told Dillenbeck that if he did this it would make it easier for him to get a job on the ship. Cahill tried to get the letter entered into evidence.

> *I am enclosing a letter that I have written and I want you to rewrite this letter on your typewriter and address it in a plain envelope to the address that I will give you. Then take the letter to New York and mail it from there. This is very important. . . . This will tip him off as to what to expect and at the same time, having been mailed in New York when I am in Cuba, it will not involve me. When I get to New York I will get another junior who will be assigned to the ship temporarily so that when you get your ticket there will be no trouble*

*getting you assigned here with me. This must be done as soon
as you receive this letter so that he will get the letter in New
York when we arrive there. Don't fail me, please. Will try to
see you this trip.*

The letter Rogers had asked Dillenbeck to rewrite and mail from New York was the note suggesting Stanley Ferson quit his job as chief radio operator of the *Morro Castle.* Dillenbeck also produced a second letter Rogers had asked him to rewrite, the one in which Ferson was warned that trouble on the ship would not settle down until he was "out of the picture." Together, the two letters had scared Ferson off the ship in August 1934, setting into motion a chain of events that resulted in George Rogers becoming chief radio operator of the *Morro Castle.*

Simpson objected to the letters being used as evidence, but he knew it was too late. Even if Brown refused to admit them, the judge now knew about the trick, and could see that it fit a pattern of removing people who got in his way. Simpson was livid.

"Are they now going to charge us with blowing up the *Morro Castle?*"

Cahill argued that the letters were pertinent because they demonstrated "the diabolical frame of Rogers's mind"; they showed he would do anything to get ahead. Brown ruled the letters "entirely too remote" to the case, but the damage had been done. The papers picked up on it and the stories of the threatening letters to his old boss on the *Morro Castle* made the afternoon editions. Suddenly, George Rogers did not look so heroic.

The Dillenbecks' trip to the courthouse was not wasted, however. Brown allowed Anita Dillenbeck to recount remarks Rogers made to her in June 1936, just days after getting his job with the police department. Rogers had shown her his badge and claimed that soon he would have an even better one.

"This is a silver one, but I expect to have a gold one someday. There are ways of getting those things," Rogers had said. "I am a very ingenious young man."

On the final day of the prosecution's case, Cahill put every member of the Bayonne police force on the stand so that each one could swear he did not type the note attached to the bomb. By the time the state rested, Cahill had called 226 witnesses. It was a stunt that attracted the attention of even the *New York Times.*

During the noon recess that day, Doyle was sitting alone at the prosecutor's table when he noticed a woman on crutches in the courtroom doorway. She motioned him outside with a jerk of her head.

They walked to the marble balustrade circling the rotunda, where no one in the lobby could hear them. She introduced herself only as a stewardess from the *Morro Castle* and claimed the burns she had gotten from the fire kept her hospitalized for eighteen months. And she believed Rogers was the cause of her suffering.

"Please stick to it until you convict that beast," she said.

Doyle asked the woman if she had any evidence, anything that could tie Rogers to the fire. Anything at all.

"I had enough evidence, circumstantial though it may be, to convict him of arson when the ship burned, but my lips are sealed by—" and she stopped, refusing to say anything more.

After she left, Doyle asked a friend to follow the woman, see what he could find out. Although he was just a radioman in the police department, Doyle felt very much like a detective, certain that he was close to cracking an even bigger case. He looked up at the ceiling, at the angels painted there, and perhaps he prayed for justice.

Alexander Simpson opened the defense's case by calling George Rogers to the stand. The lawyer asked questions that allowed Rogers to say he did not build the bomb, had nothing to do with the incident and did not want Doyle's job.

"We were the best of friends," Rogers said.

Simpson's strategy was to give the prosecution nothing, to make them prove a case for which they had only circumstantial evidence. He had Rogers offer his own "expert" opinion that a fish-tank heater could explode on its own without any prompting. And, in an attempt to diffuse the prosecution's case, Rogers admitted he had sent Preston Dillenbeck the letters that prompted Stanley Ferson to leave the *Morro Castle*. Simpson thought it would be good to show that no violence had come to Ferson. Judge Brown stopped Cahill from asking, on cross-examination, if Rogers had not gotten a promotion as a result of those threats.

Still, Cahill's questioning of Rogers was brutal. He asked how Rogers's bloody thumbprint came to be on the note, whether he had read it before Doyle—he had told the police conflicting stories—and if he had been the one to hand the package to Doyle. Rogers hesitated before answering anything, often simply muttering, "I don't know." For most of his time on the stand, Rogers—once brash and cocky—now seemed bewildered.

The only other witnesses Simpson called were Edith Rogers and her brother, who testified that George Rogers had not owned a fish-tank heater. It was, by nearly any standard, a pretty weak defense.

Cahill's closing argument lasted one hour and twelve minutes. He laid out a scenario in which a jealous and vindictive Rogers plotted to kill Vincent Doyle in order to take his job. The prosecutor said the "ingenious and diabolical" letter sent to Stanley Ferson on the *Morro Castle* was proof enough that George Rogers would stop at nothing to get what he wanted.

"If he did it to Ferson we can properly expect he would do it to Doyle. Isn't it strange that although he lived 21 years in Bayonne he didn't produce a character witness? He is afraid to expose his character."

Simpson spoke for only a few minutes, arguing that the police had proven nothing and the case should be thrown out. He said the detectives had devised a complicated and conspiratorial story that would have confused most juries—that is why the defense asked that only the trained mind of the judge hear the case.

"I'm not criticizing the police, but they made a terrible mistake," Simpson said.

The first hint of bad news came quickly. After Cahill's short rebuttal, Brown congratulated him and the police department for their masterful work. The good ole boy system was not on Rogers's side this day. The judge ruled immediately.

"It is true that the bulk of the testimony and the case against this defendant is built on circumstantial evidence. While the law requires that all circumstances must be consistent with one another and must point directly to the innocence or guilt of the accused, it is the solemn conclusion of the Court, having this in mind, that the defendant is guilty."

Brown ordered a psychiatric evaluation for Rogers and said he would be held in the Hudson County Jail until sentencing. The judge had discretion to give Rogers between five and twenty years and, before Brown adjourned court, he asked what Doyle suggested.

"Give him the maximum allowed by law," Doyle said.

When it was over, reporters swarmed Doyle. He told the *Bayonne Times* writer that he had become convinced of Rogers's guilt within a week of the accident, after seeing the evidence detectives had collected. He said that he felt sorry for Edith Rogers, for certainly she "doesn't know the type of man she's married to." As for his recommendation of a maximum sentence, Doyle had no regrets. As he spoke to the reporters, he rubbed the stumps of the three fingers he had lost.

"I hardly feel sorry for him," Doyle said.

Two weeks did nothing to calm Judge Brown's ire. He lectured Rogers for more than half an hour at the sentencing hearing on December 15. Brown had reviewed Rogers's past record and proclaimed it had not "inspired the Court in the slightest degree."

Although the judge never saw Francis Xavier Fay's report, he spoke of a history of unruliness and theft that could have been recited straight from it. He mentioned rumors of Rogers offering 25 cents to a young Bayonne boy in "an attempt to commit an unnatural crime." And Dr. Charles E. Clark, a psychiatrist with the New Jersey State Hospital for the Criminally Insane, had tested Rogers and rendered his own verdict. Clark said that George White Rogers had a psychopathic personality.

"Your crime is one of a most diabolical nature and it fell short of murder only by the intervention of Divine Providence," Brown said. "It is the type of crime ordinarily only executed by a man with a mind of a fiend."

Brown sentenced Rogers to twelve-to-twenty years in the state prison.

Rogers was moved from the county jail to Trenton just after Christmas 1938. By then, rumors had spread around Bayonne that the feds were sniffing around town, asking questions, talking to police. Word on the street was that the *Morro Castle* investigation had been reopened. Someone was very interested in George Rogers, people whispered, and they were looking very closely.

CHAPTER FIFTEEN

The War Effort

In January 1939, J. Edgar Hoover ordered his agents to send him everything they had on the *Morro Castle*. There was a lot to read, several thousand pages of reports, interview transcripts and newspaper articles crammed into file cabinets from Washington to New York. Agents had investigated the fire for nearly a year, but when no evidence of a Communist link was found, Hoover had lost interest. And since the chief agent on the case, Francis Xavier Fay, resigned in 1935, precious little new evidence had been found. But the rumors in Bayonne were not entirely accurate; the *Morro Castle* case had not been reopened—it had never really closed. And George Rogers wasn't a new suspect, he was the only suspect.

Rogers's conviction for the Doyle bombing caught the attention of Dwight Brantley, who had replaced F. X. Fay as the special agent in charge in New York. Fay's work on Rogers was fascinating, Brantley thought, and attempted murder certainly fit the psychological profile in the Fay report. Brantley had monitored the trial but was in no position to pursue a five-year-old case until Hoover became interested. And suddenly, he was very interested.

A sucker for conspiracy, Hoover was intrigued by an anonymous letter he'd received that reeked of it. Someone in Penns Grove, New Jersey—possibly a *Morro Castle* survivor—had sent him a long, rambling note about George Rogers, comparing his trial in Bayonne with the efforts to implicate George Alagna for arson years earlier. Whether the letter came from someone with a grudge, or just some local interested in the case, it was an astute observation.

Why was Rogers trying to make it appear that some one had set the ship on fire? He must have had some thoughts bearing on that particular idea and gave merit to his inner nervousness by trying to throw the blame on someone else. Now since he is convicted of such a dangerous crime I am all the more convinced that he had something to do with the death of the captain and setting that ship on fire. He was pretty clever with electricity. I think if you will use some of your most clever methods of crime detection on Rogers you will solve a great mystery.

Hoover recognized the opportunity, if not the significance, of this suggestion. He saw a chance to close a case that would bring his Bureau attention and continued prestige. It never hurt to enhance the reputation of the FBI.

In his fifteen years as head of the Federal Bureau of Investigation—as it was renamed in 1935—Hoover had built an impressive empire. He started in 1924 with 400 agents in 9 field offices and now commanded a network of 42 offices and more than 650 agents across the country. He added more people every week, and his power showed no sign of abating. Hoover had become accustomed to having things his way, following his whims. And on this day, his whim was the *Morro Castle*.

The cruise ship, it seemed, was everywhere. Hoover had gotten updates on the Rogers trial from New York, and had just received a request from the Ward Line asking permission for one of his agents to testify in a lawsuit. The insurance companies still had not paid for the loss of the cruise ship, and the Ward Line was suing. It gave Hoover pause. Perhaps, he thought, the insurance companies had a good reason not to pay. Hoover denied the Ward Line's request to use one of his men. The investigation was still open, he said, and anything the Bureau knew was confidential. Within a week, Hoover reversed himself and allowed George Starr to testify. He never said why.

Dwight Brantley visited the U.S. Attorney's Office in Manhattan a few days later. In a long afternoon, Brantley laid out what the Bureau had on

Rogers. He gave Lester C. Dunigan, the assistant U.S. attorney, a copy of the Fay report that Hoover had withheld from Martin Conboy in 1934. He drew comparisons between Rogers's earlier crimes, including the suspected arson, and what had happened on the *Morro Castle*. Rogers was a psychopath, Brantley said, and given this conviction for attempted murder, it might be a good time to make the arson case, perhaps even charge him with multiple counts of murder. If he knew Rogers had confessed the crime to Vincent Doyle, Brantley did not put it in writing. He said only that Hoover was interested.

Brantley, as it turned out, was wasting his breath. Dunigan was dismissive, said the case had been thoroughly investigated and properly tried in court. What more could they gain with an expensive, arduous—and possibly unsuccessful—trial.

"Rogers is already in jail—what more can we do to him?" Dunigan asked.

Rather than call Hoover on the telephone, Brantley delivered the bad news in a memo. It said, briefly, "No further investigation is desired."

Hoover was upset and perhaps even surprised. The U.S. Attorney's Office in Manhattan had changed considerably in four years. In 1934, he had to fight Martin Conboy to keep him from taking over the *Morro Castle* investigation. But Conboy was gone. In 1935, Francis W. H. Adams briefly replaced him to prosecute William Warms, Eben Abbott and Henry Cabaud. By the end of that year, Lamar Hardy had been appointed the U.S. attorney. Dunigan was one of Hardy's chief assistants.

The prosecutor's snub seemed to end Hoover's interest in the *Morro Castle*. If not for that slight, things might have developed differently. Six months later, in the summer of 1939, President Roosevelt replaced Lamar Hardy. *Time* magazine said it was part of FDR's shake-up of the Justice Department, and one White House source told *Time* that John Thomas Cahill had been brought in to replace the "lethargic" Hardy.

Perhaps another prosecutor might have reacted differently to Hoover's idea. But even though the *Morro Castle* file remained open, no agent would ever talk to Cahill—or any other prosecutor—about George Rogers. The Department of Justice let the case files gather dust in the same file cabinets for nearly seventy years, even after what came next. It was a decision that would cost people their lives.

* * *

The New Jersey Supreme Court denied Rogers an appeal in May 1939, just as the state court of errors and appeals would do two years later. No one was the least bit interested in the technicalities of law that Rogers said had violated his rights. It appeared he would linger in the state prison until at least 1947, when he would first be eligible for parole.

If nothing else, he made a passable prisoner. Rogers caused no trouble and accepted few visitors, mostly his wife and his friend George Brown. He spent much of his time working on his appeals or lying in his bunk reading dime-store novels, but soon graduated to the Bible. Some people in Bayonne, mostly a small circle of friends who still thought him a hero, believed he had been framed by the police, and his newfound faith gave them faith that they were right. After all, the evidence was circumstantial. Rogers said little about the case, and nothing about Vincent Doyle. For once, he went about his business as if he were trying to avoid attention.

His salvation came three years later, on December 7, 1941. That Sunday, not long after Rogers attended morning worship services at the prison, word reached the East Coast that Pearl Harbor had been attacked. The United States was now drawn into the war, and tragedy led to one of the country's proudest moments. Many boys lied about their age just to go into the service, eager to fight for their country. There was no shortage of troops, but few of these volunteers came trained as specialists.

In an inspired act of patriotism, the New Jersey Court of Pardons in 1942 solicited applications for parole from first-time offenders who wanted to serve their country. More than 350 prisoners applied, including George Rogers. In his letter to the board, he said that "the armed services need radiomen and I want to serve my country."

Although dozens of people wrote the War Department, the Department of Justice—even the president—asking that Rogers not be released, he was one of only thirty-one who received a conditional parole. But because the military would only accept men who had been given an unconditional parole, Rogers was upgraded. His clemency was granted in November 1942. A week later, Rogers took the exam to renew his operator license. He was a radioman once again.

Vincent Doyle was livid. Rogers had not served one-quarter of his sentence, and now he was being released. He could not believe the military would take him, grossly overweight and convicted of a violent crime. Most of the others released had been bank robbers, embezzlers—not especially violent psychopaths. In four years, Doyle had become an expert on Rogers and his criminal record. He knew more about it than even the FBI, so it particularly infuriated him for the parole board to consider him a "first-time offender."

Doyle could only think of one place it might do any good to complain—he wrote to the Federal Communications Commission. In a letter to the chairman, he pointed out that Rogers, who claimed to have distinguished himself on the *Morro Castle,* was the same fiend who had tried to kill him, and was supposed to be serving out a twelve-to-twenty-year sentence in the state prison. He suggested they not issue him an operator's license.

> *The purpose of this letter is to give your honorable body fair warning that what happened on the* Morro Castle *when he was chief operator can very easily happen again if Rogers gets a suitable opportunity.*
>
> *This "fiend" loose on one of our ships as an operator may prove embarrassing to any official who may be instrumental in allowing him another opportunity to practice his criminal tendencies.*
>
> *For my part his employment aboard ship would be consoling. He would be away from Bayonne and me. I am concerned, however, with the possibilities of what might happen aboard that ship and the resulting consequences to some other innocent victim.*
>
> *The problem is yours. It is my duty to inform you. No doubt the FBI can and will substantiate these assertions if an investigation is made.*

Doyle had no luck convincing anyone to revoke Rogers's parole, but he was right about one thing: the military did not want him. Even with his new radio operator's license, Rogers could only get as close to the war as the SS *Walter Colton.* The *Colton* was one of 2,751 Liberty Ships, square-hulled merchant marine vessels that carried everything from food, mail and ammunition to troops in the Pacific. The "ugly ducklings," as FDR called them, could move jeeps and airplanes and move them fast, but they were built quickly, on the cheap, and were not particularly safe. At 441 feet, they were only slightly smaller than Rogers's last ship, the *Morro Castle.*

Even in a military environment, during a war, Rogers seemed drawn to trouble. In his abbreviated stint on the *Colton,* he was interviewed at least twice by the FBI, but this time as an informant. Rogers's role in these incidents, however, was suspicious to the Bureau at best.

In May of 1944, Rogers cooperated with an investigation of a man accused of stealing military supplies—binoculars and watches, mostly. Rogers admitted he tried to buy some things from the man but claimed it was "only to collect evidence." As proof of his intentions, Rogers offered to testify against the man.

One month later, Rogers spoke to agents investigating charges of treason against Oscar Niger, captain of the *Walter Colton.* Rogers and two other officers on the ship claimed that Niger, born of German parents, was sympathetic to the Nazis. They said Niger left confidential information about the ship's course lying around in plain sight, called American radio reports a bunch of "bull" and got "very gruff" when reports of sunken Japanese ships came in over the telegraph. For good measure, Rogers added that the man was anti-Semitic and racist. Niger was replaced as captain, but no one ever proved he was a traitor or even a Nazi sympathizer.

In the summer of 1944, his service on the Liberty Ships quickly over, Rogers returned to Bayonne. He claimed he had been discharged because of a medical disability—just as he had left the navy—but Doyle heard that Rogers had been arrested in Australia and returned to the United States in chains for committing "enemy alien activities." The story spread, but Rogers denied it and sent a threatening letter to the admiral of the Coast Guard asking them to refute the rumor.

Whether the story was true, it seemed that Rogers had done little of consequence, because he soon had a job with a defense contractor in Jersey City. Rogers impressed the bosses at Eastern Manufacturing so much that he was soon promoted to foreman. For Rogers, the work was easy and the location convenient. He had to be in Jersey City the last Tuesday of each month anyway to see his parole officer, a fringe benefit he did not disclose to his new employers. By the time they found out, company president

Nathan Leonard was so happy with Rogers's work that he let that résumé omission slide.

The company, a subsidiary of the Super Electric Company, built static dischargers for U.S. Army Air Force bombers, and the government wanted 90,000 of these dinguses a month. To keep up with the demand, the company opened another plant in Brooklyn, where Rogers was sent as a floor supervisor. In June 1945, he became boss to many of the plant's eighty employees, most of them women.

He enjoyed being in charge once again. Rogers being himself, there was of course one man he did not get along with. He believed another supervisor, Henry Alfeld, was after his job and spread several nasty rumors about the man. Alfeld dismissed his quarrels with Rogers, telling anyone who asked, "That guy's got a screw loose."

Most people thought Rogers, now forty-four years old, was silly, fawning over a girl on the assembly line. He spent much of his time trying to impress this young woman, bragging about the action he'd seen in the Pacific during the war, his heroics aboard the *Morro Castle.* He even told her that he'd won the Purple Heart. As part of his pathetic courtship, he bought her expensive presents, including a nice wristwatch.

The woman found George Rogers sad. Despite his bravado, and exaggerations so obvious that even an innocent Jersey girl could see through, she sensed a certain melancholy in him. At times, Rogers seemed overly sentimental—a side of him no one else had ever noticed. But he also could be violently jealous, flying into a rage whenever she spoke to another man at the plant. Because she did not want to upset him, the girl allowed Rogers to call on her at her mother's house. A few times, she even went out to eat with him.

Rogers thought he was in love. He told the girl he was getting a divorce and wanted to marry her, offering to buy her a big diamond ring— anything she wanted. The girl tried to gently laugh off his proclamations of love, teasing that he was way too old for her. In truth, she already had a fiancé, a sailor, but did not dare tell Rogers. She did not know what he might do. Soon enough, she found out.

Rogers showed up at the girl's house one afternoon while her sailor was visiting. Enraged, Rogers demanded to know who the man was, why he was there. He swore he would kill her and any man she chose to marry. After that, they didn't speak for nearly a week, the girl doing all she could to avoid Rogers at work. Still, on July 8, he proposed to her again, even showed her the ring. She said no.

A few days later, the girl left work violently ill. No one thought much about it—nearly everyone in the plant had been sick lately. Stomach flu was going around, or so they said. Dozens of people called in sick every morning that week, and as many as forty people—half the workers in the plant—were absent a few times. Production fell behind schedule. It got so serious the company was threatened with losing its defense contract.

Rogers was there every day, looking forlorn and complaining to the other women that his marriage was a disaster. He confided to a few that he had a "special relationship" with one of the women on the assembly line, as if no one had noticed how he followed the girl around like an old fool.

George Rogers's love did not return to the plant. She quit by telephone, ran off and married the sailor. When he heard the news, Rogers was devastated. He did not show up at the plant for a week and, when he did, he told the women on the line that he had been sick because "my girlfriend recently got married."

The absenteeism became so serious that, on July 24, the company president visited the plant. In a meeting with supervisors, Nathan Leonard asked why there had been such a slowdown and warned that it could lead to layoffs. Most blamed Rogers for the laxness; conversely, he said the problem was all the absences and a time study conducted by the company that had interfered with production.

After the meeting, Leonard followed Rogers to his line on the third floor, perhaps trying to judge whether the criticism of him was justified. Along the way, he paused at the water cooler for a drink, but Rogers stopped him.

"Don't drink that," he said.

"Why?"

"I think it's been poisoned."

Leonard had been so impressed with Rogers's work that he forgave the radioman for not disclosing a felony conviction on his job application, but now he wondered if he had made a mistake. Rogers had seemed tense during the meeting and now he was talking crazy. Leonard ignored the warning and had two cups of the water. He said it tasted fine to him.

The next day, Leonard returned to the plant on other business, and Rogers went out of his way to ask, "How do you feel?" Leonard thought it odd and, before he left, asked the company chemist to test the water cooler. "Find out what the devil Rogers is talking about."

That afternoon, the chemist called Leonard in a panic. The water in the cooler had been tainted with a high concentration of potassium thiocyanate, a chemical used in making the static dischargers. It was a lethal poison—an ounce could kill a person.

The police were called and their chemists came up with the same results in separate tests on the water. It appeared that the only cooler affected was on the third floor, where Rogers worked. And oddly enough, Rogers had complained about the water several days ago, the company chemist told investigators. He had said the water tasted funny, suggested it was the reason everyone was sick and even speculated that the cooler had been poisoned. At the time, it had seemed a stupid statement. Now it appeared damning for Rogers. The trouble with his astute observation was that potassium thiocyanate had no smell or taste.

The FBI was at the plant the next day. Because it held defense contracts, the federal government was most interested in any problem with the company, and agents got the picture quickly: The water was delivered every few days by a local business; they were the only ones who were supposed to handle the coolers; it was in a spot on the floor where someone could always see it. There was hardly a time it could have been tampered with, as most people left work at the same time every day—except the supervisors, Alfeld and Rogers. They were often in the building until well after 8 P.M.

By the end of the day, agents had interviewed nearly everyone in the plant except Rogers. Now he claimed to be sick. His wife had called that morning to say that he was going to the hospital. Although it sounded serious, Edith Rogers said he would be back to work "in a few days."

The FBI visited Rogers in Bayonne, where he claimed to be recuperating from a strange illness. He told the investigators that he had been to the doctor twice and that he believed he had been poisoned. Rogers accused Alfeld of contaminating the water in a jealous plot to get his job. It was, at least, a scenario he understood well.

The investigation lasted most of a week, but the evidence was weak. The poison had come from the plant's own lab, but there was no way to prove who had put it into the water—any number of people could have gotten to the potassium thiocyanate. The FBI suspected Rogers, as most people at the plant did, but there was no proof, only speculation. Agents checked Rogers's story with the hospital, where two doctors said they had treated him, but only because he asked. Dr. Frederick A. Finger told agents that Rogers had come in on July 25—the day the police were called to the plant—complaining of stomach pains. Finger said he could not find anything wrong with Rogers, but prescribed a mild sedative with some codeine.

Eventually, the FBI and the police gave up their investigation. For a while, the water was tested every day, but it was never again tainted. There were suspicious glances cast at Rogers, and peopled talked, but they said nothing to him. The war ended, and George Rogers left the company before the end of summer.

Time passed. George Rogers felt like an outcast in Bayonne. Many people would not speak to him, and what few friends he had were the radiomen who'd known him before his time in jail. He saw Vincent Doyle around town often, but they did not speak. Rogers acted as if his former friend did not exist, and Doyle went out of his way to avoid contact.

Rogers returned to the television and radio repair business but could no longer afford to rent a storefront on Broadway. He set up shop in his living room and made house calls in a new panel truck that advertised the business without mentioning his name. It was nowhere near as profitable as his factory job, which had paid $85 a week (about $900 in 2006 dollars). Now he had to scrape by just to live and was forced to do odd jobs for the few people in town who believed he got a bum deal. Rogers was always broke.

One of his few friends was William Hummel, who lived a block down the street. Hummel, in his late seventies, was a retired printer who had worked for New York magazines and the *Bayonne Times*. The two shared a love of electronic gadgets and photography, and talked endlessly about Scripture. When tape recorders became affordable—and Hummel could afford quite a bit—he bought one and recorded himself and Rogers talking. Soon, they even learned how to tape telephone conversations. Hummel's wife had died and he lived with his daughter, who was a few years older than Rogers but had never married. In all the hours he spent at the house, Edith Hummel paid Rogers little mind.

Hummel thought Rogers an odd bird—he often told stories that didn't quite make sense and wore the same pair of gray pants every day—but considered him his closest friend. Rogers had developed what Hummel believed to be a profound spirituality since his days in "Trenton"—his euphemism for the state prison. He wrote to his old friends at the *Bayonne Times,* repeatedly asking them to run editorials that would clear Rogers's bad name. This reputation, Hummel said, prevented Rogers from making money; he was nearly starving. Hummel felt Rogers was a good man who had been unjustly jailed. He chose not to believe all the horrible stories; in fact, he trusted Rogers enough to give him a key to his house.

In May 1947, Rogers came to Hummel with a plan to make money buying government surplus from the federal War Assets Administration. Rogers said he could get two 8–16-millimeter Bell & Howell sound film projectors for $150. If Hummel would advance him the money, Rogers said he'd give him one of the projectors for $75 and they could sell the other to pay for it. Hummel wrote his friend a check for $175—the extra $25 "for your trouble." Rogers was down on his luck and Hummel was glad to help, and he liked the idea of owning a projector. It was just the kind of gadget Hummel had wanted—perhaps he'd even mentioned it. The next day, Rogers showed him a receipt from the War Assets Administration that said the projectors were on the way.

A week later, the projectors still had not arrived, but Rogers had come across another deal. He could get two TV receivers, two recorders and some blank tapes for just $550. Rogers offered Hummel the same deal, and again the old man wrote his friend a check.

When the equipment did not arrive after a few months of waiting, Rogers suggested they hire an attorney, and Hummel gave Rogers $1,000 to do so. He left the business dealings to Rogers—it gave him something to do. This wrangling went on for a year, Rogers explaining that the government moved slowly. In August 1948, he produced a letter from the WAA that apologized for the oversight and promised to send more equipment to compensate them for their trouble. Shipping and packing charges on all this equipment would run another $1,200. Hummel paid, but that shipment never arrived either.

The only correspondence Hummel ever saw were requests for insurance fees and shipping charges. Hummel paid it all until he had advanced nearly $7,500 to Rogers. Eventually, Hummel confided to his brother-in-law that he was worried, afraid that Rogers was being scammed by someone at the WAA, or perhaps even this Washington attorney. If Hummel had considered he was the one being scammed, he did not admit it. But he could hardly avoid the possibility after talking to his brother-in-law, who said the WAA letters looked fake.

Repeatedly, Rogers apologized for getting his friend into the mess and constantly updated him on his efforts to get their equipment or money back. Hummel sometimes was short with Rogers, even nasty on occasion, but he did not say too much. He came to be afraid of Rogers, knowing that he was temperamental. He feared that if he made George Rogers too mad, he might never get his money back.

Three more years passed. Rogers's business did not improve, nor did it go under. In May 1952, he was released from parole, which had been reinstituted after the war. It made little difference to Rogers; his life didn't change. Most days, he and Hummel spent their time recording phone conversations. Rogers worked on Hummel's television and radios for free as a gesture of goodwill between them. The missing equipment and the money rarely came up in their conversations, and then only when Hummel brought it up.

On June 18, 1953, a Thursday, Rogers stayed late at the Hummels' house repairing their television. That night, Hummel broke the news that he and Edith were leaving town. They had decided to retire, which was funny since he was by then eighty-three and Edith was nearing sixty. Their plan was to move to St. Petersburg, Florida, where they would buy a little house or apartment on the Gulf of Mexico and enjoy the salt air. Bayonne could be a cold and depressing place in winter, especially for old bones. Hummel announced that he had just sold his house and would soon have all his local business concluded. He asked Rogers if he could repay the money he had lent him over the years. Besides the money for the equipment that had never arrived, Rogers had often borrowed $75 here and $100 there to pay for newspaper advertisements or business expenses.

Rogers was quiet as Hummel chattered into the evening. When he finished working, Rogers told Bill and Edith that he would miss them, and promised to get their money before they left town.

The next morning, Bill Hummel stepped out of his house just before 10 A.M. He walked west, toward Broadway, planning to stop at John Harding's newsstand to pick up a *New York Herald Tribune*—as he did every day—on his way to the bank, the First Savings & Loan. He and Edith were leaving Saturday for Bloomington, N.Y., where his brother was in poor health. Hummel wanted to pay some of his brother's bills and visit for a week or so before returning to finish packing for the move to Florida.

That morning, Hummel had many things on his mind—there was so much to do, preparations to make. He most likely also thought about Rogers and whether he would really ever see any of his money. He could not have been optimistic.

A moment later, as he stood at the corner of 37th Street and Avenue E, just a block from his house, George Rogers rolled up in his red flat-panel truck.

"If you're going downtown, Bill, I'll give you a lift," he said.

CHAPTER SIXTEEN

The Death Hammer Falls

Monday morning, June 22, George Rogers walked into Paul Scheff's radio repair shop at 12th and C. He dropped by nearly every day, much to the irritation of Mrs. Scheff, who thought his standing around "chewing the rag" disrupted business. The Scheffs did not consider Rogers a close friend and assumed he came in only because he was bored. It was no secret that Rogers had little work himself.

Normally, he didn't show up before lunch, but on this day Rogers was early. Scheff figured he had come in to brag about the stool he delivered to the store Friday afternoon, a gift that he called a "Father's Day" present. Rogers was a notorious cheapskate, so Scheff had been touched by the gesture, if not a little wary. Surprisingly, Rogers said little about the stool this morning. Instead, he talked about how much weight he'd lost, enough that he was forced to get another pair of slacks.

"The pair I've been wearing are so big for me now I have trouble keeping them on," Rogers said.

Scheff found it ironic that, of all things, a diet had forced Rogers to abandon his ratty old pants, which were a running joke in town. For two years, he had worn the same gray work pants every day—most people assumed it was the only pair he owned. He now wore a nicer, but not new, pair of khakis.

Rogers talked about nothing for a few minutes—the weather and local gossip—then turned as if to leave. For a moment, he paced around the store, Scheff would later say, "like an actor waiting offstage for his cue." Then Rogers began to speak in a low voice, as if he were telling a secret.

"There's a bit of a mystery up in my neighborhood," he said. "Two old people left home to go up to New York State, and they haven't arrived there yet. Nobody knows what happened to them."

Scheff was afraid that if he showed too much interest, Rogers might get started on some long tale with no point and never leave. Mrs. Scheff would not like that. But to avoid being rude, he asked the obvious.

"Who is it?"

"Bill Hummel and his daughter," Rogers said.

He did not say anything else about it, and left soon after that. Scheff thought it mildly odd, but nearly everything about George Rogers was odd. He did not realize that, in fact, Rogers had let him in on a secret. On June 22, no one else knew the Hummels were missing, and wouldn't for another nine days.

The first heat wave of the summer had struck Bayonne. On July 1, it was 95 degrees, with humidity that stifled movement. The police couldn't tell if it improved or hurt the crime rate: fewer people were out, but those who were seemed to be in an irritable mood. Just after 4 P.M. that day, Louis Smith, captain of detectives for the Bayonne Police Department, was about to take off when a lieutenant escorted two elderly men into his office. The old men looked bewildered, perhaps even nervous.

Henry Schuct and Gottlieb Aeckerle introduced themselves as brothers-in-law of Bill Hummel. They had driven down from Jersey City looking for Hummel, who they claimed had not been in touch with them for more than a week.

"Henry here received a letter from Bill's brother in Bloomington, New York," Aeckerle said. "Henry Hummel, that's the brother, sent a letter that said Bill and his daughter, Edith, were due to go to Bloomington to see Henry. They were supposed to arrive up there on Saturday, June 20, and they never arrived. Henry asked us to find out why Bill and Edith didn't get up there."

They had phoned the Hummel residence repeatedly and, finally, after more than a day of unanswered calls, drove down. They went to the house and rang the bell but couldn't see any sign of anyone inside. The windows were closed, the doors locked. The old men didn't know what else to do, so they had come to the police station.

"In this weather, I don't know how anyone can be in there without any fresh air," Aeckerle said. "We walked over to the next corner and asked Mr. and Mrs. Rogers if they could tell us anything about the Hummels. They said they may have been staying up in Bloomington longer than they expected to."

"This Rogers you speak of, is he the fellow that lives at 38th Street and Avenue E?" Smith asked.

"Yes," Aeckerle said. "George Rogers said that maybe Bill and Edith decided to go to Florida and not bother going up to Bloomington to see Henry. . . . Well, that I could not believe. Bill Hummel would not do that. We feel certain that something has happened to them."

Smith thought for a second, and then called in two officers to take the men back to the Hummel house while he radioed another car to meet them. On the surface, it did not seem like a police matter, but Smith did not like the sound of their story. Something about it disturbed him.

Lieutenant Irving Horweck and Patrolman Harry Rubenstein arrived at the house first. The porch was cluttered with floor lamps, wooden barrels and boxes like someone was getting ready to move, but the screen was latched. When Aeckerle and Schuct arrived in the other police car, Rubenstein asked the old men for permission to cut through the porch screen.

Rubenstein crawled through the small opening that he cut and then flipped the latch so the others could join him. The front door was unlocked, but when he pushed it open, the stench inside the house nearly knocked all four of them backward.

William Hummel was on the dining room floor, his body bloated, black and lying in a pool of blood and body fluid that was swarming with maggots. A pair of glasses and a set of false teeth lay between his legs on the flowered rug. Somehow, Rubenstein managed to avoid vomiting before he ran out of the house.

The patrolman allowed Aeckerle and Schuct inside just long enough to identify the body. While Horweck called for backup, Rubenstein walked back inside, a handkerchief over his face. In the kitchen, he discovered an even worse smell and a pool of fluid in the floor. Soon, he figured out that this dark goo was dripping down from the ceiling.

They found Edith Hummel upstairs, halfway underneath her bed as if she had tried to get away from something. Her head was smashed, her body was bloated, a scene nearly identical to the one downstairs. The mattress was stained with blood, as if she had lain there before rolling off. Both the Hummels had been dead a long time.

That evening, Louis Smith inspected the house with Anthony Vatalaro, superintendent of the New Jersey Bureau of Criminal Identification. Vatalaro estimated the Hummels had been dead about ten days. Bill Hummel lay where he was killed, but it looked as if Edith had been attacked elsewhere. There was no sign of struggle in the room where she was found.

"What do you make of it, Tony?" Smith asked.

"Murder and suicide?"

"Can't be," Smith said. "In the first place, who murdered who? Neither one of them could have been the suicide. Nobody could possibly inflict such punishment upon himself and then hide the instrument that was used to do it. Someone came into this house, found one of them alone, killed that one and waited for the other."

"There's no other way," Vatalaro agreed.

Smith ordered the officers outside to corral the gathering crowd and then sent a couple of detectives to interview the neighbors. As Smith stood in front of the house trying to draw a fresh breath, he looked up the street at the white house on the corner. *Why isn't Rogers outside rubbernecking like everyone else? If he were buddies with Hummel, you'd expect him to be the first one down here.*

Smith motioned for two officers to follow him up to Rogers's house. Smith didn't care for the radioman—no one in the police department did. Vince Doyle was a good fellow, and Rogers had embarrassed the Bayonne Police Department. The guy was trouble.

George Rogers answered the doorbell as if he were surprised, as if he hadn't seen them walking up the sidewalk from his window.

"What's on your mind?"

"George," Smith said, "do you know the Hummels?"

"Oh yes. They were my dearest friends."

Past tense. Smith caught it, looked to see if the others had. Only the cops, the two brothers-in-law and the killer knew the Hummels were dead.

With little prompting, Rogers told Smith he'd been over at the house on Thursday, June 18, and had given Bill Hummel a ride to the bank the next day. He hadn't seen either of them since. Rogers was cooperative, friendly, but he never asked why Smith wanted to know all of this, why all the cops. He never asked if anything bad had happened to his friends.

The next day, Rogers was arrested as a material witness in the murders of William and Edith Hummel.

George Rogers had gone to the police station as soon as he heard the detectives wanted to talk to him. During questioning, he contradicted some things he had said to Smith the day before, and that's all it took. As a material witness, he was free to roam the jail, but not leave the station. His bail was set at $25,000—an unheard of sum for a mere witness. It suggested the police thought he was more than just someone with information.

Police made good use of their unfettered access to Rogers. They questioned him twice a day, a drill he seemed to take in stride. Rogers chain-smoked through interviews, going through a pack of cigarettes in just a few hours. The more civilized pipe he used to carry had long since been abandoned.

Rogers swore he knew nothing about the Hummels' death, but he showed no real grief over the loss of his "dear friends," as he called them. He simply kept repeating that he was innocent. When he wasn't being questioned, Rogers read from a pocket Bible, a cigarette dangling from his lip. He played the role of a martyr with considerable skill, often calling for the police chaplain to pray with him. Once, he asked to send a note to his wife and, when an officer read it, he found Rogers had simply transcribed a passage from the Bible, the same one he had written on the wall of his cell.

This behavior in no way matched the profile of the killer that detectives were developing. The person who murdered the Hummels had been vicious, unmerciful. The autopsies showed both William and Edith had suffered a fractured skull—they were beaten to death. While Edith may have bled to death, her father died from a single violent blow that left a large hole in the back of his skull.

Everything the police found suggested they died on June 19. No one had seen Mr. Hummel after he left the bank that morning; the mail and the newspapers dated back to June 19; they had not left on a trip scheduled to begin the next day.

Robbery was the motive, at least that's what Smith told the *Bayonne Times*. After all, the $2,400 Hummel had withdrawn from the bank was missing, and people had died for far less. In truth, Smith wasn't sure why they were dead, but he believed Rogers killed them, and called in the best person he knew to help with the case.

Smith visited Doyle with two detectives. He explained that the investigators would do most of the legwork but also follow his directions. They needed his insights into their suspect if they were going to make this murder rap stick. At first, Vincent J. Doyle begged them to leave him out of it.

"I cannot play any official part in this investigation," he said. "Everyone knows I am prejudiced against Rogers. Who wouldn't be if he were in my shoes?"

"They have orders to keep you out of it."

Initially, they turned up nothing. They searched the sewers and woods near Rogers's house for a murder weapon, but it was nowhere to be found. No one in the neighborhood remembered anything strange. A few people admitted they had smelled something but assumed it was a dead cat in the alley. The Hummels had not been seen in two weeks, although one lady claimed Mr. Hummel called to wish her daughter a happy birthday on the afternoon of June 19. A few neighbors thought it odd they had let the newspapers and mail pile up, as they usually asked someone to collect it when they traveled. Truth was, most people didn't much care—they found the Hummels a bit eccentric. Before Rogers was arrested, many neighbors even speculated the old man killed his daughter and then himself. Fueling this rumor was a neighbor who said she heard them arguing over the size of the home they were going to buy in Florida. Mr. Hummel wanted two rooms; Edith preferred four.

Doyle told the detectives to dissect Rogers's testimony, for he was most likely lying about something. Rogers had said it was nearly 11 A.M. when he picked up Hummel that Friday and claimed he then went to Paul Scheff's radio shop before returning home for lunch. They started by checking his alibi. Reluctantly, Doyle went with the detectives to visit the repair shop.

Scheff did not want to get involved and, at first, his answers were vague. He claimed he wasn't there when Rogers visited that day, June 19, but Doyle reminded him that he'd already said he was in the shop all that morning. Yes, Scheff said, he was—but Rogers didn't come in until that afternoon, when Mrs. Scheff was minding the store.

Shirley Scheff said Rogers was only there a moment. He dropped off the stool, made a phone call and then hurried out. He had said he was busy painting—in fact, he had paint all over his pants. Doyle asked what color the paint had been.

Why, Mrs. Scheff said, it was red.

Doyle believed Rogers had built extra time into his entire day. A man at the newsstand said Hummel picked up his *New York Herald Tribune* at 9:55 every morning, and was never late. Bank receipts indicated Hummel had withdrawn his money before 11 A.M., several minutes before Rogers claimed he picked up his "dear friend."

They tried to follow the money. Hummel left the bank with more than $2,000 in cash, but it was not in his pocket or at the house. The killer likely had the money, the detectives knew, or had spent it. Doyle asked around in local electronics stores he knew to see if Rogers had been in lately. With just a few phone calls, he found nearly $350 worth of equipment Rogers bought on June 22 alone. At one store in Jersey City, Rogers had spent $296 and paid with three $100 bills. Rogers, Doyle knew, hadn't seen a $100 bill he'd earned in ages.

Doyle took two detectives and Anthony Vatalaro from the Bureau of Criminal Identification to Rogers's house. They asked Edith Rogers about every piece of equipment in the house and soon discovered that he had a number of Hummel's tape recorders. They found Rogers's old gray pants, still stained red. Edith swore her husband had gotten paint on them "months ago," but they looked and smelled as if they had been washed a number of times. Doyle suggested Edith not lie for her husband, that she might be his next victim if he thought disposing of witnesses would save his neck. It took little coercion for her to break down.

"He's been nothing but trouble since the day I met him thirty-odd years ago, and if he murdered my two friends, he deserves no sympathy," she said.

"Edith, you have my deepest sympathy," Doyle said. "I have known for many years that your husband broke the hearts of both your father and mother. He alienated your brother Bill. He killed your dog because you went to the funeral of a cousin when he told you not to. He killed the captain of the *Morro Castle* before he set fire to that ship, killing 134 more people. But for the intervention of Divine Providence, he would have killed me. He killed your friends, the Hummels, and spent the money which he robbed from Bill Hummel's dead body. You are right when you say he deserves no sympathy."

Edith looked at Doyle blankly as he turned and walked away. She looked at Vatalaro and asked, "Who is he?"

The police took most of a week searching the Hummel house. It had taken days just to air out the place enough to stand the smell, and it was still rank beyond belief. They found an endless array of electronics equipment—the old man had enjoyed his gadgets—and also tape recordings, including a voice from the grave: a phone conversation between Hummel and Rogers. On it, Hummel asked about some man who had evidently just gone to Washington. Hummel seemed aggravated; Rogers, evasive. Hearing the conversation between Hummel and his likely killer gave the detectives a cold chill. The next day, they stumbled upon something even worse. Hidden beneath the basement steps, the police found a 2-pound sledgehammer caked with dried blood.

On July 8, police looking through Hummel's bank statements noticed some canceled checks were missing. The detectives paused for a moment, wondering whether this was a clue. And then, among the paperwork, they found the kind of evidence most detectives can only dream about. It was a note in Hummel's handwriting: "The following is an account of my transactions with George W. Rogers."

It seemed Hummel had been Rogers's own personal bank. Bill Hummel had paid George and Edith Rogers for tending to his wife before she died in 1947, and even took care of the bills from the *Bayonne Times* when

George took out ads for his business. The note detailed loan after loan that Hummel gave Rogers to buy government war surplus material, mostly electronics that they had planned to sell and split the profits. It had cost Hummel $7,500—a sizable sum, considering Hummel's house had sold for only $10,500.

"It may have been unwise on my part to continually advance money, but Rogers is very temperamental and I was in constant fear that he might have reneged on the purchase from the WAA and I would be in danger of losing everything," Hummel wrote.

Doyle thought the scheme had cost Bill Hummel much more than $7,500. And when Smith learned of Hummel's accounting of business deals with Rogers, he declared that the detectives had enough evidence. They had their case.

Rogers had hired Maurice A. Cohen, a former assemblyman and city attorney, as his lawyer. When he wasn't praying with the police chaplain, Rogers spent most of his time discussing his predicament with Cohen. The lawyer tried to get his bail reduced, just to get him out of there, but he was repeatedly turned down. Cohen had no idea why the police continued to hold Rogers without charges, and he filed motions to get him released. He said detaining a man as a witness for nearly three weeks was crazy. The day Cohen was scheduled to discuss this with the judge, Rogers was charged with two counts of first-degree murder.

George Rogers spent more than a year in the Hudson County Jail awaiting his trial. The first, in May 1954, was declared a mistrial when three jurors were excused in four days. One juror's father died, and a second became so ill the judge called in a doctor to examine her. She was diagnosed as "too sick" to serve. The third, another woman, was excused when her health deteriorated. Some said she became too nauseated to sleep or eat after seeing the crime scene photos of William and Edith Hummel.

Before the judge called a mistrial, Bayonne heard much of the prosecution's evidence: the money Rogers extorted from Hummel that he could not repay; the stained pants he stopped wearing the day after the Hummels were last seen alive; the bloody sledgehammer that the *Bayonne Times* dubbed, in a sensational headline, "The Death Hammer."

His second trial began on September 13, 1954, and in its first day, only six jurors were seated. The publicity surrounding the case had permeated the county, making it hard to find anyone who had yet to form an opinion about Rogers. County Judge Paul J. Duffy, already weary of this hoopla, announced that he might hold court on Saturdays to speed the trial along.

It was, without question, the most high-profile case the county had seen in some time, perhaps since Rogers stood trial for the Doyle bombing in 1938. Every day throughout the trial, reporters and onlookers would crowd into the building in hopes of catching a glimpse of the disgraced *Morro Castle* hero. Few of the people wandering into the building knew the history of the Zodiac murals, ornate gold elevator doors, bronze railings and colonial paintings on the courtroom walls—the connection to Millet and the *Titanic.* Rogers found the most historical significance in the second-floor courtroom where he was on trial. It was the same room where he had been sentenced in 1938.

Doyle attended the trial every day, attracting his own share of attention. He said nothing, gave no comment to reporters. No one thought it particularly strange that he was there: who could blame him for wanting to see Rogers get his final comeuppance?

The assembled crowd got their glimpse of Rogers that morning as he was led into the courtroom, and he looked the same as he would for the entire trial: wearing his one suit, a cigarette stuck to his bottom lip, his hands cuffed. He stared ahead vacantly, meeting no one's gaze.

After Maurice Cohen's standard request for a mistrial was denied, Rogers watched the prosecution and defense wrangle over jurors into the fourth day of the trial. Ultimately, only two Bayonne residents would serve on the jury: Thadeus Romanowski and the appropriately named Joseph Hammer. Out of the fourteen, five of them would be women, including the last seated, a sixty-year-old housewife from Hoboken named Eugenie Iff.

From the beginning, there was a war of words in the press. Julius Canter, the assistant prosecutor, announced that the state would seek the death penalty. Rogers, through his wife, declared his innocence and said his faith in God would set him free, but it was not long before the jury heard Rogers himself speak. Early in the first day of testimony, Judge Duffy asked if he could hear the description of the crime scene from John O'Donnell, assistant superintendent of the Criminal Identification Bureau.

"I can hear him talking, but I don't understand everything said," Rogers said.

"Have you ever used a hearing aid?" the judge asked.

"No, sir, if I run a radio and TV set where I can adjust the volume and sensitivity, I can hear perfectly."

Duffy ordered the guard to move Rogers closer to the witness stand.

Canter once again hauled out the Death Hammer and the bloody pants, although Cohen forced the state's expert to admit he could not positively identify the blood type on them. The most damaging testimony, however, came from Paul Scheff, who told jurors that Rogers had spoken of the Hummels' disappearance on June 22, 1953—more than a week before anyone else suspected they were missing. Scheff noted that Rogers was wearing different pants than normal that day, a pair of khakis, and had even mentioned it.

For the first two days, it seemed the entire state's case was based on Rogers knowing the Hummels' fate before anyone else. Mrs. Henry Hummel of Bloomington, whose sick husband had since died, said that she did not make any calls or write letters to her brother in Jersey City inquiring about William and Edith until June 30. Hummel's brothers-in-law, Henry Schuct and Gottlieb Aeckerle, testified and got their picture in the paper after recounting that hot afternoon when the bodies had been found more than a year earlier. And George Squire, who owned an appliance store in Bayonne, said that Rogers came into his shop the day after the bodies were found.

"He said, 'They have had me down for questioning already.'"

"Are you sure he said, 'already'?" Canter asked.

"I'm sure."

Canter looked at the jurors and said, "Remember that word, 'already.'"

Captain Louis Smith introduced the motive with his testimony, reading from Hummel's own notes about the money Rogers owed him. Smith said Hummel's records showed $7,538 Rogers had taken from the old man, but that only went up to 1949. In fact, Smith claimed, Rogers owed William Hummel more than $14,000. Hummel wanted the money back before he moved to Florida, and Rogers could not repay the loan. So, Smith said, he killed them both.

The prosecution was methodical in laying out its case. To support Smith's allegation, Canter called to the stand the bank teller who had helped Hummel on June 19. She said Hummel's withdrawal had included three $100 bills. Next, the prosecutor called the owner of a Jersey City store who showed Rogers had paid his tab with three $100 bills on June 22.

By the time Canter finished on Wednesday, September 22, he had called fifty-five witnesses, exhibited a lot of circumstantial evidence and offered a motive. Abraham Miller, Cohen's cocounsel in Rogers's defense, tellingly argued that the state "had not produced the slightest scintilla of evidence to show that Rogers committed murder in the first degree on Edith Hummel." He said nothing, however, about Bill Hummel. Duffy denied the defense attorney's motion to dismiss the charges.

On Thursday morning, Maurice Cohen looked nervous as he walked into the courthouse. He stopped briefly to speak to reporters, noting that "we have an important decision to make in the next twenty or thirty minutes." If he left the newspapermen wondering what that decision might be, they were not guessing for long. When the court convened, the defense and prosecution retreated to the judge's chambers for forty minutes. When they emerged, Cohen stood before the jury and said, simply, "The defense rests."

Rogers would not testify, and his attorneys would not call any witnesses. The strategy was meant to imply he needed no defense, that the state had not made a case worth arguing against. It was a gamble, but it avoided what Cohen and Miller feared most: George Rogers under cross-examination.

Julius Canter spent much of the seventy minutes of his closing argument talking about Rogers's failure to testify. It was not a matter of innocence, Canter argued to the jury, but a chance to prove he was not guilty. Rogers's silence, he said, was telling.

"You were saying to yourself, 'Now let's hear the defendant. Maybe he has an explanation. Surely he has something to say. Surely they will produce witnesses who will help us decide.

"George Rogers, help us. Is there any doubt where you got the hundred-dollar bills from? These pants, aren't they yours?

"Did you stop wearing them after the 19th?

"Help us, George Rogers. We are the jury who must decide your fate.

George Rogers, help us. We are ordinary, average citizens. We don't want to send you to the chair. Help us, George Rogers. Tell us. Nobody knows but you."

Canter claimed the stool Rogers gave to Paul Scheff was his alibi, a way to put him in a different place at the time of the murder. He said Scheff's testimony was damning because the radio repairman "is not a cop, not my friend, but a friend of George Rogers," yet he felt compelled to tell his story of how Rogers knew the Hummels' fate before anyone else.

Canter took the Death Hammer in his hand, raised it above his head and described in graphic detail the murder of Edith Hummel. He said Rogers arrived at the house within minutes after taking William Hummel to the bank. He walked into the house and bludgeoned her in the cellar. Mortally wounded, she ran upstairs to hide, to die.

"Then Rogers lay in wait. He waited for the father to come back from the bank," Canter said, the hammer still above his head. "And when Hummel came into that room and dropped his hat upon the small table there, Rogers raised the hammer"—Canter swung it as if he were driving a railroad spike into a track—"and brought it down on Bill Hummel's skull. He killed him."

Canter said Rogers deserved the death penalty and told the jurors that, when they considered showing George Rogers mercy, they should think back to those photographs of the Hummels lying dead on the floor, their heads split open.

"Give Rogers the same mercy he showed them."

It was a hard act to follow, and Maurice Cohen did not have material nearly as compelling. Instead, he ridiculed the case against Rogers, called it flimsy and accused the police of framing the radioman, not through malice but through incompetence. He claimed that Scheff's testimony had been coerced, that the police had failed even to prove there was blood on Rogers's pants and, if so, whether it was even human. *Why had the police not confronted Rogers with the pants? Why did they hide the evidence? And if Rogers had committed such a violent and heinous crime, why was there but one stain on the pants?* Cohen attempted to raise reasonable doubt, the only card he could play. He said the day the Hummels were killed was terribly hot—everyone was outside on their porch. How could a killer escape unseen?

"Why wouldn't someone see a man the size of Rogers coming in and out of the Hummel house?"

The jury was out three hours. In that time, most people loitered in the courthouse rotunda, their voices echoing off the stone walls, their shoes clicking on the marble floors. They stood and smoked cigarettes, talking quickly, in hushed tones.

Vincent Doyle believed everyone now saw Rogers as he did. He had little doubt Rogers would be convicted—how could he not be? The prosecution had stayed away from some things they knew Rogers had done: called a neighbor pretending to be Hummel; tried to bribe a jail inmate to implicate another man in the murders. Doyle thought Rogers killed Bill Hummel not with the same hammer used to kill Edith, but instead with a microphone that was missing from the house. But these were things the jury would never hear. Canter thought such supposition would confuse jurors, so he conveniently avoided it.

As Doyle stood there waiting for the verdict, Maurice Cohen walked up—another bored soul with nothing to do until the jury came back. He tried to appear confident.

"What do you think, Vince?"

"First degree and life."

"Ridiculous," Cohen said. "It will be a hung jury."

They argued for a minute, Cohen finally walking away as he muttered to himself. Doyle didn't believe a jury with five women would hand down a death sentence without hearing from Rogers. Cohen had saved Rogers's life by not putting him on the stand, Doyle knew. If he approved or disapproved, Doyle never said.

He stood at the rotunda railing for a long time, waiting for the jury, hoping that he was right, that this was the end. Above him, angels hovered and Vincent J. Doyle thought to himself that George Rogers will never see them.

Just after 6 P.M., the jury sought instructions from Judge Duffy—a question about the difference between first- and second-degree murder—and by 6:45 they had reached a verdict. Duffy had them back in the courtroom at sunset, just minutes before 7 P.M. Twelve of the fourteen jurors who heard the case were chosen to decide and the first name drawn by lottery was the foreman. That duty fell to Eugenie Iff—the last juror selected was the first drawn from the pool.

As she stood up to read the verdict, Mrs. Iff was aware that everyone in the courtroom and outside on the lawn was waiting to hear what she would say next. It was a powerful, overwhelming feeling, perhaps one that she even savored. She took her time when Duffy asked if the jury had reached a verdict.

"Yes, we have," she said, and then paused.

"We, the jury, find the defendant guilty of murder in the first degree . . . and we recommend life imprisonment."

Doyle watched Rogers, standing between two guards, as each juror stood up in turn and said the same words: "Guilty, first degree, life imprisonment." Rogers did not say a word, but Doyle noticed with some satisfaction that the radioman's knees buckled. If the guards had not caught him, George Rogers would have fallen to the floor.

Moments after the jury delivered its verdict, Judge Duffy sent Rogers to the New Jersey State Prison for the rest of his life. George Rogers would not spend another day outside a cell. Imprisoned, he became more fervently religious, stranger than even he had seemed before. The diabetes that had afflicted him for years worsened, and he spent much of his time in the infirmary. He did not mind too badly; he could read in a hospital bed just as well as on the bunk in his cell.

The warden made good use of Rogers's one true talent. Within months of his arrival, he had the prison radio system working flawlessly. With a headphone jack in every cell, inmates could listen to AM radio from their bunks. It kept them quiet and kept Rogers busy. He caused little trouble, and mostly minded his own business. Occasionally, he would be relieved of his duties after disagreements with other inmates in the radio shop. Even when he had nowhere else to go, when there was nothing to gain, Rogers could not get along with other people. He could not change.

Upon his return to Trenton, he found the celebrity that had eluded him most of his life. The requests for interviews were constant: reporters, writers, psychologists—they could not leave him alone. One doctor after another examined him and all walked away with similar conclusions. George Rogers was a mechanical genius, he had above-average intelligence, and he was undeniably psychopathic. He could not tell the truth to save his life; his reality changed on a whim. Rogers did not see right or wrong like most people, but only what he wanted to see. It seemed he was capable of committing any crime and still never believed he had done anything wrong.

Rogers tolerated the doctors and played to the reporters and authors. He dangled the hint of a good story in exchange for magazines, science-fiction books, even typewriters. He always requested a Remington Quiet Writer, because it was the only one allowed in the cells at Trenton.

He never mentioned Doyle, but Rogers spoke of the Hummels often. Of all the things he had been accused of doing, it seemed he was only annoyed to be blamed for the double murder. Perhaps it was because he had lost his freedom the day after their bodies were discovered. In a mournful voice, Rogers swore to everyone he met that he had been wrongly convicted.

"William and Edith Hummel were my dearest friends," he would say. "How could I have killed them? I've never harmed anyone. I'm innocent."

Employing his best theatrics, Rogers told one writer, Thomas Gallagher, that "God will see me through," that he would not give up until his case had been heard in the "Court of Last Resort." It was unclear whether he was referring to the New Jersey state courts, or some higher, more spiritual judge.

Of course, every interviewer asked about the *Morro Castle*. It had been his finest hour, and now it had been tainted forever. He had gone from hero to murderer, and the contrast made little sense to anyone—there seemed no way for one man to be both. Everyone asked the same question, no matter how prettily they dressed it up: *Did you do it?*

When he was asked about the ship, his face hardened and his eyes went dead. He looked, frankly, as if he could kill someone. But after a moment, he would regain his composure, smile, and turn on a strange but curiously effective charm.

"What about the Court of Last Resort? If my case is brought before the Court of Last Resort, and that fails, I'll tell everything."

Leave them wanting more, isn't that what they say in showbiz? He thought back to his days at the Rialto, when everything had been good, and he smiled. He was good at teasing these people, a real pro at holding an audience. For four years, he played coy, never revealing as much as he had told Vincent Doyle that day in the radio shop. But he hinted at it constantly.

When the interviewers got tired of his games, he tantalized police with his secret. He wrote a teasing letter to the FBI, telling them he wanted to confess to "illegal activities in the 1930s." They came running, but all he wanted to talk about was cops on the take in the Bayonne Police Department. Why, he said, what did they *think* he wanted to tell them? Considering the diagnosis of the psychologists, it's not even clear he realized how evil he appeared.

The *Morro Castle* tragedy had been nearly a perfect crime. A fire so intense, so destructive, that all the evidence had been destroyed. A single spark had led to the deaths of 134 people, but no murder charge was ever filed, and not a single person spent a day in jail because of it. There was simply no way to prove it was a crime.

As such, people eventually tired of the guessing game. After those first few "confession" letters, the FBI stopped coming. And when it became obvious he would not risk his best drawing card, the *Morro Castle,* everyone else quit showing up, too.

The days dragged on unmercifully. By 1958, he looked much older than his fifty-six years. In fact, he looked at least five years older, the age he had claimed to be much of his life, just one more lie that had caught up with him. He had nothing left anymore except the secret, the did-he-or-didn't-he that kept bringing them in. Perhaps it sometimes even brought a smile to those dark, gummy lips.

On January 4, 1958, Rogers checked into the prison hospital once again. His diabetes was giving him fits, and the staff assigned him his regular bed. This time, however, he would not give them an encore. Six days later, George Rogers died of a heart attack.

The headline in the *Bayonne Times* called him the "Murderer of Hummels; Hero of *Morro Castle.* " He was famous locally for a crime, but he had been known around the world as a hero. There was no way to avoid mentioning the *Morro Castle* in his obituary because they could not take that away from him. As much as they might have been tempted to question it, they couldn't. It was a mystery that could not be solved.

In his final moments, it may have occurred to George White Rogers that, after all this time, he had done it once again.

He left them wanting more.

EPILOGUE

End of the Line

September 8, 2004

A cool breeze washed over the Jersey shore that morning, sweeping sand along the boardwalk like a light mist.

The beachfront was quiet, nearly deserted, as the old man stepped out of his car. The sound of the surf was like an echo from his past; he cast a glance toward the Atlantic before looking up at the lighthouse beacon. It was a familiar sight, one he had seen often, perhaps even spotted that night. Slowly, the man walked around the car and collected his wife, a petite lady who looked even smaller next to his considerable height. Together they walked up the steps to the porch of the Sea Girt Lighthouse.

The people there treated the man like a celebrity, which, in a way, he was. For decades, he had been a plainspoken local activist and before that a career military officer. Many people, in fact, still called him "the Colonel." But he was best known as the last surviving crew member of the Turbo Electric Liner *Morro Castle*.

It had been seventy years, and on this day he was asked to speak at ceremonies marking that anniversary. He accepted the invitation because it gave him another chance to convince people that all his shipmates did not cut and run on the night fire claimed the Ward Line flagship. More than anything, Thomas Torresson Jr. wanted to tell people the truth.

The largest room in the lighthouse was a shrine to the ship—photographs of the accident, people on the beach that day, framed newspaper headlines. The highlight of the collection was an oar from one of the *Morro Castle* lifeboats. For decades, the litter of disaster had been preserved in garages and museums along the beach, saved from the moment it washed ashore.

Many people arrived early, eager to shake his hand, relate their memories of being children on the beach that day as the survivors came ashore, of seeing the smoke through the rain. By the time Tom spoke, the building had filled to capacity and dozens had to listen from outside, through screened windows, to a man who talked very much the way he had as a teenager. He apologized for his memory lapses, and used the old man's joke: "If I'd known I was going to live this long, I would have taken better care of myself." But Tom had not forgotten much. After seventy years, he still remembered the feeling he had on the docks that winter morning in 1934.

"When I first saw the beautiful *Morro Castle,* I fell in love with it," he began.

It had been a long journey from the *Morro Castle* back to Sea Girt for Tom Torresson. In the year following the disaster, when he was still under subpoena, he met a pretty young woman named Irene Marnell. He courted her long-distance while attending Notre Dame. On break, he came back to New Jersey and took her on dates to the Rustic Inn, a roadhouse near the state line where one of the singing waiters was Irene's old high school classmate, a local boy named Frank Sinatra.

In college, Tom read a book by Beirne Lay called *I Wanted Wings* and became so entranced by aviation that he forgot the sea. He joined the Army Air Corps, forerunner of the modern Air Force, and after the war began, he became a flight instructor in North Africa. He made the military his career, even did a stint at West Point. He had seen it all, even escorted FDR's daughter, Anna, to Washington when the president died in 1945. Tom and Irene married in 1941, had a son, two daughters and more than a dozen grandchildren and great-grandchildren. After the war, he found himself stationed in West Germany.

When he retired in 1969, Tom returned to New Jersey, where he got involved with the Elks Club, the auxiliary police force of Dover Township and St. Joseph's Roman Catholic Church. It seemed he had an indefatigable energy—he was even compelled to lead campaigns against drug abuse.

It was during those busy postretirement days that a newspaper article set him off, some anniversary story about the disaster that reported how the crew ran when the fire began. Soon, Tom learned what he had missed all those busy years: that the runaway crew was one of the most common, and prevalent, myths of the *Morro Castle*. It infuriated him.

"It's all baloney," he told the audience.

Tom Torresson could not abide the slur against these men, for he considered them family. His father never worked for anyone but the Ward Line, and Tom had known his shipmates before and after the disaster. He attended Clarence Hackney's funeral when the former *Morro Castle* officer died unexpectedly in 1939. Anthony Bujia, the assistant engineer, had cut the grass at his father's house when he needed extra money. Bob Smith, the cruise director, had remained in the business, serving on a number of other ships and for other lines. And Tom had kept up with his fellow pursers for years, even had a reunion with Bob Tolman and Russell Du Vinage in the eeriest of settings. One summer he took inventory for his father on the *Oriente, Morro Castle*'s twin sister, where Tolman had taken over as chief purser. For a week, Tom worked on the *Oriente* as it sailed from New York to Havana and back. Even though he had never been aboard the ship, he could not shake the odd feeling of knowing exactly where everything on board was located. It felt like he was walking the decks of a ghost.

Few of the *Morro Castle*'s officers fared as well as Tom after the disaster, and at his talk at Sea Girt he lamented the "bum rap" most of them got.

William Warms returned to the sea following his acquittal. A few months later, in November of 1937, he found himself in the news again when a freighter he served aboard, the *Cauto,* foundered in heavy storms off Mexico. He returned to New York, where he managed port operations for the Ward Line. When the war began, Warms joined the navy and directed military port operations for several years, but he never became captain of a ship. Warms died in Queens in 1953.

Eben S. Abbott, branded the biggest coward among the *Morro Castle*'s crew, stayed with the Ward Line until he became involved in military transport operations during World War II. Ultimately, Abbott was named chief engineer of the army hospital ship *Charles A. Stafford*. He died in New York in 1956.

George Alagna never recovered from the disaster. He settled in New Jersey for a while, but ultimately drifted around the country, stopping briefly in Mississippi and California. Alagna married a Jersey girl, but it ended in divorce. He suffered from alcohol problems and finally died in October of 1990 at the age of eighty-four.

Doris Wacker did not let her horrific experience on the *Morro Castle* keep her from the water. She would take no less than a dozen cruises throughout her long life, in between marrying, having a son, divorcing and working in the office of a major department store. When she retired, Doris moved to Florida and then Georgia, to be closer to her son. In a drawer, she keeps memorabilia from all her other cruises. The *Morro Castle* warrants no less than two scrapbooks.

In October of 1953, the owners of the Atlantic, Gulf & West Indies Steamship Lines dissolved the company during a meeting in Maine. Its last operating subsidiary, the Ward Line, was divided among the stockholders. They were holding on to little more than a dream. The glamorous Cuban cruises were over, the company a shadow of its former self. In 1941, the government had collected on the promise of the Jones-White Act, confiscating the *Oriente* for the war effort. Within months, the *Morro Castle*'s twin sister was stripped of its luxurious interiors and recommissioned as the troop transport ship *Thomas H. Barry.* She remained in the military service until 1957, when she was sold and scrapped in Baltimore—just as the *Morro Castle* had been more than two decades before.

An eerie rumor, unconfirmed, followed the company to the grave. Some people whispered that the bones of the *Morro Castle,* all of the salvaged scrap metal from her hull, had been recycled and sold to Japan just as it was gearing up for war. Reincarnated, the ship had become a part of the Japanese Navy, used to kill still more people.

A few years after the Ward Line's demise, Havana was declared off-limits, the results of another revolution, and international politics. The party was over.

In the end, Tom Torresson had been right. Aside from Abbott, the chief officers of the ship—as well as dozens of pursers, stewards, waiters, band members and even cooks—stayed with the passengers, tried to save them, even if they did not have a plan to do so. The ones who fled, and there might have been more than 100 of them, were largely the crewmen housed in the forecastle. They seldom had any dealings with the passengers and, though they likely did not care, those men may have assumed the responsibility to get the people off the ship fell to others. That doesn't make what they did right, but it certainly makes this less than a clear-cut case of leaving people to die. If there was any malice in their actions, it was directed at the Ward Line, which took advantage of the Depression economy to exploit sailors, work them hard for pitiful wages while giving them scraps to eat. Some of those people probably did not care to see the *Morro Castle* burn that night, but their reality was much different than the passengers'. They did not see the romance, they had never spent an endless night dancing on the Promenade.

The cause of the *Morro Castle* fire officially remains unsolved. Dickerson Hoover's Commerce Department report said the ship was so nearly completely destroyed that it was impossible to determine what caused the fire. The evidence suggests, however, that Warms was right—the fire may have started in two places at once: the Writing Room locker and the No. 3 cargo hold. If that is the case, it certainly bolsters the case of arson. It seems unlikely that a fire in the hold could have spread to a small, hidden closet three decks higher without someone noticing. The fire detection systems never recorded a fire in the hold, but Hoover found that the crew had routed the piping outside that night to escape the smell of the hides in the No. 1 and No. 2 holds. Perhaps smoke wafted out of those pipes only to be doused from view by the rain of the approaching storm.

The same week that Hoover released his official report on the *Morro Castle* inquiry, he sent a confidential memo to his bosses in Washington. In it, he said that if the fire was not spontaneous combustion, it probably was incendiary—arson. One detail he kept quiet, and out of his report, concerned a vacuum tank which supplied fuel to the carburetor of the emergency lighting system. The tank kept gasoline in it to prime the carburetor for the generator that ran the lights. One of the few things not destroyed in the fire, the hose from the tank, was found disconnected, as if someone had siphoned gasoline out of it. Hoover suggested that gasoline might have been poured on the blankets in the Writing Room locker. That, combined with the flammable polish in the closet, would have been enough to ignite a significant blaze. That little bit of gasoline also could have powered a destructive Molotov cocktail for anyone who knew exactly which vent to throw it down.

Even if it was arson, the crew was not blameless. The fire was allowed to get out of control in a matter of minutes because the *Morro Castle* sailed into a 20-knot headwind making better than 20 miles an hour, creating a 40 mph wind to fan the flames—an accelerant nearly as dangerous as all the gasoline the ship carried. Warms did not turn the ship to get the wind off the fire as quickly as he should have, but the fault does not lie solely with him. Had his officers more accurately reported the intensity of the fire, he may have reacted differently. Warms was motivated by a desire to bring the ship in on time and without additional cost to the Ward Line. His judgment may have been impaired because of the long hours he had been working, but he was operating with incomplete information. And, after a few minutes, it made no difference. The fire was beyond fighting.

Did George White Rogers set the fire that cost 134 lives? Through bureaucracy, poor timing and a failure to communicate, he avoided indictment in the case of the *Morro Castle.* There's no guarantee he could have been convicted. The case against him would have been purely circumstantial, as were his subsequent trials. In neither of those cases did a lack of solid physical evidence save him, but perhaps it would have this time.

Police often say the best way to solve a crime is to figure out who profits from it. While the *Morro Castle* fire brought only death, misery and pain to most people, it had been Rogers's ticket to better things. The fire made him famous; the ship nearly made him rich. And, some have speculated, the disaster, and the death of the captain, may have saved him from being fired, possibly blackballed as Alagna ultimately was. As F. X. Fay realized years ago, none of this is proof of anything, but like everything else in Rogers's life, it fits a deadly pattern.

There were rumors concerning Captain Willmott's intentions to clean house in the *Morro Castle* radio room. Although the captain clearly wanted Alagna gone—Warms testified to that—there are clues that Willmott had come to suspect Rogers was not exactly a model employee, either. Over the years, more than a few people said Captain Willmott had intimated concerns about the chief radioman. He might have been paranoid, but that didn't mean he wasn't on to something. The poison incident on that final cruise seemed a little too contrived. Rogers almost certainly brought this problem to Willmott's attention, and then magically solved it within a few hours. The coincidence could hardly have escaped the captain's notice.

It would not have taken much—a stern warning, an accusatory question—to set Rogers off. Easily slighted and psychopathic, there is no way to estimate what he might have done under the threat—real or per-ceived—of losing his job. And with Willmott out of the picture, all that trouble would disappear. While William Warms knew about Alagna's pend-ing dismissal, he never said anything about a similar fate for Rogers. Was it because Rogers was cooperating with the Ward Line's defense team, pro-viding evidence that implicated Alagna in malfeasance on board the *Morro Castle*? Or, were those rumors of friction between Willmott and Rogers just idle talk?

There were several clues that Rogers was giving a grand performance during the disaster. To Alagna, he seemed near death in the radio room, but then spent hours on the *Morro Castle* bow running around like a man half his age and size, doing everything he could to earn the label of "hero." A few hours after that, however, he feigned "near-coma" conditions for the doctor on the *Tampa,* an act that led to his being carried off the cutter like a wounded veteran in front of the assembled reporters. Rogers seemed to invite this image of himself as the savior of the disaster, when in fact he would have saved more lives if he had answered those early radio calls ask-ing about a ship on fire off the Jersey coast—something he could have done without breaking any rules. But at the time it could have made a dif-ference, he sat silent. The newspapers got it wrong; Rogers was no hero.

There were a number of peculiarities that never figured into anyone's accounting. Rogers's wife, Edith, had tried to sail on the *Morro Castle* Labor Day cruise only to be told by someone—most certainly her hus-band—that all the cabins were booked. In fact, the ship was only a little more than half full. Was he protecting her, or did Rogers simply not want his wife around? And, during one performance at the Rialto, Rogers promi-nently noted that he had taken a stroll around the deck that night after his shift. Was it a hint?

In all the other known crimes he committed, Rogers had a habit of re-turning to the scene of the crime, of attempting to look as if he were the hero—calling the police after he stole from a radio shop, alerting the com-pany to poison in the water cooler, cooperating with FBI investigations on the *Walter Colton* when his part in the incident was unclear. Were his at-tempts to frame George Alagna and his detailed boasts to Vincent Doyle the same sort of roundabout confessions? In his final days, were his promises to "tell everything" a hint, a way to keep attention, or just a game? His patterns suggest that Rogers was capable of anything.

There is the matter of Captain Robert Willmott's death. The official autopsy found no proof of poison, but even Bureau of Investigation special agent Francis X. Fay conceded not all poisons could be detected in such an examination. More important, no one ever confirmed beyond a doubt that the remains recovered by Asbury Park firefighters were, in fact, Willmott's. It seems worth noting that Rogers had two alleged instances of poisoning in his troubled past—his wife's dog and the water cooler at the Brooklyn plant. Again, it's just circumstantial evidence. It likely would have been more difficult to taint the captain's food than to burn the *Morro Castle*. And Willmott did, in fact, have a history of heart trouble. No one would deny, however, that the timing of his death was uncanny.

The FBI never questioned Vincent J. Doyle about the warnings he sent to federal agencies when Rogers was released from prison in 1942. J. Edgar Hoover had believed in the case enough to seek an indictment, but after he was snubbed his agents never asked another prosecutor to look at the evidence. If federal agents had compared notes with Doyle and U.S. attorneys, they might have made a more concerted effort. But war intervened, time passed, and as one prosecutor told the FBI, Rogers was already in jail. What did it matter?

It mattered a lot to Doyle. He spent the rest of his life investigating Rogers's criminal life. It was not an obsession, and did not consume his life, but he was driven by a need to know the truth. Doyle was an upstanding Bayonne citizen for the rest of his life, even something of a local celebrity. He rose to the rank of captain in the police department and became president of a national organization, the Association of Public-Safety Communications Officials. Long after his nemesis was gone from Bayonne, Doyle's photograph appeared in the newspaper with a beauty contest winner, joking about bathing suits and the city's new blue laws. He seems to be having a fine time, a charming man without a trouble in the world. In the photo, his injured hand is discreetly tucked into his jacket pocket.

When he retired in the 1960s, Doyle began to write a manuscript. It was a fascinating, behind-the-scenes look at two police investigations, both of them focused on Rogers. Eventually, the deaths of the Hummels and the story of his injuries at the hands of a madman became a 300-page manuscript that Vincent J. Doyle titled "Beyond All Reasonable Doubt." The book was never published, but Doyle would have the satisfaction of finishing it before he died in 1970.

* * *

Tom Torresson would never know how close George Rogers came to confessing his crimes aboard the *Morro Castle.* Even as an old man, though, his memories of Rogers gave him a shudder. No less than he could forget the ship, he was doomed to remember the menacing look of Rogers and his grotesque, gummy lips. At Sea Girt that day, he said that if anyone aboard the ship was capable of setting the fire, it was Rogers. "He was a real weirdo," Tom said in his characteristic bluntness.

Tom said that whether or not the fire was set, the damage it caused should be blamed on the ship's design. Those vents that ran behind the wooden walls, carrying sea breezes through the ship like air-conditioning, allowed the fire to spread as the nor'easter fanned it. That was the "real villain," he said. For that reason, Tom believed, it was wrong to blame any one person, and he did not keep his opinion to himself. For years, he terrorized newspapers and magazines that dared to write the clichéd version of the story, calling in and demanding corrections. Sometimes he succeeded in getting a better story written, sometimes not. But he never let a slight to the *Morro Castle* crew pass without trying to educate reporters, without trying to make things right. He felt he owed it to the crew.

Thomas Torresson Jr. would not live to see another *Morro Castle* anniversary. On Thursday, August 11, 2005—less than a month shy of the seventy-first anniversary of the disaster and just six weeks before his eighty-ninth birthday—he died in a New Jersey hospital. With him, the soul of the *Morro Castle* passed away. By 2006, there were only a few scattered surviving passengers—the former Doris Wacker among them—but Tom spoke for the crew, if not everyone on that ship. He died still hoping someone would get it right.

For the final seventy years of his life, Tom Torresson was haunted by the sight of the burning cruise ship, a dead boy in his arms, bodies floating on a violent ocean. He survived one of the worst maritime disasters in American history and lived a long life to tell about it. It was a horrifying story, but one he could relate stoically, with an eye to history.

Most important, Tom could separate September 8, 1934, from the rest of his memories. For most of his life he heard nothing but horror stories about the Ward Line flagship, about the conditions, the crew, the fire. But he kept alive the notion of a grand cruise ship in its final glory days. He recalled sailing out of Havana Harbor, the band playing while the passengers danced and laughed and sang as they never would again. It was the most fun many of those people ever had, escaping the world for a week at a time when they most needed a taste of the good life. He never forgot that.

For as long as he lived, Thomas Torresson Jr. would remember the *Morro Castle* as he loved her, when she was beautiful.

Notes on Sources

The magical Jersey shore drew me to the *Morro Castle*. Years ago, I saw the classic photograph of the ship beached alongside Asbury Park's Convention Hall and thought, *I know that place.* I was there once in the 1980s, just before the Palace shut down, just before I got out of college, with my old friend Bob Formont. We wanted to haunt those dusty beach roads that Bruce Springsteen so elegantly described—and get into the Stone Pony for spring break. It was closed, and the snow that March was nearly waist-high.

By then, Asbury Park was a ghost town very much unlike the carnival resort it had been when the great Ward liner washed ashore. Madame Marie's seemed like the most vital business on the boardwalk that day. I had never seen anything like it, but did not realize how dramatic its fortunes had changed until I saw those pictures of the *Morro Castle* years later. Captured in these black and white images are the best and worst that the dark days of the Depression had to offer, a grand tourist resort and the most celebrated coastal liner of its day—one in ruins, the other destined to follow. Those photographs made me sad, and also made me realize how temporary everything is. This book was a chance to step back into that time, a defining moment in American history.

When I embarked on this project, I had no idea how much information on the *Morro Castle* disaster was out there. I soon realized it was not only the Golden Age of cruise ships and the Jersey shore, but also for newspapers and bureaucracy. More than 400 people survived the *Morro Castle* fire, and there were hundreds—perhaps thousands—of rescuers, witnesses, investigators and reporters on the scene in the days and weeks following. That many people generate a lot of newspaper articles and paperwork. I stopped gathering when I had amassed more than 9,000 pages of material. Going through all this information, I found that, of course, no story is as simple as it seems. A lot of people have said things about the *Morro Castle* over the years that just weren't right. I hope that I have corrected, and not repeated, some of those mistakes.

Much of the information in this book was taken from the records of the Department of Commerce, the Coast Guard and the FBI. Most of this material was collected at the National Archives and Records Administration in Washington, a magical place in itself. The FBI turned over about 3,000 pages of its previously classified investigation files on the *Morro Castle* and George White Rogers. Those contemporary records, declassified only a few years ago, have never been published or used by any other writer or historian. It's safe to say very few people outside the FBI have even read them. The files significantly change the history of the *Morro Castle,* and the people who sailed her, that has been accepted as fact for seventy-two years. A great deal of the story that unfolds in these pages was hidden in these records and remained untold until now.

While the FBI material is largely what makes this book different than any previous version of the *Morro Castle* story, I believe the recollections of Thomas Torresson Jr. are just as important. He brings the story to life, and I was fortunate to have met him, then eighty-seven years old, when I returned to the Jersey shore in September 2004. Listening to Tom talk that day in Sea Girt convinced me there was a new and important story to tell and, luckily, he agreed. Tom was eager to share his amazing memories with me during the last year of his life, and I will never forget him.

I feel as if I knew Vincent J. Doyle after reading his wonderful unpublished manuscript, "Beyond All Reasonable Doubt." His son, Monsignor Vincent Doyle, was kind enough to lend me the manuscript, and it added dimensions to the story I could not imagine when I began this book. Amazingly, no one who's seen that manuscript has ever reported Rogers's cryptic admission of guilt to Doyle, and I was stunned to find it. Holding the book Doyle so carefully crafted—which included corrections in his own hand—I felt that I could not get much closer to this history. I am privileged to record some of his story, to make sure it isn't lost.

The following notes document where I got the facts to build this narrative. I have listed everything except items of general knowledge—statistics about the Depression, the history of the FBI, etc. The descriptions of the Jersey shore,

Bayonne, New York, Havana and that beautiful, doomed cruise ship are my own, taken from photographs or visits. Consider this a log of the voyage.

Prologue: Verdict Imminent

PAGE

xv *They loitered:* Except for the descriptions of the Hudson County Courthouse, which are based on my own visit to that grand building, most of the details of the moments before the verdict was read came from, "Rogers Convicted, Escapes Chair; Sentenced at Once to Life Term," *Bayonne Times,* September 25, 1954.

xvi *At $1,000 a week:* "Rogers Takes Theatre Offer," *Bayonne Times,* September 17, 1934.

xix *In a few short hours:* Both *Marine Engineering and Shipping Age,* September 1930; and *Marine Review,* September 1930, made this "safest ship" boast.

xix The *Bayonne Times:* "A New Name for the Roster," *Bayonne Times,* September 11, 1934.

xix *The paper rarely:* "Rogers Gets 12 to 20 Years; 'Mind of Fiend' Hit by Judge," *Bayonne Times,* December 15, 1938.

xx *The man with the mangled hand:* Vincent J. Doyle, "Beyond All Reasonable Doubt" (unpublished, 1966–1970).

xxi *Two minutes before sunset:* The final moments of the trial, including Mrs. Iff's wonderful pause, are recounted in the tragically unbylined "Rogers Convicted, Escapes Chair; Sentenced at Once to Life Term," *Bayonne Times,* September 25, 1954.

One: The Promise of Warmth

PAGE

3 *He fell in love:* The numerous sections of this chapter that recount Tom Torresson's January 1934 cruise aboard the *Morro Castle* are taken from an interview with Torresson in Whiting, N.J., December 2004.

4 *The golden age:* This overview of the state of the steamship industry circa 1934 was culled from several sources, including Peter C. Kohler, "Triumph and Tragedy: T.E.L. *Morro Castle* and *Oriente*," *Steamboat*

Bill: Journal of the Steamship Historical Society of America, Summer 1989; and Michael Alderson, "Treasure, Revolution, and the Mysteries of the *Merida,*" *Steamboat Bill,* Summer 2004.

6 *These formal cards:* Brochure from the *Morro Castle,* n.d. Author's collection.

8 *A native of England:* "Heart Attack Kills Captain Before the Fire" by William McElligott, the *New York World-Telegram,* September 8, 1934.

8 *He showed off a watch:* Ibid.

9 *In the past year: The Submarine Signal Fathometer for Visual Echo Soundings* (Boston: Submarine Signal Company, 1933), 24.

9 *The* Morro Castle *carried:* "Ward Line Men to Be Quizzed on Mail Pacts," *New York World-Telegram,* December 5, 1934.

9 *Still, the Ward Line:* "Gala Easter Cruise," a 1934 Ward Line travel brochure, Michael Alderson collection.

10 *The ship did:* The *Morro Castle* had license to carry refined petroleum, gunpowder and firearms, and it often did, according to the ship's log of August 4, 1934, and Department of Commerce investigation notes. National Archives and Records Administration (Record Group 41, Bureau of Marine Inspection and Navigation [Department of Commerce], General Records Relating to the *Morro Castle* Disaster, Entry 217, Box 1, Folder 2).

10 *In advertisements: AGWI Steamship News,* August 1930.

11 *The Pullman cars:* The description of christening day is taken from the newsreel film, "The Launching of the Turbo Electric Liner *Morro Castle,* " 1930 newsreel, Thomas Torresson's private collection.

12 *During the christening:* Ibid.

12 *James Otis Ward:* This brief history of the steamship company comes from several sources, including A. Hyatt Verrill, *A History of the Ward Line* (New York: Ward Line, 1930); Michael Alderson, "Treasure, Revolution, and the Mysteries of the *Merida,*" *Steamboat Bill,* Summer 2004; and interviews with Alderson.

13 *Then, a bit:* "American Merchant Marine Looks Ahead to a New Era," *New York Times,* August 17, 1930.

14 *The 500-acre shipyard:* The history of the Newport News Shipbuilding & Dry Dock Co., and the fate of Albert L. Hopkins, comes from Alexander Crosby Brown, *The Good Ships of Newport News* (Cambridge, Md.: Tidewater, 1976), 2–7, 53–55.

15 *Forgetting the promise: Marine Engineering and Shipping Age,* September 1930.

16 *Ferris's bulbous bow:* "The Launching of the Turbo Electric Liner *Morro Castle,* " 1930 newsreel.

16 *Off the Virginia Cape:* "*Morro Castle* Makes 21 Knots in Tests," *New York Times,* August 9, 1930.

16 *A few days later:* "200 Leaders Hail *Morro Castle* Here," *New York Times,* August, 20, 1930.

16 *The passes were gone:* "2,000 View *Morro Castle* on Eve of Havana Trip," *New York Herald Tribune,* August 22, 1930.

17 *On August 23:* "18-Hour Rain Chills City as Heavy Storm Batters Wide Area," *New York Times,* August 24, 1930.

17 *Just before the ship:* "*Morro Castle* Sails in Quest of Record," *New York Times,* August 24, 1930.

18 *On its maiden:* The rates for cruises aboard the *Morro Castle* come from advertisements in the *New York Times* and the *New York World-Telegram* over several dates in August 1930.

18 *There was always:* The Sea Spray information comes from a 1930s *Morro Castle/Oriente* travel brochure, Michael Alderson collection.

18 *"This boat has":* This excerpt is from a letter mailed to a Mrs. H. J. Colton, postmarked New York City, April 8, 1934. From the collection of Deborah C. Whitcraft, Beach Haven, N.J.

19 *On his winter:* Torresson interview.

Two: All Aboard

PAGE

22 *That afternoon, Rogers:* Doyle, "Beyond All Reasonable Doubt," 50–59.

24 *The labor problems:* Capt. G. P. Alepis, "*Morro Castle* Fire," *Labor Front,* October 1934, 3, 5–6.

24 *The high-society image:* The disparity in pay between Ward Line employees and its chief officers is from Peter C. Kohler, "Triumph and Tragedy: T.E.L. *Morro Castle* and *Oriente,*" *Steamboat Bill: Journal of the Steamship Historical Society of America,* Summer 1989, 117.

24 *The crew's discontent:* Hal Burton, *The Morro Castle* (New York: Viking, 1973), 15.

25 *George Alagna had:* Alagna's background comes from a number of

sources, including an October 1934 report on his background, FBI File No. 45-833, Sections V–VII; and Testimony in the Investigation of the Burning of the *Morro Castle,* National Archives and Records Administration, Record Group 41, Bureau of Marine Inspection and Navigation (Department of Commerce), Entry 214.

26 *He planned to:* The attempted strike by Alagna, Stanley Ferson and Morton Borow comes up in the testimony of Alagna, George Rogers and Warms, but the facts of this account come from an internal Bureau of Investigation report, FBI File No. 45-833, Section III. The quotes in this section come from Testimony in the Investigation of the Burning of the *Morro Castle,* National Archives (Record Group 41, Entry 214).

28 *They got Borow:* Ibid, FBI File No. 45-833, Section III.

29 *He claimed more:* George Rogers's résumé changed weekly, but he made these claims in his testimony before the Department of Commerce committee investigating the fire, Testimony in the Investigation of the Burning of the *Morro Castle,* National Archives (Record Group 41, Entry 214).

29 *During his first:* Rogers's claim to be a Radio Marine Commission spy is mentioned in a report on Rogers's background, October 1934, FBI File No. 45-833, Section III; and in Thomas Gallagher, *Fire at Sea: The Story of the Morro Castle* (New York: Rinehart, 1959), 11.

30 *His opinion of:* Doyle, "Beyond All Reasonable Doubt," 54–55.

30 *There were always:* The account of Torresson family history and how Tom got his job on the *Morro Castle* is from an interview with him, December 2004.

Three: On to Gay Havana!

PAGE

36 *Ferson might have:* Stanley Ferson's visit to the Havana consul, and the story of his last month on the *Morro Castle,* is included in Bureau of Investigation inquiry notes, FBI File No. 45-833, Section IV.

37 *As you probably:* Doyle, "Beyond All Reasonable Doubt," 54.

38 *"I think you've":* From an October 1934 internal report on Alagna, FBI File No. 45-833, Section II.

38 *Surely, moving dead:* Interview with Torresson.

41 *A combination of things:* Captain Willmott's troubles with radicals are listed in Bureau of Investigation notes, September–October 1934. FBI File No. 45-833, Section I.

41 *Some of Willmott's:* FBI File No. 45-833, Section II.

41 *The polite rumor:* Interview with Torresson.

41 *Because of his absence:* The August 4th 1934 inspection of the *Morro Castle* is detailed in a January 9, 1935, letter from U.S. Attorney Martin Conboy to E. Y. Mitchell, assistant secretary of commerce. National Archives (Record Group 41, Department of Commerce, General Records Relating to the *Morro Castle* Disaster, 1934–36, Entry 217, Box 2).

42 *Since its first inspection:* The statistics of the *Morro Castle*'s sailing history are recorded in an internal investigation memo in FBI File No. 45-833, Section V.

42 *During his four days:* From the log of the *Morro Castle.* National Archives (Record Group 41, Department of Commerce, General Records Relating to the *Morro Castle* Disaster, 1934-36, Entry 217, Box 6, Folder 2).

43 *On August 7:* Michael Reynolds, *Hemingway: The 1930s* (New York: Norton, 1997), 142.

44 *Tom had come:* Interview with Torresson.

46 *Stanley Ferson got:* Doyle, "Beyond All Reasonable Doubt," 55–56.

47 *That week, Alagna:* Testimony in the Investigation of the Burning of the *Morro Castle,* National Archives (Record Group 41, Entry 214).

47 *Tom Torresson was not:* Interview with Torresson.

48 *On the August 25:* Interview with Bob Tolman. Commerce Department records, from Tom Torresson's collection.

49 *Later that cruise:* Report of fire onboard *Morro Castle,* August 27, 1934, made by Captain Robert Willmott. National Archives (Record Group 41, General Records Relating to the *Morro Castle* Disaster, Entry 217, Box 5, Folder 4); and "Earlier Fire on the Liner Not Officially Explained," *New York Times,* September 11, 1934.

49 *In a letter:* Telegram from West the Glen Winscombe, England. National Archives (Record Group 41, General Records Relating to the *Morro Castle* Disaster, Entry 217, Box 6, Folder 9).

Four: Summer's End

PAGE

51   *Eva Hoffman, a:* The brief descriptions of passengers on the *Morro Castle*'s final voyage come from bullet items in the *New York World-Telegram,* September 10, 1934.

51   *Next door, in:* Interview with Robert Lione, June 1, 2006.

51   *Doris Wacker, an:* Interview with Doris Manske, the former Doris Wacker, in Reidsville, Ga., June 2005.

52   *If Thomas Torresson:* Interview with Torresson.

53   *It would be:* National Archives (Record Group 41, General Records Relating to the *Morro Castle* Disaster, Entry 217, Box 6, Folder 2); and "Munitions Carried by *Morro Castle,*" *New York Times,* September 28, 1934.

53   *"The passengers would":* "Passengers Killed by Ship Propeller," *New York Times,* September 18, 1934.

54   *On Sunday, it:* Interview with Doris Manske.

54   *At 5:45 A.M.:* The fight between Alagna and Freeman comes from information they provided the Steamboat Inspectors in September 1934. National Archives (Record Group 41, Testimony in the Investigation of the Burning of the *Morro Castle,* Entry 214).

56   *Later that morning:* The only account of the conversation between Captain Willmott and George Rogers comes from Rogers, which in itself is enough to make it suspect. But Willmott made similar comments to William Warms and others, enough to assume that this is close to how the exchange went. The only question is whether Willmott also suspected Rogers of malfeasance. National Archives (Record Group 41, Testimony in the Investigation of the Burning of the *Morro Castle,* Entry 214).

57   *Monday night was:* Torresson interview.

57   *When he got:* National Archives (Record Group 41, Testimony in the Investigation of the Burning of the *Morro Castle,* Entry 214).

59   *It had gotten:* Carlos Baker, *Ernest Hemingway: A Life Story* (New York: Scribner's, 1969), 265.

59   *Herbert Wacker hired:* Interview with Doris Manske.

59   *Tom Torresson did nothing:* Interview with Torresson.

60   *The next morning:* Frank Crocco papers relating to the Ward Line disaster, in the *Morro Castle* files of the Stephen B. Luce Library at the State University of New York Maritime College, Bronx, N.Y.

61   *The typical menu:* The meal described is from the *Morro Castle*'s August 19, 1934, dinner menu, Michael Alderson collection.

61   *The Wackers had:* Interview with Doris Manske.

61   *Willmott was "persistently":* Gallagher, *Fire at Sea*, 14.

62   *She and Marjorie:* Interview with Doris Manske.

62   *On Friday morning:* National Archives (Record Group 41, Testimony in the Investigation of the Burning of the *Morro Castle*, Entry 214).

63   *This passenger said:* Gallagher, *Fire at Sea*, 15.

63   *That morning, William:* The scene between Warms and Willmott on the morning before the captain's death comes from Warms's testimony before the Steamboat Inspectors. National Archives (Record Group 41, Testimony in the Investigation of the Burning of the *Morro Castle*, Entry 214).

65   *Willmott tried to:* Gallagher, *Fire at Sea:* 19–20.

65   *At one point:* Interview with Torresson.

66   *"For God's sake":* National Archives (Record Group 41, Testimony in the Investigation of the Burning of the *Morro Castle*, Entry 214).

66   *Warms took his:* Ibid.

67   *Willmott summoned Ferdinand:* From October 1934 Bureau of Investigation notes, FBI File No. 45-833, Section III.

67   *Warms had just:* From Warms's testimony before the Steamboat Inspectors. National Archives (Record Group 41, Testimony in the Investigation of the Burning of the *Morro Castle*, Entry 214).

Five: Last Dance

PAGE

73   *Victor M. Seckendorf:* Gallagher, *Fire at Sea:* 23.

74   *The call from:* Investigation notes, FBI File No. 45-833, Section II.

75   *In Willmott's room:* Interview with Bob Tolman. Commerce Department records, from Tom Torresson's collection.

75   *Van Zile went:* Gallagher, *Fire at Sea:* 21.

75   *De Witt Van Zile:* "Doctor on *Morro* Served on Staff of Hospital Here," *Bayonne Times*, September 14, 1934.

75   *After he finished:* Interview with Tom Torresson.

76   *William Warms, especially:* Testimony before the Steamboat Inspectors. National Archives (Record Group 41, Testimony in the Investigation of the Burning of the *Morro Castle*, Entry 214).

76 *"All right, Chief":* Ibid.

77 *Bob Tolman arrived:* Interview with Bob Tolman. Commerce Department records, from Tom Torresson's collection.

77 *"Somebody slipped him":* This is the abbreviated form of a quotation that shows up in various forms in several places, including Burton, *The Morro Castle,* 22; and Gallagher, *Fire at Sea:* 27.

78 *For at least one:* The discussion of rank shows up in the testimony of several *Morro Castle* officers. The best is the interview with Bob Tolman. Commerce Department records, Tom Torresson's collection.

79 *The Ward Line:* Ibid.

79 *Once the initial:* George Rogers's numerous transmissions are recounted in Bureau of Investigation notes taken in September–October 1934. FBI File No. 45-833, Section II.

80 *The men discussed:* Ibid.

81 *The news snuffed:* Interview with Doris Manske.

82 *Warms said he:* Testimony before the Steamboat Inspectors. National Archives (Record Group 41, Testimony in the Investigation of the Burning of the *Morro Castle,* Entry 214).

82 *Tom had finished:* This scene is one of those moments when it became apparent Torresson was a great person through which to see the disaster. The dialogue is reconstructed, as quoted, in an interview with Torresson, December 2004.

83 *The Ward Line's response:* Interview with Bob Tolman. Commerce Department records, Torresson collection.

85 *In the purser's:* Interview with Torresson.

86 *George Rogers signed:* Testimony before the Steamboat Inspectors. National Archives (Record Group 41, Testimony in the Investigation of the Burning of the *Morro Castle,* Entry 214).

86 *But first, he:* In none of his court appearances did George Rogers mention his postshift stroll around the *Morro Castle*—a walk that would end about seventy-five minutes before Daniel Campbell found the fire in the Writing Room locker. Rogers's account of this late-night walk during a performance at the Rialto, recorded in "Rogers, in Vaudeville Turn, Accuses Aide of Desertion," *New York World-Telegram,* September 18, 1934.

87 *On his walk:* Testimony before the Steamboat Inspectors. National Archives (Record Group 41, Testimony in the Investigation of the Burning of the *Morro Castle,* Entry 214).

88 *In the Smoking:* The discovery of the fire is primarily from Daniel Campbell's testimony before the Steamboat Inspectors, with a bit of Arthur Pender's point of view thrown in at the end. National Archives (Record Group 41, Testimony in the Investigation of the Burning of the *Morro Castle,* Entry 214).

Six: This Evening's Entertainment

With a few exceptions, which are noted, the narrative of this chapter is taken from the testimony of *Morro Castle* officers William Warms, George Alagna, George Rogers, Bob Tolman and passenger John Kempf at the September 1934 Department of Commerce, Bureau of Navigation and Steamboat Inspection hearings in New York. National Archives (Record Group 41, Testimony in the Investigation of the Burning of the *Morro Castle,* Entry 214).

PAGE

91 *By a quarter of:* Interview with Doris Manske.

93 *When he first:* This account is from Clarence Hackney's testimony during the U.S. Steamboat Inspection license revocation hearings, November 1934. Copies of the transcript are in the *Morro Castle* files of the Stephen B. Luce Library at the State University of New York Maritime College, Bronx, N.Y.

97 *The smoke woke:* Eben Abbott's discovery of the fire and subsequent actions are taken from his testimony during the U.S. Steamboat Inspection license revocation hearings, November 1934. Ibid.

102 *The Bodners had:* Interview with Doris Manske.

106 *"I'm going to":* This funny exchange in the midst of chaos is from an interview with Tom Torresson, as is the account of how he learned of the fire.

107 *Abbott called:* Eben Abbott's testimony during the U.S. Steamboat Inspection license revocation hearings, November 1934. *Morro Castle* files in the Stephen B. Luce Library at the State University of New York Maritime College, Bronx, N.Y.

Seven: Dead in the Water

PAGE

111 *One man burst:* Gallagher, *Fire at Sea,* 93.

111 *Smith waded through:* From the cruise director's testimony. National Archives (Record Group 41, Testimony in the Investigation of the Burning of the *Morro Castle,* Entry 214).

114 *The abundance of:* This accounting of the *Morro Castle*'s lifeboats, which ones were launched and which burned, comes from the Department of Commerce Bureau of Navigation and Steamboat Inspection's Report and Recommendations of Dickerson N. Hoover. National Archives (Record Group 41, General Records Relating to the *Morro Castle* Disaster).

115 *Torres tried to:* National Archives (Record Group 41, Testimony in the Investigation of the Burning of the *Morro Castle,* Entry 214).

115 *Below, the engine:* Bujia's testimony during the U.S. Steamboat Inspection license revocation hearings, November 1934. *Morro Castle* files, the Stephen B. Luce Library at the State University of New York Maritime College, Bronx, N.Y.

116 *"Well, I lost":* National Archives (Record Group 41, Testimony in the Investigation of the Burning of the *Morro Castle,* Entry 214).

116 *George Rogers believed:* Ibid.

117 *The need to escape:* Interview with Doris Manske.

119 *The operator there:* From testimony in a Coast Guard Board of Inquiry into the Guard's response to the *Morro Castle* disaster, October 1934. National Archives. General Correspondence Files of the U.S. Coast Guard (Record Group 26), File Classification No.123.

119 *Anyone who caught:* "Card Players on Shore Saw Bolt Strike Liner," *New York World-Telegram,* September 8, 1934.

119 *The* Andrea Luckenbach *was:* The movement of the responding liners comes from "The Log of the Disaster" and various other stories in the *New York World-Telegram,* September 8, 1934. More information was supplied by the Coast Guard Board of Inquiry into the Guard's response to the *Morro Castle* disaster, October 1934. National Archives, General Correspondence Files of the U.S. Coast Guard (Record Group 26), File Classification No. 123.

120 *Clarence Hackney was:* Abbott's testimony during the U.S. Steamboat

Inspection license revocation hearings, November 1934. *Morro Castle* files, the Stephen B. Luce Library at the State University of New York Maritime College, Bronx, N.Y.

121   *Apparently, the pelican:* The account of Eben Abbott's rush to escape the *Morro Castle* came from the testimony of Hackney, Warms, able-bodied seaman Morris Weisberger and Abbott in both the Department of Commerce Hearings and the November 1934 license revocation hearings. National Archives (Record Group 41, Testimony in the Investigation of the Burning of the *Morro Castle,* Entry 214); U.S. Steamboat Inspection license revocation hearings, November 1934. *Morro Castle* files, Stephen B. Luce Library of the State University of New York Maritime College, Bronx, N.Y.

123   *The fire had:* National Archives (Record Group 41, Testimony in the Investigation of the Burning of the *Morro Castle,* Entry 214).

124   *Thomas Torresson had:* Tom Torresson related his final moments on the ship to me in a December 2004 interview. Supporting his memory is the story "100 Passengers Dived Simultaneously into Ocean as Orchestra Leader on *Morro Castle* Gave Word," *New York World-Telegram,* September 8, 1934.

Eight: Adrift in the Sea of Fire

PAGE

127   *George Rogers felt:* Rogers and Alagna's escape from the radio room and last look at the *Morro Castle* bridge is from their Department of Commerce testimony. National Archives (Record Group 41, Testimony in the Investigation of the Burning of the *Morro Castle,* Entry 214).

129   *He awoke before:* Interview with Torresson.

130   *The Wackers had:* Interview with Doris Manske.

131   *By 4 A.M. ship's:* National Archives (Record Group 41, Testimony in the Investigation of the Burning of the *Morro Castle,* Entry 214).

131   *"Jump. Everybody with":* Ibid.

131   *In the final:* These final moments on the stern are recounted in brief items in the *New York World-Telegram,* September 10, 1934.

131   *Anthony Lione's free:* Interview with Robert Lione.

132   *Van Zile carried:* Burton, *The Morro Castle,* 53.

133 *Bob Smith had:* National Archives (Record Group 41, Testimony in the Investigation of the Burning of the *Morro Castle,* Entry 214).

134 *When the* Andrea: The exploits of the rescue boats are taken from "Many Rescued as Fire Sweeps Liner in Storm" and various other briefs and stories in the *New York World-Telegram,* September 8, 1934.

134 *The officers of:* National Archives (Record Group 41, Testimony in the Investigation of the Burning of the *Morro Castle,* Entry 214).

136 *Marjorie Budlong had:* "Cuban's Last Message Sent Love to Mother," *New York American,* September 10, 1934.

136 *The men held:* National Archives (Record Group 41, Testimony in the Investigation of the Burning of the *Morro Castle,* Entry 214).

136 *Nearby, Tom Torresson:* Interview with Torresson.

137 *The rescue boats:* "Rescuer of 72 Describes Men on Ship Ropes" and "Many Rescued as Fire Sweeps Liner in Storm" from the *New York World-Telegram,* September 8, 1934.

137 *Warms waved off:* National Archives (Record Group 41, Testimony in the Investigation of the Burning of the *Morro Castle,* Entry 214).

138 *One* Monarch *lifeboat:* Interview with Robert Lione.

138 *Frank S. O'Day:* "Head Waiter Sure Cigaret Cause *Morro Castle* Fire," *New York World-Telegram,* September 10, 1934.

139 *The sea was:* Interview with Doris Manske.

139 *In Brielle, where:* The story of the Bogans' and the *Paramount* rescues comes from several sources, including "Two, Rescued, Die on Reaching Point Pleasant," *New York World-Telegram,* September 8, 1934; "Fishing Crew Saved 67 Lives," the *New York Sun,* September 10, 1934; "*Morro Castle* Fire: A Rescuer's Tale," *New York Times,* September 2, 1984; and the Bogans' testimony in the Coast Guard inquiry. National Archives, General Correspondence Files of the U.S. Coast Guard (Record Group 26), File Classification No. 123.

Nine: A Parade of Lost Souls

PAGE

141 *It seemed darker:* Eben Abbott's landfall is recorded in a number of sources, including Captain Jeffrey W. Monroe (whose father, Clarence "Red" Monroe was in the No. 1 lifeboat), "*Morro Castle:* A Disaster Still Under Dispute," *Sea Classics* V, 28, No. 11, November

1995; Gallagher, *Fire at Sea,* 197–199; and the testimony of Morris Weisberger, also in the lifeboat, U.S. Steamboat Inspection license revocation hearings, November 1934. *Morro Castle* files, Stephen B. Luce Library of the State University of New York Maritime College, Bronx, N.Y.

142 *Reporters who were:* National Archives, General Correspondence Files of the U.S. Coast Guard (Record Group 26), File Classification No. 123.

142 *They couldn't even:* National Archives (Record Group 41, Testimony in the Investigation of the Burning of the *Morro Castle,* Entry 214).

144 *Lieutenant Commander Earl:* The exchange between the *Tampa* captain and the *Morro Castle* officers was pieced together from Rose's testimony at the Coast Guard inquiry and the Department of Commerce testimony. National Archives (Record Group 41, Testimony in the Investigation of the Burning of the *Morro Castle,* Entry 214) and General Correspondence Files of the U.S. Coast Guard (Record Group 26), File Classification No. 123.

145 *Tom Torresson could:* Interview with Torresson.

147 *Arthur Harry Moore:* Burton, *The Morro Castle,* 97–99.

148 *She still clung:* Interview with Doris Manske.

148 *Despite their best:* The *Paramount's* rescue of Doris and Lillian Wacker comes from "*Morro Castle* Fire: A Rescuer's Tale," *New York Times,* September 2, 1984; interview with Doris Manske; and the Bogans' testimony in the October 1934 Coast Guard inquiry. National Archives, General Correspondence Files of the U.S. Coast Guard (Record Group 26), File Classification No. 123.

150 *In the* Monarch's *playroom:* "*Monarch* Saves 72 from Liner; 7 Unconscious," the *New York World-Telegram,* September 8, 1934. After talking with Robert Lione, I became convinced he was the subject of this account, although I only say it conditionally in the narrative. Lione was four at the time, rescued by a *Monarch* lifeboat and could remember being given a model of the *Monarch of Bermuda* that morning. Lione, now 76, still has that boat.

150 *Earl Rose, captain:* National Archives, General Correspondence Files of the U.S. Coast Guard (Record Group 26), File Classification No. 123.

151 *Survivors made landfall:* The collection of scenes from the Jersey

shore and New York docks came from newsreel footage in Tom Torres-son's collection; various articles in the *New York World-Telegram* and the *New York Times,* September 8, 1934 editions.

152 *Doris Wacker woke:* Interview with Doris Manske.

153 *A trawler towed:* Interview with Tom Torresson.

154 *When the towline:* National Archives (Record Group 41, Testimony in the Investigation of the Burning of the *Morro Castle,* Entry 214).

155 *Towing the cruise:* The account of the *Tampa's* attempt to tow the *Morro Castle* comes from the testimony of Captain Earl Rose in the October 1934 Coast Guard inquiry. National Archives, General Correspondence Files of the U.S. Coast Guard (Record Group 26), File Classification No. 123.

156 *On board the* Tampa: National Archives (Record Group 41, Testimony in the Investigation of the Burning of the *Morro Castle,* Entry 214).

157 *Outside, the nor'easter:* National Archives, General Correspondence Files of the U.S. Coast Guard (Record Group 26), File Classification No. 123.

157 *For the entire:* Burton, *The Morro Castle,* 134–135.

Ten: Greetings from Asbury Park, New Jersey

PAGE

161 *On Sunday, the:* The description of Asbury Park comes in part from newspaper articles related to the disaster, but also Helen-Chantal Pike, *Asbury Park's Glory Days* (New Brunswick, N.J.: Rutgers University Press, 2005). R. W. Hodge's amazing tour of the still-burning *Morro Castle* comes from his own first-person account, "Ship So Hot Soles Burn from Coast Guard's Feet," *Utica Daily Press,* September 10, 1934.

162 *At one point:* The story of the birds was reported by the local paper, "Fantastic Tale? No, It's true," *Asbury Park Press,* September 10, 1934.

164 *When the reporters arrived:* Raphael Avellar, "*World-Telegram* Reporter Finds Liner Bent and Twisted Shambles," *New York World-Telegram,* September 10, 1934.

165 *The Coast Guard:* The arrival of the *Morro Castle* officers was covered by George Rogers's hometown paper in "Radio Chief Kept Up Calls for Aid," *Bayonne Times,* September 10, 1934.

165 *"I don't know":* "Chief Officer Ashore, Fears Living Man Was Left on Ship," *New York American,* September 10, 1934.

166 *Earlier that morning:* National Archives (Record Group 41, Testimony in the Investigation of the Burning of the *Morro Castle,* Entry 214).

169 *"I ran to":* "Chief Engineer Jumped from Rail into Water," *New York World-Telegram,* September 8, 1934.

169 *Willmott's first cousin:* "Captain's Death 'Strange,'" *New York Times,* September 11, 1934.

169 *Mathilda Willmott collapsed:* "News Shocks Mrs. Willmott," *New York American,* September 10, 1934.

170 *Meanwhile, the photographers:* "More Pictures of the Burning Steamship *Morro Castle,* " *New York Post,* September 10, 1934.

170 *That day, Tom:* Interview with Tom Torresson.

171 *Selma Filtzer fainted:* "Bride Faints at Funeral," *New York World-Telegram,* September 10, 1934.

172 *Meanwhile, Alagna felt:* National Archives (Record Group 41, Testimony in the Investigation of the Burning of the *Morro Castle,* Entry 214).

173 *That afternoon, Conboy:* F. X. Fay memo to J. Edgar Hoover. September 11, 1934. FBI File No. 45-833, Section I.

Eleven: An Agitator Among Us

PAGE

176 *The train arrived:* This scene was from one of the best newspaper stories of the day on the disaster, beginning with a most poignant lead, "The dead were handled gently in death." That line was almost stolen for the first line of this chapter. Earl Sparling, "Only Numbers Identify 47 at End of Holiday Voyage," *New York World-Telegram,* September 10, 1934.

178 *Despite his appearance:* National Archives (Record Group 41, Testimony in the Investigation of the Burning of the *Morro Castle,* Entry 214); and "Liner Fire Was Incendiary, Captain and Mates Believe," *New York World-Telegram,* September 10, 1934.

179 *That morning, Cuban:* "Fire Started by Communists, Cuban Charges" and "Fire 'Red Plot,' Says Detective," *New York World-Telegram,* September 10, 1934.

179 *A stout man:* "Hoover Finds Spotlight Only in Tragedies," *New York World-Telegram,* September 10, 1934.

179 *It would only:* "Liner Fire Was Incendiary, Captain and Mates Believe," *New York World-Telegram,* September 10, 1934.

181 *Soon, the arcades:* The flattened pennies and the Boardwalk Taffy Shop's unbelievably distasteful postcards are still out there. They show up on eBay quite often, which is where I learned of them.

181 *That afternoon, a plump:* "Looks Like Ship on Stage Drop with Pinspot," *New York World-Telegram,* September 10, 1934.

181 *Fifty years earlier:* Gary S. Crawford, *A Brief History of the Morro Castle Ship Disaster of 1934* (Neptune, N.J.: Privately published, 2004), 5.

181 *The radiomen:* "U.S. Gets Rogers' Disaster Story," *Bayonne Times,* September 11, 1934.

182 *Rogers declined to:* Ibid.

183 *At least publicly:* "Radio Chief Accuses Aide Who Saved Life in Ship Fire," *New York Journal,* September 12, 1934.

183 *It seemed attorneys:* "Lawyers of Ward Line Call Before U.S. Jury," *New York Daily News,* September 13, 1934.

184 *Because Abbott:* National Archives (Record Group 41, Testimony in the Investigation of the Burning of the *Morro Castle,* Entry 214); and "Chief Engineer Never Took Post, Abandoned Ship After Half-Hour," *New York World-Telegram,* September 11, 1934.

185 *George Rogers made:* National Archives (Record Group 41, Testimony in the Investigation of the Burning of the *Morro Castle,* Entry 214); "Couldn't Get Intelligent Order from Bridge, Says Radio Man," *New York World-Telegram,* September 12, 1934.

187 *In Asbury Park:* "Body Believed That of Captain Brought Ashore," *New York World-Telegram,* September 12, 1934; and "Remains of Willmott Found in Cabin by Chief Taggart," *Asbury Park Press,* September 11, 1934.

187 *Perhaps city officials:* "City Denies It Sought to Buy or Rent Liner," *Asbury Park Press,* September 13, 1934.

188 *Despite Taggart's find:* "Willmott Autopsy Is Ordered," *New York Sun,* September 13, 1934.

188 *Tom Torresson arrived:* Interview with Torresson.

188 *He left that:* "Articles found in staterooms," from the Frank Crocco papers relating to the Ward Line disaster, *Morro Castle* files, the Stephen B. Luce Library at the State University of New York Maritime College, Bronx, N.Y.

189 *Sometime after Tom:* Letter from William S. Taggart, Asbury Park fire chief, and a letter to Carl H. Bischoff, city manager of Asbury Park. Ibid.

189 *George Rogers returned:* "Many Tributes Paid to Rogers," *Bayonne Times,* September 13, 1934.

189 *Among the invited:* "Singer, Doyle Know How It Feels to Send Call for Aid When Ship Disaster Looms," *Bayonne Times,* September 10, 1934.

190 *Most people found:* Doyle, "Beyond All Reasonable Doubt," 72–73.

191 *Among the tips coming:* Telegram from F. X. Fay to J. Edgar Hoover, September 13, 1934. FBI File No. 45-833, Section I.

191 *Fay had little:* The Bureau's activity is recounted in various undated, unsigned memoranda and telegrams from the fall of 1934. FBI File No. 45-833, Sections I and II.

192 *A federal judge ordered:* "Alagna Freed; His Testimony Called Vital," *New York World-Telegram,* September 13, 1934.

192 *Not even his:* "Rogers, Alagna Friends Again," *New York World-Telegram,* September 14, 1934; and "Alagna Denies Charges," *New York Times,* September 15, 1934.

193 *Rogers had been:* The photograph of Rogers and Alagna shaking hands graced the pages of several newspapers that Friday afternoon, and it may be the creepiest picture ever taken. The story this account is culled from is "*Morro Castle*'s Radio Operator and Aide Make Peace; Bitterness Arising from Probe Vanishes in Handclasp," *New York Evening Journal,* September 14, 1934.

194 *While few matched:* National Archives (Record Group 41, Testimony in the Investigation of the Burning of the *Morro Castle,* Entry 214).

194 *She was escorted:* "Seaman Not Told About Fire Doors," *New York Times,* September 20, 1934; interview with Doris Manske.

195 *Later that day:* "Rogers Takes Theatre Offer," *Bayonne Times,* September 17, 1934.

Twelve: Breaking Point

PAGE

197 *"Your name in full?":* The exchange between Alagna and Dickerson Hoover comes from "Warms in a Daze, Alagna Testifies," *New York Times,*

September 21, 1934, and the National Archives (Record Group 41, Testimony in the Investigation of the Burning of the *Morro Castle,* Entry 214).

199 *The big man:* "Rogers, in Vaudeville Turn, Accuses Aid of Desertion," *New York World-Telegram,* September 18, 1934.

200 *Two days after:* Letter of George Alagna to Dickerson Hoover, Department of Commerce. National Archives (Record Group 41, General Records Relating to the *Morro Castle* Disaster, 1934–36, Entry 217, Box 2, Folder 1).

201 *Sounding very much:* National Archives (Record Group 41, Testimony in the Investigation of the Burning of the *Morro Castle,* Entry 214).

202 *Nothing new or:* Memorandum of E. A. Tamm to J. Edgar Hoover, September 22, 1934; and letter from F. X. Fay to Martin Conboy, September 29, 1934. FBI File No. 45-833, Section I.

202 *Still, Martin Conboy:* Memorandum of J. Edgar Hoover to E. A. Tamm, September 28, 1934. FBI File No. 45-833, Section I.

203 *Fay was not:* Internal investigation report by F. X. Fay, September 27, 1934. FBI File No. 45-833, Section I.

205 *Tom Torresson had:* Interview with Torresson.

205 *Doris Wacker delayed:* Interview with Doris Manske.

206 *On October 26:* Department of Commerce Bureau of Navigation and Steamboat Inspection's Report and Recommendations of Dickerson N. Hoover. National Archives (Record Group 41, General Records Relating to the *Morro Castle* Disaster, Entry 217).

207 *A panel of judges:* The account of this hearing comes from "Ward Line Puts Part of Blame on Radio Men," *New York Post,* November 5, 1934; "Ward Line Tries to Pin Late SOS on Radio Man," *New York Daily News,* November 6, 1934; and testimony in the U.S. Steamboat Inspection license revocation hearings, November 1934. Copies of the transcript are in the *Morro Castle* files, Stephen B. Luce Library at the State University of New York Maritime College, Bronx, N.Y.

208 *Alagna did everything:* Telegram of George Alagna to Franklin Delano Roosevelt, November 8, 1934. National Archives (Record Group 41, General Records Relating to the *Morro Castle* Disaster, 1934-36, Box 2, Folder 1).

208 *On November 30:* "Warms Is Arrested with His Engineer in Ship Fire Deaths," *New York Times,* December 1, 1934; "U.S. Arrests Capt. Warms

and Engineer in Morro Fire," *New York American,* December 1, 1934; "U.S. Speeds *Morro Castle* Neglect Trials," *New York Post,* December 4, 1934; "Line Indicted with Official in Ship Blaze," *New York Daily News,* December 4, 1934.

209 *Over the next:* "Ward Line Made $263,000 on Fire," *New York Post,* December 7, 1934.

209 *The charred hull:* "Pounding Tide, Wind Crack *Morro Castle,*" *New York World-Telegram,* December 7, 1934.

209 *If that weren't:* "Ward Line Faces Loss of Mails," *New York Post,* December 5, 1934.

209 *The winter brought:* "163 Saved as Liner and Freighter Collide Four Miles Off Sea Girt," *Asbury Park Evening Press,* January 25, 1935.

210 *Francis Xavier Fay:* Internal reports and memos October 1934–January 1935, FBI File No. 45-833, Sections I–III.

210 *In the early:* The details of the *Morro Castle*'s last days in Asbury Park come from various accounts in the *Asbury Park Evening Press,* including "*Morro* Is Moved 80 Feet in Storm," January 24, 1935; "Last Hides Out of *Morro Castle,*" February 19, 1935; "Balmy Weather Attracts Throng," March 4, 1935; "*Morro Castle* Is Moved 57 Feet; Beached Here 6 Months Ago Today," March 8, 1935; "*Morro* May Float Out to Sea Today," March 9, 1935; "*Morro Castle*'s Stern Is Afloat," March 13, 1935; "Few See Vessel Leave at 2:05; Reaches Harbor," March 14, 1935. The story of a curse on the ship comes from "*Morro Castle* 'Jinx' Pursues Wreckers," *New York Post,* November 26, 1934.

212 *Already, it had:* "Alagna Suit Fails," *New York Sun,* March 4, 1935.

212 *"Suggest Alagna leave":* "Alagna Warned to Leave Town," *New York World-Telegram,* March 30, 1935.

212 *Two days later:* "Alagna Seeks to Die Writing of Sea Horror," *New York World-Telegram,* March 29, 1935; "Alagna Is Freed on Writ," *New York Times,* April 4, 1935; "Alagna, Trying Suicide by Gas, Writes Note on *Morro Castle* Fire," *New York Herald Tribune,* March 30, 1935.

213 *Francis Xavier Fay:* Telegram from Federal Bureau of Investigation, New York City, to Bureau headquarters in Washington regarding the Alagna suicide note, March 29, 1935, FBI File No. 45-833, Section III.

Thirteen: A Short Fuse

PAGE

217   *Adams ridiculed William:* "U.S. Denounces Four at *Morro Castle* Trial," *New York Evening Journal,* November 13, 1935.

218   *Warms, looking even:* "'Act of God' Defense in *Morro* Fire Trial," *New York American,* November 14, 1935; and "Shed Insignia Fleeing *Morro,* Says Engineer," *New York Daily News,* January 15, 1936.

218   *On January 23:* "3 on Trial in Ship Fire Killing 136," *New York Daily Mirror,* November 12, 1935.

218   *Judge Murray Hulbert:* "Four-Year Term Given to Abbott; Two for Warms," *New York World-Telegram,* January 28, 1936.

218   *In September 1935:* "Radio Men's Strike Delays Two Ships," *New York Times,* September 15, 1935.

219   *Francis Xavier Fay:* "FBI Agent Francis Fay, 92; Probed Lindbergh Kidnapping," *Chicago Tribune,* May 13, 1990.

219   *The radioman:* Most of the information in this section on Rogers's background comes from a report written by F. X. Fay in October 1934 in FBI File No. 45-833, Section III. The information on Rogers's military time is from his veteran's records on file at the National Personnel Records Center in St. Louis, Mo.

222   *He had spent:* "Ship Hero, Through with Sea, Content with Obscurity on Eve of *Morro Castle* Tragedy's First Anniversary," *Bayonne Times,* September 7, 1935.

223   *Of all things:* The story of Bayonne and its revolutionary police car radios comes from two books: Kathleen M. Middleton, *Bayonne Passages* (Charleston, S.C.: Arcadia, 2000), 96–97; and Gladys Mellor Sinclair, *Bayonne Old and New* (New York: Maranatha, 1940): 103–120.

224   *The official position:* "Hero of *Morro Castle* Joins Bayonne Police," *New York Post,* June 9, 1936; and "Rogers Linked to Bombing as Blast Victim Testifies," *Bayonne Times,* November 22, 1938.

226   *Doyle came to:* The friendship of Rogers and Doyle is explored in several newspaper articles, although the bulk of this information comes from "Rogers Linked to Bombing as Blast Victim Testifies," *Bayonne Times,* November 22, 1938.

227   *In April 1937:* "*Morro* Fire Verdict Upset by U.S. Court," *New York Journal,* April 7, 1937.

227   *Rogers talked about:* George Rogers's allusions to his guilt in the *Morro Castle* fire are from Vincent J. Doyle's personal accounts of the conversation. Doyle, "Beyond All Reasonable Doubt," 26, 38.

228   *On March 4:* This account of the day of the Doyle bombing comes from Doyle, "Beyond All Reasonable Doubt": i–ii, 1–2; and "Mysterious Blast Maims Officer; Explosive Experts' Aid Enlisted," *Bayonne Times,* March 5, 1938. Testimony in Rogers's subsequent trial, recounted in various newspaper articles, provided additional details.

Fourteen: The Mind of a Fiend

PAGE

232   *George Rogers didn't:* The account of Rogers's minutes after the explosion comes from "Suspicion Turned on Rogers 1 Hour After Explosion," *Bayonne Times,* December 2, 1938, and photographs of the crime scene in Doyle, "Beyond All Reasonable Doubt."

233   *The department dispatched:* Doyle, "Beyond All Reasonable Doubt," 2–8.

235   *The* Bayonne Times*:* This section refers to several stories from the *Bayonne Times:* "Bomb Probe Spreads to Other Cities as Police Check Clues," March 8, 1938; "Bomb Case Hits Snag, Police Hint," March 9, 1938; "Bomb Mystery Solution Seen," March 10, 1938; "Bomb Clue Hints at Insider's Job," March 12, 1938.

236   *On Tuesday, McGrath:* "Rogers Linked to Bombing as Blast Victim Testifies," *Bayonne Times,* November 22, 1938.

237   *Police Chief O'Neill:* "Rogers Arrested in Bomb Blast," *Bayonne Times,* March 15, 1938.

237   *"No, Captain, Rogers":* Doyle, "Beyond All Reasonable Doubt," 26.

238   *At his arraignment:* "Rogers' Bail Set at $7,500," *Bayonne Times,* March 16, 1938.

239   *"If the detectives":* "Doyle Can't Believe 'Friend' Bombed Him," *Bayonne Times,* March 18, 1938.

239   *Doyle was still:* "More Doyles in Hospital—Including a Brand New One," *Bayonne Times,* May 8, 1938.

239   *He introduced himself:* Doyle, "Beyond All Reasonable Doubt," 45–47.

240   *Vincent Doyle was:* Ibid., 87–96.

241   *George Rogers seemed:* The account of the bombing trial is compiled from Doyle, "Beyond All Reasonable Doubt," 50–60, 107–145; and a se-

ries of articles in the *Bayonne Times* between November 21 and December 2, including: "Court Give Rogers Trial Without Jury," November 21, 1938; "Rogers Linked to Bombing as Blast Victim Testifies," November 22, 1938; "Expert Aids State Attempt to Prove Rogers Made Bomb," November 23, 1938; "Rogers Faces Police Ouster Even if Freed," November 25, 1938; "Rogers Due for 2nd Day of Grilling," November 30, 1938; "Closing Pleas Made in Bomb Case Today; Judge Delays Ruling," December 1, 1938; "Rogers Facing Sanity Tests After Conviction as Bomber," December 2, 1938.

249   *Two weeks did:* "Rogers Gets 12 to 20 Years; 'Mind of Fiend' Hit By Judge," *Bayonne Times,* December 15, 1938.

Fifteen: The War Effort

PAGE

250   *In January 1939:* Memo of J. Edgar Hoover to Dwight Brantley, January 30, 1939, and an anonymous letter from Penns Grove, New Jersey. From FBI File No. 100-278950, records relating to George White Rogers.

251   *Dwight Brantley visited:* The FBI's inquiry into prosecuting Rogers is detailed in a report dated February 27, 1939, written by Dwight Brantley. From FBI File No. 100-278950.

253   *The New Jersey:* "Court Denies Rogers' Plea on New Trial," *Bayonne Times,* May 15, 1939.

253   *In an inspired act:* "Rogers Paroled from Prison to Enter Service," *Bayonne Times,* September 4, 1942.

253   *He could not believe:* Vincent Doyle letter to T. J. Slowie, Federal Communications Commission, November 30, 1942. FBI File No. 100-278950.

255   *In his abbreviated:* The account of Rogers's time on the *Walter Colton* comes from an internal FBI report from the San Francisco office dated June 5, 1944. FBI File No. 100-278950.

255   *Rogers impressed the bosses:* This account of the water cooler incident and subsequent investigation comes from an internal FBI investigation report from the New York City office dated August 4, 1945. FBI File No. 100-278950. Some additional details come from Doyle, "Beyond All Reasonable Doubt," 148–149.

256   *The woman found:* Ibid. The young woman that Rogers was courting,

or terrorizing, has been left anonymous to history. The FBI has blacked out her name in all reports related to this incident.

259   *One of his few:* This account is from Vincent Doyle's recitation of the police investigation into the Hummels' murder and comes from the second half of his book, in which he adds a subhead and begins pagination over. Doyle, "Beyond All Reasonable Doubt (The Second Episode)," 83–91.

262   *That morning, Hummel:* "Rogers Held in Hummels' Murder; Robbery Called Motive in Killings," *Bayonne Times,* July 3, 1953.

262   *"If you're going":* Ibid.

Sixteen: The Death Hammer Falls

PAGE

263   *Monday morning, June:* Doyle, "Beyond All Reasonable Doubt (The Second Episode)," 23–29.

264   *Just after 4 P.M.:* Ibid., 2–19, and "Rogers Held in Hummels' Murder; Robbery Called Motive in Killings," *Bayonne Times,* July 3, 1953.

267   *His bail was:* "Rogers Fails to Raise $25,000 Bail," *Bayonne Times,* July 6, 1953.

267   *Rogers swore he:* Ibid.

268   *He explained that:* Doyle, "Beyond All Reasonable Doubt (The Second Episode)," 23–24.

268   *Initially, they turned:* "Police Search for Murder Weapon," *Bayonne Times,* July 8, 1953.

269   *Rogers had said:* Doyle, "Beyond All Reasonable Doubt (The Second Episode)," 23–30.

269   *They tried to:* Ibid., 46–50.

269   *Doyle took two:* Ibid., 64–67.

270   *The police took:* Ibid., 57–91.

271   *Rogers had hired:* "Rogers to Be Charged with Murder," *Bayonne Times,* July 16, 1953.

271   *George Rogers spent:* The account of the first Rogers trial for the Hummel murders comes from a number of articles in *Bayonne Times,* including "Jury to Be Shown Death Hammer," May 21, 1954; "Blood-Stained Pants Linked to Rogers," May 22, 1954; and "Mistrial Declared; Rogers' Lawyers Will Ask for Bail," May 24, 1954.

272   *His second trial:* "Second Trial of Rogers Opens; Juror 6 Named," *Bay-*

onne Times, September 14, 1954; and "State, Defense to Open Today at Rogers Trial," *Bayonne Times,* September 15, 1954.

273 *"I can hear":* "Blood-Stained Pants to Go Before Jury Today," *Bayonne Times,* September 16, 1954.

273 *The most damaging:* "Hummels Missing, Rogers Said Here," *Bayonne Times,* September 17, 1954.

273 *Captain Louis Smith:* "Hummel Lent Rogers $7,500," *Bayonne Times,* September 21, 1954.

274 *On Thursday morning:* "Rogers Offers No Defense; Rests, Calls No Witnesses," *Bayonne Times,* September 23, 1954.

274 *Julius Canter spent:* Canter's closing argument is reprinted, nearly verbatim, in Doyle, "Beyond All Reasonable Doubt (The Second Episode)," 127–146. Other information from the close of the trial comes from "Rogers Case Goes to Jury Today," *Bayonne Times,* September 24, 1954; and "Rogers Convicted, Escapes Chair; Sentenced at Once to Life Term," *Bayonne Times,* September 25, 1954.

276 *As Doyle stood:* Doyle, "Beyond All Reasonable Doubt (The Second Episode)," 147.

276 *Just after 6:* "Rogers Convicted, Escapes Chair; Sentenced at Once to Life Term," *Bayonne Times,* September 25, 1954.

277 *Rogers did not:* Doyle, "Beyond All Reasonable Doubt (The Second Episode)," 148.

277 *The warden made:* Harry Camisa and Jim Franklin, *Inside Out: Fifty Years Behind the Walls of New Jersey's Trenton State Prison* (Windsor, N.J.: Windsor Press, 2003), 51–53.

278 *He always requested:* Gallagher, *Fire at Sea,* 256–259.

279 *When the interviewers:* An internal FBI memo, April 23, 1971. FBI File No. 45-833, Section I.

279 *The days dragged:* "Rogers Dies in Trenton Prison," *Bayonne Times,* January 11, 1958.

Epilogue: End of the Line

PAGE

282 *In the year:* Interview with Torresson.

283 *William Warms returned:* "Warms Dies; Chief on *Morro Castle,*" *New York Times,* May 16, 1953.

283 *Eben S. Abbott, branded:* "Eben S. Abbott, 76, Nautical Engineer," *New York Times,* August 25, 1956.

284 *George Alagna never:* Interview with Gary S. Crawford and information from the Social Security Death Index.

284 *In October of 1953:* "Stockholders to Weigh Dissolution of the West Indies Line on Oct. 14," *New York Times,* October 6, 1953.

284 *An eerie rumor:* This rumor started solely on the basis that Japan bought much of the scrap American steel on the market in those days, no doubt on a buildup to war. This theory comes from Burton, *The Morro Castle,* 171.

285 *The same week:* A confidential memo from the Department of Commerce director, October 25, 1934. National Archives (Record Group 41, Bureau of Marine Inspection and Navigation [Department of Commerce], Entry 217, General Records Relating to the *Morro Castle* Disaster, Box 5, Folder 2).

286 *Over the years:* The idea that George Rogers was going to be fired at the end of the Labor Day cruise is one of the most puzzling aspects of this story. If it's true, then Rogers had a clear motive for burning the *Morro Castle.* Unfortunately, with Willmott's death, there is little way to determine whether it's true. If the captain wanted to dismiss Rogers, he did not tell his officers or Ward Line officials. Of course, some think Willmott's misgivings about Rogers were well known, but the company needed the "hero" radio man on their side. But that is a theory that leaves us only a step or two from a grassy knoll and a lone gunman. References to Willmott's plans to fire George Rogers are found in the FBI File No. 45-833, Section III; Gallagher, *Fire at Sea,* 14–15; and Doyle, "Beyond All Reasonable Doubt," 45–47.

288 *When he retired:* "Vincent J. Doyle, a Police Captain," *New York Times,* February 10, 1970.

289 *Tom Torresson would:* Interview with Torresson.

ACKNOWLEDGMENTS

I could very nearly fill up the first dinner sitting on the *Morro Castle* with all the people who helped me with the research it took to write this book.

I am most indebted to Thomas Torresson Jr., who shared his story with me over the course of a year before he passed away. He was generous with his time, and I listened to him for hours in person and over the phone. We spent a day at his home in Whiting, New Jersey, watching film footage of the *Morro Castle* and reliving his summer on the ship before he and his lovely wife, Irene, drove me to the Jersey shore for a dinner I will never forget. He was charmingly blunt, but touched me with his sincere hope that the *Morro Castle* story finally would be told accurately. I hope I have done that. Tom once told me, "I just hope I live to read it." It's one of my greatest regrets that he didn't see the first word of the manuscript. More than that, though, I simply miss him. I felt I had made a good friend.

Another friend I have gained as a result of all this is Michael Alderson of Louisville, Kentucky. He is probably the foremost expert on the Ward Line, and he graciously opened his extensive archives, read the manuscript for errors and passed along countless helpful tips—as well as supplying some of the photos and artwork in this book. Anyone interested in learning more about the storied history of the cruise ship company—and this is just one of its stories—should visit Michael's Web site at www.wardline.com.

Michael indirectly put me in touch with Doris Manske, the former Doris Wacker. I had chosen Doris to represent the *Morro Castle*'s passengers months before I met her, based solely on newspaper accounts of her horrifying ordeal.

When her granddaughter, Carrie Manske, contacted me, I knew this project was blessed. Doris has been a sweetheart and, after reading so much about her, I felt like I was meeting a celebrity when I first shook her hand. Thanks to Doris, Carrie and Doug Manske. I also owe thanks to Robert Lione for finding me and sharing his fragile memories of a tragic childhood.

I want to thank Martin Beiser, my editor at Free Press, for trusting me to disappear into this story for a year. His suggestions gave me a clear course to follow, and his confidence that I wasn't running aground somewhere meant a lot. From day one, we have seen this book coming together exactly the same way, and you just can't do any better than that. He gave me many ideas that made this a much better book. Thanks also to everyone else at Free Press and Simon & Schuster, especially Andrew Paulson.

None of this would have been possible without my friend and literary agent, Tracy Brown at Wendy Sherman Associates. Tracy has guided my publishing career one way or another since 2000, and I couldn't ask for a better voice in New York. Not only has he tirelessly promoted this book and pushed me to write it as best I could, he has provided his considerable editorial talents to reading the manuscript.

Much of this story came from the archives of museums, libraries and government agencies, and I was fortunate to find many people who care about their jobs—which made mine easier. Mark Mollan at the National Archives in Washington went far beyond the call of duty. Every time I thought I had it all, Mark sent me a new nugget that added layers to this story. He made my visit to the Archives especially smooth, and his interest made this a much better book. I'm also deeply indebted to Sidney Moore and the library staff at the Mariners' Museum in Newport News; Shafeek Fazal at the SUNY Maritime College in the Bronx; Patty LaSala at the Asbury Park Public Library; Debbie Beatty and David M. Hardy at the FBI; Karen Gallagher and John Rooney with the Bayonne Police Department; the staff of the Bayonne Free Public Library; William G. Seibert at the National Personnel Records Center in St. Louis; Megan Fraser at Independence Seaport Museum; and the reference staff at the Charleston County Public Library, particularly Linda Stewart, who tracked down obscure microfilm and books during the long winter.

At my newspaper, the *Post and Courier,* a number of people helped out, including librarian Libby Wallace; Bill Thompson, book editor, advisor and friend; Tom Spain and Leroy Burnell, who helped me with their photo wizardry; and the ones in charge—Larry Tarleton, Bill Hawkins, Steve Mullins, Marsha Guerard and Rick Nelson. What little fun I had during the last year came at the poker table with Fred, Tom, Schuyler, Mic, Ben, Steve, Dave, Bryce, Robert and especially Arlie.

I owe a very special thanks to Monsignor Vincent J. Doyle, the son of Bayonne police captain Vincent J. Doyle, who provided me with his father's manuscript for "Beyond All Reasonable Doubt." Doyle's insights, recollection and record of the events added to this book immeasurably. I included as much of his story as I could because, more than anything, he wanted the story told.

A number of folks provided recollections, advice and research assistance. Thanks to Ms. Raegan Quinn; Deborah C. Whitcraft; Jim McNamara; F. X. Fay, Jr.; Capt. Jeff Monroe, whose father was on the *Morro Castle* that night; Marie F. Wright at the National Railway Historical Society, North Jersey Chapter; and Jim Bogan, who spoke at the Sea Girt anniversary ceremony along with Tom Torresson. The guys in Sea Girt, particularly Conrad Yauch and Bill Dunn, have been great—even if they thought I was crazy to drive 700 miles to attend their anniversary ceremony. Fellow *Morro Castle* historian Gary S. Crawford of Neptune, New Jersey, filled in a big blank on George Alagna, and we had fun trading notes. My eternal gratitude goes to friends Sally M. Walker, Fran Hawk, and Jim and Mary Fortune, who were kind enough to read this in manuscript form and give me valuable feedback. And, of course, we wouldn't be here if not for all that Bruce Springsteen music, which first lured me to Asbury Park and provided the soundtrack to all those trips up and down the Turnpike.

My family endured as much as I did during the work on this book. Thanks to everyone in Tennessee and Georgia—particularly Judy Hicks—but especially Beth, Cole and Nate Hicks for tolerating the long absences and a quiet house while I wrote. Beth not only read the manuscript more times than I had any right to ask, offering valuable feedback, but she also kept the rest of the world running while I was cruising through history. Thank you for putting up with it all. Cole waited patiently, taking my free time when he could get it, and Nate sat on my lap and typed the "b" key for me every now and then.

Finally, I have to say good-bye to Michael J. Davis, one of my closest and oldest friends, who died unexpectedly while I was writing this book. I will be lucky to ever have a friend half as good. A lot of people miss you, Mike, only a few of them more than me.

Brian Hicks
Charleston, South Carolina
July 4, 2006

INDEX

ABOUT THE AUTHOR

Brian Hicks, a senior writer with the *Post and Courier* in Charleston, South Carolina, is the author of *Ghost Ship: The Mysterious True Story of the Mary Celeste and Her Missing Crew.* He is coauthor of two previous books on maritime subjects: *Raising the Hunley: The Remarkable History and Recovery of the Lost Confederate Submarine* and *Into the Wind: The Story of the World's Longest Race.* The recipient of the South Carolina Press Association's award for Journalist of the Year, Hicks lives in Charleston with his wife and two sons.